THE ILLUSION OF TECHNIQUE

Besides a long and distinguished academic career as a professor of philosophy, William Barrett has been active in the intellectual and literary life of the country. He was an editor of *Partisan Review* during the years following World War II, and served later for a time as literary critic for the *Atlantic Monthly*. He was also among the first of that small group of philosophers in this country who, shortly after the war, introduced European Existentialism to America. This combination of interests—in technical philosophy and human issues—gives him his unique quality as a leading contemporary thinker. Barrett is the author of *Irrational Man* and is one of the few philosophers of our time who is able to communicate from his special field to the public at large.

THE ILLUSION OF TECHNIQUE

*A Search for Meaning
in a Technological Civilization*

———————◆———————

William Barrett

ANCHOR PRESS/DOUBLEDAY
Garden City, New York
1978

*Portions of this book first appeared
in* Commentary *magazine in different form.*
Copyright © 1967, 1975, 1976 by the American Jewish Committee

Doubleday & Company, Inc, would like to thank Harcourt Brace
Jovanovich Inc., for permission to reprint a quotation from *Collected
Poems 1909–1962* by T. S. Eliot.

Library of Congress Cataloging in Publication Data

Barrett, William, 1913–
The illusion of technique.

Includes index.
1. Philosophy, Modern—20th century. 2. Wittgenstein,
Ludwig, 1889–1951. 3. Heidegger, Martin,
1889–1976. 4. James, William, 1842–1910. 5. Technology
and civilization. 6. Liberty. I. Title.
B804.B358   190
ISBN: 0-385-11201-7
Library of Congress Catalog Card Number 77–27765

To Julie

This book was begun during the freedom of a year made possible by a fellowship from the Guggenheim Foundation; and was completed during the following year when I was a Senior Fellow of the National Endowment of the Humanities. I wish to express my gratitude to both organizations.

Very particular thanks are due to three lovely young women of the Doubleday staff. Loretta Barrett, as directing genius and driving force, was all that an editor should be. Angela Cox and Harriet Rubin alternately cajoled, corrected, encouraged, and generally kept the pages from getting lost. I shall miss them.

CONTENTS

Prologue   "Mind-forged Manacles"   *xi*

PART I   TECHNIQUE

1   The Illusion of a Technique   *1*
2   Technique, Technicians, and Philosophy   *17*
3   The Mystique of Logic   *27*
4   Mysticism   *51*
5   Open Language   *59*
6   Mathematics, Mechanism, and Creativity   *79*

PART II   BEING

7   The Two Worlds   *109*
8   Homeless in the World   *133*
9   The Cash Value of Being   *157*
10   Technology as Human Destiny   *177*
11   "Utopia or Oblivion"   *203*

PART III   FREEDOM

12   The Moral Will   *229*
13   The Will to Believe   *253*
14   The Faith to Will   *271*

PART IV   THE SHAPE OF THE FUTURE?

15   The Shape of the Future: American Version   *297*
16   The Shape of the Future: Russian Version   *317*

Epilogue   Nihilism, Faith, Freedom   *333*
Index   *347*

Prologue

"Mind-forged Manacles"

A BOOK BEGINS FOR ITS AUTHOR FAR BACK OF ANY PARTICULAR experience that he might fix on as its beginning. But sometimes there may be a passing incident that he likes to associate with its early shaping:

Some time ago (February 1974), the New York *Times* printed a column by Anthony Lewis reporting a conversation with a Soviet behavioral scientist in Leningrad. The scientist was not named, but the reporter clearly took him as representative of a point of view influential in the Soviet Union. It is a view not altogether unknown to us from our own behavioral scientists. The difference is that in the Soviet Union these scientists can expect to have their methods put sweepingly into effect. So this Soviet scientist could look forward confidently to the day when the techniques of his science would completely shape the new Soviet man. Dissent in any form would then cease to be a problem for the state. The drives of the individual would be so channeled to the uses of society that no trace of disruptive individualism would ever again reappear.

Now, Mr. Lewis is not among those given to being unduly nervous about the Soviet Union—indeed, his journalistic efforts are often directed at restraining those who get too exercised on the subject. But this particular conversation with the Soviet scientist had evidently shaken him. Dictatorship, when it acquires the more rational methods of science, begins to worry even the purest liberal. The revolution according to Marx has become the society according to Pavlov. The prospect was enough to waken Mr. Lewis, for

the moment at least, from the slumbers of détente. "What about individuals like Solzhenitsyn?" he asked. The Soviet scientist's answer
was prompt and categorical: There simply would not be any more
Solzhenitsyns.

At the time I was reading *Gulag Archipelago*, and could not help
thinking that Solzhenitsyn's inquisitors already commanded some
potent techniques of their own for discouraging dissidents. True,
the methods were crude and brutal, and lacked scientific sophis-
tication. Worse still, they were administered after the fact, or the
imputed fact, of the crime. Why not prevent the crime of dissent
before it arises? The more polished techniques of the behavioral scientist might shape the mind beforehand so that it would never be
tempted into any dissenting path. That would be a great step in
efficiency. Why go to inordinate lengths to break a man's spirit if
you can mold him so that he has no spirit to begin with? Simply as
a matter of economy, too, the saving would be enormous: The elaborate "sewage system" for disposing of the rebellious, on which
Solzhenitsyn reports, would become unnecessary. All just a matter
of finding the right technique.

The techniques of shaping behavior are the preoccupation also of
our own American psychologist B. F. Skinner, whose book *Beyond
Freedom and Dignity* had appeared at about this time, though I had
not yet gotten around to reading it. Now suddenly this passing column in the *Times* brought the two authors—Solzhenitsyn and
Skinner—to the forefront of my attention, and I could not resist the
impulse to place them in imaginary dialogue with each other. Professor Skinner, after all, might do as an American stand-in, with due
allowances made for their political differences, for that unnamed
Soviet behaviorist with whom the *Times* reporter had talked in
Leningrad. I had never thought that Mr. Lewis would be a catalyst
for me in anything; but one never knows from what quarter the
light may suddenly strike. At any rate, his column set me about the
intellectual experiment of reading two books side by side—or, more
accurately, in counterpoint with one another.

And they do make a very striking counterpoint amid the general
disorder of contemporary events. Both books appeared close
enough in time so that they can be considered as virtually simultaneous products of our period. Both had large sales, yet must have
reached different audiences, for there was no public indication that
anybody drew comparison between them. And yet both dealt, in

their different ways, with the subject of freedom, which has now become the paramount issue of our time.

To be sure, they deal with this issue so differently that their paths might not seem to cross ideologically at all. The American psychologist does not discuss political liberty as such. He is simply concerned to deny that anyone as a matter of fact is ever free under any circumstances at all, whatever the political form under which he lives. Yet this sweeping metaphysical position is not altogether without political consequences. The society according to Pavlov would not be innocent of political implications. The ideal of the free and self-governing (autonomous) personality is a traditional part of our thinking in law and political philosophy. For Professor Skinner this idea is not only an illusion, but also a pernicious relic of the past that stands as a barrier to our future progress. A thoroughly scientific program for the advancement of mankind demands that we scrap it. So he does come on as something of a social crusader after all.

Solzhenitsyn, on the other hand, gives us a powerful and horrifying picture of what life is like for millions of people who have in fact been deprived of their freedom. The Russian had been imprisoned and then exiled for espousing liberty. The American, who denigrates the idea of individual freedom as a metaphysical belief, has been the recipient of the highest academic honors in this country. We are a free country and would not have it otherwise. Clearly, we live in a strange time.

I.

We need not pursue this imaginary confrontation farther at this point. Its upshot is to place the whole idea of scientific technique in a new and glaring relation to life. In a society more and more dominated by technique, it is likely that human technology will be systematically attempted and even come to assume a commanding place. The behavioral scientists themselves force this claim upon us. What we need to cure our present ills, Professor Skinner tells us, is a "technology of behavior." And he is confident that this technology is already at hand. "The techniques are there," he repeatedly assures us; we have only to put them to work.

If we step back for a moment to take stock of this situation, we note an extraordinary shift here in the problem of free will as compared with the nineteenth century. The people of that earlier period felt that determinism was something forced upon them by nature itself. It seemed to be the residual picture of the universe at which physics, the most exact of the natural sciences, had finally arrived. The molecules in nature ran their course according to inalterable laws; and as the molecules of your body moved, your mind and person were swept along with them. There was nothing you could do but submit to this scheme, for it was forced upon you as the last word of science. Hence the great wave of melancholy among the educated, who felt that human effort in the face of such a universe was void and ineffectual.

That scientific picture is gone, and physics no longer lends the determinist its support. Now it is not nature, but the technicians, who would compel us to give up the idea of freedom. The behavioral scientist who has elaborated techniques of conditioning in the laboratory brings these forward as the basis of his claim that freedom is an illusion. The "technology of behavior," not physics, becomes the chief weapon in the arsenal of determinism. The irony here should not pass unnoticed. The human mind, which creates those techniques of conditioning in the first place, is to be ensnared in the prison of its own devising.

Usually the prevailing thought of an era proceeds against the background of some dominant image. For the older Newtonian determinism it was the image of the heavenly bodies—the stars and planets moving inalterably in their courses. This inalterable pattern was to be transposed down to the smallest particles of matter, of which we humans were fragmentary aggregates. The equations that govern human beings were the same as those that govern the heavenly bodies in their inertial circling. And though a little more complex, these equations would eventually be written. The newer determinism invokes a different image: not the cosmic image of the stars in their courses but a piece of man-made technology—the computer —is the background against which this thinking moves. And the question on which the future of freedom hangs is whether we can simulate the human mind completely in a computer.

William Blake spoke against the "mind-forged manacles" in another context. The most visionary of the Romantic poets, Blake saw the traces of such manacles in the faces and voices he encountered in the streets of London. These stunted and blasted lives were not the work of nature, but of the mind of man working against itself. The note of social protest here was only incidental to Blake's purpose. The libertarian ideas of the French Revolution were but a stepping-stone to the visions of Swedenborg. The enemy always in the background for him was a certain mechanism of mind that begins to prevail in modern society, stifling the imagination and producing a consequent stultification of life amid the routines of convention and the narrowness of a priggish morality. Our context here is somewhat different, and certainly more restricted, but Blake's great phrase still rings with meaning. The "mind-forged manacles" reappear in a different guise in the contemporary appeal to a "technology of behavior."

In all of this the determinist is driven by a thoroughly human and obstinate impulse common to all intellectuals. He has a conviction, and he wishes to prove it at all costs. If nature no longer obliges by conforming to his position, he will proceed to produce thoroughly determined humans. The physicists tell us we can no longer speak of nature as a machine in the simple-minded fashion that philosophers and scientists once did. No matter; the determinist now will make up for that by producing mechanical humans. No doubt, practical advantages are usually offered to conceal this sheer intellectual obstinacy. We are promised that the technology of behavior —or the engineering of human beings, to put it more bluntly—will diminish social conflict, make society run more smoothly and efficiently, and perhaps—who knows?—eliminate personal neurosis altogether. Still, manacles are manacles, whatever the imaginary benefits they are supposed to confer.

Clearly, then, anyone who would argue for freedom today has to concern himself with the nature of technique—its scope and its limits—if his thinking is to engage itself with the possible patterns of conditioning that may some day be visited upon us. The question of technique is, in itself, an important one for philosophy—and more important particularly for modern philosophy, which has so often let matters of technique blind its vision. More significantly still, the question bears upon the uncertainties of a whole technological civilization, which even as it wields its great technical powers is unsure of their limits or possible consequences.

II.

The book that follows was not born of that accidental conjunction of events—a passing newspaper column and the reading of two current authors that it provoked. That would be making matters a little more dramatic than they were, and perhaps giving the particular journalist more credit than I am willing. When I happened upon his column, I was already embarked upon a study of contemporary philosophy that sought some overview of its subject without the fragmentation into schools that usually occurs. A survey proved temperamentally impossible. Indeed, as I proceeded, I found myself lopping off more and more extraneous material. The twentieth century has a definite shape, intellectually speaking, which we seem to perceive quite clearly at times; yet we are still in the midst of it, and our vision of this shape must be partial and uncertain. More disturbing still, the pattern we discern, the significant steps that seem to have been taken here and there, could all be reversed by the events of the next two decades and the possible collapse of a civilization that these events might bring with them. What I aspire to here, then, can be no more than a sketch toward a history of philosophy in our century. And the story, I decided, could be told better in terms of certain representative figures to whom I feel particularly attracted.

Accordingly, the three philosophers I concentrate on are Ludwig Wittgenstein, Martin Heidegger, and William James. It might seem that James, whose activity belongs in great part to the previous century, is a little out of place here. But the justification of him as a contemporary will be made later in context.

At first glance these are three unlikely bedfellows. However, if we are not to let philosophy degenerate into isolated camps, each armed against the other, we must attempt communication across the barriers that some philosophers, out of their sectarian frenzy, seem intent on erecting. At the least, these three figures can be taken as representative of certain major types of philosophizing that have held the field in this century. Yet each is so markedly individual that he raises the question whether a philosophy that amounts to anything is to be completely fitted into the pigeonhole of a "school." The more individual a thinker the more truly and deeply representative he is, but that is something very different from being typical.

Thus Wittgenstein can be taken as representative of what has come to be called "analytic philosophy." The label is something of a makeshift, though. Wittgenstein's procedure is synthetic and intuitive throughout, all swoops and darts of insight, rather than the laborious dialectic practiced by other members of the school.

Heidegger serves as our representative of phenomenology and existentialism, yet he is so uniquely himself that the classification is purely provisional. "I am not an existentialist," he declared at one point, seeking to separate himself from the popular movement that had been launched by Sartre. What Heidegger says is certainly true if we measure him by Sartre. But if we push the meaning of the word farther, we shall find that he is "existential" at a deeper level than Sartre's thought can ever reach. Once again, the labels are somewhat makeshift.

James is our exemplar of pragmatism. Yet in the unashamedly personal tone of his philosophizing as well as his bold adventure into religious belief—precisely the aspects for which we take him up— he has always been something of an embarrassment to some fellow pragmatists.

Allowing for these creative unorthodoxies of the three thinkers, we may at least make some claim that our treatment is well rounded. The pursuit of such symmetry, however, was not part of my deliberate intention when I started. It simply happened through the gravitation of personal attraction. Amid the shifting currents of this century one cannot be sure which will lead us safely into a deeper channel and which will merely spend itself in the sand. One cannot stand aside and attempt to calculate the caprices of future judgment of current reputations. One does better in the end to fol- low the things that truly engage one. The value of a philosopher lies in the degree to which he stimulates one's own thinking. In any case, one philosophizes best in dialogue with philosophers whose thinking one finds congenial.

Yet in retrospect I should perhaps conclude with a less grudging acknowledgment of Mr. Lewis's column. True, the reading of it did not beget this book, nor shape in any way the philosophical mate- rials dealt with. But had it not been for the chance encounter with that item in the newspaper—and, more particularly, the parallel reading of Solzhenitsyn and Skinner it provoked—the emphasis and even the form of my exposition might have been quite different. For the book as it now stands, besides being an exploration of cer- tain contemporary thinkers, is also an attempt at a connected argu- ment for human freedom.

There are good philosophical reasons why we should make free- dom the central issue in philosophy. Immanuel Kant held that the three great philosophical questions were God, freedom, and immortality. These are the questions we all want answered, but that science can never answer for us. Toward the end of his life Kant came to hold that the question of freedom had a certain priority among these three. The matter of freedom is something that lies more directly within our own hands, so to speak; its reality is present within us and becomes, if only in part, present in our experience; and, finally, as we pursue the question of freedom, it opens up into the other two grand questions, of God and immortality. I think Kant had good reasons for his view; and indeed I will be re-creating that view, though in a very different language from his, in some of the pages that follow. But these formal reasons recede into the background when we place figures like a Solzhenitsyn and a Skinner in brutal confrontation. Then we catch a glimpse of our actual freedom, and philosophy itself, perched precariously on the edge of a technical civilization for which reasonings like Kant's may no longer be even understandable. And thus our argument for freedom has to take on a different and more urgent emphasis.

Since this argument is embedded in our exploration of three philosophers, the reader may be helped if we present its skeleton here as a kind of preliminary guide. It falls into three parts, and in each part one of our three thinkers serves to develop and orchestrate one aspect of the central theme:

I. The lesson of Wittgenstein's career for us lies in the failure of logic to determine a philosophy. (It is not the only thing he has to teach, nor the only thing we gather from him, but it is the lesson we emphasize.) At a certain point formal logic has to give way to the more haphazard insights of common sense. The insistence upon exactness has to bow to the requirements of adequacy.

The formal logic in this case is mathematical logic, a technique that seemed powerful enough to some philosophers earlier in this century to resolve all the disputes among philosophers. Its failure to bring such peace ought to tell us something then about the limits of technique generally. A highly technical civilization that sought to run itself on its accumulated techniques could not escape the contingencies of decision and creativity that are needed to keep the machine going. Decision and creativity! We are landed back in the human condition of freedom once again.

II. Human techniques, however, do not operate in a void. Embodied materially and socially in the form of our technology, they shape a new human environment for us. They place us as human beings in a new relation to our environing nature, to the cosmos, and so ultimately to ourselves.

With the explosion of the atom bomb we caught some glimpse of this new domain of being we have entered—a glimpse, but hardly an understanding. Since then, we have had floods of journalism, pro and con, on the subject of technology, but despite all the words shed, it is questionable whether we have arrived at a philosophical comprehension of what has befallen us.

Heidegger is a useful guide through some of these thorny questions. The question of technology, which is central to his later writings, is in fact the issue on which his thinking comes into most direct confrontation with the modern age. Superficially, technology looks like the pure servant of freedom: By increasing our powers it multiplies our opportunities to be free. But in attaining those powers we could very well lose the direct and organic sense of our relatedness to nature that humankind once knew; or, in Heidegger's words, we could attain a mastery over beings but lose the sense of Being itself. We can thus imagine a technical society of the future that had conquered its material problems but was afflicted with a loss of meaning that its own technical thinking left it unable even to grasp.

Here the function of philosophy may not lie in providing answers but in keeping a question open.

But we as individuals have to answer another question for ourselves that inevitably takes us a step beyond Heidegger:

III. Both Wittgenstein and Heidegger, at certain moments and in certain aspects, are religious thinkers of a kind. But if their thought brings them to the threshold of the religious, they themselves do not cross over. The question of freedom, however, cannot stop there; it has to push beyond this threshold to explore the individual's need and his right to risk religious belief. Religion is not an adventitious issue attached anyhow to the problem of freedom. Simply in the interest of his own freedom, the individual is compelled to put the religious question to himself—however he may answer it. Accordingly, any philosophical defense of freedom would be incomplete if it did not put this question to itself.

And here (in Part III) William James becomes our chosen companion. To choose James for this purpose would seem to be obvious enough since he has dealt with the will to believe as a central theme;

but there is an added reason for our choice in the fact that he is *almost* the last modern philosopher who sets the individual before us in the full concreteness of his needs and options. This last might seem a surprising claim in view of the prominence of certain existentialist philosophers in our time. Do we not find the individual everywhere in the pages of Heidegger and Sartre? Not really in the sense we are after. For all the depth and power of Heidegger's analysis of human existence, the individual is replaced by a structure of possibilities; and that is as it must be in the scheme of his thinking. In Sartre the individual disappears into the demonic and melodramatic possibility of his own freedom. Like that Pierre, in his own chosen example, who perpetually haunts the cafe by his absence, the individual ends by becoming absence: no longer a person like you or me but the figment of his own abstract and impossible fantasy of liberty. We have to go back to James to meet ourselves in our actual quandaries and uncertainties; and that is why I think it profitable, particularly in the present situation of philosophy, to renew his mode of thinking, however far we may have to diverge from him in the end.

So, in this brief outline, the reader has the whole design of the book in hand.

Some readers might exclaim at the absence from our scheme of any explicit treatment of social issues. Nowadays it is difficult to write on the subject of freedom without having the social question —how we are to preserve and if possible extend liberty—push itself to the forefront. This social question, as such, lies beyond the scope of the present undertaking, though in two final chapters (in Section IV) we touch indirectly upon it. Our concern is with the philosophical—and, indeed, metaphysical—question of freedom for the individual, and not with the specific forms and problems of political liberty. In the long run, however, I do not think the two kinds of question can be separated; and it seems to me the course of events now at loose in the world is beginning to bear this out.

Part I

Technique

Chapter 1

The Illusion
of a Technique

LUDWIG WITTGENSTEIN FIRST ARRIVED IN CAMBRIDGE IN THE FALL OF
1911. By the following spring he was enrolled as a student of Bertrand Russell; but in his own brusque and imperious fashion Wittgenstein passed very quickly from student to friend and collaborating gadfly on the problems that then occupied his teacher.

The time of his arrival was an auspicious one. A year earlier, Russell and Whitehead had published the first volume of *Principia Mathematica*, their epoch-making work on logic and the foundations of mathematics. They were now busy on the subsequent volumes, which would appear shortly in the next few years. Wittgenstein was too late to be a collaborator; the work had already taken its inalterable shape without him. Yet even now, in being personally close to Russell, Wittgenstein had become a full participant in the questions that the whole enterprise provoked.

The spectacle of three such extraordinary men, huddled around the same infant, is one to quicken the imagination. The image is intellectually true if not physically accurate. What exchange Wittgenstein had with Whitehead must have been slight, and happened through the mutual acquaintanceship with Russell. Whitehead, in fact, had by this time removed to London, and his collaboration with Russell proceeded largely through the mails and the telegraph. Nevertheless, from the point of view of intellectual history, the image of these three minds centered on the same subject and book remains entirely valid despite these minor separations. We have further to imagine these three against the background of the years just prior to the Great War, as the British still call that conflict. The intellectual ambience of Cambridge, particularly, shone with a kind of quiet radiance that never quite came back to the world again. Though the individuals who bathed in it were not aware, it was the end of a chapter in European civilization. But so far as the fortunes of this book, the *Principia,* and its subject, mathematical logic, were concerned, those years were an opening chapter in a very adventurous career. Looking back, then, we are justified to single out the historic moment when these three minds were concentrated along the same path. They are the three Magi, in the traditional tableau, come to kneel at the advent of something new in the world. Only this cradle does not contain a Christ child but a treatise on logic.

It is rare to find three minds of this magnitude together in the same place and time; rarer still to find their attention centered around the same subject and even the same book. The unity in which they are held together for the moment is all the more heightened by the extraordinary differences in personality of the three men themselves. Indeed, if one were to search through the whole human spectrum, one would be hard put to come up with three more distinct specimens, both in their backgrounds and in their individual traits. From what deep springs of character our personal philosophies issue, we cannot be sure. In philosophers themselves we seem always able to notice some deep internal correspondence between the man and his philosophy. Are our philosophies, then, merely the inevitable outcome of the body of fate and personal circumstance that is thrust upon each of us? Or are these beliefs the means by which we freely create ourselves as the persons we become? Here, at the very outset, the question of freedom already hovers in the background. But whatever our final answer may be, we can at least note now that these personal wellsprings of character could scarcely be more different than they are here.

Russell, as the most public figure of the three, would seem to be the most easily accessible in personality. Yet his biography leaves us with the sense of something strange and unrealized in this life, a portion of his being that never quite came fully into consciousness. An orphan and an aristocrat, he was marked thus with a double and contradictory loneliness; and all his later adventures into love and notoriety never quite filled the inner void. He pursued feeling as an abstraction, but never quite realized it concretely in his own life. He helped found a school for deprived children, but left his own children feeling unloved. He was a liberal and champion of humanitarian causes; but against a philosophic antagonist he was not known to be overly fair. His political views were democratic and socialist; but his people had been prominent statesmen in the councils of England, and in philosophical debate Russell could assume their mantle as if he were a lord in Parliament dismissing a backbencher with a scathing quip.

Whitehead came from another class, and this at a time when differences of class in England were matters not only of social status but of spiritual heritage as well. His people were "local men," yeomen schoolteachers and parsons, attached to the countryside of East Kent, and Whitehead inherited from them his deep sense of piety toward the land and the life rooted in it. It is entirely fitting that he should eventually gravitate, even in his philosophy, to the poetry of nature found in Wordsworth and the other Romantics.

It may be that the deepest difference between any two individuals lies in the degree and kind of the religious impulses each is susceptible to. If so, Russell and Whitehead are indeed diametrical opposites. Russell is the ingrained rationalist, for whom religion is alien and antithetical, ultimately no more than an absurd hypothesis about matters of fact for which there is no evidence. For a while he kept up a certain flirtation with mysticism; but it was a mysticism of little religious content if any—no more than an intellectual intoxication with mathematics, which faded as the years went on. Whitehead's religious impulses, on the other hand, are deep and genuine. However liberal his theology, he is nevertheless deeply orthodox in the quality of his piety. His religious feelings are spontaneous and unforced. They rise to the surface wherever the occasion permits. But their ultimate expression is an entire metaphysical system itself, which, though sweeping in its generality, has its roots in the line of his forbears, those "local men" attached to their region. Whitehead gave them and their traditional piety a metaphysical voice.

Both Russell and Whitehead belong in good part to the civilization of the nineteenth century. We can imagine Russell in the line of John Stuart Mill, liberal in politics and utilitarian in morals, though with certain skeptical and dissonant notes added, as befits modernity. Whitehead recalls us at times to the England of Newman. One can imagine Whitehead a generation earlier as one of those who would have been touched by Newman's fervor, but who resolutely remained within the piety of his region and its local church. His prose itself at certain times seems to invoke the comparison. A certain clerical murmur that runs through it puts us in mind of Newman, if one could imagine that impeccable stylist for a moment writing just a little bit sloppily.

When we come to Wittgenstein, however, there is no doubt about what century we are in and that it is our own. It is not a matter of new and dissonant chords added to an old tonality. The key itself has been changed, or rather has disappeared: We are in our own atonal world. The difference is not merely one of years, though those particular years were a turning point in civilization. At the period we have in mind, Whitehead was fifty, Russell forty, and Wittgenstein a youth of twenty-two. The difference in background was more considerable: Wittgenstein came from Mittel Europa, from Vienna, which was a spawning ground for modernism in a variety of forms, and therefore a cultural antipodes to the England of that time. He expresses his insights in brilliant fragments, in line with so much of the deliberately fragmentary nature of much of modern art. In his religious longings he is as far from the witty disbelief of Russell as from the solid piety of Whitehead. Deeply religious, Wittgenstein practices a religion of asceticism—in this case, a self-denial that starves his own religious impulses. This self-starvation resembles somewhat the frightening example provided by the great modernist writer Franz Kafka. The deeper you feel the more silent you must be about your feeling. Wittgenstein, in short, is another embodiment of the neurotic genius, and as such a thoroughly representative figure of our age of neurosis. Nothing seems wanting to establish his claims to modernism, including the fact of his homosexuality and the bitter conflicts that came with it.

What, then, was the power of the idea that could bring together the minds of three such very different human beings? How could a particular logic ever have been expected to unite them permanently under the banner of one philosophy?

For most of us, logic is not that powerful and central a subject. Life seems to get along at times with a minimum of logic. And as for mathematical logic, it seems even more remote and rarefied—an intricate discipline for specialists. But this *Principia* was no ordinary textbook of logic; and coming when it did, it made no ordinary claims. The nineteenth century had seen the first decisive steps taken in the mathematicizing of logic; and by the end of the century there had been a number of brilliant explorations by various logicians along this line. What Russell and Whitehead set out to do was, first, to codify all of these previous explorations, and so set forth the whole body of logic in a precisely symbolic, or mathematical, form. Thus for the first time in human history, it appeared, there would be a complete and exact representation of the structure of human thought.

More than this, the authors had a second and even bolder aim in mind: Beyond codifying all of logic, they were also seeking to "reduce" mathematics to logic. Reduction here means the attempt to exhibit a way in which all the truths of mathematics might be expressed within a purely logical language and so be revealed as essentially logical truths. The *Principia* thus promised to shed a new and perhaps final light on the foundations of mathematics—an area that, for a variety of reasons, had become particularly troubling at the turn of the century. After age-old uncertainties and doubts, these foundations would at last be secured by being established within the simpler, purer, and more basic structure of logic itself.

For the visionary, the advent of the book was like a dream come true. More than two centuries earlier, at the beginning of the era of modern science, the great philosopher and mathematician Leibniz had sketched a project of creating a *caracteristica universalis*, an exact and universal language to be used by the scientists of all nations and in all disciplines. The work of Russell and Whitehead seemed to be the fulfillment of that project. Here, after all, was a universal language, since it expressed the logical core of all languages. Anyone who would speak logically, no matter what his field, must ultimately be speaking within this framework. Special theoretical languages may be constructed for the particular uses of certain sciences, but they too would still have to operate within the general matrix of logic. As the ideal logical language, *Principia* would then be the language of languages.

Russell and Whitehead did not talk explicitly of technique. The word did not then figure so prominently in the intellectual vocabulary; and it would have had an alien ring in the philosophical atmosphere of Cambridge before 1914. When American pragmatism, in the writings of William James and John Dewey, had come to the attention of British philosophers, the reigning minds of Cambridge

—G. E. Moore and Russell himself—had raised disdaining eyebrows at it. Only American philosophers could be so crude and common as to bring practical considerations into philosophy. Thus Russell and Whitehead set forth their logic as a piece of pure theory. Nevertheless, insofar as they claimed to bring forth an ideal and exact language, considerations of an instrumental and practical nature could not altogether be absent. Language has to be regarded, in one of its aspects at least, as a tool or instrument. Indeed, it is the most potent instrument and advantage that humans command in relation to the other species. Viewed as the language of languages, *Principia* would also provide us the technique of techniques: it would, in fact, be the most potent instrument of thought yet devised. And Russell hastened to proclaim it as such. Ordinary English, he insisted, is confused and misleading; and only through this new formal language was clear and exact thinking possible.

I.

The prestige of Russell's and Whitehead's achievement was not really slow in growing when one considers the initial difficulties presented by their text. Bristling with strange symbols, the *Principia* seems at first glance incomprehensible to the ordinary understanding. One critic has remarked that the book is in fact mainly about notations. The remark is ironic but not distorting. Beneath the prolix wealth of symbolism, the basic ideas of the work are very simple and well within the comprehension of the intelligent beginner who sets his mind to it. And once these ideas became current, it was their very sweeping simplicity that made for the powerful appeal of the work.

The first impact was upon specialists—logicians and those mathematicians who were interested in the foundations of their subject. During the 1920s, however, the ripples spread among philosophers, and by the 1930s these had become a tidal wave in some philosophical circles. Professor C. I. Lewis of Harvard, for example, a distinguished philosopher and logician in his own right, declared that the book marked a turning point in human thought. And the emergence of logical positivism at about this time served to reinforce this view.

What the positivists did was to take over the empiricism of David

Hume and annex to it the new technique of mathematical logic. In their actual philosophizing, however, it was the latter that provided the more potent and aggressive weapon. It appeared to give them a more exact and more "scientific" language in comparison with their adversaries. Only within the framework of this language—or so it seemed then—could philosophic problems be raised with any degree of precision at all. Otherwise you might be deluding yourself about pseudoproblems, thin and vaporous as mist. And the positivists, when they turned this weapon back upon the past, lay about with wholesale slaughter. The great philosophic problems of the past were to be declared pseudoproblems, and the great figures of the past were portrayed as men fighting with empty shadows. The resulting scheme that issued from positivism had at least the virtue of overwhelming simplicity. All problems were either questions of fact or questions of logic. The former were to be dealt with by the sciences, and philosophy disappeared without residue into a certain kind of logical analysis. Thus when philosophy, which originally was supposed to question everything, turns to question itself, it finds that it has vanished.

There should be nothing surprising in this position. Ever since Kant, modern philosophy has been engaged in searching for and recasting its legitimate role. The modern period might even be described as the one in which philosophy has become most uncertain of itself. Positivism at least had a clear-cut answer to this uncertainty. Amid all the jockeying of the philosophic schools, amid all the varied proposals as to what philosophy is or ought to be about, none was more candidly suicidal than that of positivism.

Whether or not you were caught up in the disputes that raged around positivism at that period, mathematical logic haunted the general intellectual ambience. For a young student then entering philosophy, this book, *Principia Mathematica*, lay squarely across your path. It had become a kind of modern *pons asinorum*, the bridge that had to be crossed to get into the real terrain of philosophy beyond. No matter what your particular field, you felt you would be adequate to it only if you had some preliminary competence in the logic of this book. Only within the terms of this language—as our thinking then ran—could philosophic questions be raised with any degree of precision at all. And if they could not be raised within the framework of that language, so much the worse for them: They could be dismissed or ignored. There was a prevailing faith that logic, in its mathematical form, provided a technique that was decisive for philosophy.

That confidence has very largely waned among philosophers today. Yet the belief in the decisive role of technique has not vanished; it has passed from the philosophers into the culture at large. It has become a general faith, widespread even when it is unvoiced, that technique and technical organization are the necessary and sufficient conditions for arriving at truth; that they can encompass all truth; and that they will be sufficient, if not at the moment, then shortly, to answer the questions that life thrusts upon us.

Thus the case of our three philosophers becomes of crucial significance. History is usually so unclear and unsymmetrical in the unfolding of events that we are hard put to gather whatever lessons we can from it. But very occasionally, as in the present case, history seems to provide us with crucial experiments of its own—situations where we have only not to be blind to draw the moral. The separate philosophical developments of Russell, Whitehead, and Wittgenstein is such a test case, which the twentieth century has left with us. Not to profit by it is to entrench ourselves more deeply in our current illusions about technique. Those who do not learn from history, as Santayana has said, are doomed to repeat it.

Turn again to our initial situation. We fix our attention upon three philosophers of extraordinary abilities at the moment when they are coming into possession of an instrument of thought of extraordinary power. Moreover, all three are convinced of the great value and significance of this instrument. Now, if technique were decisive in the forming of a philosophy, then we should expect that all three, in their subsequent development, would travel more or less the same path. One would allow for minor divergences in accordance with different personal interests and styles of expression. In the main, however, their later philosophies should move more or less parallel with each other—at least if the common technique were the decisive factor. The historical reality, of course, turned out to be altogether different. All three philosophers, in their subsequent development went off in drastically different directions from one another.

It turns out, in fact, to be difficult to trace any definite role that logical technique plays in forming the philosophies of the two men, Russell and Whitehead, who authored the *Principia*. In *The Problems of Philosophy* (1912), two years after the first volume of *Principia* had appeared, Russell's position is developed independently of mathematical logic. The position is Platonism, elaborated in rebellion against the idealism in which Russell had been brought up. His reasons for holding it do not derive in any way from the apparatus of mathematical logic. In retrospect, we are able now to make the opposite judgment: We can see how much of the Platonist structure of the *Principia* itself was shaped by an independently formed philosophy.

In 1914, in *Our Knowledge of the Eternal World*, Russell takes the new tack and proclaims that *"Logic is the essence of philosophy."* He would thus assign a determining role to the new technique. His simple statement here—"Logic is the essence of philosophy"—sums up the core of logical positivism well before that movement had yet appeared. Nevertheless, in the ensuing years, Russell's position tacks back and forth so much that we can only conclude that if logic is indeed issuing the directives, it must be giving very uncertain and inconclusive ones indeed.

It is worth taking a brief, if schematic, look at this development. In 1912 Russell's position was a dualism along standard and traditional lines. Experience is split into two worlds—a private or subjective and a public or objective world, the worlds of sense perception and of physics. This is the doctrine of the two worlds, which will be a recurring theme throughout this book, and we therefore call attention to it here at its first appearance. It is a doctrine that has shaped the intellectual climate of the whole modern age, and one against which philosophers in this century, whatever their different schools, have felt called upon to struggle. Russell himself is not comfortable with it, and in 1914 he seeks to take a step beyond it. He tries to build a bridge between the world of mind and matter—or, as he now puts it, between psychology and physics. For this purpose he borrows from Whitehead a logical technique for deriving the abstract concepts of physics from the concrete data of sensation.[1] If the fundamental concepts—of space, time, and matter

---

[1] Whitehead called it the method of "Extensive Abstraction." It was essentially the procedure in *Prinicpia* for dealing with the mathematical problems concerning Dedekind's "cut" and the existence of irrational numbers. Instead

—in which we frame our notion of the physical world can be exhibited as deriving from our sensory experience, then the gulf between the two worlds seems to become less impassable. Notice, however, that there are still two worlds to begin with—otherwise why struggle so elaborately to build a bridge between them?

Accordingly, Russell took the farther step, which does not appear in fully explicit form until 1921, in his *Analysis of Mind*. Instead of a dualism between two worlds, there is now a doctrine that he calls "neutral monism." (The terms, as well as the initial suggestion, were borrowed from William James, though they are put by Russell to a rather un-Jamesian use.) There are now not two worlds, mental and material, but one world, which can be viewed alternately as mental or as material, depending on the way in which we construct it from elementary constituents that in themselves are neither mental nor material—therefore, to be called "neutral." Russell chose as these basic building blocks the elementary data of sensation. The table on which I write, for example, is an assemblage of data—color, shape, hardness, and so on. My mind contemplating it is also another such assemblage, but of different data—namely, all those data of sensation that make up the stuff of my personal biography.

The doctrine is a baroque and spectacular effort, though of dubious success. But its success or failure is not our question here. We

---

of postulating the existence of an irrational number, like $\sqrt{2}$, as a distinct entity, you "construct" it as a class of rational numbers. Consequently, Russell thought you need not postulate the existence of ordinary physical objects, like tables or chairs, but simply "construct" them as classes, or collections, of sensory data.

To "construct a class," for Russell, was simply to have an adequate notation for writing it down. Later on, Wittgenstein was to reject this peculiar idolatry of notation. His thinking on mathematics had changed, under the stimulus of Brouwer, and he demanded much more definite requirements for constructivity. You construct the class only as far as you compute the number. You end thus, however far you go, with a finite decimal, which falls short of "*the* irrational number" you seek. See Chapter 6.

Around this isolated but very significant bit of procedure we could develop a whole chapter on the relative roles of philosophy and technique. Thus:

(1) Two philosophers, Whitehead and Russell, embrace the technique. However:

(2) In the hands of each man it yields an altogether different philosophical interpretation of the nature of experience. Meanwhile:

(3) A third philosopher, Wittgenstéin, rejects the technique altogether on philosophical grounds!

Decidedly, technique here is subservient to the philosophic outlook with which one comes at this technique.

ask instead: Why did Russell choose sense data as the elementary building blocks of reality? Did the choice follow logically from the new logic, which was supposed to be "the essence of philosophy?" If anything was "neutral" in this snarled situation, it was the logical technique itself, as between two rival views of experience. Thus Russell acknowledged his indebtedness to Whitehead for the particular technique, but in Whitehead's hands that technique issued in an altogether different philosophy. And it did so because both men started from an altogether different vision of experience. For Russell, experience comes to us partitioned into discrete atoms; for Whitehead, every sense perception is an immediate disclosure of the world, into which all the details of background enter, though in different degrees of relevance. Russell arrived at his sense data as the basic building blocks of the world through a process of thought —or lack of thought, his critics say—that did not in the least derive from mathematical logic. His choice of these elements came out of a particular grasp and elaboration of experience—a peculiar phenomenology, to use the term of another school—that was anterior to the application of the technique.

Without following all the involutions of the intervening years, we may pass to a final position of 1948, in *Human Knowledge*, where at last Russell has turned full circle and declares that logic is not a part of philosophy at all! By this time he had read the handwriting on the wall: Mathematical logic had become a specific and voluminous field of research for mathematicians and so had finally settled down into a quite special discipline within mathematics itself. It was no longer the *caracteristica universalis*—that universal and all-embracing language of which Leibniz had dreamed as a possible key to all knowledge. From 1914 to 1948—in a third of a century —logic has passed from being the center of philosophy to forming no part of it. If this last conclusion holds, then philosophy would be exactly where it is if *Principia Mathematica* had never been written. But we have to give Russell all due credit for the path he has traveled. He has given us thereby the accurate summation of all those years: Not one substantive philosophic position of his during that time really derived from the particular technique of logic.

The role of mathematical logic is not any more determinative of Whitehead's philosophy, and in some respects its presence is even harder to trace. True, he does use some of the techniques of *Principia* to elaborate his views of space and time in subsequent writings. But the techniques are in the service of a fundamental intuition that is itself part of larger vision of the universe. And Whitehead does insist on this larger vision. He is one of the few philosophers of our period who holds to the necessity of speculative philosophy and develops such a system of his own.

"Speculative" here means exactly what it says. The philosopher seeks a generality beyond the boundaries of science; he attempts to frame a comprehensive and coherent framework of ideas within which the partial results of science may become more intelligible. The effort is an unpopular one nowadays, at least among philosophers, for scientists in a holiday mood do not disdain to make such ventures. Yet, Whitehead held, it is a frustration of our human intellect not to attempt such rational conjectures. We stultify ourselves if we cease to wonder about the universe, about all that is, and about God as the bottom ground of actuality between Being and Nothingness. Cut off from such questions, the human mind becomes cramped and pettifogging in its horizons. Thus his unpopular espousal of speculative philosophy came actually to be directed against the dominance of the technique he had helped to father. His words shortly before his death, "*The decline of speculative philosophy is one of the diseases of our culture*," were aimed against the narrow positivism that at that particular time was battening upon the technique of the *Principia*.

More than this. The fundamental premise of Whitehead's philosophy runs counter to the logic he had coauthored with Russell. Whitehead holds an organic view of the universe. The parts of an organism stand in internal relation to one another within the whole. Their connections are not merely external, but bonds of intimacy one with another. In the logic of *Principia*, however, all connectives are "extensional"—they link facts externally. In that language you cannot express the intimacy of facts A and B beyond saying that A and B happen to be found together. You can state their coincidence but not their active interplay. Whitehead never turned back to make any detailed critique of his work with Russell.[2] He proceeded

---

[2] One exception, a single paragraph in a late essay, "Mathematics and the Good," is a devastating comment on the Rule of Types, which Russell had introduced into the work. The rule is a practical crutch, Whitehead observes, adopted only to make the system work. But in its actual operation this rule would make arithmetic actually unworkable! Since this rule was distinctly Russell's contribution, Whitehead may be paying off old scores. But the point itself is very important, and we shall return to it in Chapter 6.

philosophically as if the collaboration had never taken place. His whole later philosophy could have been substantially what it is if the *Principia* had never come into existence.

Oddly enough, it is the younger follower, Wittgenstein, whose philosophic evolution is more wedded to the fortunes of mathematical logic. He was the only one of the three who tried to take seriously Russell's dictum that logic should become the essence of philosophy. Wittgenstein began, at any rate, by constructing a total view of the world within the framework of mathematical logic. But he did not stay there. His further stage was to renounce the domination of formal logic for the language of everyday use as a more adequate vehicle for philosophical clarification. The pretensions to exactness are given up for the more real satisfactions of adequacy to experience. But his revolt against Russell leads him even farther. Not only is the technical apparatus of logic too impoverished for philosophic use, and therefore in need of being supplemented by the everyday language; but also this logic, so Wittgenstein holds, has in fact become a positive disaster for some mathematicians and philosophers because the mere use of a symbolic notation can seduce them to get by without having to think clearly. Thus, with regard to this one particular technique, Wittgenstein runs the gamut from the extreme of acceptance to the extreme of rejection.

III.

The century has receded fast, and Russell, Whitehead, and Wittgenstein have taken their place in it. We are able, with some degree of clarity, to see each figure as a whole. In each case the man and the philosopher are wedded inseparably in our vision of them: We see the man through the philosophy and in the philosophy; and the philosophy as that without which that particular man would not be who he was. And, in each case, we have to conclude that a particular technique—in the present instance, mathematical logic—played little part in the formation of these philosophies. Their ultimate view of things came out of an area of experience and personality—which is to say, an area of freedom—deeper and prior to any particular technique of which they may have made occasional use.

What leads us to the philosophies we eventually adopt for ourselves? Or, more simply, what makes us as individuals see things as we do? There is no sure answer to this question, but one amusing anecdote about Whitehead and Russell may shed a little light on the question. The incident occurred during the days of their collaboration on the *Principia*. Whitehead had been puzzled and fascinated for some time that in almost all matters Russell came at things from a different angle from his own. Finally, he observed to his friend: "You know, there are two kinds of people in the world: the simpleminded and the muddleheaded." And when Russell waited for the application, Whitehead immediately gave it: "You, Bertie, are simple-minded; I am muddleheaded." The terms are playful and ironic, but their intent is serious and their perceptiveness acute. We are reminded of William James' classification of "tough-minded" vs. "tender-minded" thinkers. But "tough" and "tender" connote certain factors of aggressiveness and of the will, while Whitehead's distinction is more purely intellectual. The "simpleminded" fasten upon the clear fragments of fact that lie in the foreground to the neglect of the complex background of reality against which those facts emerge. The "muddleheaded," on the other hand, are so engrossed in this complexity of background that enters into every atom of fact that clarity of expression emerges dimly if at all.

Whether or not Whitehead's distinction holds for philosophers throughout history, it was certainly to prove apt for Russell and himself. Both went about their subsequent careers as if they were intent on confirming it. Whitehead created a thoroughly muddleheaded philosophy that required an unusual and special vocabulary of its own. Russell remained resolutely simpleminded to the end, never deviating from a clarity that illumines its point for a moment, only to leave us afterward with all the puzzles of its oversimplifications.

And Wittgenstein? He seems to oscillate between the two poles, exhibiting alternately the matter-of-fact simplicity of the engineer looking for simple material models and at other times the flair of the artist for what can be only barely or indirectly communicated, if at all.

This duality is another in that bundle of conflicts that makes him a "modern." That is one reason why we choose Wittgenstein as the special case to study in subsequent chapters. He seems to draw into himself all the conflicts that modernism has brought into our culture; and in examining him, we may perhaps come to some deeper understanding of the climate under which we still labor. There is a second, and more systematically philosophical reason, for singling him out. His philosophic development is more explicitly wedded to logic; he has pondered the basis and significance of logic more deeply than either Russell or Whitehead; and consequently we should be able to see in him, more clearly and in detail, the relation between technique and philosophy.

So far we have found no decisive relation between logic and the separate philosophies of these three men, and it might seem therefore that we were making out the development of modern logic to be an unimportant matter. On the contrary—and we must insist on this strongly—the development of this logic has been of enormous philosophical significance. Only that significance has not come in the shape of some earlier dreams. Logic has not provided a key to traditional philosophical problems, like matter and mind, as Russell dreamed. It does not liquidate ethics, aesthetics, or metaphysics, as the more aggressive positivists once hoped. Its value has turned out at once more limited and yet sweeping in its consequences. It is the only one of the modern sciences that has produced its own critique, in the Kantian sense of that word—that is to say, it has shown its own limits. And in showing the limits of its formal systems, it shows the limits of the techniques and the machines that man may design.

For the prospects of a technical civilization that is a conclusion of major consequence.

Chapter 2

———◆———

Technique, Technicians, and Philosophy

WHAT IS A TECHNIQUE?

The Yurok Indians are a tribe living on our Pacific Coast who subsist very largely on the salmon that swim out of the ocean into their rivers. Before the season the salmon begin running, the Yurok build a dam to trap the fish in order to ensure a good catch for the winter. The building of this dam is preceded and accompanied by much ceremony and ritual. There are mass enactments of the tribal myths, purification baths, fasting from certain foods, sexual abstinence, and a taboo against certain kinds of incontinent talk. When the fishing has been done, and the catch is in, there follows a corresponding short period of détente, a kind of bacchanalia in which sexual freedom and verbal license are tolerantly allowed to run their course.

The dam itself is a fairly complex technological achievement; but for the Yurok the rituals that accompany it are as much part of the whole technique of hunting the salmon as the act of building or the preparing of nets and other gear. To the civilized mind this represents a failure to separate subjective and objective components in the business of the hunt. The primitive does not understand this separation, and if he could be made to understand, would rebel against it. All his inherited ways teach him the wisdom of not separating man from the nature within which he moves. Thus he comes to think of the fish that are caught as a gift of nature, and even the skill of the fisherman as another such gift. Consequently, the whole hunt is not a sheer self-assertion of the human will against nature.

Belatedly, we have come to recognize that these rituals may have a "psychological" efficacy. But this acknowledgment itself shows that we cannot return to his condition, for the terms in which we would honor it are also altogether alien to it.

In the broad anthropological sense, all rituals may be considered as techniques; and a culture is the sum of its rituals. Some rituals still attend our own technology. When a hydroelectric dam is completed, there may be various ceremonies in celebration: a crowd gathers, politicians speak, a band plays; and if the occasion warrants, there may even be a prayer delivered by a clergyman. But such pomp is halfhearted, if we compare it with the Yurok. The detached anthropologist would note that, in the whole spectrum of human cultures, ours is one in which ritual becomes more perfunctory and external in relation to its technology.

The imposing structure of technology, as the dominating presence in modern society, tends to assimilate the meaning of "technique" to itself. This assimilation shows itself more plainly in other languages than English: in German, for example, *Technik* signifies technology, and in intellectual discussion is likely to be used more often than its cognate, *Technologie;* and similarly for *technique* and *technologie* in French. The assimilation of these two terms to each other is the great fact of modern history. What we are dealing with here, and what we shall be dealing with throughout, is the single phenomenon indicated by the hyphenated form *technique-technology.*

The two, in fact, have become inseparable. The majority of us have only minimal techniques in relation to the machines we use. We know how to press buttons, and most of us drive our automobiles without knowing what a carburetor is. But if our civilization were to lose its techniques, all our machines and apparatus would become one vast pile of junk. We would not know how to produce the power that keeps the machines running, and we would not know how to replace those machines that wore out. We would roam amid a landscape of dynamos, factories, and laboratories, and with all this equipment still intact as so much sheer physical matter, we would nevertheless be a civilization without a technology. Modern science and technology are the offspring of *method* and they persist only so long as we command this method. *Technology is embodied technique.*

We do, of course, still use the word in other areas, as in the arts, which appear alien to technology. We commonly speak, for example, of a painter's or a writer's technique. We even give studio courses in these subjects. And if we enroll as students, we seek to learn to paint or to write, as the case may be. But even here, and perhaps most of all here, if we watch how the various meanings grade off, we get a glimpse of the more precise and limited sense of technique. The teacher may give us certain quite simple and mechanical rules to get started. But if the pupil persists and develops, he eventually reaches a point where the teacher has to tell him he is on his own, and there is no prescribed technique that will paint his picture for him. Then other words have to be invoked—a special knack, a gift, flair, talent, or, most remote of all, genius. Indeed, it was a simple consideration like this that led Kant to define genius as the ability to produce something over and above any rules. Genuine creation is precisely that for which we can give no prescribed technique or recipe; and technique reaches its limits precisely at that point beyond which real creativity is called for—in the sciences as well as the arts.

But it is just at this point in the arts, where technique ceases to be sufficient, that we catch a glimpse of the meaning that is central to technique-technology. A technique is a standard method that can be taught. It is a recipe that can be fully conveyed from one person to another. A recipe always lays down a certain number of steps which, if followed to the letter, ought to lead invariably to the end desired. The logicians call this a *decision procedure*.

As children we became familiar with such procedures in our elementary arithmetic. Adding, subtracting, and multiplying were perfectly automatic procedures, even if they sometimes strained our attention. Problems in long division were a little more vexing because, for the sake of speed, they sometimes involved a certain amount of shrewd guessing. But if you went slowly, they were no different from the other operations. All you had to do was follow a routine method carefully, and you came out with the correct answer. Quite early too, in school mathematics, we encountered other kinds of problems that could not be solved in such mechanical fashion. In high school geometry, for example, you can prove some theorems only be devising a certain *construction:* You have to draw a line or figure that is not there in the original data. For this you had to be inventive; and if you weren't clever enough for that, you were forced simply to memorize the proof in the text—which had originally been the creation of genius by some ancient Greek. These two procedures—free construction and the rigorous application of a rule or rules—are antithetical but complementary. Together, they define the substance of mathematics.

Thus, even though we cannot formulate it, we come very early to know what the logical essence of the machine is, and consequently the meaning of technique that is central to technology. A machine is, logically speaking, an embodied decision procedure. By going through a finite and unvarying number of steps it arrives invariably, so long as it is not defective, at a definite result. When your car starts up in the morning, it is solving a problem by going through a number of prescribed steps. It is performing the same kind of operation, logically speaking, that you did as a child when you had to perform simple long division, though it is to be hoped more quickly. All that we desire from a machine of this kind is that it go through the routines written into it. The last thing we want from it is that it be creative or inventive in any way. When your automobile starts to sound in the morning as if its starting up were a matter of improvisation or invention, it is usually time to trade it in.

I.

Stripped down thus to its logical essence, the machine would hardly seem to be a threatening thing. It merely performs routine actions in our service; it does our long division for us, so to speak. It is when the machine becomes more clever that we begin to fear it. It may become cleverer than ourselves, and something we cannot control. There is also the fact that clever people can sometimes become quite thoughtless in pursuing their goals; thus the more complex and subtle the technology the more likely sometimes it is to carry with it damaging side effects that were never expected.

But whatever its source, there is no doubt that the suspicion of technology has become so widespread that the dominant myth of our time may very well become that of Frankenstein's monster. And, as should be the case with myths, this one has begun to have a strong grip not only on the intelligentsia but on the popular mind as well. The horror movies, for example, are mostly a re-creation of this myth in one form or another, and their audience has grown steadily. Most of science fiction, as a prophecy of the future, is one prolonged horror story. For the student of our culture, this situation has a very curious and striking ambiguity about it. While our writers, and some of the best of them, were seeking to re-create myths in literature for the sake of an age that seemed to have lost the capacity for myth, all this time technology was bringing in one very big myth through the back door. And there is the further irony about this: While technology is something essentially pointed toward the future, it has nevertheless been able to stir in the unconscious of the modern audience the primeval fears and horrors of monsters and ogres with which the old legends and fairy tales abound.

It would be pointless here to repeat the legitimate complaints that have made us fear technology. The cause of the environment has now found its champions and, it is hoped, will find more as time goes on. What is to the point, and particularly on a philosophical level, is to try to call attention to the very mixed and intricate nature of the matter of technology, especially when there is a tendency to drastic oversimplification on one side or the other. The real depth of the problem begins when we see how difficult it may be to separate out the beneficial and detrimental effects of technology. Chemical fertilizers, for example, have enabled our agriculture to become enormously productive, and so feed millions of people who might otherwise go hungry; yet these same fertilizers leach off into streams, pollute our waters, kill fish, and turn lakes into stagnant ponds. Medical technology has reduced those age-old enemies of mankind, plagues and pestilence, all over the world; and as a result we now face the threat of overpopulation, which may become the most serious problem humankind will have to deal with in the next century. In cases like this, technology does not seem like the alien monster of a horror story, but very human indeed—ourselves writ large. We seem to carry over into technology that deepest and most vexing trait of the human condition itself: that our efforts are always ineradicably a mixture of good and evil.

We seem thus at once to have both too much technology and hardly enough. We do not as yet, for example, have enough technology actually operant to feed all the people on this planet.

Our ambivalence is further compounded by the fact that, complain as much as we do about all the hardware of technology, we secretly nourish a fascination with technique itself. The publishing market is regularly flooded with "how to" manuals of all kinds. We turn to books to learn how to make love, and in consequence sex

comes to be thought of as mainly a technique. Treatises on mental
health appear that carry with them their own built-in little self-help
kit of psychotherapy. All of this would be comic if it weren't also
so pathetic—and ultimately dangerous. This worship of technique is
in fact more childish than the worship of machines. You have only
to find the right method, the definite procedure, and all problems in
life must inevitably yield before it. Our ambivalence here toward
the whole phenomenon of technique-technology could scarcely be
more complete. I do not know that there are any statistics on the
matter, but I suspect that a good many persons who put their trust
in manuals of sex may be the very same persons who take up the
cause of the environment and rail against technology.

Philosophy has a very special relation to this muddled state of
affairs, if the philosopher would only stop to think about it. Philosophy is, in fact, the historical source of technology in its modern
sense. This claim may seem surprising at first sight, but we have
only to recall our earlier discussion to see that it is in no way exag-
gerated. We pointed out then that technique, in its strictly technological sense, involved two factors. (1) There must be a clear and
distinct separation of the subjective and objective components in
any situation in order for us to take rational hold of the problem.
(2) The objective problem, thus isolated, is to be dealt with by a
logical procedure that seeks to resolve it into a finite number of steps
or operations. Both these conditions were the creation of philosophy.
Descartes ushered in the modern age by establishing the primacy of
method, in the course of which he fixed the distinction between subject and object as sharply as could possibly be done. And as for logic
itself, that was originally the creation of philosophers in the ancient
days of the Greeks.

Thus the whole of technology, as we now know it, is the late, and
maybe the final offspring of philosophy. There is not the least exag-
geration in this judgment. It merely reports the simple historical
course of things.

But being a parent does not now confer any special privileges
upon the philosopher. He is absorbed into the technical scheme of
things with everybody else. One of the chief characteristics of the
technical society is the specialization of labor. This follows from
the logical nature of technique itself. Since technology is merely the
embodiment of a logical procedure, and this procedure divides the
problem into a number of partial and successive steps, therefore the

social accomplishment of the task will be divided into the accomplishment of these component parts. Consequently, we are each assigned our particular slot in the society.

The philosopher has to feel a little uncertain here. He is still secretly committed to a discipline that is uneasy before such specialization. Voltaire described his Dr. Pangloss, the ridiculous metaphysician in *Candide,* as "professor of things in general." The irony was meant to be devastating. Talk about everything in general fails to be specific about anything, and is therefore empty of sense. Ever since, philosophers in the modern period have labored under the shadow of Voltaire's censure. Moreover, unlike their ancient brethren, they now have to contend with modern science, which did speak—and triumphantly so—about very definite and specific things. Yet the philosopher, uneasy as he may be, is still condemned to the tag of his calling. So far as he is still assigned to the profession of philosophy, he must seek to frame some general scheme of ideas, however tentative, about the way things are. He is condemned to be a "professor of things in general." The ghost of Dr. Pangloss still haunts him.

An escape seems to beckon by way of social imitation. Simply as a social being, the philosopher will feel this push anyway. In any society the individual has to establish his social status by demonstrating competency in the ways that are normally approved by that society. In a technical society this means that the individual establishes his technical proficiency at some kind of task. Since there are no privileged exceptions, the philosopher is dragged into the net like everyone else. He seeks therefore to justify himself and his existence as a peculiar kind of technician. There are even "technical" journals in philosophy, as in mathematics and physics. The philosopher thus adopts a protective coloration that helps him escape notice in his society. But if he stops to think for a moment, he will realize he is playing a game: The so-called technical publications of philosophy do not resemble those in mathematics and physics. If he thinks a little longer, he will conclude that philosophy is the kind of subject in which there cannot be technical journals of that kind. But these considerations easily get lost in the heat of the battle. Prestige and personal vanity involve one in controversy; the technique of the philosopher has to do with words, and arguments about words; and the more he immerses himself in hair-splitting debates the more he can feed his illusion that he is a genuine technician. He becomes absorbed into what was at first his protective coloration. The philosopher disappears into the technician. From a larger historical perspective, there is an amusing but very somber irony here: Philosophy, which was the original sire of technique, is now about to be devoured by its own offspring.

Pulled by these opposing forces—on the one hand, to become a specialist and lose himself in technical details, and on the other hand still to maintain contact with the larger questions of his ancient calling—the philosopher experiences a great sense of relief if he should happen upon a technique that seems to satisfy both requirements at once. Such was the response when *Principia Mathematica* appeared on the scene. It was a technique, and a sufficiently intricate one, such that the ability to understand and handle it gave one the credentials of technical competence. On the other hand, it was not a narrow technique; it seemed to have the most universal implications, and so far from shutting one off in a narrow technical cubbyhole, it seemed to open a broad highway into other disciplines. Thus one could be a "professor of things in general" without having to hang one's head in embarrassment.

But technique also has the characteristic that it sometimes breeds its own obsolescence. Just as the material products of technology become worn out and obsolete, so too the technique that begot them has to be replaced by another. In philosophy this usually means a total change in style and language.

The turnover in philosophic styles has been very rapid in this century. Perhaps that is fitting in a technical civilization, which seems to accelerate history in its every aspect. If one persists long enough as an academic philosopher one sees these styles in philosophy come and go, and one strives to attain some normal human balance between enthusiasm and disillusion. If the rapid succession of reigning orthodoxies does not seem to serve philosophy, which is supposed to aspire after perennial truth, still there are some advantages to be gained from the turnover. At least one narrow technique will yield to another, and one error is driven out by the next. Whether truth is ever attained thereby, we cannot be sure; but at least one hopes that it may hover somewhere over the whole process. And if one does not become disillusioned altogether, there can also be certain moments of illumination in the very shock of change, as in the following story:

My colleagues and I were met to revise the course of studies for students majoring in philosophy. The particular bone of contention in this case was the requirement of mathematical logic, which some students felt was not really relevant to their particular interests. Most of my colleagues, and I myself, felt that some minimal exposure to the subject was a necessary discipline to go through. The vigorous dissenter in this case was an active young colleague, who made his position very plain: He had never had training in the subject, had never felt the need of it, and did not see why students should have to spend their time in going through with it. Had he been a humanist in his general tendencies, the dissent would have been understandable, though it would probably have been offered much more diffidently. But in fact he was a technician of sorts, and altogether convinced of the value of his own chosen technique. He was now immersed in linguistics, and was convinced that this discipline would provide the definite and final key to philosophy.

There are certain moments when the passage of time strikes us with its brutal illumination, and this was one. I felt that this young man and I could be interchangeable across the gap of a generation. Twenty-five years ago this young philosopher would have been urging that mathematical logic was central and indispensable to philosophy. And were I twenty-five years younger I might very well be exhibiting his total passion for the new technique. *Autre temps autres moeurs.* This young philosopher believes that the whole of what we traditionally know as philosophy will disappear without a trace into linguistics. The particular technique has changed, but what persists unchanged is an underlying conviction of our era, that technique of some sort is decisive for philosophy.

So the case of Russell, Whitehead, and Wittgenstein is worth returning to. Its lesson, apparently, has not yet been learned; and that lesson, one of the really significant legacies from an earlier generation, might help to deliver the present generation from some of the illusions about the omnipotence of its current techniques.

Chapter 3

---◄◆►---

The Mystique of Logic

HAD HE WRITTEN NOTHING, HAD HIS INFLUENCE NOT BEEN SO enormous over four decades of philosophers, Wittgenstein would still have been one of the extraordinary personalities of our century. The degree of his influence indeed is not altogether separable from the powerful impression he made upon pupils and disciples, who carried the words of his doctrine through the long years when he chose to remain unpublished. What must have been the attraction of this personality that years later, after the turbulence of their friendship and its final break had long since subsided, Russell wrote: "Getting to know Wittgenstein was one of the most exciting intellectual adventures of my life." These are remarkable words for a man as cool and worldly as Russell to have uttered about anyone. They are positively amazing if we stop to reflect that when they first met, Wittgenstein was a youth of twenty-two and unknown, while Russell himself was a mature man of forty and already famous.

Wittgenstein was extraordinary too in the number of his gifts. He showed precocity in engineering and technical matters; at the age of ten, we learn from the charming account of his sister, he constructed out of bits of wood lying around the house a sewing machine that actually worked. Trained as an engineer, he first went to England in 1911 to work in aeronautics at Manchester. He even took out some patents that, we are told, anticipated later inventions in this field. Combining engineering and art, he spent two years (1926–28) building a house in Vienna for his oldest sister, which was at its time a remarkable contribution to modern architecture. Sensitive to music and literature, he also wrote very well. Thus it would seem that a career as engineer, artist, or literary man might have been open to him. That he happened to become a philosopher might look then like a mere matter of chance, but in retrospect it is hard to think that he could have become anything else.

The profusion of gifts suggests a Renaissance figure, lavish and outgoing in its energies. The direction of his thinking is exactly the opposite. He restricts himself, narrows his horizons, absorbs himself in what appear as small and commonplace questions. He remarks ironically of himself that he philosophizes somewhat like an old woman who has misplaced her keys or spectacles and is rummaging for them. Several times in his life he tried to escape from philosophy and turn himself to some less reflective and uncertain profession. In vain; he is pulled back into the ceaseless questioning that claims him as a philosopher. A homeless being, he could find a home here, for philosophy is that area where man seeks himself out as homeless. No matter what casual item he touches, Wittgenstein philosophizes with a peculiar intensity that we can only call religious.

The family he was born into in 1889 was wealthy and influential —his father was an important industrialist and a minister of state. The familial origins were mixed Jewish and Christian, but predominantly the former. Intermarriages between Jews and Christians had long been commonplace in Austria, and the attempt to separate racial lines was not attempted until Hitler. Wittgenstein's mother was Catholic; he was baptized as Catholic, and listed that officially as his religion. There is no indication that he ever thought of himself particularly as a Jew. A rather remarkable fact: a Jew who never thinks of himself as a Jew!—homelessness compounded.

The family was also very cultivated, and from the earliest age, Wittgenstein was exposed to the various currents of the cultural life of Vienna. (It was also a family haunted by tragedy: All of Wittgenstein's brothers ended their life in suicide.) The attempt has been made—not always convincingly, I believe—to establish detailed influences from this environment upon the formation of Wittgenstein's thought. Nevertheless, the general intent of such studies seems to me sound, whether or not they hold up on particular details, for there does seem to be some very deep sense in which Wittgenstein belongs to the spiritual milieu from which he sprang.

What was the atmosphere of the capital of the Austro-Hungarian Empire like in the early years of this century? We have one unforgettable and powerful portrait of it in Robert Musil's great novel *The Man Without Qualities*. Musil calls the place *Kakania*—a name that speaks its own derision—and he depicts it as frivolous and empty, alternately yearning and despairing, pretentious and nihilistic. But Musil's pen was dipped in acid, and we get only a negative, if searching, vision of this Viennese world. On its positive side, out of this same spiritual milieu, Vienna produced two of the most powerful and symptomatic movements of modern culture—psychoanalysis and atonal music—both voices that speak of the homelessness of modern man. Perhaps Wittgenstein's in philosophy is a third voice to set beside these two. On its social side, Vienna was the glittering and elegant capital of empire. But if this gaudy part of its life was ever encountered by Wittgenstein, it left no traces. The religious earnestness of his own temperament seems to have passed it by unnoticed.

His sister records that these marks of seriousness and intensity appeared quite early, and caused the family to worry about him. She took consolation, however, from Dostoevski's words about his saintly character Alyosha in *The Brothers Karamazov*. Alyosha appeared unworldly and helpless, yet people would always come forward to help him, and he would land on his feet. Some benign angel hovered over Wittgenstein through the events of his life; and though it did not spare him his torments, it enabled him to survive.

Wittgenstein did not enter philosophy in the creeping and tedious fashion of the usual graduate student; he leaped, almost as if without preparation, in *medias res*. He found in Bertrand Russell and mathematical logic both the man and the subject to focus his questions. Russell was generous in this relationship; he said that he learned more from Wittgenstein than he taught him, and quite early on announced that it would be this young man, as yet unpublished, who would make the next decisive step in philosophy.

Varying and conflicting things have been said about the relationship of the two, usually spurred on by the philosophic animus of the particular commentator. The simple human truth of the matter is expressed in a letter that Wittgenstein wrote Russell in the first year of their friendship. They cannot be friends, he says; he will always revere Russell, and be very grateful to him for his help and kindness; but friends they cannot be, for their values are too

different to permit it. Now, Wittgenstein was a difficult person in
many ways; he set a high value upon friendship, and in turn was
likely to be an exacting friend. But there is no petulance in this letter. What is amazing is the singular maturity in a young man who
had just turned twenty-three. Wittgenstein does not upbraid Russell
for his values—they are as personal to Russell as Wittgenstein's to
himself; but being thus radically different in their values, they cannot really become friends. (No more, we may observe in passing,
than they could ultimately be expected to have the same philosophies.) On this particular occasion Russell seems to have quickly
smoothed matters over, and their friendship continued as it had
been. But the letter was prophetic; when the final rift came, in 1922,
the occasion was relatively unimportant; they were simply too
different to remain permanently close friends.

The difference is shown in their response to the outbreak of war
in 1914. Russell, opposing the war, was imprisoned for a while as a
dissenter. Wittgenstein promptly returned to Austria and volun-
teered for service in the army. Radical as he was to prove in his
thinking, in life he felt a deep and spontaneous loyalty toward any
authority that he considered legitimate. His religious sense of life
moved him to seek out some kind of service and self-sacrifice. Sta-
tioned away from the front, he made repeated efforts to be sent
closer to the fighting. It is part of the comedy with which the
world looks at really serious personalities that these efforts were
regarded by the authorities as an attempt to evade service. Eventually, though, he did get to the front and ended as a lieutenant in the
artillery.

The intensity of his inner life continued during all the outward
turmoil of the war. In the little town of Tarnev near the front he
picked up a copy of Tolstoi's version of the New Testament, was
deeply impressed by it, and kept it by his side. His troops knew him
as "the man of the book," because he carried it everywhere with
him. He was the man of the book in another sense too; he was also
carrying around with him the manuscript of what was to be his first
work, the *Tractatus Logico-Philosophicus*, while laboring to complete it. That a work so concentrated and compact in form should
have been conceived and largely brought to completion amid the
life of the trenches cannot but fill us with awe at the intensity of
mind of the thinker himself. Shortly before the Armistice of 1918
Wittgenstein was captured by Italian troops, and it was in an Italian
prison camp that the book was finally completed.

Russell had no word of Wittgenstein during the war, and, in fact, did not know if he were still alive. The two did not see each other again until the end of 1919, when they met in Holland. Russell has left us, in a letter, a record of that meeting that is of the utmost importance in understanding Wittgenstein's state of mind at the time. Without it, we might not grasp the depth of religious feeling that lies behind the *Tractatus,* and therefore miss the intent of the work itself. Writing to Lady Ottoline Morrell on December 20, 1919, Russell says: "I had felt in his book a flavor of mysticism, but was astonished when I found he had become a complete mystic. He reads people like Kierkegaard and Angelus Silesius, and he seriously contemplates becoming a monk." We note Russell's surprise that what he had taken to be only "a flavor of mysticism" turns out to be a matter on which Wittgenstein is really dead serious—and which he intended, in fact, to be the central message of the work. Russell further observes that Wittgenstein is passionately attached to the novels of the Russians Tolstoi and Dostoevski, particularly the latter. It all started, Russell goes on to say, from Wittgenstein's reading of William James' *Varieties of Religious Experience* back in Cambridge before the war. Much as one admires James' book (which, by the way, remained a lifelong favorite of Wittgenstein), one cannot quite believe it all started with that reading. James does not have that evangelical fervor or power to have effected a conversion where no previous disposition existed. From the start, Wittgenstein seems to have been that rare phenomenon among human beings—a genuinely religious personality.

Finally, there is one remark in Russell's letter that is more revealing than he is aware of: "He [Wittgenstein] has penetrated deep into mystical ways of thought and feeling, but I think (though he wouldn't agree) that what he likes best in mysticism is its power to make him stop thinking. . . ." To stop thinking, to be free for a while from the devouring jaws of the intellect!—that is a cry of thinkers like Pascal and Kierkegaard, with whom in his own peculiar way Wittgenstein has a kinship. In that book he had picked up near the front, Wittgenstein would have read and understood Tolstoi's magisterial sentence in the essay that accompanies his Gospel translation: *"The more we live by our intellect, the less we understand the meaning of life."* Wittgenstein probably would not have disagreed with Russell's remark about the need to stop thinking. Certain parts of experience are only grasped if we stop thinking and let be. But all of this would have been foreign country for Russell.

Back in Austria, Wittgenstein made efforts to get a publisher for
his manuscript. After running into difficulties, he was at one point
ready to drop the whole matter. The questions the book dealt with,
after all, lay behind him; he was engaged in the attempt to escape
from philosophy and its questions, finding work as a gardener in a
monastery and then as a country schoolteacher. It was through Russell's intervention that publication was finally secured. The English
edition, with facing German text, appeared in 1922, together with
an Introduction by Russell. Wittgenstein objected to the Introduction, and thereafter the friendship between the two men was
never quite restored. The subsequent fortunes of the book are now
part of the philosophic history of this century.

I.

Now that the controversies and misunderstandings it originally provoked have faded, the *Tractatus* is at once a simpler and richer
work to read. Subsequent developments in logic have moved beyond the book, and show us that while on some points Wittgenstein
made a few prophetic hints, on others he was groping in the dark.
No matter; the author continues to interest us as a philosopher, not
as a technician. The book was strange and mystifying to its readers
when it appeared. For us it has long since become familiar; and yet,
when we come back to it after his later writings, we find it stranger
in another sense because it strikes us as more extreme and arbitrary
in its assumptions and conclusions. Yet it has the peculiar stamp, the
intensity of Wittgenstein's genius, about it; it continues to live as
the unique and thoroughgoing expression of a particular philosophic
vision that haunts the modern mind more deeply than it is aware
of or often cares to acknowledge.

What is this vision? The position may be labeled as "Logical
Atomism," a phrase previously introduced and put to use by Russell. But Russell advanced this new style in philosophy merely as a
mode of procedure: as a kind of philosophical analysis that proceeds
by the piecemeal decomposition of any complex subject into its logically ultimate components. Wittgenstein cannot abide in this halfway house of method; with his usual abruptness, he pushes the matter of procedure to its root. What must the world be like if your
only reliable mode of analyzing it is to take this logical form? And
he wastes no words in telling us what his vision of this world is at

the very beginning of his book. The world is the totality of all facts, and these facts have a peculiar relation, or nonrelation, to one another: *"Any one fact can either be the case, or not be the case, and everything else remains the same"* (1.21).

We have to catch our breath at the audacity of this last statement. We have slowly to let sink in how austere and bleak a picture of the world Wittgenstein is painting for us. The facts that constitute the world are utterly disconnected and lie external to each other within logical space. There is no internal, necessary, or organic bond between them. We may be prepared for this position a little, but only very little, by some other expressions of fragmentation in modern culture. The modern imagination indeed has been haunted by the image of a fragmented world, and in the arts has sought from time to time to give some expression to this feeling. In the novel, particularly, there have been certain bold attempts, and even the elaboration of special fictional techniques, to convey this aspect of experience as the brute flow of random detail. But nowhere has this picture of an ultimately fragmented world been given *intellectual* expression so starkly and tersely as in the single proposition of Wittgenstein: *"Any one fact can either be the case, or not be the case, and everything else remains the same."*

This is an astounding statement to fling in the face of our ordinary experience. To be sure, our everyday world has its gaps, discontinuities, irregularities, and nonsequiturs; and we ourselves, if we took notice, are far more fragmented beings than we care to admit. Still, connectedness is more generally the case than not. One fact does make a difference to others; and if certain facts did disappear, it seems to us that everything else would surely not remain the same. In our dealings with others we like to think that our personal existence does make a difference to some people, just as we feel that our own lives have been different because of a few people here and there whom we have come to know and love. But these feelings of ours, if we follow Wittgenstein's doctrine, would only hold for the superficial *appearance* of things; the *reality* of the world that underlies them would be totally different and alien from them.

What leads Wittgenstein to this peculiar view? The *Tractatus* is written in an aphoristic and oracular style; it does not give the reasons that lead its author to the conclusions he expresses. Yet it is not difficult to reconstruct those reasons from his text. And indeed his reasoning here, we shall see, is not a piece of personal idiosyncrasy, but has about it a massive simplicity that expresses a whole ideological epoch.

We have to grasp, first, what it is that the book seeks to do. Wittgenstein's aim is to tell us what the world is ultimately like insofar, and only insofar, as it can be expressed in a logical language. The attempt has, *prima facie* at least, as much justification as Kant's effort to describe the world from the structures of human consciousness. If the world in itself should be different from those structures, then —so Kant tells us—we would not be able to think it. Analogously, with Wittgenstein, if the world were altogether differently structured from the forms of our logic, we could not express it in language—at least not in any kind of logically exact language. "We could not say of a nonlogical world what it would be like."

Two things, however, have to be noted specifically in this attempted inference from language to the world. Everything turns (1) on the particular form of language one chooses; and (2) on the particular relation one takes to hold between language and the world. Our view of the world could be quite different depending on what choice we made on either of these matters.

1. For Wittgenstein at this stage, the pivotal choice is the language of mathematical logic—and, specifically, the logic of Russell and Whitehead. It has been remarked that he seems to be describing the world as if God had created it after the image of *Principia Mathematica*. The joke is not inaccurate. To be sure, he has serious quarrels in matters of detail with this logic; but on the whole he takes it as the model or paradigmatic language that provides the framework within which to see the world. What justifies his choice of this particular language, and for this particular purpose? He does not tell us. But the reasoning behind that choice would seem to be clear: if we are to construe the nature of the world from language, it would be best to start from the logically most exact form of language that is available.[1]

2. Between this model language and the world there must be a definite relation if we are to infer from the former to the latter. And for Wittgenstein, at this stage, this relation is very simple and clear-cut: language is a mirror that reflects the world, and, accordingly, we may infer from the image in the mirror to the thing or things it mirrors.

---

[1] Later he was dramatically to reverse this choice. The language of mathematical logic, he decides, blocks our efforts to see the world adequately.

Wittgenstein is captured by this metaphor of a mirror, and by the simple line of reasoning that leads him to it. Suppose we take it as fundamental that the business of language—for Wittgenstein at this stage it is the sole business—is to state facts. In order to state its fact, the statement must be in some way a representation of that fact. But it can represent its fact only if the constituents of the statement correspond one-to-one—as the details in the mirror correspond to the details they reflect—to the constituents of the fact. "The statement is a *picture* of the fact." Analogously, the musical score is a picture of the sounds of a symphony: for each sign in the musical notation there corresponds a distinct sound to be heard when the music is played.

Now we have to take only one tiny step further in order to arrive at the logical atoms that make up the world. Logic analyzes statements into two kinds: complex or molecular statements, on the one hand, and, on the other, the atomic statements into which these are resolved. But what holds for the items in the mirror must also hold for the realities the mirror pictures. Hence, in line with our picture theory of language, the world must ultimately be made up of atomic facts that correspond to the atomic statements with which logical analysis terminates. And the various groupings of these atomic facts make up the complex facts that constitute our experience. We thus arrive at the full-fledged doctrine of Logical Atomism.

If we sum up this line of reasoning we have just traversed, omitting the intervening steps, we could say quite simply that Wittgenstein believes there are atomic facts because there are atomic propositions in the logic of Russell and Whitehead. That is a condensation, but not really a travesty of his doctrine. And if it sounds cruel in its concision, it nevertheless places proper emphasis upon the underlying fact of how completely his thinking here was bound within the framework of the logic bequeathed to him by his teacher.

What these ultimate facts are—whether the data of sensation or the particles of physics—Wittgenstein does not tell us. That is a matter for empirical determination, and philosophers are supposed to remain strictly within the limits of a purely logical analysis. Neither Russell nor the Positivists who followed Wittgenstein were so cautious. Russell's Logical Atomism attempted to construct the ordinary physical objects of our experience, like tables and chairs, out of the elementary data of sensation. Following him, the Positivist

Carnap, in his early work *The Logical Structure of the World* (a rather peculiar title for a philosopher who would renounce metaphysics), attempted systematically to build the world out of the same sense-data. Later the attempt was abandoned by the Positivists as being too tedious, cumbersome, and in fact altogether unnecessary for the purposes of scientific knowledge. In fact, however, the whole project is so riddled with initial ambiguities that it has never been successfully carried out. Wittgenstein is spared such embarrassments: he insists only upon the existence of the atomic facts, not their nature.

II.

Wittgenstein seems to philosophize apart from any historical reflection, as if he were confronting problems nakedly and face to face. But there is always a risk for a philosopher, or any man, to attempt to be ahistorical. In trying to approach a problem from scratch, with a clean slate, he may very well end by reproducing, despite the flourishes of orginality, a pattern of thought which is already familiar to the world and has suffered the fate of varied and vigorous criticism. The ahistorical thinker too is likely to be the unwitting child of the immediately prevailing climate of opinion. And in the present case, we can see quite clearly that the Logical Atomism of Wittgenstein results from the historical convergence of two powerful currents that flow into modern philosophy.

The first is the famous analysis of causation by David Hume in the eighteenth century. When we say that A causes B, Hume tells us, we do not assert any internal or necessary bond between the two phenomena. We mean only that when in fact A occurs, B occurs. Fire burns; the two phenomena, flame and heat, are conjoined facts. And that is all we can say about any so-called "causal relation" between the two. And if we were to say that fire "implies" warmth, we can mean only that it will not be the case that the fact of fire occurs and not the fact of warmth. Toward the end of the nineteenth century, physicists like Mach and Helmholtz took over Hume's analysis and pushed it forward in their own science. The notion of cause or force as an occult power or inner bond between phenomena was to be banished from the physical sciences. Science states only the co-presence and co-variation of facts within the world. And having thus apparently acquired the blessings of science, the Humean view became basic dogma within the prevailing climate of empiricist opinion.

The second stream to swell this current was the emergence of the new mathematical logic itself. Not that this logic as such says anything about the doctrine of causation, but as a calculus it provides us with certain devices that permit us to move more easily and familiarly within a Humean world. If the reader has little or no mathematical logic, that should be no hindrance here; he has only to grasp the simple and momentous idea that lies at the basis of this discipline in order to see how, interpreted in a certain way, it will lead to Wittgenstein's Logical Atomism.

The first step in transforming logic into a mathematical calculus was to change our understanding of its fundamental element: the statement or proposition. In the older tradition of logic of Aristotle, when we say that A is B, we wish to exhibit what kind of thing A is, and specifically that it is of the kind B. A proposition, in Aristotle, is a *logos*, a saying or sentence. But not every sentence is a proposition: a prayer, entreaty, and question are sentences but make no statement of fact. A proposition, therefore, is a particular kind of *logos*—a *logos apophantikos;* and the root of the latter word in Greek is the verb meaning to appear or cause to appear; to bring something out into the open. The statement brings the thing before us and shows it to us as it is. We stand here in a primary relationship to language which, as we shall see later (Chapter 8), is a basic concern to a philosopher like Heidegger. But the mathematical logician steps boldly beyond that relationship:

Thus to transform logic into a calculus we must take a giant step at the very beginning—we have to abstract from the intrinsic character of A and B, and from any intrinsic relation that holds between them. When we say that all A is B, we mean merely to say that the instances that fall under A, whatever A may be, occur in conjunction with the instances that fall under B. *The proposition states a certain distribution of facts within logical space.* The facts so distributed may "have nothing to do with each other," in the usual understanding of these words. Notice too that we say logical, not physical, space: A and B may occur at opposite ends of the galaxy, and still be represented by means of the same logical diagram. We are to think of two intersecting circles: Then the facts tabulated under A fall inside, outside, or part inside and part outside of B. There thus seems to be a certain kinship between the mathematicizing of logic and the picturability of its facts. Indeed, the class calculus, with which this logic was launched, may be regarded as a kind of elementary topology of closed spaces. And it may have been this affinity with possible diagrams that disposed Wittgenstein to imagine a proposition as a picture in the first place.[2]

The logic of Russell and Whitehead, pushing this abstractive process further, provides a calculus of propositions based upon the notion of "material implication." Usually when we say that A implies B, we take it that there is some intrinsic bond between the two. The logician abstracts from that: When he asserts "A implies B," he intends no internal bond between the two; he merely asserts that the facts are so distributed in logical space that in no case will an instance of A occur without the occurrence of an instance of B. There is, for example, the fact denoted by the proposition A, "Twice two is four," and the fact denoted by the proposition, "Snow is white." For our ordinary experience, these facts have nothing to do with each other, they are utterly disconnected; and in our ordinary language we would not say that A implies B. But the logician has no hesitation at all in saying this. These two propositions have the same truth-value (both are true), and they therefore satisfy his condition for implication: the first will not be true and the second false. Accordingly, then, the proposition "If twice two is four, then snow is white," is a perfectly proper, and indeed true, statement for the logician. The statement jars our habits of ordinary speech, and may seem strange to us initially. But it is precisely this kind of device that provides mathematical logic with its unique powers of manipulation and calculation.

Thus the facts may be as intrinsically disconnected as you please, and the structures of logic will still apply. For the level of generalization toward which logic strives, and where its full powers come into play, this disconnectedness of the facts is an indifferent matter. But what happens now if you take this logical language as a picture of the world? What you find in the mirror you will find in the reality it mirrors. The disconnectedness permitted in logic will mirror the possible disconnectedness of facts within the world. *"Any one thing can either be the case, or not be the case, and everything else remains the same."*

---

[2] Would he have said that a proposition is a picture of a fact if the Venn diagrams had not already served as pictures of facts? We can always say, in any case, that a proposition is a picture of a Venn diagram.

Wittgenstein has simply followed out to the bitter end the two lines of influence within the prevailing empiricist climate of opinion of his time. If one holds to Hume's analysis of the causal relation, together with a metaphysical projection of an extensional logic upon the world, then the conclusion is unavoidable: the ultimate constituents of the world, whatever they may be, will be disconnected. We can note of them only their mutual occurrence or nonoccurrence as the case may be. Why they come and go in relation to each other would be finally inexplicable. We face a blank wall. At bottom, the world remains ultimately irrational.

It is the disconnectedness, even more than the atomicity of this world, that brings us up short. Almost three centuries ago Leibniz constructed his own picture of a similarly atomized world. In the Leibnizian system, the ultimate constituents of the world, the monads, do not act upon or communicate with each other. "The monads have no windows," in his famous phrase. These ultimate atoms of the world are so sealed off from one another that there is no aperture through which they may look out, perceive, affect, or be affected by other monads. Yet these monads are all interrelated and communicate with each other in the Monad of Monads, God. No such possibility relieves the blankness of Wittgenstein's universe. Since he does not specify what the atomic facts are, we are free to imagine them as the most valuable kind of entities that our hearts might desire. They might all be blessed and good—let us say, so many beautiful angelic beings. Still, if they are to be thoroughly external each to each, if they in no way communicate with each other so that the existence of one makes some difference to the other, then we would have to find this world decidedly lacking. At least the monads of Leibniz could all sing together as a choir in celestial harmony within the all-monad God. Wittgenstein's atomic facts, on the contrary, are doomed to silence and solitude. The dictatorship of logic leads us to a sterile world.

III.

But if logic plays an exalted and dictatorial role, he nevertheless proceeds to deflate it. Logic is at once all and nothing to him at this stage. The structures of logic may map the structures of the world, but the propositions of logic themselves say nothing at all about the world. They are mere tautologies. They say only that A is A.

This view is so commonplace now that we tend to forget what a bombshell it was at the time against the Platonic position of Russell. As a thoroughgoing Platonist, Russell had originally held that the entities with which logic deals *subsist* independently of space, time, and the human mind. His views on this "subsistence" were shifting meanwhile, but as late as 1920 he wrote in the *Introduction to Mathematical Philosophy: "Logic is concerned with the real world just as truly as zoology, though with its more abstract features"* (p. 169). Since the statement is not explicated in context, we may find it worthwhile to stick for a moment with this zoological parallel. The zoologist deals with giraffes, lions, marmosets, lemurs, and other interesting creatures; and he tells us significant facts about their biological and anatomical structures. These creatures are real, they exist in time and space, and the zoologist adds to our store of information about them. But if the propositions of logic are tautologies, if they merely say A is A in various complex and interesting disguises, then it is hard to see how in any way these can be compared with the propositions of the zoologist or any other natural scientist. Russell's zoological comparison becomes quite senseless. One is then forced to take another view of what logic is and what kind of reality it deals with.

Wittgenstein seeks to exhibit the tautologous character of logical statements by the device of truth-tables. List all the possibilities of truth and falsehood for the component parts of a proposition in logic, and the result for the whole will be truth in any case. Thus the proposition of logic is true whatever the facts may be. And, consequently, it can say nothing about the world. The logical proposition, "Either it is raining or it is not raining," is necessarily true whatever the actual weather may be. But it is true vacuously; it tells me nothing about the weather.

The die-hard Realist might respond that it tells us about the weather in any possible world. We have therefore to seek a more convincing model in order to exhibit this tautological character of logical truths. It seems to me a more forceful and vivid illustration is by means of a picture—and it is odd that Wittgenstein, whose imagination was so possessed by this metaphor of pictures, did not use this device. We make use thus of the ordinary Venn diagram from elementary logic, and we take as our example of logical truth the basic and traditional syllogism: "If (1) All A is B, and (2) All B is C; then (3) All A is C."

We proceed to picture the first premise, which says that there is no instance of an A which will not also be an instance of B, by shading out the part of circle A that falls outside B in order to indicate that it is empty.

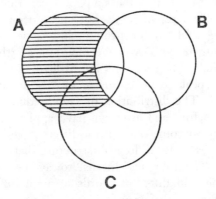

Similarly, with the second premise, all B is C, we cancel out all the Bs that fall outside C.

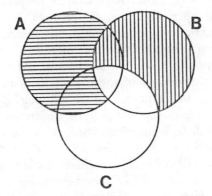

We have thus pictured the distribution of facts within our little world as expressed by the two premises, and we proceed now to the conclusion. This says that all A is C—i.e., no instance of A falls outside C. We are therefore to shade out in the diagram that part of A that falls outside C. But when we look now to the diagram, we see that this has already been done. The premises have already pictured the facts the conclusion would state. The conclusion adds no further information that is not already there. The distribution of facts within the universe is exactly what it was before and after we apply our law of logic. Hence the logical truth tells us nothing about the world.

In the light of this model—the simplest I can think of to exhibit the tautological character of logic—not only does Russell's comparison with zoology fall to the ground, but some serious questions occur about Wittgenstein's own sweeping talk of "the logical structure of the world." When we look at our little diagram, what sense does it make to speak so portentously of "the logical structure of the world" at all? The distribution of facts within the world is exactly what it is before and after we have applied our logical law. We only manage to come out with a different verbal statement at the end. There is only a logical structure between statements, within language. "Tautologous" means "to say the same thing." We say the same thing in different words or with different symbols. Logic gives us a system of transformations by means of which we can change one set of expressions into another, *for our own purposes*, while we continue to speak of the same facts. The conclusion of our little syllogism above, for example, simply serves to focus our interest in another way upon the facts as they stand. Logic is thus a human instrument devised for certain practical human purposes. Wittgenstein stands paradoxically here at a halfway house between a newer view of logic, which he was not to elaborate until years later, and the vestiges of the older Russellian position whose foundations he was in the process of demolishing. On the one hand, he pushes the emphasis upon tautology to deflate the claims of logic. On the other hand, he is intoxicated still with the rhetoric of Russellian Realism and speaks of logic as a "world-mirror," and, even more exaltedly, of "all-embracing world-mirroring logic."

Years later, he would speak of "the bewitchment of the mind by language," for which human failing philosophy must strive to be the cure. He himself, however, is now bewitched by the metaphor of a mirror; and it happens to be a particularly misleading metaphor in the present case. Consider, for example, a room in which there is no mirror. The objects in the room, and their spatial relations, are accessible without any mirror. If we bring a mirror into the room, we find the images of these objects duplicated now in the glass, but they were already fully accessible without it. According to the metaphor of the mirror, then, the "logical structure of the world" should be given to us just as plainly and fully even if we had never articulated logic at all! Which seems patently absurd. Yet, Wittgenstein might say, "we could not say of a nonlogical world what it would be like." Precisely; and that is also another reason why we cannot think of logic as a mirror. We could not *say* of a nonlogical world what it would be like, because our saying would be language, and language must be logically articulated to some minimal degree at least. Here language becomes our human condition for having a world at all. The world comes to be for human beings only through and within language. Language, world, and human being are co-ordinate terms. But we are involved here in the meanings of world and human being for which Wittgenstein's philosophy provides no analysis and for which we have to turn for interpretation to a philosopher like Heidegger.[3]

And what of philosophy itself? In Wittgenstein's world where the facts stand external to each other, and logic deals only with the identities within a formal language, what is there left for philosophy to do? Very little indeed, when we think of the traditional aims of philosophers. If we wish to make statements about the world, these fall within the province of the empirical sciences, and are to be tested by the methods of those disciplines. On the other hand, there are the tauotological statements of logic, which have a formal interest and may be manipulated for practical use, but tell us nothing about the world. All our human questions must fall into one or the other camp; and philosophy, accordingly, divides dichotomously into questions of fact or questions of logic. And in that division it virtually disappears. The traditional parts of philosophy—metaphysics, ethics, aesthetics—fall by the way, since they emerge, according to this perspective, a confused mixture of questions of fact or questions of logic, which it is the business of logical analysis to sort out. So far as ethics, for example, deals with human desires, values, and choices, these are facts within the world to be explored by psychology and the behavioral sciences. The philosopher must content himself merely to analyze the logical syntax of value statements. Where philosophers make metaphysical speculations about the cosmos, if these have any factual content, they pass over into possibly suggestive hypotheses to be dealt with more efficiently by the natural sciences—physics, chemistry, or biology, as the case may be. Any statements philosophy might try to make beyond these

[3] See later chapters 7 and 9, particularly the latter.

would be, strictly speaking, nonsense: They would not make sense.
Henceforth, there will be left to philosophy no doctrine at all, but
only the logical activity of clarification, which consists chiefly in
sorting out statements into their factual and logical components.
Only by such radical surgery could one hope to relieve philosophy
of muddle and obscurity.

So the young Wittgenstein, not yet thirty, drew up the complete
blueprint for Logical Positivism before even the name of this philosophical school had been coined. This movement, begun in Vienna
in the 1920s, proceeded to make great headway in the Anglo-
American world of the 1930s and 1940s. Though not now so prevalent, or at least in its originally more aggressive form, it has left its
deep mark upon the current philosophic mind. And much of the
philosophy that succeeded it in the Anglo-American world, though
it would disclaim the name, has been and remains thoroughly Positivist in spirit. The vocabulary has changed, but the fundamental
pattern of thought remains. It was, in one way, a very strange
movement for an individual like Wittgenstein to have fathered. In
the matter of temperament and personality, he stands alone and at a
great distance from other prominent Positivists. They were men, as
I knew them personally, for whom the sense of mystery simply did
not exist. For Wittgenstein it was very real indeed, but he wished to
keep it out of philosophy. In the same spirit he could cheerfully
consign ethics to psychology because his own ultimate values were
not facts within the world: "The meaning of the world lies outside
the world." He was a divided man, and the Positivists took half of
his mind. Some ardent followers of the later Wittgenstein have in-
veighed against Positivism as a total misunderstanding of him. The
charge is excessive; there is in fact a strong Positivistic streak in
Wittgenstein that continues throughout his thinking to the end,
though it is not the only component. The Positivists were not false
to his thinking, but they did take over only a part of it, and that
part indeed—as we shall see in the next chapter—which he thought
relatively unimportant.

IV.

What are we to judge, then, of this world that Wittgenstein has
pictured for us? And, first of all, what would it mean, what at best
could it mean, for us to be free in such a world?

Here, as usual, Wittgenstein is consistent with his assumptions. Human freedom, in a world of atomic facts, lies only in our ignorance of the future. "*The freedom of the will consists in the fact that future actions cannot be known now.*" This is the only kind of freedom possible for us in the fragmented world of Hume, where there is no bond between the present and the future. The future is open to us only in the sense that we stumble into it blindly. We are like blindfolded children, seeking to pin the tail on the donkey, and free only to stumble over any odd piece of furniture that happens to come in our path. This is a freedom of pure negativity—a freedom of impotence and ignorance.

Yet we know a very different kind of freedom as we go about our ordinary tasks in the everyday world. This quite ordinary freedom lies not in ignorance but in our ability to direct the future in ways that we desire. The present is not abysmally and totally severed from the future, but flows in some partially manageable way into it. But this ordinary practical freedom of ours becomes a theoretical impossibility in the fragmented world of Hume and Wittgenstein. In that world there is no continuity of becoming at all—no causal influx of the present into the future. One atomic fact follows another without connection. I reach out to grasp my pen in order to put these words down, and what I thus perform as the simple and continuous act of my will is now supposed, in the Humean view, to fall apart into disjointed fragments. There is no longer that seamless flow of becoming from my impulse to take this simple object, my grasping it, and putting it to use to set down the thoughts I intend. Instead, there is supposed to be a disconnected succession of discrete events—a desire, a movement of an arm forward, fingers closing around the pen, and the various jerky movements that have left these tracings upon paper, at which I then gaze back as a stranger. I cannot say simply that I took up my pen and wrote down these thoughts, for the reality of the doer, and indeed of *doing*, has disappeared from this world. Freedom, as we normally understand it, can have no meaning here for the simple reason that the continuity of process itself has been abolished. The present does not flow meaningfully and effectively into the future.

The discrepancy with common experience, which we have noted earlier, is not something that would have stopped Wittgenstein in his tracks at this stage. The controverting of ordinary experience at certain crucial points is by deliberate design rather than negligence

—the design of a particular kind of metaphysics. We say "meta-physics" deliberately, for despite Wittgenstein's Positivistic rejection of this discipline he has in fact presented us with as thorough-going a metaphysics as one could wish. It is all very well for him to say at the end of the *Tractatus* that everything he has said is to be regarded merely as a ladder that we are to throw away after we have used it to climb to the height of his vision. The ladder, if we are to climb by it, must have rungs solid enough on which to plant our feet, whatever we decide to do with it afterward. The rungs in this case are definite statements about the world, which in fact add up to a metaphysical doctrine. And this metaphysics, moreover, is of a particular historical kind, which *on principle* must run counter to ordinary experience because it finds that everyday world to be Appearance and not Reality. The Logical Atomism of Wittgenstein, in short, gives us but another version of the *Two Worlds*—a doctrine that has held Western thinking in its grip since the seventeenth century.

We remarked earlier that Wittgenstein's thinking is not so ahistorical as he, or his close followers, may have imagined. His assumptions belong to the empiricism of his immediate period. But that period has, in turn, to be imbedded in the larger and deeper pattern that defines the modern age. Without Descartes, and his two worlds, Hume would not have been. No man, least of all the thinker, can succeed in being ahistorical. The roots of our being reach further and deeper into history than we are usually aware. Wittgenstein is no exception. He is an original mind, intensely so, but his originality here succeeds only in producing a novel version of a very entrenched and traditional view.

This view finds it necessary to divide reality into two parts. There is, on the one hand, the world of our day-to-day experience, with all the characteristics and qualities that are familiar to us. On the other hand, science presents us with a world that is very different and seems to make greater claims to truth. We therefore call the latter the "real" or "objective" world; and the former is labeled "subjective"—as the mere "appearance" of an underlying "reality." Wittgenstein does not use such words; but since his Logical Atomism rides roughshod over large parts of our everyday experience, it is just as much a version of the Two Worlds as if he had availed himself of the usual terminology. What is significantly different in his case are the grounds on which he is led to make the division. For a philosopher like Descartes, the compelling reasons for splitting the two worlds apart came from physical science, the framework of which he was in fact helping to create at the time. Thus the familiar qualities of our world—colors, sounds, smells, and the rest—were to be replaced by configurations of matter in space. The Atomism of Wittgenstein, on the other hand, claims to follow, not from the results of physical science, but from an analysis of mathematical logic itself. And just because it seems independent thus of any particular empirical discoveries, it might strike some minds as being more rigorous.

Whitehead has labeled the doctrine of the Two Worlds a form of "scientific materialism." It seeks to reduce the world of concrete experience to the more general *material* components that underlie it. Since Wittgenstein does not tell us what his atomic facts are, and makes no appeal to the material conclusions of physics, the label is not so appropriate here. But if we change the phrase to "scientific reductionism," then Wittgenstein's thought might be accurately named a form of "logical reductionism." In any case, his thinking follows the same pattern as the older doctrine—a pattern that, turning to Whitehead again, we may call "the fallacy of misplaced concreteness." The exact but highly abstract concepts of logic (not physics, as in the older doctrine) are taken to characterize the ultimate matters of concrete reality. The mathematical logician looks away from the everyday world in order to construct more general and abstract relations among entities. He is intent on a scheme general and powerful enough, for his *practical* purposes, to encompass disconnected and unrelated facts within its structures. For his purposes, this disconnectedness, in the everyday sense, does not matter. But what Logical Atomism then proceeds to do is turn the whole scheme on its head: The abstract structures are taken to indicate the underlying and ultimately concrete features of the world. It is as if we had a mirror—to resort to this questionable metaphor for the last time—that somehow filtered out all the varied features of a face and gave us back the images of people as bare silhouettes. And we then concluded from this mirror that in reality, as distinguished from their ordinary appearance, people were nothing but such silhouettes.

How can we escape from this bleak picture of the world that Logical Atomism paints? We could renounce mathematical logic as the ideal or paradigmatic language, and that indeed is one step Wittgenstein was later to take. But we need not go so far in this rejection as he ultimately does. Suppose one wanted to hold on to the logic of *Principia* and yet did not want to succumb to the doctrine of atomic facts. What would be required for that? The remedy is not so difficult as one might think. One would simply have to give up the notion that the relation between language and fact is one of simple picturing. That logic has atomic forms of statement, then, would carry no implication about the nature of the world. We merely need such elementary statements in order to assemble the machinery of the calculus and set it going. A logical calculus thus becomes a practical instrument, like any other human device or technique, and in itself lays down no fiat as to what the world must be ultimately like. We would thus pass over into a radically different view of language itself—as a practical activity in the service of life. Wittgenstein was not to take this giant step until several decades later. But make no mistake: When he does take that step, it is not out of any quirky shift in taste for the nuances of our common language, but because he is compelled to restore its full measure of truth to our everyday world, which he had here so thoroughly travestied in his obsession with a formal technique.

One final point that bears very much on what will follow.

The bleakest aspect of the book really consists in something that scarcely drew much attention in the furor of its early reception. This is the underlying assumption that logic and mathematics are closed systems. A system is closed when there is some mechanical means by which we can determine whether any combination of symbols is a true or false statement. A computer could scan any such combination and either accept it as a tautology (a true statement) or reject it as a contradiction (false statement). Thus Wittgenstein could exhibit the tautological character of certain logical statements by the purely mechanical device of the truth-tables—a device that an elementary student of logic now learns at the beginning of his course. In the excitement, however, it was forgotten that this mechanism served only for a small and quite elementary part of logic, the so-called Calculus of Sentences. The unspoken assumption was that what had proved true for the part would hold for the whole of logic. Indeed, so unspoken was the assumption that it came to be held almost as established fact.

This point did not attract much attention because the atmosphere, in logical circles, was heady with the great triumph of the *Principia*. It looked as if logic had reached, or was just about to reach, its final and definitive form. Moreover, mathematics seemed to be traveling a parallel path at this time. Had not mathematicians, particularly those of the Formalist school, been inching toward a complete axiomatizing of their subject, that is, toward laying down certain rules by the mechanical application of which one could grind out all the truths of mathematics. Thus one could turn over all the work of mathematicians to some vast computing machine. And now that there was in existence a comprehensive system of logic that seemed to embrace mathematics within itself, did not this goal look imminent? Surely, underneath all the operations of logic there must be some underlying simple forms that would exhibit all logical reasoning as a purely mechanical process.

Now, remember that for Wittgenstein at this stage mathematical logic is the model of all language. Presumably then all ordinary human desires, needs, actions, or plans could be expressed with both exactness and adequacy within the form of this language. And if this language is determinate and closed, then the possibilities of our human existence would be similarly closed. All human developments would be mechanical combinations of already given elements. Creation, genuine invention, novelty—the hallmarks of freedom— would vanish. This would be the bleakest consequence of Wittgenstein's thought. No wonder then, that beyond logic and its mechanical manipulation of facts, he had to find another realm of "the Mystical."

This general confidence at the time that logic had reached a definitive form, as well as Wittgenstein's youth (which we should not forget), helps to explain the extraordinarily dogmatic tone in which he asserts his convictions. "The *truth* of the thoughts communicated here," he tells us, "seems to me unassailable and definitive." And further that "The problems have in essentials been finally solved." Alas for humans when they begin to dogmatize in this fashion! Indeed, mechanism as a philosophic doctrine might be defined as the belief that the last machine which human ingenuity has created gives us the final form of reality. What usually happens is that human ingenuity and freedom create a machine which supersedes the previous one, and reality in consequences exhibits a different pattern. It is a fairly reliable rule that whenever men of

science are sure that they have reached some final formula or statement about the ultimate way things are that the scientific situation
itself is reaching a stage where it is likely to be blown wide open.

And this, of course, is exactly what did happen with logic. The
fact that logic and mathematics turn out to be open rather than
closed, that no mechanism can encompass them and exclude the
need for invention and creation—these are facts that should be of
greatest significance for the philosopher. For if language—even in
the most strict and elemental form of logic—is open, then so too
must be our human existence, which in fact transpires within language. Wittgenstein's subsequent career was to be an adventure into
this openness.

Chapter 4

Mysticism

To MAKE A MYSTIQUE OF LOGIC IS TO ASCRIBE TO IT EXTRAORDINARY and almost magical power—the power to lay down the structure of the world and to dissolve the traditional questions of metaphysics. At the very opposite pole from such a mystique lies true mysticism, and Wittgenstein discovers it precisely there, where logic abdicates its powers.

The first part of the *Tractatus*, so far as substantive contributions to logic are concerned, is largely of historical interest. The subsequent progress of logic, as well as Wittgenstein's own development, were to absorb some of his questions, displace others, and generally transform the nature of all of them. But it is the last part of the work—and, strictly speaking, not so much a part as a few pages tacked on almost as an afterthought, so it might seem to the careless reader—that give us the real sense of Wittgenstein's thinking in this book. They are likely to prove the more enduring pages, for they tell us of the ideas that kept the man Wittgenstein alive.

The place of "the mystical" is identified quite simply and tersely: "*That* the world is, is the mystical." Science tells us *how* the world is; it describes the myriad kinds of phenomena, their behavior, and their mutual interactions one with another. But before the sheer fact of the world's existence, *that* there is a world at all, that anything at all exists, in Leibniz's telling phrase, we can only stand in silent awe. Before this primal mystery of Being our human chatter falters. Here language can only point, and then pass into silence. "Of that whereof we cannot speak we must be silent."

Yet it is just this domain of what cannot be spoken that Wittgenstein personally valued most and that he believed to be the most important part of human life. Only if we enter that zone of silence are we truly human. And here he is at the uttermost remove, personally and existentially speaking, from the great body of his positivistic followers. Silence would put the academic philosopher out of business; where nothing is to be said, one cannot hope to write a paper in logic.

The importance Wittgenstein attached to the mystical is shown most forcefully and unmistakably in a very revealing letter he wrote to the German publisher Ficker:

> The book's point is an ethical one. I once meant to include in the Preface a sentence which is not in fact there now but which I will write out for you here, because it will perhaps be a key to the work for you. What I meant to write, then is this: My work consists of two parts: plus all that I have *not* written. And it is precisely this second part that is the important one. My book draws limits to the sphere of the ethical from the inside, as it were, and I am convinced that this is the *only rigorous* way of drawing those limits. In short, I believe that where *many* others today are just gassing, I have managed to put everything firmly into place by being silent about it.[1]

This letter is of crucial importance for the student of Wittgenstein. In the first place, it gives us a quite unambiguous declaration of his own meaning in writing the book; and second, it gives us another description of—or, more exactly another pointer toward—the domain of what cannot be uttered: The mystical is also the ethical, or the source of what is truly ethical in life.

How can this be so? How can the awareness of the mystery of existence have ethical substance for us—indeed, if we are to follow this letter to the publisher Ficker be the decisive factor, ethically speaking, in human life? To speak at all, for Wittgenstein at this stage of his development, is to speak clearly; and if we cannot speak of the mystery, beyond that mere verbal gesture that points toward it, how can we draw any definite ethical prescriptions from its acknowledgment?

[1] Paul Engelmann, *Letters from Ludwig Wittgenstein, with a Memoir* (New York: Horizon Press, 1967), p. 143.

Wittgenstein does not have anything like a system of ethics. One has to construct what his ethics would be like from a few scrimpy remarks that he has left us. On one side—and it is the negative side —his view is tolerably clear, and it is thoroughly positivistic. So far as our will and our ethical behavior are facts within the world, they fall under the empirical sciences of behavior. Our moral statements, under logical analysis, turn out to be expressions of our own emotions—of desire or aversion, as the case may be. Such was the general position that the positivists, allegedly following him, used to discredit traditional ethics.

But this is only one side of Wittgenstein's thought, and he has something more and very different to say on the subject. The meaning of the world, he tells us, lies outside the world. Consequently, the striving of the will, so far as it is engaged with this meaning, is pointed beyond the world. (The world here, remember, is simply the totality of all the facts.) Thus, whatever Wittgenstein's positive ethical views may be, we know at least what they are not: They are not those of a strictly naturalistic or utilitarian ethics. The ultimate good could not be defined finally and completely as happiness or the greatest balance of pleasure over pain. These are states of human being that, if they occurred, would be facts within the world; their meaning—like the meaning of the world itself—would point beyond them. The happiness of mankind, for example, if it ever should come to pass, would still leave men asking: Why? What point to it? To what end? Wittgenstein's position here—though this may come as a surprise to some—shows a definite family resemblance to the Kantian ethics.

Kant held that the requirements of moral action lead us beyond the phenomenal into the noumenal realm. The world of phenomena is accessible to us in perception and can be articulated by the concepts of our understanding. The noumenal is the realm where our concepts fall short. We enter it on faith and by postulating what we can never prove; but enter it we must as spiritual beings. Otherwise, the voice of moral conscience, the central part of our human personality, would become irrational and absurd in urging us to pursue the good no matter the cost to ourselves. Kant brings to bear, in a quite legalistic way, the whole theistic apparatus of God, Providence, and immortality. But these are what Kant calls *Ideas*, practical makeshifts, of which we can have no definite concepts. On the surface his ethics would seem to have little similarity, if any, to

Wittgenstein's. But in both, the ethical turns ultimately on what cannot be articulated in definite concepts.

Suppose, now, we gather together the various hints that these last pages of the *Tractatus* give us about this region beyond language. They fall under three headings:

1. "The mystical" is the sheer fact that the world exists, that there is anything at all rather than nothing. This is the cosmological awe at the mystery of existence.

2. This region of the unutterable, that of which we cannot speak, is also of supreme value to man. It is the whole "ethical" point of his book, as Wittgenstein says in his letter. In our ethical striving we reach toward it as the domain in which our actions and we ourselves would find their "meaning."

3. At this point our second and third headings overlap. When we speak of something we call "the meaning of life," we are but speaking in another mode of the ethical. At times, in our worst moments, we feel that life is without meaning; at other times it seems to us to have meaning. But we may be hard put to state in any concrete, factual way the difference between the two conditions. We are driven by a desperate need that our life should have meaning. Yet this "meaning" that we seek is inexpressible—at least by the strict standards that the *Tractatus* would impose: We cannot state it as a simple fact or any of the combinations of facts that logic permits. *"Is this not why men to whom the meaning of life, after long doubting, became clear, could not say wherein this meaning consisted?"* (6.251)

Suppose we now put these three kinds of hints together; we take them then as so many indications coming from somewhat different directions but all pointing toward one and the same region of experience that our life touches from time to time. Wittgenstein's mysticism would embrace all three. Intellect and will here meet: The mystery of the cosmos before which our mind stands in awe becomes one with the mystery within us by which we ethically strive; and both come together in the sense that somehow, in a way inexpressible to us, it is all meaningful. Our point here is reinforced if we consider further what Wittgenstein says about immortality. If we had eternal life, he tells us, that would not solve the question life puts to us. We could go on endlessly burdened with the sense that existence generally, and our own particularly, is meaningless. What can redeem life, if it is to be redeemed at all, are only those moments of "eternity in the present"—when the mystery of the world and we ourselves as ethical beings belong together in some unfathomable feeling that all is well. So understood, Wittgenstein's fragmentary utterances add up to a quite traditional and sound mysticism.

I say "sound" deliberately. The traditional excesses of some mystics—their extravagant language, bizarre actions, or even more bizarre cessations of action—create the misunderstanding that the concerns of mysticism are remote from the ordinary conditions of life. We need to be recalled to the fact that the occasions from which mysticism springs are not very far from common experience. The ordinary person, however, moves within the mystical without being conscious of it. And I do not mean here that he is aesthetically unaware of the miracle of existence itself, but that he is unaware of the ground of his ethical existence. In the sphere of the ethical this man may build up his virtues through the routines of benevolent action. Habit, decency, or an engrained kindness may carry him along the more routine paths of ethics. But in moments of extremity—and these are always lurking—the routines of habit will not always work for him. They may not be sufficient to spur him to strive when striving seems hopeless or the world has deserted him. At such moments the concepts of ethics themselves may suddenly sound empty and distant. Those grand-sounding goals—the greatest good of the greatest number or one's own perfection as a rational being—do not seem then to have any connection with that tiny corner of action in which he is caught or the smallness of the task he has to perform there. Under such circumstances, the moral man if asked, or if asking himself, the question "Why do you go on?" cannot put into words any satisfactory answer. Yet that which he cannot put into words, which keeps him going and prevents him from sliding into the pit of nihilism, is the core of his life and thus the most valuable part of it for him. It corresponds precisely to that "unwritten" part of Wittgenstein's book, which—so he tells his publisher—is more important than what he has written.

Sketchy and brief as the hints he gives us are, there is nevertheless the value of a certain logical austerity in the way Wittgenstein exhibits his mysticism. It does not come at us as the deliverance of any special state of mind, special revelation, or sublimely hysterical vision. In its very terseness of expression it is presented as binding on

all of us and not merely on the mystic as a peculiar kind of temperament. The mystery that the world is, engulfs us all. We do not
reach it by any peculiar hallucinatory or paranormal experience; we
have only to push our reasoning about language and facts far
enough, and it is there waiting for us. No doubt, for the great bulk
of mankind the awareness of this mystery occurs, if at all, only on
the margins of consciousness. But were it to fade altogether from
those margins, we would become a race of narrow technicians.

And it is precisely here that the tactic of silence becomes a debat-
able one. No doubt, Wittgenstein's exploitation of this silence has its
own dramatic effectiveness. On our first encounter with his text,
this silence seems positively thunderous; thereafter, however, it begins to diminish a bit in its power over us; we would really like a
little more to be said. No doubt too, most of those who venture into
this region are "gassing," as Wittgenstein calls it. Few indeed, amid
all the varieties of religious writers, are humanly convincing; and
those who succeed must often use all those devices of what
Kierkegaard calls "indirect communication." Silence before the incommunicable at least retains its own peculiar dignity. Yet there is a
danger in such silence adopted as a deliberate tactic. The positivists,
for example, who professed to follow Wittgenstein took this silence
to be a sign that there was nothing there at all to talk about. For
them, indeed, there was nothing there; the part of life Wittgenstein
valued most simply did not exist for them. They are not unusual
and strange in this. Indeed, they are representative of one powerful
tendency of our culture today, which in its sheer thirst for information becomes ever more positivistic in spirit. It insists on facts, but
the fact must be tailored to the means of communication. We come
to accept as real only what can be communicated in some tidy and
precise bulletin conveyed by television or radio. Whatever eludes
such neat capsulation goes unnoticed or forgotten. Silence, permanent silence, in the face of this drift can only assist in making the
mystery vanish altogether.

Most of all, though, to pursue the tactic of silence is perhaps to
bow a little too obsequiously to the formalist restrictions upon language. What is suggested is that the mystery is merely a flaw in
language, as if we merely happened to have hold of an instrument
deficient in this respect. The mystery that the world exists is not,
first and foremost, a peculiar fact about the limits of language. In
stressing those limits, in locating the mystery on the other side of

language, we tend thus to place it at a distance from ourselves. But the mystery, in fact, encompasses us; we and our language exist within it. And here the emphasis shifts from language to Being.

It will be interesting later to note the option taken by another philosopher, Heidegger, in this matter. He too, though by a different route, arrives at the region of "the nameless," where concepts in the ordinary sense cease to apply. What then is the philosopher to do? To pass into silence would be to give the game away to the enemy. The philosopher has to take the risk of a different vocation for thinking, whose task is the "poetic utterance" of Being. (The German word here, *Dichten,* is at once more poetic and earthy than "poetize.") And this not out of any rhetorical impulse for "gassing" but out of the sobriety of thought, which is called upon to keep the mystery alive for a culture that might otherwise let it perish.

In any case, Wittgenstein could not abide within the stark limits of the *Tractatus* forever. The logic of Russell began to appear as a much too rigid framework in which to cast reality. The attempt to understand language itself through the model of a single paradigmatic language—and that, mind you, a formal language that is artificially constructed—is fruitless. It does not show us the multiple uses that language serves in the actual flow of life. And as for attempting to construe the world from a logic like the *Principia,* that is like looking at a landscape through a grid and then carving out its parts in geometrical form without following the natural contours of the terrain.

In the next and mature stage of his thought Wittgenstein sets out on a course, equally original, to seek out these living contours within language as we use it.

Chapter 5

————◆————

Open Language

WHILE HIS BOOK HAD BECOME THE TOPIC OF PHILOSOPHIC CONVERSA-
tion at Cambridge, Wittgenstein remained in Austria, a lonely figure
searching for a vocation. For a while he found employment as a
gardener's assistant in a seminary. Perhaps at this time the idea was
still strong to enter a monastery and become a monk. A little later
he took the job of country schoolteacher in some of the poorer
Austrian villages. The desire for service or sacrifice of some kind
was still with him.

His sister Hermine, who visited his classes on several occasions,
tells us how passionately Wittgenstein flung himself into teaching
his country schoolchildren. He made models, taught the children to
build simple engines and to create their own visual pictures for
what he was trying to teach them. "Show and tell" is the name of a
common classroom game for children. Perhaps all teaching is in its
way a version of this game; and the philosopher who teaches children may learn from them something more essential about the nature of language than he would from any formal calculus. To tell is
to show: to bring something into the open and make it clear. Wittgenstein had a genius here that he was to carry over into his later
writings, which exhibit a tireless capacity for inventing models and
examples—a quality that makes at once for the unusual richness of
his thought and the despair of anyone seeking an easy summary of
it. It is a gift that also places him in an ambiguous relation to the
philosophic school that is too loosely and easily labeled "analytic
philosophy." He is not an "analytic" philosopher in any sense com-

parable to those who earn this title by grinding away at the consequences of this or that particular proposition, as if filing a legal brief. On the contrary, his procedure is synthetic and imaginative throughout—constantly projecting new pictures, models, and points of view from which to look at the most ordinary states of affairs. Philosophy is a way of seeing rather than the tedious business of a lawyer's brief. Wittgenstein's invention in the matter of examples was a gift of nature and not something learned. But nothing prevents us from seeing the episode of schoolteacher as a stage on his life's way. It can sometimes be a more enlightening experience to instruct elementary pupils than advanced scholars. With the latter we can fall all too easily into the embrace of an available abstract language whose presuppositions thus remain hidden to us. In teaching the young you have to satisfy the schoolchild in yourself and enter the region where all meanings start. That is where, in any case, the philosopher has perpetually to start.

All the same, his sister felt his teaching school was a waste of his great talents. It was, she said, like using a precision instrument to open crates. She was voicing the family's anxiety for what appeared to be Ludwig's drifting and uncertain state of mind. On the whole we know little of his life during this period of the 1920s and particularly the conflicts in which his homosexuality involved him. Wittgenstein's answer to her reveals under what deep tensions he was passing: "You are like someone who, looking through a closed window, can't explain the strange movements of a passerby. He doesn't know what kind of a storm is raging outside and that this person is perhaps only with great effort keeping himself on his feet."

These words bring up inevitably the morbid aspects of his temperament. His student and friend G. H. Von Wright declares: "It is probably true that he lived on the border of mental illness. A fear of being driven across it followed him throughout his life." A hostile critic could easily distort these words. It is a mark of one kind of religious personality, as William James has pointed out, to be infected with a certain degree of morbidity. The religious man lives at the farther edge of existence, from which most of us keep clear, and he is therefore likely to show traits that will seem morbid to us. But what really counts here—again following James—is whether the so-called morbid disposition is ultimately destructive of the personality and the life, in which case it is genuinely pathological, or whether it somehow brings the life and work into some more con-

centrated unity. And by this criterion there can be no doubt of the
health of Wittgenstein's later writings: They are in their own way
a celebration of the ordinary world and of the everyday vision of
things.

In 1929 he was recalled to Cambridge and the teaching of philosophy. Here his external biography falls into line: The rest of his
life, with some brief interruptions, was spent in Cambridge teaching
and writing.

It was an austere existence, the more austere by Wittgenstein's
own choosing. He slept on a simple cot. His rooms were almost
bare of furniture. He preferred to eat alone in his chambers rather
than to dine in the Commons with the other dons. The conversation
there, he told his colleague and friend John Wisdom, was "neither
of the heart nor of the head"—the academic chatter of dons—and
he preferred not to join it. There was nothing of the theatrical gesture here; Wittgenstein wanted to simplify his life, and he followed
the simplest course that most of us might like to but would not have
courage enough to take. In the same spirit he had simultaneously
renounced his fortune and given up wearing a tie in the 1920s.
These were not acts of bohemian defiance; he wanted simply to rid
his life of as many encumbrances as possible. In his bare chambers
there were few books. He read detective stories for diversion, need-
ing the simplest pulp fiction to turn his mind off. As for more serious authors, he maintained his attachment to William James' *Varieties of Religious Experience*, a book that—as Russell notes—had
been a powerful influence years earlier. And Wittgenstein delivered
himself of the judgment that Kierkegaard was "the greatest writer
of the nineteenth century."

In a sense, then, Wittgenstein did fulfill the plan of becoming a
monk and entering a monastery that he had spoken of to Russell in
their 1919 meeting—only the monastery was a monastery of one,
and was located within Cambridge. Otherwise, Wittgenstein's life
shows all the marks of a religious dedication. For us, who are so nat-
uralistically inclined by our culture, the inevitable question is: Was
it a happy life? His pupil Norman Malcolm reports—in the same
vein as Von Wright—that Wittgenstein lived for the most part in
perpetual torment. Yet Malcolm also notes that at the end Wittgenstein declared his life had been "wonderful." Malcolm in turn finds
it wonderful and mysterious that he should have said this. It would
not have been puzzling to Dostoevski, who gives to his tormented

character Kirillov the redeeming vision that all of us, if we but knew it, are happy. In the end, the religious man declares that all is well.

Yet, as a religious life, this is one of strange self-denial. The traditional ascetics denied the flesh in order to luxuriate in the spirit. Wittgenstein, in effect, denies the spirit by remaining silent about that part of life he held most valuable. Now, denied speech, and without ritual expression through attachment to a church, the religious longings are likely to grow thin and anemic. There is a story by Franz Kafka, "The Hunger Artist," one of his most compelling and frightening, that we feel has a particular application to the author himself. The art of "the hunger artist" is fasting, and he carries on his protracted fasts before the public, which finally grows bored with them. Eventually, all skin and bones, he starves himself to death. Physical fasting here can be taken as a parable of spiritual denial. The religious impulses, when not nourished, grow into a starved specter of themselves. Kafka had a deeply religious temperament, but a curiously ironical and dialectical rationalism stood in the way of his spiritual fulfillment. "A spike grew out of his forehead," he observes of himself in one brutal and telling image; and elsewhere he sums up his life by saying that his head had conspired against him. Wittgenstein, like Kafka, is a hunger artist of the spirit. In this respect they are kindred souls, both thoroughly representative figures of the "modernist" spirit in its simultaneous longing and self-denial. The religious note sounds throughout Wittgenstein's life, as it does through Kafka's, but with a curiously self-frustrated, muffled tone—like a strangled prayer.

I.

Picasso once remarked about the painting of Cézanne: "If there were not anxiety behind those apples, Cézanne would not interest me any more than Bouguereau." The word "anxiety" here may not be the right one; it suggests nervous flutterings that are alien to Cézanne as a painter. The father of modern painting was not a modernist. He stands as solidly within nature as any painter in the tradition, and as no painter has stood since him, while the essence of modernism lies in its break with nature. Yet Picasso's intent was clear enough, and his judgment profound: He meant to refer to the intensity of inner life that, in the right hands, can make even an apparently trivial subject matter of absorbing significance. And so understood, his remark may be fittingly transcribed to apply to Wittgenstein's *Philosophic Investigations*.

If a philosophic reader of the nineteenth century were brought back to life, handed this book, and told it was one of the major works of our period, he might find himself very startled at that claim. A major work that talks only of such small and trivial occasions of ordinary speech! That goes on without beginning, middle, or end from one isolated paragraph to another! It would be in vain for us to cite Nietzsche's occasional aphoristic style in comparison. The aphorisms in Nietzsche break the expository flow, or they themselves add up into some sweeping generalization about the universe and man. In Wittgenstein there is never the eruption of any generalization beyond the matters that our ordinary language talks about. The philosopher does not step outside the everyday to intimate any comprehensive world-view. Yet this book, like the apples of Cézanne, acquires a certain monumental life of its own in our mind.

The *Investigations* rings us around from that encompassing zone of silence toward which the *Tractatus* had pointed. In that earlier work this final silence had been thundered at us, but here it is not even announced; it is present, if at all, only through its absence. The *Tractatus* had spoken of the world as seen from above, even though Wittgenstein professed to be kicking away the ladder by which he had climbed to that height. In this later stage of his thought there is no height and no ladder; we are totally immersed in the world of ordinary language as we go from one particular example to another. Critics have spoken of the world of Franz Kafka's fiction as one of "baffled transcendence." The characters are always haunted by some transcendent world beyond the banal one they inhabit, yet they are perpetually defeated in their attempt to make contact with this other sphere, and they always return to the flat contours of the everyday. But Wittgenstein does not appear to be haunted by even this kind of transcendence. The renunciation of that other and higher world must be so complete—at least for philosophical discourse—that we must even forego any nostalgia for it. "Philosophy leaves the world as it is."

A work of such ambitious renunciation brings with it its own peculiar difficulties. Wittgenstein's delay in publication is a symptom of the unusual enterprise that its writing was. The book was substantially completed in 1945; yet he held onto it, still adding and correcting; and it remained unpublished at his death in 1951. It did not appear until posthumously, in 1956. Had he lived longer, he could have held onto it indefinitely. One could always add more. The form of the work did not indicate when one had arrived at completion. In this respect the *Investigations* resembles some works of contemporary art that seek to break with the traditional concepts of form. In a piece of atonal music—there may be no development toward a climax, no resolution, and no coda. The piece begins abruptly and breaks off abruptly. It is completed when enough has been given to draw us so fully into the work that its reality has become valid and convincing to us. So Wittgenstein's book, organized more or less around two basic themes, gives us enough to draw us completely into the point of view from which it is written.

This is obviously a dangerous form to imitate, and Wittgenstein's followers have not always been as lucky as the master. The preoccupation with ordinary language can degenerate into triviality. Even in Wittgenstein himself one chafes at a certain fragmentary quality, the indisposition at times to push an insight toward more systematic and coherent shape. Bertrand Russell remarked about the ordinary language movement in philosophy that it showed an unseemly preoccupation by philosophers with "the silly things that silly people say." Russell's wit was catty, as usual, but there were times when some of the more derivative practitioners seem to have earned his barb. What is the difference in Wittgenstein? We have to go back to Picasso's remark on Cézanne. What makes Wittgenstein different is the intensity of mind at work through the apparently trivial subject matter, so that often as we may turn away from his text frustrated at not finding the answers we seek there, just as often we come back to find our thinking quickened by it. His reputation was, I believe, inflated in the previous decade, and is now in for very extensive deflation; but however far the deflation may go, we should not forget this living quality of his thinking. The man is always there, alive in and through his thoughts. And when one considers how much of our philosophy has become routine and academic, without the sap of life or spirit, this vitality of his is no small recommendation.

II.

The monumental change from the *Tractatus* to the later Wittgenstein lies in the shift from the formal language of logic to our ordinary language as the chosen subject and medium for philosophy. This choice has far-reaching consequences. Our ordinary language is not a single monolithic structure. We speak differently at different times and according as we address ourselves to different subjects. The logician considers language only as the vehicle of statements or propositions. But in fact we use language for a great many other vital purposes. At the end of a long and informal catalogue of these, Wittgenstein concludes by asking us to reflect on how we use language when we go about "asking, thanking, cursing, greeting, praying." (No. 23) Thanking, cursing, praying[1]—these are a far cry from the province of logic, yet they are very significant parts of life, and therefore the philosopher ought not to exclude them.

Thus our common language, far from being a single homogeneous whole, is in fact a family of overlapping languages. Here Wittgenstein introduces his now famous notion of "language games." The word "games" may seem a poor choice, suggesting something frivolous and inconsequential. But we need only recall Bobby Fischer and chess to realize that a game may be a deadly serious matter. The term "language game" is apt for two very good reasons: (1) A game is a form of vital activity, an exuberant and adventurous display of life. (2) A game is played in accordance with rules; but note that these rules have been set up by human beings, and, equally important, they are subject to change.

Consider this latter point first. Our American games of baseball and football have been played year in year out, generation after generation, and yet the rules are still undergoing changes. Sometimes a rule is changed to eliminate indeterminate situations; the infield-fly rule in baseball was such a case. Sometimes the change is to make the game more interesting. Thus some changes presently proposed for baseball are aimed at speeding it up. The game, it is said, belonged to an older and more leisurely period; our present life-style has speeded up and consequently demands a more rapid rhythm and tempo in the games we play. Here the total context of our life comes into play as a force to change the rules.

But are not such strict disciplines as logic and mathematics out-

---

[1] It is rather to be regretted that Wittgenstein did not devote himself to an analysis of the grammar of prayer. What we call "the philosophy of religion" might now wear a different face. In Chapter 14 we try to fill this gap.

side of this vital context? Not at all. The history of mathematics exhibits changes in the same fashion as other games. When the Greeks discovered irrational quantities, they might have chosen—as some ardent Pythagoreans would have wished—to exclude them from mathematics altogether. Arithmetic would have been confined to counting, and mathematics otherwise would have become less powerful and interesting. Newton and Leibniz violated old rules when they introduced infinitesimals in the seventeenth century, but this new calculus enabled them to develop the science of mechanics for the mastery of nature. The paradoxes so introduced were not removed until the nineteenth century, when Cauchy and Weierstrass adjusted the rules to accommodate this invention. And so it goes. The present "crisis in mathematics" has to do with fundamental choices about the way the mathematical language is to be used in that particular form of activity we call mathematics. It is always a matter of *free choice*, but the options that are open are those afforded or required by the wider context of the activity.

We are now in a position to understand the reason for Wittgenstein's shift from the *Tractatus* to his later immersion in the everyday language. As usual, he condenses the point into a vivid image, leaving it to us to piece it together with the whole. To deal exclusively with a formal logical language is like walking on ice. "There is no friction and so in a certain sense the conditions are ideal, but also, just because of that, we are unable to walk. We want to walk: So we need *friction*. Back to the rough ground!" (107) The more abstract and ideal the language the more remote it is from the concrete conditions of life.

His general position thus is one of a very radical and thoroughgoing pragmatism—as thoroughgoing indeed as anything William James and John Dewey could wish. If Wittgenstein had developed his book in anything like demonstrative form, its fundamental axiom would have been a sentence that we come upon only far on into the text, as if he had worked to his true starting point only near the end:

"What has to be accepted, the given, is *forms of life*." (226) This is the fact, the given, from which all thinking must start; and thinking, which starts from this fact, is in turn itself but another form of life. *Primum vivere deinde philosophari* says the old adage; and it is right to emphasize the primacy of living, but wrong to suggest that philosophy is an adjunct added onto life, when in fact it

should be a vital activity we carry on to clarify our way among the
tangled affairs of the everyday. Formal logic is not a framework
that encloses this life, but a deliberately restricted language that we
use for our own purposes, and so it falls within the total context of
this life. If Wittgenstein is no longer absorbed within that narrower
formal language, but chooses instead to immerse himself in the everyday language, that is because here we are engaged with the more
enveloping and concrete conditions of our life.

All of which reverses the traditional doctrine of the two worlds.
Logic no longer dictates an ultimate structure of the world. There
is no ultimate reality lying behind or beneath ordinary experience to
which we turn intellectually as the court of last appeal. All meanings are born within the human world of the everyday, and have to
return there to be tested. A split between inner and outer, private
and public, worlds becomes equally unfeasible. Ordinary language
moves between both these opposed poles. When we deal with formal logic, the operation is usually one of pencil on paper, the manipulation of a calculus. But our everyday language is speech, and
takes place not inside our separate heads but out in the open. However, this common language, on certain occasions, may express an
intimacy we share with each other. No metaphysical curtain is
drawn to divide our language into mutually exclusive private or
public universes of discourse.

There is one curious restriction that Wittgenstein imposes upon
our use of the ordinary language as compared with games. We are
free, if we wish, to change the rules of a game—including the game
of mathematics. But Wittgenstein insists that we are not to tamper
with the ordinary language; we are to take everything as it is and
work within that framework. Why this restriction? Is it that we
may be spared the possibilities of individual aberration by following
the guidance of collective wisdom that has shaped the common language? Here is one more point on which we might prefer that
Wittgenstein did not proceed by oracular jumps but pursued the
more usual reflective path of other philosophers. Now, the rules of
our language were not consciously constructed at any time in the
past, so far as we know. They grew up organically somehow in the
dark backward abyss of time. These rules also change in the course
of time, not at the fiat of any given individual, but subtly and gradually in accordance with the whole life of a people. A great philologist, Wilhelm von Humboldt, observing this shaping force of lan-

guage from generation to generation, concludes: "It is in language that each individual feels most vividly that he is only an effluence (*Ausfluss*) of all mankind." A living language becomes in this way a repository of wisdom that transcends the individual's own poor powers if left on his own.[2]

III.

Granted this radical opening move, that our colloquial speech is to be the medium within which we philosophize, what then does Wittgenstein have to say? What is his doctrine?

And here, of course, the paradoxical answer is that he does not have a doctrine at all to communicate. There is a definite emphasis and orientation, but no body of propositions that could conceivably be taken as a philosophic system. This seeming paradox, however, is quite in line with his purpose: The activity of philosophy is for the sake of clarification; and if it has done its job, it should return us to what is plainly and obviously there in the first place, if we had but the eyes to see it. "Philosophy leaves the world as it is." It can alter nothing in that world; nor can it, like science, advance into territory unknown to our ordinary perceptions and powers; it can only bring us back to what must be our perpetual starting point.

The emphasis and orientation, however, are sufficiently distinct that we may quarrel with them—and so to that extent at least they will do for a doctrine. Wittgenstein's subject is restricted enough. The lively motley of remarks, asides, illustrations, and queries that make up the *Investigations* center around two principal themes:

1. Language and the problem of meaning; what used to be called the meaning of meaning.
2. The problem of mind and body; how mental experiences are to be spoken of correctly in relation to overt bodily behavior.

The two themes are not unrelated, and Wittgenstein's treatment of them is to bring them together as close as possible. In both cases his

---

[2] Still, with the deepest of respect for tradition, one has to raise a question here. Suppose the evolution of a language were such that certain meanings became lost to it. Would not an individual thinker in that case have to struggle against the forms of language in order to retrieve those lost meanings? This is a question we shall have to come back to later in the case of Heidegger.

intent is the same: to get rid of a Cartesian model of the mind as some distinct container, or closet, in which peculiarly "mental" experiences, ideas, or meanings are harbored. We are not to think, for example, of meaning as a kind of halo that surrounds a word; or to change the figure, as Wittgenstein so often does, as a kind of mental nugget that we keep in the treasury of consciousness. The meaning of a word has to do with the way we use it within the total web of our discourse. The force thus of Wittgenstein's emphasis upon the intrinsic connection of meaning and use is to turn us away from the fictitious inner cabinet of the mind into the open and public world, where people talk and behave toward each other in the ordinary situations of life. The emphasis is thus plainly behaviorist throughout. The question remains: How far does this behaviorist tendency in Wittgenstein go? Indeed, how far can it rightly go if ordinary language is taken as an arbiter?

For one thing, the reduction of meaning to usage cannot be carried through. We look up a word to learn its meaning, and we find a list of its uses. But we have to understand the meaning of those uses if we are to be enlightened. Of course, these latter meanings can be explicated by citing further uses, but the meaning of these latter has in turn to be understood. And if we end with behavior, as the behaviorist would wish, as our final means of explication, we have still to understand the meaning of the behavior in question. An American, for example, is quite startled to learn at firsthand that when a European audience whistles, it *means* to express not approval or adulation, but the most jeering condemnation.

However far we push the reduction of meaning to usage, and in the last instance to behavior, we end with a world in which there are meanings. We begin there too. We are not the blank tablets, of Locke's imagination, on which separate experiences impinge. To have any experience at all, or to explicate any meaning at all, we have to presuppose, to borrow Heidegger's terms, that we already exist within a world in which there are meanings. What Wittgenstein has to say to us thus on the connection of meaning and use comes down to a general heuristic phrase: "If you want to know the meaning of a word, look to its use." This is good practical advice, though we must always have some meanings in our grasp in order to carry it out.

What does the behaviorist seek? In one sense or another he wishes to reduce our mental life to overt bodily behavior. The reduction can take place by denying outright that there are any distinct kinds of things as mental processes or states at all; or the behaviorist may claim that our expressions about such processes or states, wherever meaningful, can be tranlated into equivalent expressions about bodily behavior. Wittgenstein claims that he is not seeking to eliminate the fact of consciousness as such. "Why should I deny there are mental processes?" he asks at one point; and he goes on to explain that he doesn't want to deny them, he merely wishes to show how we can talk about them correctly. Yet the bulk of his text, the sheer accumulated weight of his examples, all tend in the other direction: They are of the simpler kinds that serve to indicate nearly always how a statement referring to consciousness is to be replaced by one that refers to overt behavior.

It is this simplicity, or even simplemindedness, of the examples that are most troubling. Our heaviest grievance against the behaviorist, after all, may be for his impoverishment of our psychological life itself. Since he deals with overt behavior, he restricts himself to the more elementary kinds because it seems that these can be described without injecting "inner states" into the data. Hence the psychic life that emerges is one without depth, complexity, or inwardness. Professor Gilbert Ryle, for example, lacks Wittgenstein's genius, but Ryle is a more consistent behaviorist, and we may see the process of oversimplification more clearly at work in him. Ryle pursues the flat and obvious case so ploddingly that we can hardly find anything to quarrel with in his account of mind—as far as it goes. The question is how far it goes; and this is the doubt that is raised in a very acute remark of Iris Murdoch. Ryle's world, Murdoch observes, is one

> in which people play cricket, cook cakes, make simple decisions, remember their childhood, and go to the circus; not the world in which they commit sins, fall in love, say prayers, or join the Communist Party.

Nor, she might have added, a world in which anyone would write a novel—at least an interesting novel. Murdoch is both a philosopher and a novelist, and she would not want to forget as a philosopher what she knows as a novelist. Reading the great novelists—Dostoevski, Proust, Henry James, or Jane Austen, for that matter, who in her own way is as complex and subtle as any—we move constantly and easily within the minds of their characters, and at the

same time within the world they inhabit. We understand what goes
on in the character without having always to pin this understanding
on some small twitch of behavior. We do the same in real life, with
the people who are our intimates, though not with the radiant clarity that it is the power of art to bring us. Indeed, as soon as we invoke this comparison with the novel, how meager and paltry the
behaviorist's world looks.

What leads the philosopher to this poverty is an admirable intention. Professor Ryle wanted to get rid of the Cartesian dualism between mind and matter, for which doctrine he coined the now famous phrase, "the ghost in the machine." The ghost is consciousness
taken as an immaterial substance; the machine is the human body,
mechanistically conceived; and the former is somehow hidden inside
of, or mysteriously haunts, the latter. Such was the picture left to us
by Descartes; and nearly all philosophers in our century—in England, America, and on the Continent—have been at one in their
struggle against it. Indeed, this struggle against Cartesianism seems
to have been the common bond amid all the diversities of schools
and sects. The result has been a great enrichment in the exactness of
our philosophic talk about consciousness. But Murdoch's observation leaves us with a nagging doubt of all this great accomplishment. Perhaps it is the fact that she is also a novelist that suggests another perspective; for as soon as we think of the novel—of
the prodigious breadth and depth of acquaintance with the inner
lives, indeed the souls, of its characters, that it leads us into—we
have to find that the human soul stands very poorly with modern
philosophy. In attempting to dispel the ghost from the machine, we
have banished more than we wanted to. We have become behaving
organisms rather than conscious subjects. To be a conscious subject
is not at all to be a Cartesian subject; but it is also much more than
being a behaving organism.

In his sudden and abrupt fashion Wittgenstein lets fall the observation:

> My attitude toward him is an attitude toward a soul. I am not of
> the *opinion* that he has a soul. [178e]

The statement dangles there in the text, and is not given the further
exploration it cries out for. I do not think my friend *has* a soul, in
the sense of some Cartesian substance hidden inside his head or

diffused throughout his body. Nevertheless, my attitude toward him is still that toward a soul. It would be more correct to say that he *is* a soul, rather than that he *has* one—just as, by the way, it is more correct to say that he is a body rather than that he has a body. Is the attitude merely fanciful, fictitious, cute, or is it real and earnest? Wittgenstein has written elsewhere at length to show that belief is not an isolated mental state; to believe something is to hold fast to and act upon it. If I act, talk, and think in relation to my friend as toward a soul, then I do earnestly believe that he is a soul. It is true that I know of no philosophic analysis of the soul that is quite satisfying to me. But must I wait upon such an analysis before I have the attitudes that I do toward those I love? And even were there an analysis that dispensed with the soul, my attitude would remain what it is—unless love and devotion were to vanish altogether.

Wittgenstein's observation about the soul leaps out at us like a sudden thrust of lightning, but as quickly fades away. Had he pursued examples of this sort, his text would wear a different aspect. He himself has given one of the best warnings against some of the more simpleminded and monolithic types of behaviorism:

> A main cause of philosophical disease—a one-sided diet: One nourishes one's thinking with only one kind of example. [593]

Yet we cannot escape feeling that he himself has not heeded his own admonition. True; we should expect him to deal with simpler examples—and remember, that for Wittgenstein at this stage philosophy is almost completely a matter of individual cases—in order to make clear for us his orientation and point of view. But at a certain point, we feel, he might have sought out more complex and subtle instances for his material.[3] The fact is that the streak of positivism,

---

[3] Less simple-minded instances might be drawn from scientific behavior just as well as from the novelistic situations Iris Murdoch suggests. There is, for example, the story of Galileo's invention of the telescope. According to the contemporary biographer: Galileo, having heard that a certain Dutchman had contrived an enlarging glass, retired to his study, and "after one night's prolonged meditation" invented the telescope. This might be set down in the usual stimulus-response pattern. Stimulus: Galileo hears about an enlarging glass; response: Galileo invents the telescope.

But what interests me here is the hyphen in this stimulus-response situation: namely, that night of prolonged meditation. Surely, that intense and concentrated thinking is the crucial factor without which the telescope would not have been fabricated.

When the behaviorists sets out to study the behavior of a rat, he has to

the simplemindedness of the engineer, runs deep in Wittgenstein, and he was never quite free from it. And the characteristic of the positivist is above all that he must ban the meaningless from discourse, the result of which is often that the more complex and voluminous matters at issue are also shut off from our vision. Thus the data of introspection, the inner life itself, have become suspect to our analytic philosophers. But Wittgenstein should have had more trust in the powers and richness of his chosen medium, the ordinary language. Our common speech may be in good part geared to our transactions with things, but it is also saturated with human inwardness and subjectivity. How could it not be, since it is the medium within which human souls have communicated with each other over the generations? It is, after all, in this common speech that writers whom Wittgenstein admired—Dostoevski and Kierkegaard, for example—express themselves; and they manage to communicate to us modes of our being that, as yet, have not submitted to behavioristic reduction. An intelligent reader, even without any philosophy, understands Kierkegaard very well on the subtle modes of despair. It would be a pity if this reader, after studying philosophy, were to find Kierkegaard "meaningless."

IV.

But where is freedom—our chosen theme—in all of this?

Wittgenstein does not discuss the question of free will as such, and his observations about the will itself are very brief and compressed into a barrage of remarks about intending and doing. As usual, these observations are stimulating, but also, as usual, fragmentary. Wittgenstein helps us to think, but he does not give us a philosophy; we have to form our own from what he says.

The tenor of what he has to say is that we are not to regard the will as a substantial entity in its own right, whose acts parallel or trigger the body's actions. The will is not an independent agent operating within us, nor is it an instrument that we make use of to

---

single out from all the animal's random scurrying that kind of behavior he finds relevant to his study. And this is what he calls "operant behavior." The rat, for example, pushes a certain lever with his nose and receives a pellet of food in return. This little bit of behavior changes his world. Galileo's long night of meditation, then, would certainly have to be considered "operant behavior" on this account: It certainly changed the world. Indeed, thinking may bring about more changes in the world than any amount of overt behavior.

perform an action. When I raise my arm "voluntarily," I do not make use of my will as an additional lever, so to speak, between me and the movement.

All this is quite obvious. The will is a high-level abstraction that serves to single out one aspect of that seamless web of becoming what we call a voluntary action. This abstraction, however, does designate something real; and Wittgenstein is so intent upon expelling the ghost from the machine that he does not do justice to the will as an inner and motivating power in our life. Thus he asks us to consider the case where our body may be incapacitated for one reason or another and does not respond as we would like:

> We can say "I will, but my body does not obey me," but not "My will does not obey me." [Augustine]/[618]

St. Augustine had experience enough in the discipline of the will that we should perhaps listen to him here. To be sure, the will is not an independent creature, like a dog, whom we teach to obey us; but still there are many matters in life on which we try to change our will. "I do not wish to wish these things," sings T. S. Eliot in *Ash Wednesday;* and if we dislike enough the kinds of things we wish, we may actually set about changing our wants. Of course, this usually involves changing the kinds of things we *do*—our habits of behavior; but the latter in turn overflow into and change the kinds of things we want.

Imagine a doctor who tells his patient: "Cigarette smoking has become very dangerous to you in your condition. You must contrive some way to give it up." If the prospect of life without cigarettes seems so grim and cheerless that it is not worth the effort, the patient will have no motivation to forsake his habit. (Motivation and will we take here to be equivalent.) But if he treasures his life, he may be moved to initiate a strategy of behavior that will enable him finally to quit smoking. This is freedom, and it is a fact that some people achieve it. The motivation, or will, is here the central source of the change—the manuals on how to stop smoking always insist on this: You have really to *want* to stop smoking in order to give it up. But it is also the case that the change in behavior aims at altering his will. Thus it would hardly be a satisfactory solution of matters if the man gave up smoking but lived in the perpetual itch and uneasiness to light up. A satisfactory cure must deliver us from the desire. This too sometimes happens with people who have changed their behavior about smoking; they may have come so to dislike the smell of smoke that they find it unpleasant even coming from others. I know of such cases.

Might we not venture to say, indeed, pushing past such reformations of our external behavior, that the change we often most ardently desire for ourselves is a transformation of the "inner person" —a change in our feelings, desires, and will, in our fundamental attitude toward ourself and the world? The route we may have to travel may be a change in behavior, but the goal that we seek is a change of heart. The rites and practices of religion are modes of behavior directed at transforming the will. Where they work for the individual, they enable him to come to peace with his will. If this religious example be uncomfortable for some readers, we may take the more secular case of a patient in psychoanalysis. Such a patient may come to therapy not to rid himself of a particular noxious habit or disturbing tic; he may be afflicted with some more general and less localized malaise—a lassitude of the will, declining motivation, a vague sense of the meaninglessness of things. If he had lost motivation altogether, his case would be hopeless; but then, of course, he would not even have come forward for treatment. The psychiatrist must use what motivation is still there and reroute it into whatever channels of activity are possible in the hope that this may bring back some new and different resurgence of the will and its energies. If the treatment succeeds, the change in the patient will have been total: He will look at the world and himself with different eyes, and he will find new and different values therein. That, of course, would be the ideal psychoanalysis; but something remotely like it does sometimes happen.

As soon as we shift our gaze from some isolated fragment of behavior, like raising an arm, to the larger question of motivation, a new perspective on human freedom opens before us. The question of this freedom enters then another dimension. Where Wittgenstein may help us in this problem, then, does not lie in these brief remarks on the will but in the whole drift of his book itself—in the sense and import of the philosophic reversal from the *Tractatus* to the *Investigations*. In the earlier work he had taken formal logic as his model. He believed, like others at the time, that this language was closed—that it provided a mechanism for determining automatically the truth or falsity of any proposition uttered in it. The change to the ordinary language is thus a shift from a closed to open language. The rules of the latter are indeterminate and flexible; we have to improvise, create, and choose as we go along. But this change from closed to open language is also a passage from a closed to an open world, for our world—the concrete world in which we live—does not come to us as something independent of language; we do not construct a language independently and then add it on to experience; our world transpires within language. Consequently, the essential openness of the language that we have to use for the purposes of life means that the world of our experience is correspondingly open. And that the world should lie open to us is the real and concrete meaning of freedom to which we aspire. For what is the depressing sense of unfreedom that steals over us at times but the feeling that the world has closed in upon us, that we are in a prison all the doors of which have been locked, and that we are trapped in a routine that never opens out upon any fresh possibilities?

We must guard ourselves, however, against a too sensational and external misunderstanding of this open world. Here the demon of Sartre's freedom winks and beckons. This Sartrian freedom is absolute and dizzying; at any moment it holds before me the possibility of some radical and gratuitous act into which I may plunge my future totally. If I have the money, I can take a plane to Tahiti and start life anew. Alas, I have not fled from myself; I carry with me the same flesh and blood, the same psyche, and I have now to recreate their fortunes under other conditions. The sense of an open world does not lie in these glittering possibilities of a leap into another mode of existence, but in something much more mundane and humble. In fact, that sense of the world's being open may be assisted, not hindered, by some sustaining routine.

Philosophers, dealing with the question of freedom, have thrown too much emphasis upon the question of the single act. In this they have been captured by the language game of the law. In a criminal trial we have to debate whether the defendant was in control of himself at the time of a particular action. Was he in his right mind or temporarily deranged by passion at that unique moment when he committed the act? We ask such questions as part of the fabric of our social and legal life, where it is necessary to establish degrees of guilt. The prisoner must wait in the dock for our judgment, but the question of freedom itself is not to be so confined. That question cannot be contracted within such horizons. It is perhaps time that all those examples of isolated fragments of action, like the raising of an arm, be retired to the philosophical oblivion they deserve. We should ask, instead, whether an individual is free or not in his concrete "form of life." We need, in short, to remind ourselves of Wittgenstein's axiom: "What has to be accepted, the given, are *forms of life*." That would be a good starting point on this as on other questions. In the light of this principle, the question of freedom is to be raised, not for an isolated act like raising one's arm, but for the given individual in his total and actual form of life. Is that particular life a free one or not?

Consider the case of Immanuel Kant, who took his daily walk so regularly and precisely at the same time each day that the townspeople of Koenigsberg set their clocks by it. Was Kant nothing but a robot in this? Not at all; he was acting voluntarily. He had set up the arrangement himself as part of the discipline of his life. Suppose, however, that the habit had become so ingrained that he could not change it? Suppose—to borrow the lingo of psychiatry—a repetition compulsion had taken such a deep hold on him that, even had he tried, he could not have pried himself loose from it? He would still have been a free man. The openness of his life lay elsewhere; for on that daily walk, so regularly timed, he was nourishing thoughts that were to transform the intellectual history of Europe.

Kant, of course, is one of the very great figures in the history of culture. It is given to very few of us to be open in our life toward momentous intellectual or artistic creation. Yet, humanly speaking, none of us need lock ourselves in the prison of a closed world. There comes to mind suddenly the remembrance of an older man who kept a stationery and newspaper store on a corner near where I lived years ago in New York City. Each morning he opened at the same time, and at evening closed his shop with equal punctuality. His life was in this respect an unvarying routine. Yet it was always cheering to drop in and chat with him; he left one with the sense, without his ever overdoing it, that each day was a fresh adventure, bringing its small bundle of curiosities awakened and partly satisfied, a gift beyond anything he had been led to expect. He had raised two sons to enter the professions, one as a doctor, the other as a lawyer; and he had thus this sense of accomplishment behind him, of a life that had served some purpose and meaning. The varied routine of the shop came as an added bonus to round off his days.

I never asked—the quality itself seemed too simple and unforced

to require questioning—what was the particular secret of his un-
failing zest. We need not be creative geniuses to find the world
open before us. It may require little, very little, for the doors of our
prison to spring apart—perhaps only some simple change in our
inner attitude. For, contrary to any behaviorism—even so flexible a
one as Wittgenstein's—this inner attitude is not a peripheral and
dangling accompaniment to our actions, but the other way around:
It is doing that is subordinate here to being, our actions to the consciousness that can irradiate them and give them meaning.

The freedom of any individual life is thus inseparably bound with
the presence or absence of some sense of meaning in that life. The
question of human freedom, therefore, turns ultimately on the question of what makes a life meaningful or not. And it is in this form
that we shall have to pursue it in our later pages.

But we have not yet quite done with Wittgenstein. We have to follow him to the end, to his final judgment on the technique from
which he had started. It is only there that we can measure the extent
of his rebellion against Russell. Wittgenstein had begun, following
Russell, by enthroning logic as dictator of our philosophical decisions. The step into ordinary language might have seemed to some
merely to add a further province to philosophical analysis by annex-
ing informal discourse to the domain of formal logic. In fact, however, Wittgenstein wishes to upset the dictatorship altogether. Not
only is the formal logic of Russell an insufficient key for unlocking
our philosophical puzzles, but—so he finally concludes—it is often a
positive hindrance to clear thinking. The rebellion against Russell,
in short, is total.

Chapter 6

Mathematics, Mechanism, and Creativity

IN 1928 WITTGENSTEIN HEARD BROUWER, THE LEADER OF THE INTUI-tionist school in mathematics, lecture in Vienna.[1] The following year Wittgenstein returned to Cambridge to resume his philosophic career after a decade spent groping for another vocation. The hearing of Brouwer thus coincides more or less with his return to philosophy.

It would be possible to make too much of this conjunction of dates—especially if we were to imagine some immediate and total conversion on the spot as a result of that lecture. In fact—and we can see this from the succession of notebooks that his editors have so helpfully and intelligently brought to publication—it took Wittgenstein some years and the toil of much reflection to work himself away from his older views. Nevertheless, the encounter with Brouwer was a direct exposure to the most powerful spokesman for a point of view on mathematics and logic that was diametrically opposed to the views of Frege and Russell, on which Wittgenstein had been brought up. And Wittgenstein's own views, when they eventually took shape, were to move very much in the intuitionist direc-

---

[1] Brouwer delivered two lectures in Vienna on March 10 and March 14, 1928: "Mathematics, Science and Language," and "The Structure of the Continuum." They are among his more pregnant essays, but neither has yet been translated into English. The themes of both are echoed in Wittgenstein's subsequent thoughts about mathematics. The first lecture is particularly relevant philosophically, since it seeks to embed mathematics in the total human context. Though Brouwer's language is subjectivistic, and Wittgenstein deals with the same matters objectively and behaviorally, both seek the same embedding. This relation of Wittgenstein to Brouwer has yet to be fully explored.

tion of Brouwer. And without this change in his fundamental views of mathematics, Wittgenstein could not have taken his later step into the philosophy of ordinary language.

It may come as something of a surprise to some readers to learn that there are rival schools of intuitionists and formalists in mathematics. Why should there be different schools of opinion in this subject at all? Mathematics is supposed to be the most rigorous and objective of disciplines, and therefore the one in which men should, if they are capable of it at all, reach complete agreement. Yet in this century a kind of civil war has been raging among mathematicians over the foundations of their subject; and the outcome of the conflict has yet to be decided. Disagreement has in fact been so violent that at one point, after a mathematical congress early in the century, Poincaré, the great French mathematician, exclaimed: "Men do not understand each other; they do not speak the same language." We might wonder why, if men are technically competent, they should not understand each other's language. But the issue here is no longer one of technical competence but of the basic premises of insight. And on this terrain men are likely to carry their own particular dispositions to see things as they do. One can scarcely have a clearer indication how all of us, mathematicians like the rest, can be chained to philosophical premises, and how potent these premises are even in grasping the apparently most "objective" matters. There is no such thing as a pure technique that isolates itself completely from the insight that decides what that technique is about and what it is for. Technique has no meaning apart from some informing vision.

These disagreements among mathematicians should remind us that mathematics, whatever else it may be, is a part of the historical life of mankind. An adequate philosophy of mathematics cannot view it as less. That it is such a part of our historical life ought to persuade the reader not to turn his back on the issues it raises. It is remarkable how educated and intelligent people are put off by the first sign of a mathematical idea, however simple it may be. I had an experience of this timidity some years back when I looked over the shoulders of my children as they suffered the unseemly trials of the New Math. When I spoke to other parents, perhaps hoping to rally them to some mild protest, they shied away from matters that they professed were beyond them. Yet these were the same people who could follow the stock market meticulously, compute their income tax carefully, and who were delighted by the exhausting complexities of bridge. Yet they believed that mathematics belonged to some formal and sacrosanct sphere distinct from these activities of calculation—a belief which, with Wittgenstein, we shall here be concerned to demolish. I hope, therefore, that my reader will not skip this chapter simply because of its subject.

The New Math is now somewhat out of fashion because it proved to be a pedagogical failure. Yet a failure in practice—as we have been told by the pragmatists—is usually the sign of deficient theory. The New Math was presented to teachers and pupils as more "scientific" and yet it was in fact a bold *philosophic* adventure on the part of the educational powers. They chose to plump for a particular philosophy of mathematics, believing it to be fashionable, though it turned out to be a fashion thirty years out of date.

Had Wittgenstein been studied, they might have been deterred from their reckless adventure. The result is that our school system is now saddled with millions of dollars of textbooks, which had been part of a vast selling campaign for this program. One could scarcely find a plainer or more materialistic example of how philosophy—in this case a particular philosophy of mathematics—can make a difference in life, and sometimes enter the marketplace with the most gross economic consequences.

The obstacles in the way of philosophic readers here are of a different order. Some of Wittgenstein's admirers would discount his later writings on mathematics—I suspect partly because of his uncomplimentary remarks about the misuses of mathematical logic. For the most part they are bound, more than they are aware, by Russell's ideas on the subject, and cannot see beyond these. It is hardly consistent to admire Wittgenstein as a "great" philosopher, and yet find his mathematical thoughts negligible—in view of the central position these held in his thinking. If these mathematical writings seem fragmentary, they are not really less so than his thinking on other matters. The obstacle, I suspect, is that American philosophers are unfamiliar with the thinking of Brouwer and the intuitionists, and have not yet thought their way into the questions that Wittgenstein pushes even more radically. My own view is that his notebooks on mathematics contain some of the boldest and most stimulating thoughts that Wittgenstein has to communicate to us. They are not complete, of course; they do not resolve all the questions they raise, and in the end they lead us before a great and glaring gap—but that is a gap that mathematical philosophy has not yet crossed. Nevertheless, fragmentary as they are, they do add up to a coherent position.

Their coherence can be presented under three headings. (1) We have first to deal with his rebellion against Russell's logic, and the sense that that logic would make of mathematics. (2) Second, Wittgenstein has some significant things to say against the axiomatization —or, in his pregnant phrase, the mechanization—of mathematics proposed by formalists. (3) In the third aspect of his thought he pushes his pragmatism to its extreme, to a kind of conventionalism, from which mathematics emerges fundamentally as a network of human norms or conventions. And it is here that we shall encounter the serious gap we have mentioned.

I.

"ARITHMETIC WITH FRILLS"

Russell claimed to have reduced mathematics to logic—that is, to exhibit a way in which statements of mathematics could be translated into purely logical statements. The aim of the reduction was to secure the foundations of mathematics more firmly.

Wittgenstein's objections take a general turn at first. Our "feel" of the different domains of mathematics goes against this homogenization—this smelting down of specific differences into the underlying stuff of logic. He wants to defend something he calls the *Farbigkeit* (the colorful variety and heterogeneity) of the separate mathematical disciplines. The styles of thought in one field may be quite different from those in another. Someone who works in number theory (consider that amazing phenomenon Ramanujan) may be called upon for different powers of construction, imagination, and insight than a geometer. A mathematician skilled in one field may be an indifferent artisan in another. To say that logic gives us the essence of mathematics is like saying that the craft of the cabinetmaker consists essentially in gluing the pieces together.

Then again, why do these separate branches of mathematics need to have their foundations secured? Are they insecure otherwise? If I acquire a simple theorem in arithmetic—say, that there is no last prime number—the proof is presented in English with the accompanying simple algebraic notations for numbers, multiplication, and addition. And in these terms I find it entirely convincing, evident, and self-sufficient. What would be secured by translating it into logic? Would it become any more certain thereby? On the contrary, it becomes so much more complicated and that much less "perspicuous." And a proof, Wittgenstein insists, should be "perspicuous"—it should be such that we can grasp it clearly as a whole if we are to be convinced by it.

Moreover, if logic is to provide a foundation for mathematics, what will serve as its foundation? *Quis custodiet custodem?* Who will guard the guardian? Is logic more certain and sure than, say, arithmetic? We shall see later that it is in fact much less secure than elementary arithmetic. Why should not mathematical logic, then, be regarded merely as a specific mathematical discipline, one among many, rather than that it should arrogate to itself a doubtful hegemony over all the others?

Let us turn now to the specific manner of the reduction proposed by Russell. To convey mathematics into logic, we should succeed with the simplest cases first—for example, with the simple natural, or counting, numbers. Thus we are to exhibit the elementary mathematical truth of *Two plus two equals four* as a statement that contains only purely logical expressions. To make matters more concrete, consider the fact now present before me: There are two apples, and two bananas in the fruit basket on the table; and consequently four pieces of fruit. Logically expressed, this runs: There is an *a* and a *b* that are members of the class apple; *c* and *d* that are members of the class banana; and therefore *a*, *b*, *c*, and *d* are either apples or bananas. The translation is now complete; we have transformed the original statement into a purely logical one, where no specific mathematical terms occur, but only the logical notions of individuals, class membership, if-then, and either-or.

It all seems so marvelously simple! And with the natural numbers taken care of in this way, we go on to exhibit the real numbers, using the method of Dedekind's "cut," as classes of natural numbers; and mathematical functions in turn as classes of real numbers. And thus, from that first simple step, the whole prodigious garden of mathematics opens before us.

However, in the seeming simplicity of this first step, we encounter a snag. I pick up this bunch of grapes (I have counted them; there are twenty-five) and throw them into the basket. Now there are *Two plus two plus twenty-five* or twenty-nine pieces of fruit on the table. How do we transpose this into the logical calculus? We run out of letters and are forced to use numerical subscripts. Whatever device we adopt, we are forced, if we wish to produce a true statement, to count out twenty-nine operators accurately! We have not escaped arithmetic and counting after all. The logical statement has merely wrapped the arithmetical statement in a great deal of flimsy gauze. It has not replaced arithmetic, but merely given us, in Wittgenstein's telling phrase, "arithmetic with frills."

Someone might say, Well, this operation of counting concerns us, but not "the proposition in itself." But what is this proposition in itself? What meaning does it have except as it fits into our discourse and the use we make of it? What meaning does a language have apart from any or all use? Well, someone might say, why not have two arithmetics: a "theoretical" one in Russell's language, which we never use, and the ordinary arithmetic, in which we do our counting? We could imagine the theorems in this "theoretical" logical calculus engraved in some monumental tome that is kept in a guarded and sequestered place. Even so, we would still have to count the operators (letters) in those statements to be sure we were engraving true ones. Then everything would go on in our lives as if those sacred tomes did not exist.

There are two separate but related points in Wittgenstein's argument here: (1) It is a mistaken conception of the "theoretical" to think of it as having meaning apart from human practice, operations, and usage. (2) Arithmetical or numerical structure, contrary to what we had been led to believe by our early training in Russell, is in fact more basic than logical structure. A structure *A* is more basic than another structure, *B*, if *B* presupposes all the elements that appear in *A* plus some additional ones of its own. Thus the logical translation reproduces all the elements of the arithmetical statement plus some additional features—what Wittgenstein calls "frills" —of its own.

(That arithmetical structure is more basic becomes clear, it seems to me, in the various "limitative theorems," to which we shall come in a moment, and most spectacularly in Gödel's celebrated result. Gödel showed that a proof could be exhibited as a particular way of counting off the theorems of a system. He then constructed a formula such that, if it should ever be counted off, the system would become contradictory. Here arithmetic does the work; it shoulders the main burden of the argument, and indeed makes the whole proof possible. Then at a certain moment, as it were, logical syntax arrives on the spot to observe what our arithmetical constructions had achieved.)

The doubtfulness of attempting to define numbers in terms of logical classes may be illustrated by a story that comes out of World War II. I cannot vouch for the truth of the story, and it is rather gruesome in tone; but even its gruesomeness may serve to fix its lesson securely in our memory.

A company of American soldiers operating in the South Pacific came into contact with a tribe of headhunters, whose sympathies they were able to engage against the Japanese. The natives, among other things, showed a particular fondness for American cigarettes. The American captain promptly struck a bargain: For each Japanese head brought in, the native would get a pack of cigarettes. One enterprising hunter arrived one day with an extraordinary catch of twelve heads. The officer congratulated him, and carefully counted out twelve packs of cigarettes. He expected the native to be delighted, but instead the fellow looked at him in dismay. What was wrong? It was finally necessary to align the twelve heads on the ground, and beside each, one by one, a pack of cigarettes. Then and only then did the native gather up his prizes and go off cackling with joy.

The number 12 did not exist for this native; he could not count that far. Yet he could perfectly well pair off sets, one by one, in the manner of Frege and Russell. Clearly, the pairing of sets cannot give us the notion of any definite number. And we therefore cannot, by these means at least, secure the reduction of mathematics to logic.

We would do well to linger a moment longer on our gruesome story, for its anthropological overtones bring out the question of mathematical existence more starkly. (The anthropological context is also part of the total context in which Wittgenstein would have us examine mathematics.) The New Guinea natives have devised quite subtle strategies to cope with life; they have extensive knowledge of local flora and fauna, and can recognize the various natural signs within their environment; they have language, rituals, and a fairly complex kinship structure. But in their various shifts to survive they have not found it necessary to devise or construct a number system. Should we say that the number 12 exists but that they have not yet found out about it? It is easy for us to say this since we already have the number in our reckoning. It has become second nature to us, and so we tend to think of it as a part of nature, so to speak. Suppose the human mind had not evolved beyond the stage of this New Guinea native's; the number 12 would not then exist at all for anybody. Would it exist, waiting, so to speak, for discovery by mankind? America was there before Columbus discovered it. But America was a vast mass, existing physically in space and time, and mathematical entities are clearly not of that kind. These entities must, then, if they have being independent of the human mind, subsist in some kind of Platonic heaven beyond space and time. But such an assumption leads us back into ancient metaphysical fantasies.

We have entered here into the old question of the existence of mathematical entities—a question that currently divides Platonists and intuitionists in the philosophy of mathematics. Platonists hold that these entities have a reality independent of the human mind, intuitionists that they are human constructs. Plato and Kant might be chosen as historical ancestors of both positions. Wittgenstein holds to the latter position; but he differs from an intuitionist like Brouwer in holding that mathematical entities are not so much mental concepts as functioning parts within that total network of behavior he calls language.

Why are there still Platonists at this late date in history? "The bewitchment of our mind by language"—this is the constant intellectual temptation against which Wittgenstein is preaching. We think of this injunction as one directed only against woolly minded metaphysicians; but mathematicians too can become the victims of their own language and end by reifying the objects of their symbolism. It is easy to decide that the number 12 does not float around in any kind of independent existence. But when we come to more subtle matters, like infinite series, mathematicians can easily be bewitched by the intricacies of their own language, and slide into unconscious Platonism. But this particular point we shall have to postpone for the moment till the next section of this chapter.

We come back now to the business of numbers and classes. There is a simpler and more powerful argument against the attempted reduction of numbers to classes than any that Wittgenstein makes, though it is implicit in his pages. Let us try to make it explicit. The reduction of mathematics to logic claimed to secure the foundations of the latter. Thus the implication is that classes must be simpler, more certain, and more secure than the notions of the natural numbers. In fact, the natural, or simple counting numbers are among the most clear-cut and definite conceptions that we have; and it is the notion of class that turns out to be vague, uncertain, and ambiguous. The evidence of this is that the theory of sets had scarcely been brought into mathematics than it developed antinomies; while elementary arithmetic has been with mankind for centuries upon centuries and has yet to exhibit a contradiction. The method of *notum per ignotius*—to explain what is clear and definite through what is less uncertain and more vague—is surely a very irrational procedure. Arithmetic is more certain than logic; the abacus breeds no antinomies.

It may be worthwhile to review Russell's famous antinomy to make our point clearer. In its easier and more popular form this runs as follows: In a certain town there is a barber who shaves all those, and only those, who do not shave themselves. Does he shave himself? If he does, he doesn't; and if he doesn't, he does.

Of course, such a barber is impossible, and we may discard the supposition promptly. But the generalization of this paradox by Russell is not so easily disposed of. Russell's mode of presenting the paradox is itself very revealing: We are to consider, first, that most classes are not members of themselves. Thus the class of teacups is itself not a teacup. We may call these *ordinary* classes. But there seem to be some unusual or extraordinary classes that are members of themselves; thus the class of things that are not teacups is itself not a teacup. Now let us form the class *w* of all these ordinary classes—of all the classes that are not members of themselves. Is *w* a member of itself? If it is, it isn't; and if it isn't, it is. In other words: the class *ordinary* is itself extraordinary; and if it is extraordinary, then it is ordinary. When Russell first communicated this paradox to the venerable Frege, the latter lamented: "Alas, arithmetic totters!" He was wrong; it was not arithmetic, but his own logicizing of it, that tottered.

Russell's remedy for the paradox was to invoke his rule of types. The expressions of the system are to be classified into levels and types such that the members of a class cannot be on the same level as the class itself. Thus it no longer becomes grammatically permissible either to affirm or deny that a class is a member of itself. The rule is a purely practical crutch created ad hoc to make the system work. We thus arrive at a peculiarly ironic situation: The logical calculus was supposed to provide a more purely "theoretical" basis for arithmetic; yet this calculus can be made to work only if we prop it up with a purely practical makeshift. Pragmatism thrust out the front door returns by the back door—and with a vengeance.

And this practical makeshift does have some very impractical features. The rule permits us to establish a definition of number at one level, but we cannot apply the number at that level. We cannot speak of *two* ideas on *two* pages of text in the same sense of *two*. If we were really to carry on mathematics within this system, we would find ourselves involved in almost unbearable complications. Moreover, even with the rule of types, the ghost of the old antinomy still haunts the system. If at any moment, while we are manipulating the calculus, we stop and ask ourselves what we are doing, we cannot form any legitimate conception in answer. For example: We are dealing with classes. What classes? Well, since the theory is general, with any or all classes permissible by the rule. But this class of permissible classes is itself not permissible. As a purely practical decision, to keep the calculus working, we do not write the paradox down, but we continue to think it.

A more radical reflection by Russell on his own quaint example— the class of things that are not teacups—might have led him to doubt the notion of class itself. What belongs to such a class? God, angels, men, trees, rocks, prime numbers—well, everything at all that is not a teacup. Its outlines are blurred and indefinite. The term "class" as such is an uncertain term. Whether a class is clear or not depends upon the entities that make it up. We may think of it in analogy to a parenthesis: The parenthesis is clear only if what falls inside the two parentheses is clear and definite. By contrast, the natural numbers 1, 2, 3, . . . are hard, sharp, and definite in their outlines: there is no uncertainty about their meaning. Why, then, attempt to define the clear by the unclear?

Behind this claim to hegemony by logic there lurks the dominance of a particular metaphor. Bertrand Russell observed that mathematics ceased to be interesting to him when he came to see it as one immense tautology, which could be directly apparent as such to a superhuman mind. This is the ennui of a god who has stepped outside of the human condition. There could hardly be a more drastic case of the bewitchment of the mind by its own metaphor. When one considers the actual history of mathematics with its constant creations and surprises; new concepts and fields constructed that had not been dreamed of before, or, if so, only dimly; with its constant nourishment by the problems encountered in nature; then one clearly has in Russell's metaphor a view that, precisely because it is severed from the actual life of mathematics, ends by being lifeless and sterile itself. Yet it is a metaphor under which most Anglo-American philosophers, whether aware of it or not, still labor.

But beside this image of mathematics as a self-enclosed and self-contained tautology, there is another metaphor that bewitches our thinking, and that is fetched, it would seem, from an altogether different quarter of the imagination: the metaphor of mathematics as a machine mechanically grinding out its results.

II.

MECHANIZATION

The impulse toward axiomatizing mathematics was a positive step in the nineteenth century toward securing greater mathematical rigor. In the century following Newton there had been an immense expansion of mathematics; but this prodigious enrichment of the subject had left a great number of uncertain methods and concepts in its wake. In order to make mathematical thinking more rigorous, it would be necessary to insist that it remain strictly within the framework of its initial premises and that the mathematician draw on no assumptions, tacit or otherwise, that he had not explicitly postulated. The axioms lay down the rules according to which the game of mathematics is to be played.

But this demand was not enough. The impulse toward axiomatization once launched, a certain *hubris* of spirit—perhaps the spirit of mechanism endemic at that period—gradually took over. It is not enough that there should be rules; the rules must be of strict and definite kind, if they are to prevent an appeal, covert or otherwise, to intuitive evidence of any kind. They must abstract from all meanings, and merely specify configurations of symbols and operations on those symbols that a machine, properly programmed, could perform. And the purpose of the whole mathematical enterprise, if it were ever to be successfully completed, would be to produce a gigantic machine, or group of machines, that could automatically grind out all the truths of mathematics. The mathematician himself, in his traditional creative role, would thereby become obsolete; he

would become, if he survives at all, merely a mechanic tinkering
with a machine that in all essential respects would be already complete. We observe too that the ordinary idea of a proof as a procedure for showing something—for bringing something out into the
open and making it evident to us—would disappear.

So arrogant a venture, however, was to bring its own insecurities.
Quis custodiet custodes? If the axioms are to guarantee mathematics, what is to guarantee that the axioms themselves do not lead
us into a contradiction? Since we are not to rely on self-evidence
and perspicuity at any point, whatever conclusions we draw, however partial and restricted, will have to depend upon the integrity of
the whole structure. What, then, is to ensure that our mathematical
machine does not at some point grind out a contradiction, which
would make the whole system senseless? Hence the demand for
consistency became the great order of the day among the formalists.
If the axioms were consistent, one need not understand what one
was talking about in operating the machine; one could still be sure
that no contradiction would come out of its operation.

Yet mere consistency would not be enough. Rules that had been
established somehow as consistent would nevertheless be trivial if
they were sufficient to produce only a handful of mathematical
truths. The axioms must therefore be *complete*—that is, sufficient to
generate all the truths of a mathematical system. Moreover, beyond
these demands of consistency and completeness, there was another
requirement that Hilbert, the leader of the formalist school, came to
insist upon more strongly as the movement gathered force. The ultimate desideratum of a machine is that it produce its results automatically. You would not want an automobile, to use our earlier example, whose starting every morning you would have to improvise.
When you turn on your ignition switch, you expect the machine
automatically to go through those finite and unvarying steps (a "decision procedure") that get the motor running. Every morning that
your car starts promptly it automatically solves its little problem according to the axioms of procedure imprinted in it. What good
would the axiom systems be if they did not automatically produce
their conclusions—if, that is, despite the axioms, the mathematician
were still condemned to create, to grope, and to flounder about in
the old way, in order to come up with any results? It would be like
having a beautiful car that would move only if you got out and
pushed it. Thus the mathematician would be doing mathematics in

the old way, using whatever intuition, imagination, and inventiveness he could command; while the axioms would come in at the end only as decor, as a vehicle of presentation. Hilbert was, then, entirely consistent when he urged his followers that the finding of decision procedures within the various mathematical fields was the most important task for them if the axiomatic program were to be really productive.

Alas, all three of these dreams were to be rudely shattered. The first blow fell in 1931 with Gödel's celebrated proof of the incompleteness of arithmetic. Less spectacular, but equally significant, there followed shortly the studies of Church, Turing, Tarski, Post, and other logicians on the question of the undecidability of systems. All told, these "limitative theorems," as they have come to be called, are the century's greatest contribution to logic, and perhaps as great as any in the whole history of the subject; and their effect is to render impossible the dream of mechanizing mathematics totally. It is therefore worth our while to take the briefest of glances at what they accomplish.

Gödel showed that even such a relatively simple system as elementary arithmetic is too rich to be encompassed by any set of axioms. It will always contain more truths than the axioms can yield. The direct consequence of this for the question of consistency is momentous. One cannot prove arithmetic to be consistent without presupposing means that are richer—and therefore less certain—than arithmetic itself. The hope thus of establishing the consistency of mathematics generally dwindles.

What strikes us here is that so small a piece of reality constructed by the human mind as is the field of the natural numbers, apparently so simple and transparent in its nature, should yet prove so refractory and elusive to the axiomatic method. And this elusiveness shows itself just as drastically, though differently, in the complementary results of the Norwegian mathematician Skolem. While Gödel showed that the axioms are too meager to encompass arithmetic, Skolem has shown that they are too loose to fit the body of arithmetic snugly. Other systems, different from arithmetic at significant points, are covered equally well by these axioms.

The metaphor of a suit of clothes suggests itself here. A good suit fits the body adequately and snugly. But here the suit (the axiom system) is at once too skimpy, so that the wrists and ankles protrude and remain uncovered; while at the same time it is too loose and floppy, so that several different people can be fit into it at once. We are reminded of the incident in *Gulliver's Travels* when the tailors of the fantastic kingdom of La Puta construct a suit of clothes for the hero by very elaborate mechanical means; and which, when put on, turns out more ill-fitting than any garments fashioned by ordinary methods.

The discoveries on decidability are even more striking for a theory of machines. Only very minimal systems, it turned out, are decidable—that is, provide an automatic means of deciding whether any given statement in the system is true or false. Or, in other words, provide an automatic means for solving all problems that arise within the system. You have but to take a small step forward, introduce the least bit of complexity, and the system is such that it no longer permits an automatic decision on its problems. You have to grope, flounder, and create in order to solve your problems— even within the framework of the most elegantly framed axioms.

Wittgenstein had no hand in any of these discoveries. Some of his critics have pointed out, and quite truly, that he did not keep up with the newer developments in logic. But the remarkable thing is the way in which his philosophy fits in with these later findings, and indeed seems to be the view of mathematics they point toward. Wittgenstein remarks that his aim is to *vorbei reden* (speak past) Gödel. This does not mean to speak against or in disregard of Gödel's result; but to concern himself with the more simple and elemental things we do when we do mathematics, such that Gödel's result on incompleteness should be what we would expect.

It would be well if we paused here for just a moment in order to bring out the human point of these logical matters. The contrast between logic and life has been one of the standard conventions of our thought, and philosophers in the past have made use of it from time to time. The difference, as usually represented, is between the closed and the open, the complete and the unfinished, the fixed and the indeterminate. ("There is a system of logic, but no system of human existence," says Kierkegaard.) But what emerges from these newer developments is, rather, a striking similarity in one fundamental respect between logic and the human condition.

If we had thought to escape from the particularities and contingencies of our actual life into a timeless and perfect logical world, we were greatly mistaken. Logic, in its way, gives us back a picture of our own human condition. People who have a fear of freedom seek to box themselves into a situation where control will be complete, where every emergency can be met by a predetermined technique that will be routine and automatic in its efficacy. But the routine character of such a world, even if we could maintain it, begets boredom, monotony, and in intense cases, neurosis. In logic, analogously, if we wanted completeness and decidability, we could restrict ourselves to those minimal formal systems that permit it. But it would be like confining ourselves to playing the match game, in which he who picks first invariably wins. You might have the thrill of victory at first, but its monotony would soon become tiresome. The human spirit craves a certain amount of openness in its world, a certain measure of indeterminacy and adventure; otherwise every future prospect already palls in anticipation. We pay for this open world by a certain measure of risk and insecurity. We cannot be sure whether the elements out of which we have built our world will hold together consistently; never know for sure whether our techniques and resources will be sufficient to meet all problems; and particularly to meet our emergencies. We have to rely on invention and ingenuity that cannot be pre-programmed. The price for freedom is risk, uncertainty, and inevitably the measures of anxiety that accompany these; but without such qualities life would lose its zest and adventure.

"Man is condemned to be free," Sartre has remarked in commenting upon the various human devices and deceptions by which we try to evade the burden of freedom in our life. A whole generation of mathematicians labored to abolish their subject by turning it over to the mechanism of axioms. The mechanization failed; and the mathematician, to borrow Sartre's apt phrase, is now condemned to be free. "Mathematical thinking is, and must remain, essentially creative," mathematician-logician E. L. Post sums up in commenting upon the various limitative proofs that modern logic has produced.

These "limitative theorems" should in fact be called "liberating theorems." They show us that human creativity exceeds any mechanism in which it might seek to contain its own constructs. We are always more than any machine we may construct.

Undecidability, as an intrinsic character of mathematical systems, throws a very searching light on the ancient and vexed question of the existence of mathematical entities. It becomes more questionable to detach these entities from the human operations of calculating. Consider Wittgenstein's example of the number π, which designates the ratio of the circumference of a circle to its diameter. We know that this is is an irrational number, which goes on as an endless nonrepeating decimal, 3.14159 . . . Somewhere in this expansion, where our calculation has not yet reached, we imagine that there may occur the sequence 777. Does it or does it not occur?

And precisely here, our imagination becomes bewitched by language. We invoke the sacrosanct law of logic, the law of the excluded middle, and say: Either there is a sequence 777 somewhere in the expansion of this number, or there is not. One or the other *must* be true. What is happening here? We imagine we are looking down that expansion like a long corridor stretching away, and somewhere beyond our sight is the triad 777. (Or, on the other hand, it is definitely *not* there!) But of course there is no such corridor; the expansion exists only as we calculate it step by step, and only so far as we calculate it. The human race might go on calculating this decimal to a million places, and not find 777 occurring. Still, that is no proof that it might not turn up in the next million, if we calculate that far. But to think of it as already there—as it were, waiting for us—is to think of that whole expansion as independently subsisting quite apart from our activity of calculating.

And here our bewitched imagination is tempted to call God to its aid: A divine intelligence, we imagine, taking in the whole infinite expansion of the decimal at a single glance can see immediately whether or not 777 occurs in it. But Wittgenstein wants to reject even this beclouding fantasy. Not even God can see an infinite expansion as something it is not—as something closed and finished, rather than as an endlessly unfinished process.[1]

III.

CONVENTIONALISM

One of the seductive promises of the axiomatizers was that we would eventually be able to carry on mathematics without having to understand what we were doing. It was sufficient that we should

[1] Wittgenstein also extends this line of reasoning against the famed Dedekind "cut," which is supposed to define the nature of the real numbers. Thus the square root of 2 would be defined as a "cut" between all the rational numbers less than or greater than itself. But this is to talk as if these numbers *were already there*, whereas they come into being only as we calculate the decimal in successive steps, 1.4, 1.41, 1.414, 1.4142 . . . etc.

Here again, the point is that we cannot ascribe existence to mathematical entities independently of the operations by which we establish them.

be able to manipulate the symbols according to the rules. We need not concern ourselves with the meaning or truth of our postulates but only with drawing necessary consequences from them. The proofs of consistency would ensure that what we were doing would turn out well. Now, however, that we know that these proofs of consistency are not to be forthcoming, we have to take a very different view of these matters. We have to be concerned with questions of meaning and truth—with the meaning of our concepts, and both the meaning and truth of our statements. And as for proof, we have particularly here to return to a more traditional view of evidence and cogency.

The proof, Wittgenstein tells us, must be "perspicuous." It must be eventually transparent that we may grasp it as a whole so that it becomes clear, cogent, and compelling to us. Wittgenstein has put the matter elegantly in one of the most pregnant sentences he ever uttered:

> It is not something behind the proof, but the proof itself that proves.

A proof is not something that takes place behind the scenes, through the invisible mechanism of axioms into which we do not catch a peep. Wittgenstein's sentence rang bells for me when I first came across it because at that time I was party to the sufferings of some young students in the toils of the New Math. These children, for whom mathematics had been presented as a tedious affair of bookkeeping, had no notion at all that a proof was ever something they were supposed to *see*. But if mathematical reasoning is never to be clearly *seen*, then it becomes something taken merely on trust, no matter how sophisticated the computers we turn its operations over to.

Yet precisely here there arises a difficulty for Wittgenstein. That mathematical procedures should ultimately be clear, evident, and cogent, so that we *must* accept their results, is the *phenomenological* demand that we place upon this discipline. There is no truth that does not rest ultimately upon what is evident to us in our own experience. On the other hand, the *pragmatic* dimension has also to be considered. Mathematics is a human activity, and as such is part of the stream of life, which does not usually permit us to hug our isolated nuggets of clarity to our bosom in isolation from the rest of experience. Thus the originally evident proof may have to be fitted alongside other mathematical facts, and we might wish to modify its expression or re-evaluate its import in relation to later clarities. Somehow the philosopher must strike a balance between these two claims. But as between these two aspects—the phenomenological and the pragmatic—Wittgenstein throws preponderant emphasis upon the latter. He wants a pragmatism so extreme that he can regard mathematics as essentially a "network of norms"—a network of human conventions.

Now, we tend to forget what an enormous role our conventions play in mathematics, and it is useful to have a thinker remind us of this. The convention of the decimal system, for example, has probably advanced the development of mathematics more than any single high-level theorem. Nevertheless, Wittgenstein's conventionalism seems excessive in its scruples.

What troubles him particularly is the notion of *necessity*, from which he would like to escape if he could. Mathematics is commonly said to differ from the empirical sciences because it deals with necessary truths, and the latter give us only probabilities. But Wittgenstein would not want to leave this distinction so absolute. The two are not thus sundered, after all, as they enter the fabric of our ordinary language, which is the decisive context for Wittgenstein.

Thus the statement of a proof fits into the web of mathematical discourse, and this in turn into the larger fabric of human language. Language itself is a system of conventions, within which we humans live. As life changes, the conventions of language change with it— and in ways we cannot always foresee. Now, a convention *compels* us to follow the consequences of its use; if a symbol is used in this or that way, then you *must* say such-and-such. The whole philosophical question here turns on this matter of necessity, on what it is that words like "compels" and "must" bind us to. May we not *choose* to alter the original convention because we do not wish to follow its consequences at a certain point? If a language is open, it will not necessarily determine every situation that comes up; we have the *freedom* to alter the rule in the face of the facts as they arise. Notice how words like "choose" and "freedom" enter now, as compared with the previous words of necessity—"must" and "compels." What is the relative scope and role of these two sets of expressions in relation to each other? That is the problem of conventionalism as it presents itself for the philosophy of mathematics.

There is, of course, no general solution of this question. The only law that holds here is case law, to be worked out in particular situations. But even in some of his particular cases, Wittgenstein's emphasis upon convention seems excessive.

Take his simple example of a multiplication, 7 times 3 equal 21. How do we know this? Wittgenstein tells us it is a rule we have been taught, thereby suggesting that we "know" it only through habit or custom. At least, he leaves this conjecture hanging. Suppose we perform the multiplication and it does not come out to 21. We must have made a mistake. Why do we say this? Couldn't we possibly think of changing the rule of multiplication? But surely this is an unprofitable line of inquiry on Wittgenstein's part. We are not dealing here with an isolated rule that we have simply learned by rote. The number system has such a network of interrelations that any simple assertion like "7 times 3 are 21" is, in fact, *overdetermined*. To change this apparently simple rule of multiplication we should have to change the whole of elementary arithmetic.

Under what circumstances then, we may press on to ask, would we change this rule and with it the whole of elementary arithmetic? Well, we do not know, and cannot imagine, any such circumstances. Our claim of necessity here turns into a confession of the inability of our imagination. The question of certainty, for Wittgenstein, comes down practically to this: What beliefs of ours would we give up last if we were compelled to? I would find it harder to give up elementary arithmetic than the principle of contradiction as a universally valid law. Indeed, this principle does not seem to hold for certain psychological states, like those of ambivalence, for example. Our psychological vocabulary may never be exact enough to exclude the possibility that in a certain situation we shall have to say a certain man loves and hates the same object at the same time and in the same respect. To assert the universal validity of the principle of contradiction is to assert that we will never encounter some universe of discourse where our vocabulary cannot be made precise enough to exclude our having to say that a thing is both A and not A at once. And this, of course, becomes an assertion about experience and the fate of our language. Here the logical and empirical turn out to be not altogether disjoined.

But if Wittgenstein is not altogether satisfying on the subject of conventionalism, we have to remember that his thinking here is tentative, probing, and deliberately provocative. His genius lies in going to the limits of a position and showing us what happens there.

In the *Tractatus* he had taken the whole apparatus of mathematical logic as providing the fixed and rigid framework of the world. Now the shoe is on the other foot; the emphasis has shifted to the flexibility, irregularity, and particularity of the situation we encounter within the language game of mathematics.

Thus even some of his bizarre examples turn out to have a very good gadfly effect upon us. At various times he asks us to imagine some strange world in which our measuring rods bent, our rulers sagged like dough, and numbers slid on the page as we wrote them. What kind of mathematics would we construct in such a world? Under such circumstances it might be enormously difficult to build any mathematics at all. But should we succeed, we feel that though its expression might come out very differently, mathematics would nevertheless be the same in some ways as our own—identical under certain transformations, as the mathematicians say. Is this faith an illusion? We cannot be sure.

On their positive side, however, these bizarre imaginings should serve to remind us how much of our actual mathematics has developed out of our constant intercourse with the physical world around us, how much we depend on the steady properties of the instruments we use and of the physical bodies about us. The whole history of mathematics stands there to attest to this relation between the mathematical mind and nature. Geometry and the calculus, for example, developed out of our need to deal with things of the physical world. Some modern mathematicians, however, tended at one point to sever this tie with nature. In the exuberance of formalism they were led to imagine mathematics itself as a free excursion in the void. Modern philosophers have abetted this tendency. One of the disservices of positivism (for which the early Wittgenstein bears some responsibility) was to erect into dogma the slogan "Mathematics tells us nothing about the real world." The dogma should have been suspect from the start. It is entirely unlikely that we should have been able to build airplanes or launch rockets without the aid of mathematics. The mistake was to take this or that isolated proposition and ask to what particular fact in the world it corresponded; and of course the answer would be negative. The later Wittgenstein suggests a more sensible way of regarding the question. We do not isolate the single mathematical proposition from the body of mathematical discourse; and in turn we take the latter as part of our total language; and, as this functioning part, mathematics serves to tell us a great deal about the things of our world.

And it is precisely here, I think, that we may find the key to the question of conventionalism—a key, moreover, that Wittgenstein himself does not seem to grasp. The conventions we adopt must somehow "work": They must serve us in coping with nature. We might, for example, decide to change our mathematical conventions and drop the notion of irrational numbers altogether. After all, they have been a troublesome part of mathematics, and no altogether satisfactory theory of them has yet been worked out. But the diameter of the square would still be there to be measured. And it is this need to deal with nature that ultimately takes the measure of our various conventions—mathematical and others.

At present the philosophy of mathematics is divided between Platonists and intuitionists, and it has been suggested that some mediation between them be found. If Plato and Kant are the two ancestors of these rival schools, then we might suggest Aristotle as the third tutelary figure between them. We need the notion of the mind as itself a product of nature and related to nature in its most fundamental modes of operation. The entities of mathematics do not subsist in a timeless Platonic world—they are human constructs; but they are constructs that have their use and their being in relation to the natural world that encompasses them. All human thinking takes place against this background of nature. But it is this sense of nature —of our encompassing involvement with it—that Wittgenstein's philosophy lacks, and for which we must turn elsewhere in the following section.

One concluding word, however, has to be said on Wittgenstein and conventionalism. It is, I think, the real and ultimate sense of what he has to say on the subject, though he does not quite bring it out explicitly. When he questions the necessity by which we must follow logically the consequences of a given convention, is he not raising a question about our practical adherence to logic itself? Is consistency such a bugbear that we should strive to follow it at all costs—even were it to be an impediment in some living situations? It may very well be that truth comes to be for us in some areas when we have left logic behind us. We have it on some of the greatest authority that this is so. St. Thomas Aquinas, so it is reported, had at last a vision, after which he said that all his writings —all those massive, logically ordered *Summae*—were but as "straw." And, from a very different tradition, there is the Buddha, who refused either to affirm or deny the logical queries put to him by some of the Brahmanical dialecticians. The truth he was after, so he believed, lay in neither yes nor no to the logician's questions. And if these examples seem too transcendental for the reader, he may perhaps summon up some more mundane one for himself. For myself, there comes to mind a moment from the past, when the woman I loved, her cheeks blazing with anger, exclaimed, "You're so goddamned logical!" She was right, and I have ever since tried to take heed of her lesson. At certain points we do well not to press on in our mania for logical consistency if we are to grasp the substance of what the living occasion brings us.

So we would hope too that a highly technical civilization might still be able at some point to set aside its logical adherence to its techniques in order that it might possibly learn to live and love.[2]

In any case, Wittgenstein warns us, if we seek to absolutize logic, then we should remember the ghost of inconsistency that still haunts it. Russell enunciated a practical rule of types to make the system work by forbidding us to write down certain expressions. The ghost of contradiction, however, still haunts the system if we try to think what the system is about—that is, all the classes or sets it permits. For his part, Wittgenstein is willing to let the contradiction remain—perhaps as a salutary reminder. If it is practical for some uses to have the system without a contradiction, it may be useful for other purposes to have the contradiction still potentially present. And we may leave him thus with this impish and oracular image:

Why should Russell's contradiction not be conceived as something that towers above the propositions and looks in both directions like a Janus head?

Logic was never less certain and never more interesting.

---

[2] An example: Even if such research as that of Masters and Johnson on sex were to be made technically and logically perfect, one would hope that a civilization were able to say, "Yes, but it misses the point."

Conclusion to Part I

AFTER THE INTRICACIES OF THE LAST CHAPTER IT MAY BE WELL TO pause for a moment to take note of the place to which our argument has brought us. At the least, the reader who has been dragged through all those matters might need to be reassured that they really bear upon the question that launched us.

That question concerns the increasing involvement with each other of the ideas of freedom and technique in the modern world. The "technology of behavior," after which behavioral scientists yearn, ascribes the most sweeping powers to technique. It is assumed, or proposed to us as an hypothesis, that the techniques exist that can shape human beings completely for all the situations of life. We have only to put them to use and we shall be able to mold mankind in whatever ways we might find desirable—and thus transform the human condition itself.

The results from logic suggest that matters may be a little more complex than this. Even the much simpler and more manipulable entities of mathematics and logic prove elusive to the rules we try to lay down for them. Individual cases occur that are not automatically governed by the rule and that have to be dealt with through improvisation and invention. We are back in the old human quandary again. If we try to flee from our human condition into the computer we only meet ourselves there. The inevitable game of "choice and consequences" is still to be played out, though on a different level.

Here a small story may be to the point. It is not an uncommon story; tales of this kind abound, and enough of them may eventually accumulate to make up a unique contribution of our age—the creation of a distinct genre to be called "folklore of the computer." This one came to me from a friend, who at various times serves as a consulting engineer on computer ailments. He had been called in by the telephone company because they were having trouble with a particular program. They had wished to work out an efficient schedule so that there would be adequate personnel on hand for the peak hours and no redundancies during times where there was less demand for telephone service. The variables that entered into the problem were what you would expect: absences due to illness, times off for meals and for coffee breaks, repairing to the rest rooms, etc. One ingenious and rather brash programmer had come up with an algorithm—a general formula—that seemed to govern all these variables; and, accordingly, all the data were fed into the machine. But the results did not turn out as expected. The staff turned out more irregular in their comings and goings than the computer projected. Not totally so; but enough so that a day-to-day patching of the schedule had to be improvised, which in turn created considerable confusion and was beginning to cost the company a good deal of money. It was at this point that my friend was called in.

It seems, I remarked, that people will go to the bathroom unpredictably. It was my small effort toward a joke, but it did not lighten his mood. He was in the midst of a problem that was defeating him. Usually the arguments about undecidability take place in the pure and rarefied atmosphere of metamathematics; but here this devilish indeterminacy of a system was present in something so humdrum and mundane as a schedule of working hours. And here the indeterminacy was spread throughout the whole system; not only was the computer unable to encompass all the irregularities of scheduling, but also one could not determine where lay the sources of error. The trace-back tapes, when played, failed to give a picture of exactly where the snarls occurred, so that these particular parts might be changed and the rest of the data and the program be salvaged. When most of us make mistakes in the humble kinds of computations we perform in practical life, we can usually trace back and find out where our arithmetic erred, correct the mistake, and proceed accordingly. But in the case on which my friend had been called in, no such partial correction seemed possible; the indeterminacy infected the whole system. In the end, there was nothing to do but scrub out all the data already fed into the machine, at the cost of thousands of dollars to the company, and start over—with no necessary guarantee of success this time either, except that the programmer would now be considerably less ambitious in his aims.

A short while thereafter I happened to meet socially a young executive of Bell Laboratories. When I told him this little story, he frowned impatiently. He thought I was attacking the computer, which I was not. The story merely indicated, he said, the stupidity of the original programmer. Precisely. The computer only gives us back ourselves. It is a faithful mirror that reflects the human traits that are brought to it. In this case these had been a certain overingenuity and brashness, which, because they proved so costly, were—as this executive grumbled—thoroughly stupid. But there could be other human faces that the computer might give back to us —the face of arrogance, of ruthlessness, of the lust for power.

Imagine thus a dictator who takes it into his head to plan the life of a whole community. The needs of food, housing, etc., are researched, and the data fed into some computer. (This programming in itself, by the way, might be quite costly, but who ever said that planning was economical?) Suppose now this planning experiment should run the same course as our telephone scheduling. Not only does our computer grind out results that are at variance with the irregularities that occur in the human situation, but also it is impossible to trace back and find out where, if at all, partial corrections might be made to make the whole program work. No matter. The dictator has power to compel his subject people to submit to the bed of Procrustes that the computer has designed for them.

In the popular imagination the faith in hardware expresses itself in the images of technological gigantism: Just make the computer mammoth enough and it will solve all problems. But the intrinsic logic of a problem remains what it is even if we had at our disposal a computer gigantic enough to cover a modern city. The absence of an intelligent idea in the grasp of a problem cannot be redeemed by the elaborateness of the machinery one subsequently employs.

But at this point I imagine the behavioral scientist growing restless and exclaiming: What has all this subtle business of logic to do with the concrete task of shaping human beings? These facts about the incompleteness of formal systems may be surprising and interesting in their own right; but surely it is an irrelevant procedure to drag these matters into the alien field of human behavior and the ways we may find to shape it. Human beings, in fact, are pretty malleable stuff, and in this respect are simpler than the complex systems they excogitate.

Well, there is a point in the logical parallel. To condition a human being, from the sheer determinist point of view, is logically similar to programming a computer. In either case we imprint certain rules from which future actions are to follow. The completeness of the rules therefore becomes a very pertinent issue. Now, if a system of the mind's devising so elementary as that of arithmetic proves recalcitrant to formalization, is it likely that the mind that created it will be less complex and more easily constrained within rules? That, I admit, is the more idealistic and long-term view of the matter. It is part of my faith, if you will, that the human mind will never finally acquiesce in the surrender of its freedom. In the short run, however, I might agree with the cynicism of the behavioral scientist. Human beings do run with the herd, and they are surprisingly docile to conditioning in a great number of ways. And history furnishes plenty of examples of great minds who pliantly bowed the knee to authority. Still, the question remains how far we can make a man's responses thoroughly determinable. Can we turn a human being into a closed system so that we have imprinted in him the axioms from which all his future actions inevitably follow?

I imagine that this is less than the behaviorist, at least in the liberal Western world, would be satisfied with. He wants, after all, to produce a human being who is adult and mature; and that means flexible enough to meet the contingent situations of life as they arise. No one doubts that there are techniques that can permanently maim people, turn them into zombies, or reduce them to feeble imitations of a mechanism. The difficult thing is to condition people in some positive way that will lead them to be free to develop whatever possibilities they have. And this is indeed a difficult matter, an affair of tact and improvisation rather than system, as those who have had experience of child-rearing know only too well. It is much easier to cripple rigidly than to shape flexibly. Indeed, one great evidence of the power of conditioning, as found in the bulk of the psychoanalytic literature, centers around circumstances and deprivations in childhood that were damaging in their effect.

In the Eastern bloc, however, behavioral scientists might be satisfied if conditioning begets routine and obedient members of society. For the purposes of the total state it might be enough to produce subjects who will be unswervingly loyal Communists. But this still leaves open the question: What is it to be a loyal Communist in this or that particular situation? A good Communist, we might say, is one who blindly and unswervingly follows the Party line. But what about the leaders who have to fabricate that Party line? What is good Communist policy in this or that particular exigency? All their early indoctrination may not automatically provide an answer. We encounter again the individual case that has not been determined by any preassigned rule, and we are thrust back into the region of improvisation and invention that is freedom. The totalitarian rulers may enjoy an enormous advantage from the docility of their peoples, but in the long run the rulers may lose just as much in the possibilities of positive creation that come with individual initiative.

The business of conditioning people, however, has been a subsidiary issue in this first section. Our principal question had to do with the more fundamental relation of philosophy and technique, and particularly the role the latter placed in shaping the former. And it was from the point of view of that question that we looked at the historical example of three philosophers—Russell, Whitehead, and Wittgenstein. There was the crucial case, the reader will remember, where a comprehensive technique, available and believed in, did not determine the philosophies of the men involved. The case is not finally conclusive; there will be other techniques, and other philosophers making use of those techniques to try to make them do more than they possibly can. Meanwhile, however, that historic example seems to offer us good reason for concluding that philosophy must take precedence: Every technique is put to use for some end, and this end is decided in the light of some philosophic outlook or other. The technique cannot produce the philosophy that directs it.

But enough, for the moment, of the question of technique as such. So far we have argued against the belief in the omnipotence of technique in terms of its inherent limitations. But technique, as it is embodied in our technology, does not exist in a void. Despite the great triumphs of a technical civilization, humankind still exists in the bosom of nature: We are creatures utterly dependent upon a delicate planetary environment—a thin crust of soil and a fragile layer of atmosphere. And despite too the specialization of our culture, which seems to assign each of us to our narrow slots, we are still cosmic animals, haunted by some imagination of our place in the scheme of things. How does technology change our relationship to nature? The question goes beyond the specific problems of the environment, however pressing and important these may be; it asks, rather, what fundamental pieties toward the cosmos are still left to us today. In short, how does technical man exist in relation to Being?

To this question we now turn.

Part II

Being

Chapter 7

———◆———

The Two Worlds

THE QUESTION HAS BEEN WITH US ALL ALONG. HOW COULD WE HAVE escaped it when it has haunted the philosophy of the past three centuries? So far we have taken note of it only as the occasion arose, and then merely in passing, as if to ticket it for later examination. Now we must face this specter, which has been waiting in the wings.

And it is a specter, this doctrine of the two worlds. We find it upsetting to learn that the world disclosed to us by our senses, this familiar and intimate world in which we live, is only appearance, while the real world, which science discovers for us, does not resemble it at all. Eddington's example of the two tables is a little shopworn by now, but it may serve once again. There is the familiar table on which I write, on the one hand; and on the other, the table of which science informs me. The first is brown, smooth, continuous, solid to the touch, and quietly at rest within itself. The table science tells me of, however, is not in the least like this. It has no color, and is neither solid nor continuous; in fact, it is mainly an empty space in which tiny particles, far from being at rest, are incessantly athrob and moving. Were it merely a matter of tables, we might leave the perplexity to philosophers, who seem to have a penchant for worrying about that particular article of furniture. But the unreality alleged here infects the whole of our daily world and down to its deepest fibers. The fullness of this world, its richness and variety of qualities, above all the vivid perceptions of value that we take from it—all these are to be somehow shunted aside into a realm labeled "subjective." The objective world is something other and alien. And we ourselves, in consequence, seem shunted aside as strangers who do not belong to the other world.

We should not be surprised then that the New Science, as the seventeenth century called its great revolution, even while vastly expanding the frontiers of human knowledge, brought with it a new note of uneasiness. Pascal, with a remarkable prescience, was one of the first to grasp this disquietude and give it eloquent voice. The infinity and silence of this new universe beget anxiety because they bring with them the uneasy sense that mankind may be only a tiny and meaningless freak within nature. The malaise has been with the modern consciousness ever since, and the enormous increase of our technical powers has not dispelled it. So long as the thinking of a technical civilization still harbors within itself this division between the two worlds, we continue to suffer from the wound of absence. We are homeless in the world.

The problem here, at bottom, concerns the mind and its relation to nature. The subjectivity of our human world, which the doctrine alleges, cannot come from our sense organs. Considered merely as portions of matter, these organs are denuded of qualities and therefore congruous with the physical world around them. And so too with our brains: We do not find in them, as bits of matter, the kinds of qualities that make up the world of experience. The mystery comes at the end of the process, when consciousness somehow supervenes. Then we see the green of the trees and the blue of the sky, and we smell the scent of the rose. The world as we know it comes suddenly into being, and then only within the mind. Indeed, if we follow the doctrine literally, the mind fabricates a good many things that are not there. And it is this very odd trait alleged about human consciousness that creates the whole puzzle in the first place.

And it is quite natural thus that when the doctrine of the two worlds first finds its full expression in Descartes, it should lead him to doubt about the essential relation of the mind to material nature. We may find it worthwhile therefore to glance back for a moment at his reasoning. Though we shall be traveling a well-worn path, we may nevertheless come upon some surprises—particularly as these touch upon our theme of freedom. We shall also be able to mark off precisely the point where the German philosopher Edmund Husserl, about the year 1913, chose to diverge from Descartes and launch a new movement in modern philosophy.

I.

DESCARTES—THE ANCESTOR

The year, if we wish to have exact dates, may be set down as 1629. Actually, the initial vision had occurred ten years earlier, but now at last he must collect his thoughts about it and write them down. René Descartes, a young French nobleman, mathematician, and philosopher, but more lately soldier-at-arms, retires to an inn in Holland to think amid the confusions of his time and the clamors of war.

Descartes had shown precocious gifts in mathematics. In our age of specialization, which ironically he helped to usher in, a youth so gifted would have been long since locked away in a research institute. But he was part of the Renaissance, which had its own idea of the complete man. Besides books, it was necessary to know the world and its ways. So Descartes was to spend the most vigorous part of his youth frequenting the circles of the fashionable and learned in Paris, and then for seven years follow the armies of various European kings in the field. This experience of the world was not lost on Descartes; he was a shrewd observer, and a very worldly awareness of his own age and the role he was to play in it was never far from him—a point that we as interpreters of him should not forget. Nevertheless, his destiny is to think, and for that he must retire from the world into solitude. What was to emerge from that solitary room in the Dutch inn was nothing less than an intellectual outline of the modern age to come.

The time is a confusing one. The excitement of new discoveries and new perspectives is in the air. The New World has been discovered, is now being actively explored, and is a part of everybody's thinking. The geographical horizons of European man have thus been vastly extended, and his intellectual horizons even more spectacularly so by new discoveries and promises of discovery. The outlines of a new science—mechanics—are being sketched by an Italian named Galileo. An Englishman named Harvey has discovered the circulation of the blood, and the fact that the heart is a pump suggests that the whole body (and the whole of nature too) may be simply an elaborate machine. An age rich in discoveries (like our own) is likely to be rich in confusions (also like our own). The new facts and theories upset the old framework, but as yet bring nothing to replace it. Amid the uncertainty of his time, amid his own uncertainties, Descartes seeks a way out of the confusions. He must find some solid ground on which to stand.

He must therefore follow the path of doubt. He will proceed to doubt each of his beliefs and reject each in turn, if it is in any way dubious, until by this means he either arrives at something he cannot doubt, which is therefore certain, or else he concludes sadly that he must rest forever in the dark night of uncertainty. Thus begins his famous systematic doubt, under whose shadow the next three centuries of philosophy were to labor.

He begins by doubting the senses. They would seem to be easily doubted, for on many single occasions in life we do make mistakes in our perceptions. And if in some cases, why not possibly in all? How can we be sure that when we seem to be awake we are not actually dreaming? We open our eyes, shake our head, extend our hands, and so on, and these may be all delusions. Descartes, with a superb dramatizing sense, brings the whole abstract process of doubt down to the immediate and familiar fact of the body that we live with day by day. "Let us reflect that neither our hands nor our whole body are such as they appear to be." Indeed, the new science was to project a perspective of nature in which all bodies, our own included, simply as bits of matter moving in space, were "really" very different from what they appeared to be.

But if the senses deceive us about bodies, why may not the space and time in which those bodies are located be really different from the way in which they present themselves? And how about the most elementary truths of mathematics, as when Descartes adds three and two together to get five? His evidence for this latter truth is that he has repeatedly counted the numbers out to get that sum. But he has often found himself mistaken in certain computations, and why not therefore in this?

Descartes proceeds now to gather all these doubts under the famous fiction of the Evil Demon who has contrived the whole apparatus of heaven and earth into a semblance of objective order and reality merely to deceive him; and here the prose itself reaches a passionate crescendo of incertitude:

> I shall then suppose that some evil genius not less powerful than deceitful has employed his whole energies in deceiving me; I shall consider that the whole heavens, the earth, colors, figures, sound,

and all other external things are nought but the illusions and dreams of which this genius has availed himself in order to lay traps for my credulity; I shall consider myself as having no hands, no eyes, no flesh, no blood, nor any senses, yet falsely believing myself to possess all these things. . . .

Never was the plight of the skeptic put more melodramatically. Yet, as every reader knows, the ending here is a happy one; light breaks through, and within this dark night of uncertainty there shines the luminous ray of the consciousness that doubts. Even if the Evil Genius deceives me in all immediate matters of the external world, I must at least be conscious in order to be deceived. In this certainty of self-consciousness Descartes proposes to lay before us the starting point for all philosophy and science. And in the usual manner of crusaders he compresses it into a rallying slogan: *Cogito, ergo sum* (I think, therefore I am).[1]

It seems a small truth against the enveloping darkness, but Descartes has mammoth ambitions for it. The *Cogito* will provide the marks—self-evidence and clarity—that distinguish truth, above all the truths of mathematics. Mathematical method must therefore be given primacy as the most certain means of mastery in all fields of knowledge. Behind the faltering steps of the doubter marches the conquistador. The systematic doubt of our everyday world is the first step into the era of technique, which is what our modern age has become.

A very different assessment of Descartes and his historic role is given by Hegel, who was writing at the beginning of the nineteenth century in the high tide of German idealism, with its glorification of human consciousness. And his words in this connection are worth pondering:

> Only now do we arrive at the philosophy of the modern world, and we begin it with Descartes. With him, we in fact enter into an independent philosophy which knows that it is the independent product of reason, and that the consciousness of self, self-consciousness, is an essential moment of truth. Here, we may say, we are at home; here, like the sailor at the end of his long voyage on the stormy seas, we may cry "Land"! . . . In this new pe-

[1] In the usual manner of slogans, this one too is misleading. It is not the existence of Descartes the man that his thinking certifies, but only of the existence of his consciousness—and then only in the moment he brings it to full self-awareness: when, in short, he is aware that he thinks. The certainty attained thus falls far short of what the slogan claims.

riod the principle is thinking, thinking proceeding from itself. . . .

It is altogether appropriate that Hegel should borrow his metaphor
from the voyages of discovery that opened our modern age. These
discoveries, however, only opened men's eyes to the external world;
to give this period its full historical triumph there would have to be
a complementary discovery internal to the human spirit itself. All
philosophy—indeed, all human life—is a struggle toward self-awareness. When philosophy posits self-consciousness as its starting
point, however, we have entered a new stage of human history.
Hegel could thus fit the new philosophy into his pattern of triads:
the ancient, the medieval, and the modern worlds. The Greeks, despite their extraordinary brilliance, remained, spiritually speaking, at
a level of naïve objectivity; the Middle Ages brought an inwardness
of spirit into history, but it remained tenuous because, being otherworldly, they had lost their grip on this world. The modern age
comes forward to synthesize and complete these two antithetical attitudes of mind: Modern man emerges as the creature who triumphantly takes possession of his world and at the same time asserts
the value of the human spirit in its complete and radical self-
awareness. Hence, the philosophy of Descartes is the fitting prelude
to the new epoch of human enlightenment, of which Hegel saw
himself as the consummating philosopher.

Nowadays we are likely to be a little more cautious in our assessment of Descartes. The discovery of self-consciousness may be a
great step forward for the human spirit, but here it brings with it
some entangling liabilities. It is a strange affirmation of consciousness, this of Descartes, that begins by abolishing our everyday
world. For the Greeks and the medievals, whatever subsequent use
they might make of it, that world was quite evidently there. Their
thinking began there and remained congruous with it. The primacy
of self-consciousness in Descartes projects us into all the quandaries
that beset the privacy of mind. How do we cross from this private
mind to an external world that it has placed in question? How is
this mind related to that individual body to which it is so peculiarly
attached? The exaltation of self-consciousness, which Hegel admires, splits the mind off from a realm of objects, which it proceeds
now to understand in quantitative terms very different from those
of everyday life. How can the private mind be sure of the existence

of any other minds but its own? And so on and so forth. There enter into philosophy a whole host of puzzles that had not been troubling before.

These difficulties are now commonplace to the philosophic reader. But what is not generally observed is the way in which freedom and the will assert themselves at the core of the Cartesian reasoning. The doubt, Descartes observes, is laborious and difficult. Insensibly a certain lassitude leads him back into the course of his ordinary life. Everything within us and without us conspires to make us believe in this illusion of the everyday. But we must not let be; letting be would bring us to assent to the overriding convictions of our everyday world as these manifestly and powerfully press upon us from all sides. Instead, the will in its freedom must choose to force us, against all our natural inclination, into another path: that of the doubt. And what lies at the end of the doubt? The discovery of a method that will enable us to wrest nature's secrets from it. This mathematical method has since found its greatest triumph in physics, which has transformed our world. But Descartes insisted it was *the* method for every field. His own efforts in physiology met at best with indifferent success, but even here he has found subsequent justification: Biologists tell us that in the construction of hypothetical mechanical models, which are now extremely productive in their science, he was a prophet. What, then, is the whole strategy of Descartes' thought? *The will in its freedom chooses to go against nature and natural impulse in order to conquer nature and its secrets.* Here is the first step toward the metaphysics of power that will dominate the modern age.

But as with many revolutionaries, Descartes had one foot firmly planted in the past—enough indeed to rescue him from his own ultimate perplexities. Once arrived at the certainty of self-consciousness, he had to cross over to the world outside it—and for this he needed the guarantee of God. A benevolent God would not create us such that our minds, at least when we thought clearly and distinctly, did not in some fashion mirror nature truly. Descartes retreats to the belief of the Middle Ages even at the moment of launching a revolution that will eventually abolish it. The modern reader is surprised at how little of his *Meditations* is taken up with the doubt, and how much the greater part with the intricacies of theological reflection. This work is not an epistemological treatise on skepticism, as some modern interpreters would like it to be; but as its full title indicates, *Meditations on First Philosophy*, its subject really is "First Philosophy," which is here understood in the unbroken tradition since Aristotle as metaphysics that culminates in God. Descartes, like the rest of the seventeenth century, thinks within and toward God. We who stand outside that conviction have to find other strategies of thought to deal with his quandaries.

II.

PHENOMENOLOGY

Suppose we follow Descartes only up to the point where he retreats into the medieval framework. We have suspended our naïve belief in the objects around us, and by this means have arrived at the discovery of consciousness itself. What then? We are not bankrupt, we do not find ourselves in a void with empty hands. On the contrary, there is a vast deal of material at our disposal on which we, as philosophers, can set to work. This was the great and original insight of Edmund Husserl in the early years of the century. Inspired by it, he proposed to launch a new philosophic discipline, *Phenomenology*—which in time was to become the most significant movement in Continental philosophy of our period. Let us see how he goes about the launching.

At the moment when consciousness imagines itself hovering outside of its world, ready to abolish that world in doubt, just then does the whole multifarious data of that world lie spread before it. In the room where Descartes raises his hand and asks if it be real, he may indeed be dreaming. But whether he dream or not, nothing is changed in what appears: the things that manifest themselves are there for consciousness to explore in all the concreteness of their qualities and interrelations. We may thus suspend the question whether these things have a real existence outside the mind while we go about the business of describing them. We neither affirm nor deny that they exist independently of us; we simply place the question of that existence in brackets and set it aside.

This procedure of "bracketing" is the essential first step, according to Husserl, by which we enter the domain of phenomenology. But it is important that this bracketing not be misunderstood. It is not identical with the epistemological doubt whether the object really exists; and it is not the postponement of this question for a later answer. It seeks to bypass this question altogether in order to find its way into a more fruitful field of philosophizing. Thus the bracketing has a twofold force. On the one hand, it places the question of existence in brackets and sets it aside. On the other hand, it puts the whole world and its data within brackets in order that consciousness, poised outside the brackets, can scan that world more dispassionately and acutely.

More commonly, Husserl speaks of this as the phenomenological *Epoche* or Suspension, borrowing a term from the ancient Stoics. For these ancients the term denoted the suspension of judgment necessary to procure rational equanimity of mind against the turmoil of the passions. It was thus originally a term loaded with moral meanings; for the Stoic it indicated the path toward salvation, the means of attaining human freedom from the enslavement of the passions. For Husserl, the term belongs only to theoretical reflection; it signifies that act of thought, which, disencumbering us of our prejudices, secures the purity of our detachment as observers and describers.

Nevertheless, like the Stoic suspension of belief, this Husserlian bracketing involves its own violent rupture with our ordinary attitudes. In everyday life we move amid things and other people carrying about with us the spontaneous and seemingly invincible conviction of their independent reality. Husserl calls this everyday attitude the natural standpoint or sometimes the natural consciousness. We are not to deny the convictions of this natural standpoint; on the contrary, Husserl in a later stage goes to extraordinary lengths, virtually tying himself in knots, to validate our ordinary beliefs in external things and other minds. But this natural attitude of consciousness is too immersed in its own concerns to be aware of its presuppositions. We have therefore to place it too in brackets the better to see and describe what its conditions are.

Thus the whole of philosophy is to become an effort in systematic description. Here was to be a radically new point of departure for philosophers. Philosophy was no longer to be the battleground of that ceaseless dialectic by which one generation of philosophers refutes its predecessors only to be refuted in turn as the old doctrine takes on a new verbal dress. Speculative hypotheses were to be rejected, as well as all concepts that were but empty and arbitrary constructions. Every idea, to be legitimate, must exhibit its sources within experience. Phenomenology would thus be, at one and the

same time, the most radical of empiricisms and the most radical of
rationalisms. "To the things themselves!" became Husserl's rallying
call to a generation of German philosophers to join him in this con-
certed effort of description. Since experience was inexhaustible, the
effort must engage many minds and be the cumulative work of generations. What was promised was a renewal of philosophy itself;
and it was inevitable that Husserl should attract followers and
launch a movement for which he would ceaselessly be engaged in
writing and rewriting the program.

And here too, at the very entrance into his discipline, the
phenomenologist discovers the principle of consciousness itself in
this very act of bracketing the world. Consciousness, suspended outside the world, has to begin by examining itself. When it does, it is
surprised to find that it is almost nothing. It is not any kind of mind
stuff or psychic substance. Indeed, it is not a determinate kind of
thing at all; it has no describable characteristics of its own that we
can specify. If we want to talk about consciousness, we are able
only to talk about the objects of which we are conscious. When we
try to look into it, we look through it and past it. If I try to examine my "blue mood" of the moment, I find only things in the world
that now strike me as "blue." The nature of consciousness is to
point beyond itself—to whatever datum it is conscious *of*.

This is Husserl's basic doctrine of the *"intentionality"* of consciousness. The term comes to him from the medieval philosophers
via Brentano; and whether or not it is the best possible term, it has
now become fixed in the phenomenological literature. We are not
to take "intention" in its narrower sense as signifying a practical aim
or purpose. We are to think of it rather in accordance with its Latin
etymology: a tending toward, or pointing to . . . Consciousness is
essentially referential, whether or not I am able to certify the actual
entities to which it refers. American and British philosophers have
recently talked a good deal about questions of meaning and reference and their possible distinctness. But as a *conscious act*, every
meaning refers in some way. Even my most passing fantasy, or va-
grant mood, however inchoate it be, points toward or qualifies the
world in some way, though I may find no actual referent for it.
Consciousness is always consciousness of . . .

Since consciousness points beyond itself, it is in its very being a
self-transcendence. As he often does, Sartre was later to melodram-
atize this point by making consciousness a negation—a negation of
itself *toward* its object. Still, there is a certain power in this para-

doxical way of putting the point. It serves all the more strongly to discourage people from thinking of consciousness in any way as a *thing*, however subtilized. It should even deter some philosophers from talking of an idea as a "meaning," to which we then attach reference.

This principle of intentionality, indeed, throws into question some of our commonest modes of talking about the mind. We sometimes talk, for example, of "mental content" or of things that are "in our mind" as if consciousness were some kind of cabinet or container that is stocked with a variety of items. We speak of what is passing in our mind as if we might be watching a parade in the street or a succession of images on a moving-picture or television screen. The expressions are familiar and convenient, and there is no harm in such metaphors if we know what we are doing when we use them. But these forms of language have done damage in philosophy before, and their ghosts are still troublesome in contemporary discussions. If images are passing through my mind, for example, I am not watching them as I watch actual visual images pass on a screen.

This effort to decontaminate language inevitably begets comparison with Wittgenstein. Indeed, the latter's philosophical exploration of ordinary language is at bottom a phenomenological enterprise. Wittgenstein exclaims "Don't think, look!" as a warning to us not to rush into empty dialectic without seeing clearly what we are talking about. Husserl's slogan for phenomenology, "To the things themselves!" was in the same vein—an exhortation to look beyond our abstractions to the concrete data they so often obscure.

Both philosophers think that the essential function of philosophy is descriptive. Yet there is a vast difference in what they hope will come out of this description and in the methods by which they pursue it. Husserl, as the leader of a movement, is immensely more ambitious for his project: Phenomenology should ultimately provide an absolute grounding for the sciences and for reason itself. Wittgenstein speaks as the more solitary individual, and rather in a tone of resignation: "Philosophy leaves the world as it is."

Wittgenstein's medium is our ordinary language, and for the most part he speaks with an almost colloquial simplicity. Husserl has a rather unfortunate penchant for technical terminology, and at times multiplies distinctions with the indecent fertility of a Scholastic of the late Middle Ages—a rather strange procedure for a thinker who is summoning us to "the things themselves" away from beclouding abstractions. On the other hand, there is something incomplete and unsatisfactory in Wittgenstein's absorption in ordinary language. He writes at times as if the sole function of philosophy were to teach us the correct grammar of our speech. Against this the phenomenologist would insist, and rightly, that we cannot go on indefinitely discussing modes of speech or the grammar of our day-to-day language, however incidentally enlightening these may be. Somewhere along the line the philosopher has to have recourse to realities other than language. We have to check what people say against what we experience. Ultimately what is given in experience must be a datum more basic than what we say about it. And in fact Wittgenstein does have to speak as often about things and how they look and how we look at them as he does about the ways we talk about them.

III.

SCIENCE AND THE "LIFE WORLD"

Our search, remember, is for a way beyond the division of the two worlds. Does Husserl help us toward that unity?

His lifelong struggle, at any rate, is toward one kind of unity—the unity of reason with itself against its threatened fragmentation by the prodigious variety of the modern sciences. Husserl came to philosophy from mathematics, and something of the mathematician never left him. He is pulled originally into philosophy by the need for rigor—a rigor more absolute and self-validating than mathematics itself can provide. Now, this quest for certainty traditionally narrows the philosopher's options. It compels him toward certain carefully chosen modes of consciousness that seem to provide within themselves their own guarantee of certainty. On the other hand, phenomenology aimed to fling the door wide open on the whole field of consciousness, in all the profusion of its riches; and there is thus the opposite pull toward concreteness and adequacy. In the pull between these two opposing tendencies lies the intellectual drama of Husserl's own development as well as of the subsequent history of phenomenology.

With regard to the fragmentation of knowledge, two sciences particularly occupy him, mathematics and psychology, and in both he sees signs of the modern confusion.

In mathematics, as we noted in an earlier chapter, the program of mechanization had begun. Mathematical techniques abounded, and it seemed unnecessary to ask about their meaning so long as they worked. It was enough that the mathematician operated with marks on paper so long as these led to no inconsistency. For Husserl this situation was a scandal and an abdication by the European mind of its traditional goals of rationality. Mathematics, since the Greeks, had been taken as the very model of intelligibility for the human mind: a science that grounded its reasoning upon self-evident conceptions that were clear and distinct, and therefore meaningful in the strictest sense. Now it was to be assimilated to the world of technique, and the mathematician was to acquiesce in becoming a technician who merely operated a machine successfully.

A similar situation prevailed in psychology. The first experimental laboratory had been established in 1870, and research was proliferating. Yet there was a great deal of confusion as to what these experimental methods were ultimately dealing with. Behaviorism had not been launched as a sweeping program, but a kind of protobehaviorism was in the air in the materialism that issued from the laboratories. Husserl was embattled. What is the point of a psychology that is confused about the fundamental fact of human personality, which is consciousness itself? It will only end by assimilating itself clumsily to an imitation of what goes on in the physical sciences. Its researches go off in all direction but lack a unifying center.

The situation has become, if anything, more aggravated since Husserl wrote. Discoveries upon discoveries have piled up, but the unifying conceptions seem lacking. And the rate of discovery seems constantly accelerating. Each decade knows immensely more than the preceding, and seems just that much more confused than its predecessor. Is it possible for the scientist to escape the fate of the technician in our technical era? The technician is called upon to handle the instrument he is assigned to without having necessarily to know how it works. The man who comes to repair your television set is able to spot what's wrong and fix it without having to know the theories of electromagnetism. So the biologist need not know the laws of optics on which his microscope has been constructed. The characteristic of technical organization is the subdivision of labor and the specificity of the task assigned. Within science this begets the common situation where one scientist borrows and uses the results of another scientist without having to know clearly on what they are based, or what their finer meaning may be. Now imagine this procedure carried out to the farthest degree. Each link in the chain does what it does without knowing what the whole chain is about. We would end by building a tower of Babel where each layer of the structure cannot communicate with the next.

A more modern and somber parable would be Kafka's tale "The Great Wall of China." In this story the people once knew what they were doing in building the Wall. It was to keep out the nomads and thus preserve civilization; and its building was accompanied with much idealism and enthusiasm. But now they build the Wall only in sections, and each group has lost contact with the others; and, most of all, they have long since lost touch with the central capital. They do not even know whether this center still holds, or the Empire itself still stands. Yet they continue to carry on their meaningless labor, no longer knowing what their purpose is in doing what they do.

They have lost touch with the center! Precisely, Husserl would say; what is lacking to us is a unified center for the vast array of information we have accumulated. The center he would propose is simply consciousness itself. The phenomenological demand may be put in this way: Everything we pursue or achieve in the way of knowledge takes place within and by means of the light of consciousness; and it must therefore be able to come before this court and give evidence for itself; it must be able to exhibit itself within the light of consciousness as intelligible and self-validating.

A noble but perhaps impossible ideal. The responsible scientist has to be satisfied with such justification at best for only a portion of his science, while for the rest he must carry on and make do with whatever ideas or procedures work. Husserl's is really the ideal of what science would be if it were already finished and complete.

But against this centripetal pull of his thought, the other complementary and expansive push of phenomenology emerges.

Just past the midpoint of his career, and increasingly as he grew older, another motif becomes dominant in Husserl's thinking. This is the idea of the *Lebenswelt* (life world) as the region of our ordinary experience out of which all meanings, scientific and other, must emerge. For a man of Husserl's austerely theoretical temperament the rich disorder of the life world was not an immediate lure. Some commentators hold that he was moved in this direction largely through the influence of his followers, who had a more vivid interest than he in the actualities of life. But it was also the consequences of his own doctrine of consciousness that drove him in this direction.

For if consciousness is essentially intentional, then one has to affirm this intentionality straight across the board. In the case of such clear-cut matters as our percepts and concepts, this intentional, or referring, aspect of consciousness is evident. My perception of this table is to be distinguished from my other perceptions only in that it is of this actual table. Similarly, with my concepts: I can talk about my different concepts or ideas only in terms of the things those concepts are about. But what of the vaguer kinds of experience, like passing moods or feelings? As these stir vaguely at the bottom of consciousness, or filter through it, they seem much more "subjective," more distinctly to be located in the mind. They are the kinds of experience that are more likely to give rise to the notion of consciousness as a kind of impalpable *stuff* that is colored by our moods. At any rate, the object they refer to is not so immediately apparent as in my perception of the table.

But even here consciousness points beyond itself—though not to any isolated object but to the totality of objects. This mood of mine, for example, which has been with me all afternoon, heavy, restless, nameless—is it hidden somewhere inside my mind, coiled like a dragon at the bottom of consciousness? No; I do not find it in me but in the world, present to me everywhere: in the gray, sagging day, heavy with a rain that impends but will not fall; in the litter of papers on the table, which point to the tasks that also hang as heavy over me as the clouds outside. Every object I turn to look at becomes charged and heavy as the day itself. The mood engulfs my world of the moment—or, more exactly, it is the way in which the world engulfs me and makes itself present.

Husserl was compelled more and more to take notice of this totality that haunts consciousness. However I seek to isolate any perception, I must take it in always against some enveloping background. I see the table surrounded by the room, and the tree standing out against the horizon. The horizon is never precisely demarcated, and in attempting to fix it we cannot stop short of the totality. All our particular experiences take place within the framework of our attitudes, interests, and concerns. The life world is the concrete totality in which any individual bit of consciousness unfolds.

Husserl has arrived here at something very different from his original starting point. What had launched him on his path had been a search for the pure *a priori* bases of logic and mathematics. Now he seems plunged irremediably into the concrete welter of our ordinary life. Yet even here he would pursue his theoretic passion: Philosophy must still be the pursuit of *a priori* structures that are to be found within this enveloping life world. Husserl remains still the confident rationalist. We cannot be sure of the existence of things—for consciousness theoretically stands outside the bracketing it has imposed—but we can be sure of their appearance: the essences they exhibit to us. Phenomenological knowledge thus becomes knowledge of *the structure of appearance*. Here Husserl demarcates very emphatically his own pursuit of the *a priori* from predecessors like Descartes and Kant. Descartes sought the clarity of consciousness in order that it would ultimately provide him with a single method—a mathematical method—that could then be applied roughshod over all the varieties of experience. Husserl would emphasize that phenomenological scrutiny must follow the distinct essence and structures that manifest themselves within each region of experience. As for Kant, he sought the *a priori* constituents of knowledge in the structure of the human mind. But for Husserl consciousness has no structure in itself; it is characterized only in relation to the objects that it intends. The essences that enter into *a priori* knowledge belong to "the things themselves" as these present themselves in consciousness. The mind of the phenomenologist is to be a pure transparency; he must give himself unreservedly to experience as it presents itself. Husserl states this aspect of his thought in a powerful and almost axiomatic way in a late work, *Cartesian Meditations:*

> This cannot be emphasized often enough: Phenomenal explication does nothing but *explicate the sense this world has for us all prior to any philosophizing,* and obviously gets solely from our experience—*a sense which philosophy can uncover but never alter.*

Philosophy can only take what is given; it can never alter it! This is an extraordinary and potent statement—and one to which Husserl himself, as we shall see, does not ultimately hold.

If we can only explicate the world as it is given to us, then we have at least weakened the position of Descartes. The consequence of the Cartesian dualism is to denigrate the everyday world. This world may lie in the forefront of our experience, but the true world is what takes place behind the scenes, as physical science discovers it to us. Now, if we follow this principle of Husserl, the life world takes precedence. It is, after all, the reality we live, while the scientific world is a reality we conceive, and the life world must therefore come first in value to us as living persons. And with regard to ourselves as knowers, this life world has priority for knowledge too, for it is the source from which any conceptual reality has to exhibit its legitimate derivation. There may be systematic differences between the two worlds, but they cannot be ultimately inconsistent. The railroad tracks look as if they converge, but in reality they do not; but this does not consign their visual appearance to "unreality." In fact, it is from that convergence that we learn about the laws of optics in accordance with which tracks must appear to converge. The stars in the winter sky look clear and near, but "in reality" are light-years away. But if the stars appeared differently from the way they do, our astronomical conclusions about their nature and distance would have to be different. Any attempt to destroy the validity of the life world *ipso facto* undermines the scientific world.

Yet this aspiration toward unity—the effort to reintegrate the modern consciousness as a whole—turned out to be an impossible dream, both because of internal doctrinal reasons and the external course of events. Husserl is one of the exemplary figures of the century, and perhaps all the more exemplary in his failure. He had entered the lists as a crusader for what he considered to be the classical ideal of reason against the disunifying forces of the time. As the times became stormier, his struggle seemed to him to become one in the cause of European civilization itself, so far as this civilization has been built around the ideal of reason. The eruption of Nazism in Germany was like the last blow. Toward the end of his life, three years before his death in 1938, he had fallen into despair and wrote that "Philosophy as science, as serious, rigorous, and indeed apodictically rigorous, science—*the dream is over.*"

IV.

BEING IN THE WORLD

But this dream was in fact already riven by its own internal division. The shadow of Descartes still falls over Husserl. He cannot escape it, struggle as he may against it. He has laid down his thought along the line of Descartes—by a suspension of belief in the existence of objects—and he is imprisoned in the consequences of that starting point. To be sure, his two worlds are not the mental and material ones of Descartes, but their division is just as radical. Husserl leaves us with (1) a separation of essence and existence that cannot be pasted together, and in consequence, (2) there is a wall built between consciousness and Being that the former can never altogether scale. However closer consciousness may inch toward Being—like a curve approaching its asymptote—it never quite arrives there. You cannot begin by placing consciousness ouside Being and then have it reach it by a series of converging approximations.

This dualism may be expressed as an inconsistency between Husserl's starting point and the ultimate place to which phenomenology had led him. The starting point from which he would launch phenomenology was "transcendental subjectivity"—that is, the attitude of the *Epoche,* or the bracketing of existence. But phenomenology, as it develops, discovers the richness of consciousness and its intentional correlates. The life world is revealed as the concrete context within which the actual life of consciousness transpires. Moreover, Husserl insists, we can change nothing in this world; we have to take it as given: Philosophy *"does nothing but explicate the sense this world has for us all prior to any philosophizing."* But the sense that our life world has for us all, prior to any philosophizing, is one that is saturated through and through with the fact of existence. The standpoint of "transcendental subjectivity" would therefore have to be abandoned or radically altered.

Consider this business of *bracketing* now a little more closely. We are to take the objects of our experience and place them in brackets —that is, we suspend our belief that they exist independently of our experience in order that we may describe their *appearance* within experience more accurately. (Note here we already have a dichotomy between *existence* and *appearance*—a dichotomy, in fact, that Husserl will never quite abolish.) But this act of bracketing is itself an event in the life world. Every bit of consciousness is fair game for phenomenological scrutiny, and suppose we turn the eyes of phenomenology now upon this particular conscious act of bracketing. How does the bracketing exhibit itself phenomenologically? It presupposes a world, and ourselves as beings in this world, in order that we may give it meaning. Descartes must tell us about his room at the inn in order to make the doubt intelligible. We perform this act of bracketing as existing individuals: It is a device or ploy that we want to use for certain purposes. And if it makes sense, it does so because it is part of a project that may bear philosophical or scientific fruit. In short, existence already surrounds and contains the brackets we would place about it.

The paradox of his starting point should have been glaringly apparent from the moment that Husserl had become the leader of a movement. The radical subjectivism of consciousness does not seem a plausible position when one is rallying disciples under one's standard. Descartes performed his solitary journey into the dark night of the doubt alone and without disciples; Husserl believed the work of phenomenological description to be so vast that it required the collaboration of many minds and generations to achieve. The irony in the whole business is almost dramatic; one imagines Husserl calling his collaborators together and saying to them: "Gentlemen, we are going to suspend the belief in external objects and in one another's minds. This will free us for the description of the pure structures of experience as they show themselves within consciousness. We will adopt the point of view of the pure privacy of mind and—the result of this joint effort will be most fruitful. It will be a labor too that future generations will carry on."

The project to detach oneself from the world is a project to accomplish certain goals within the world. The subjectivism that we feign to adopt as philosophers is a role we choose to play before others and with others. The mind that would proclaim its own privacy is a being in the world.

Husserl is an "essentialist"—as the existentialists who followed in his wake were to label him. The label is correct; but these tags—"essentialist" and "existentialist"—have become a little frayed in use and their meaning consequently somewhat blurred. We have now to press on to the concrete items that give the label its meaning in Husserl's case.

Husserl's attachment to essence has the peculiar stamp of David Hume to it. We see the color and shape of the table, says Husserl, and consequently these are essences directly present to consciousness; but the existence of the table is not similarly present to consciousness. Hence, though *we cannot be sure that what appears exists, we can be sure of the appearance*. This is simply Hume's phenomenalism clothed in the language of essence. There is no distinct impression of existence, Hume tells us. I see the table, and have distinct impressions of its color and shape, and if I close my eyes, I can summon these to mind; but I can form no mental image at all of its existence, beyond the bundle of these distinct qualities. Hence the idea of existence itself comes to float dubiously and insubstantially in the void.

To the end of his life Husserl remained curiously attached to Hume, and professed to see in the latter's phenomenalism a precursor of phenomenology itself. But in fact Hume's view of perception is not a phenomenological exploration at all. It is a theory *about* our perception—a very abstract and constructed one that conceals its own abstractions—and not at all an accurate description of what takes place when we do perceive. Simply as a phenomenological description, it is far inferior, for example, to the traditional one of Aristotle. Surely it is silly to ask us to close our eyes and picture to ourselves (vainly, of course) the existence of the table as a distinct and isolated datum. I do not perceive the existence of a table, but I do perceive an existing table. Existence is not an isolated datum, but a fact of a much more pervasive kind. It is a character of the actually existing world, or that portion of it present to me, within which I perceive actually existing objects. I cannot expect to see existence as if it were anything like a color or a shape.

An ancient sage once suggested, perhaps in jest, that skeptics should be whipped until they became convinced of the certainty of their senses. It would be a brutal remedy, and hardly to be recommended to our time, which has seen enough brutality of its own. Yet the suggestion has a point worth our considering. It might suggest that this doubt of the senses—which is a thread running through modern philosophy and a primary source of the division between inner and outer worlds—becomes quite indefensible in certain situations. Are we to say that the pain, as an internal datum, is certain, but the existence of the whip and the man wielding it is not? We have thereby already split reality in two. That ancient suggestion might also remind us that those particular data that some phenomenologists might cherish for their luminous and tranquil self-evidence are not the only forms of consciousness that bring certitude with them. No doubt, there is a noetic delight in grasping the relations of shapes in geometry, or establishing the intrinsic order of tones and colors in a phenomenology of perception. These are the structures of appearance, which are to occupy us wholly as phenomenologists, and in comparison with which the actual occasions in which they come to exist must seem indefinite, negligible, and uncertain. But there are other data, sometimes thrusting themselves upon consciousness, that carry a very different but equally potent certitude just because they bring with them the harsh bite of actual existence—a flogging, for example, to recur to that ancient and monstrous suggestion; or stepping out into the icy blast of freezing weather and feeling the razors of the wind slice through you. Have you ever plunged inadvertently into water that was so unexpectedly hot that it was almost scalding?

More often this power of the actual invests us in a quieter and steadier way in the accumulated density of life we secrete around us. I wonder about Descartes in that room at the inn in Holland. A few touches, like the bed and the stove, he has made forever memorable to our imagination. But these details are skimpy; the room is no more than the incidental setting to his meditation. He is a bird in passage; he has not lived in that place long enough to stain it with the marks of his own existence. Otherwise he might have found it more difficult to feign the nonexistence of his surroundings. I turn to look around now at this garret of a study in which I am writing. How much of my life has transpired here, and how many of these objects face me with the accumulated density of a history that has been theirs and mine! Could I possibly pretend now, just for a little moment, and feign a doubt like Descartes'? I have an uneasy feeling that this room and its objects would laugh back at me: Whom are you trying to kid? And last night my old dog, now incontinent of feces, crawled up here and left her mess. Poor dear beast, what shall I do with her? Bracket her existence? I would have to cancel all that part of my history and the history of this room with which hers is entwined. Cleaning up after her, I was not able for one moment to pretend that what I had to dispose of did not exist. Try it some time, gentle Cartesian!

Or need we bring up as examples of consciousness those particular moods that Heidegger, coming in the wake of Husserl, was to explore? If the mood is anxiety, then existence itself is thrust starkly before us. I am anxious before my death. Here my own existence, and the existence of the world I am to lose, yawn like an abyss before me, overwhelming, palpable, and impalpable at once, uncanny and precarious. How can I really pretend to "bracket" my own death? My anxiety before it would cease to be what it is.

But these animadversions upon Husserl do not yet get to the center of our question. They serve to indicate the primacy of existence and its unshakable certitude as a fact of experience. This is the existence of the beings around me and my own existence as an actual being. It is no more than the sense of the traditional *existentia* that is grasped by medieval Aristotelians like St. Thomas Aquinas. But we need to take a step farther to gain a sense of *Being* and its fundamental relation to consciousness if we are ultimately to get beyond the division of the two worlds. We said at the beginning that the dualistic doctrine rested on the mode in which we understand the relation of mind to nature, or subject to object. But it turns out that only because we stand within Being can we make this distinction between subject and object at all. Consciousness, in short, is intelligible only in terms of our being in the world.

And indeed this should have been evident directly from Husserl's discovery of the intentionality of consciousness, though it required Heidegger to bring it out. For if consciousness always intends or refers, then it itself and what it intends must somehow belong to the same world. I say to you, "Please bring me that book"—meanwhile pointing. You ask me which one I *intend*. Well, the book I mean is the third one from the left on the top shelf. I have indicated my meaning by selecting out an item from the world around me. My act of intending can take place only within an enveloping world. Consciousness as the performer of intentional acts is thus intelligible only on the basis of our being in the world. It would be without roots or sense otherwise.

When Heidegger's *Being and Time* appeared in 1927, it was in one sense a complete reversal of the master's doctrine. Yet it is the mark of an important thinker that his thought should be fruitful enough to prepare the way for its own reversal if necessary. But such has not been the way in which some stubborn Husserlians have chosen to see this development. And here the facts of historical contingency were to play their part: Husserl seems the exemplary and heroic figure, and therefore more sympathetic to our eyes; while Heidegger's name will perhaps be permanently soiled by his adhesion for a while to Nazism. But if we look past such accidents of personality and history; if we give ourselves to the matter of phenomenology itself, as the persistent effort to let the things show themselves for what they are, then we too have to take that decisive step from consciousness to Being.

For if we begin with a consciousness disjoined from Being—a

consciousness hovering outside the brackets in which it has placed the world—then no matter how indefatigably and carefully we inch forward toward Being, we never arrive at it. We cannot inch forward to Being; we have to plunge in at once with both feet. And indeed we are already there, if we but let ourselves become aware of it, for we can give no meaning to consciousness otherwise.

This step, however, is not a mere relapse into the uncritical indolence of what Husserl calls the natural consciousness or the natural standpoint. Our natural consciousness does have a powerful light of its own, which after these Cartesian centuries we have certainly to restore to it. Lacking that light, indeed, we humans would have no other light at all. But we must not overestimate this consciousness: Whatever its other virtues, it is too occupied with its own narrower concerns to have vision for the Being within which it moves. For that we have to set about opening its eyes—which is something very different, however, from hobbling it with any artificial procedure of bracketing.

We pass thus beyond the privacy of consciousness, which would inevitably divide us between two worlds. Instead, we take as our starting point the fundamental fact of our Being-in-the-world. But this does not mean we have already arrived where we would wish to be. It remains to be seen whether we moderns can find ourselves at home in this world.

Chapter 8

-----◆-----

Homeless in the World

ALIENATION IS ONE OF THE DEEPEST THEMES IN MODERN CULTURE. It has also become, alas, one of the most hackneyed. Everybody talks about it, and the more we talk the more casual and accepted the thing itself seems to become. Alienation even becomes an "in" thing. To be alienated is a mark of distinction that sets us off from our less sensitive fellows. In the 1960s the young aspired to it, cultivated it as a way of life, and proclaimed it as their defiance in the face of their elders. Alienation thus becomes a pseudohome in which we may comfortably nestle along with other superior and lofty souls. The more easily we chatter about it, the more the phenomenon itself, in its true dimensions, becomes hidden to us.

Alienus means a stranger, and therefore someone not at home where he is. If we think about a home, and what it means to be without one, we shall begin to think a little more concretely about the matter of alienation. We may find too that we have not laid the disturbing ghost by our casual chatter.

To be homeless—how well we know it in this age of displaced persons! Great masses of people are uprooted, driven out of their homes, resettled in strange places. That is part of the history of our troubled century. Even in a so-called stable society like our own, mobility becomes constant. In the movements of people from city to suburb, suburb to suburb, city to city, our successive houses begin to resemble wayside stations. A few years ago the movie *Airport* made a popular splash. It was a poor movie, but it struck a responsive chord in the audience. An airport, with its ceaseless arrivals and departures, seemed to be an adequate image of what life today, in the global stage of humanity, has become.

After the first space flights another metaphor for our earthly existence became current. We were here on earth like voyagers on a spacecraft. The image was a well-intentioned warning: as the resources on board a spaceship are limited and therefore to be prudently conserved, so too are those of the planet Earth as we voyage with it through empty space. If we befoul the atmosphere of our cabin, we cannot replace it. In the technological era it is natural we should find a technological image for our terrestrial existence. Nevertheless, one could hardly find a more dismal picture of our homelessness than this. From the moment we think of our life on this planet as a voyage in a spacecraft through empty space, we have ceased to dwell upon this earth as men once did.

Homelessness is the destiny of modern man. This theme is persistent and recurring in the thought of Martin Heidegger, though he appears to have an ambiguous relation to it. In his earlier works he seemed to bend every effort toward showing us how man is and must be, not by social or historical accident but essentially, an uncanny stranger in the world. His later work seeks to redress this balance: to point forward to the ways in which humankind may find again on this earth a home in which to dwell, think, and build. But perhaps there is no ambiguity here. Only when we have come to understand the stranger within us at his true depth can we learn to domesticate him again.

It might seem ironical that Heidegger, the most stubbornly regional character in modern culture, should be the contemporary philosopher most preoccupied with this theme. All his long life he has been rooted to his place, Suebia in the southwest corner of Germany, near to the Alps and the Bodensee—a mountain and a lake, good companions to meditation. Only very late in life did he travel far enough from his home to see a Greek temple, something on which his thinking had long dwelt. He wanted to see the place that had once been the home of a god, and around which men could therefore build their own homes. There is then no irony about his chosen theme. Only a figure so rooted can be properly disturbed at mankind's loss of home.

This feeling for his own region may have been what led Heidegger to become a Nazi for a few years at the beginning of that regime—a nationalist party can sometimes make a strong appeal to regional feelings. We cannot be altogether sure. In 1966 he taped an interview on this Nazi chapter of his life for the magazine *Der Spiegel*, which was not released until ten years later, immediately after his death in May of 1976. As to his inner motives we are still left in the dark after we read that interview. The actors in a drama may not always be the best witnesses to the motives that drove them. What led him to break with Nazism may be more significant than what originally led him into it, for this break coincides in its dates with a definite shift in the emphasis of his thinking. Yet even here the connections between life and thought still remain tenuous and strained at best.[1]

Perhaps philosophers should not have any biography other than the life of their thought. It does not help our initial acquaintance with Plato, for example, to learn that he chose to be prudently absent from Athens during the trial of his master Socrates. In Heidegger's case, the Nazi episode seems to be the only thing in the way of biography that some critics are willing to allow him. We are therefore spared any such further details of a biographical kind and can plunge directly into the matter of his thought.

The use of this thought is to help us come to some deeper understanding of our human homelessness. The classical analyses of alienation were given in the nineteenth century by Hegel and Marx. Heidegger speaks from a further region than these great thinkers. For even if their conditions for overcoming alienation were present —if the human spirit were no longer divided and at odds with itself (Hegel), and men were to find at last a real sense of community within a socialist society (Marx)—there would still lurk a more deeply rooted alienation at the core of our human being, and in relation to being itself.

I.

MORNING

Being? You could scarcely find a word less likely to stir the enthusiasm of readers today. We want solutions to specific problems, or —if we are to dabble in generalities—ideologies that hold forth illusions of such solutions. Being is too remote and abstract for such concerns. It has no cash value, as William James would say. Perhaps

---

[1] See note 1 at end of this chapter.

the word is hopeless, after all. History has loaded it with too many distorting connotations, and modern philosophers have riddled it with too much critical buckshot. Well then, let us scrap the word and plunge instead into the everyday world and try to take note of the ways in which we *are* in that world.

You enter that world differently with Heidegger than with a philosopher like Wittgenstein. The latter permits you only the language of the everyday. You cannot rise above ordinary language to describe its nature. You can show what this language is only by examples of its use, but you remain within it. Like a fish in water, we never get out of that pervasive medium in which we live. Heidegger, however, does attempt to describe the general features of our ordinary existence, and he therefore moves both within it and without it. Indeed, one of the characteristics of the ordinary is that it harbors within it those moments that can always evict us out of it into the extraordinary and uncanny. Thus for the purposes of his description Heidegger uses a language that is often very far from ordinary language. Much has been made of the strangeness of his terminology, but that objection has long since spent its force as we have come to assimilate his meaning. A work like *Being and Time*, as we return again and again to it, begins to strike us more and more with the economy and power of its expression: It does not seem that language—in this case the German language—could have been used more simply and efficiently to convey the powerful range of what the writer has to say. As we move away from it in time, the book towers as one of the great landmarks that our century has to show for itself. In any case, it offers the profoundest description of our ordinary existence that philosophy has yet given.

Let us follow its lead, then, through one day of our everyday.

I—or you, reader—wake to the day. That in itself is as momentous a fact as it is banal. You wake to this day that is present and yet is the day that *is to be* as you set about the day's business. Time present is a future present in that presence. You do not wake in space but in your room. Physical space—the space that science constructs—is not the world in which you open your eyes at morning or close them at night. Nor do you encounter physical objects in anything like the sense of science. True, you are immediately plunged into a world of things: shoes, socks, articles of clothing, or of the toilette with which you assemble yourself for the day that is both present and is to be. The more smoothly your dressing proceeds, the more unobtrusively these familiar articles come to hand and disappear back into their framework of use, and the less they present themselves as material substances. Only if the shoe is tight, or the razor jams, does this utensil present itself in its obtrusive obstinacy as sheer materiality that resists you. Space, matter, substance—these lie at the remote horizon of our daily concerns, if at all, and though they could become themes of purely *theoretical* interest, these are not the usual cares we take up at breakfast.

Your small world now links into a larger one: You have to be on your way to work. Notice that "have to be" again. It is a phrase so banal that we do not usually observe how heavy and fateful its meaning is. We are alive and have always to be on the way to . . . You take your car, let us say, to the train. You stop at a traffic light. Red—that means *Stop*. This meaning is not something to be located "in your mind." Meaning is not, first and foremost, a mental phenomenon but an aspect of things within our daily world. Things have such-and-such a meaning as they point or refer to other things or to behavior that they elicit from us. And this is true too of that larger world that surrounds the man-made world of human traffic. This morning, for example, you may have peeped out of the window earlier to see if there were clouds that might *mean* rain—in which case you would have carried your raincoat. Signs, symbols, meanings—these do not enter as phenomena from a distinct realm of the mental but as aspects of the various things we encounter and have to deal with in our environment.

On the train you take a seat on the right because the morning sun, risen in the east, will not bother you there. So far there is no abstract physical space, but there are spatial directions that we humans mark out for ourselves. We establish places for ourselves in relation to our particular uses for them: The right side of the train, for example, allows you to read your newspaper without the glare of sunlight.

Your morning newspaper! Here another and vaster space opens before you. Events from all over the world, reported here, file before you, depressing, cheering, or boring, according as they engage your particular concerns. Man is the creature who can annihilate distance and bring far and near together. This peculiar relation to space is one of his possibilities. Notice how this thread of possibility weaves its way in and out of the tapestry of your day. This day itself is a concrete possibility present—the day that is here and yet is to be, and in such a way that what is to be already shapes what you think and do. Perhaps too the morning headlines carry the tremors of history behind them. To be involved in history, making it or suffering it, that too is one of mankind's unique possibilities, at once challenging and terrifying. Even in our tiny corner, reader, you and I, who are not principals in the historical drama, nevertheless feel the constant tug of its possibilities upon our lives. But perhaps at the moment such thoughts beget anxiety, and you would rather turn aside from the ominous possibilities your paper spreads before you and relax with the crossword puzzle.

Notice that you have not been an ego or a self or a mind throughout any of this—not in the sense, at any rate, in which philosophers have traditionally discussed these matters. You do not carry around a self inside you like a tiny substantial nugget at your center. Sitting there in the train, you are simply one passenger among many. You rest for the moment in that anonymity of the everyday that is at moments blessedly possible for us. An existentialist of a different brand like Sartre would poison even this tranquillity for us. According to him, the conductor who glances at us as he comes down the aisle has transfixed us with his stare and we are frozen in the gaze of the Other. Sartre is haunted by the world of Proust, where as you exit from a brothel or crouch to peer through a keyhole you may suddenly be caught by a hostile eye that fixes you forever in the posture of shame. As a phenomenologist, Sartre can never quite grasp the normal in the everyday; his imagination, theatrical and melodramatic, must distort, heighten, overdramatize. Significantly, his best play is also his most theatrical one—*Kean*, an adaptation of Dumas and a brilliant re-creation of Second Empire melodrama. But we are not now in the world of Proust or of Dumas but in an ordinary train; and this anonymity of the everyday, of being one among others, is emotionally and ethically neutral. Persist in it too long, of course, or against the call of other possibilities, and you become a lost soul, a faceless member of the mass.

But for the moment the respite is precious and you escape into your crossword. The puzzle is just difficult enough to engage you and just easy enough not to cause frustration. If the latter, you might be thrown into cares that would project this self lurking in the background all too violently into the foreground. It will be with you in any case all too plentifully throughout your day, always at the horizon, summoning you to be, never complete but always on the way. You are thankful then for these few moments of respite.

So we could go on, if space permitted, through the intricate details of a day, with Heidegger always at our side. It is a good exercise for readers of him to live a day in the eyes of his text. It is amazing how his book stands up to the test. Here is our human existence, not as philosophers have conceived it or as we habitually cover it over with ready-made phrases, but as we actually live it, thrusting forth into the dimensions of time, with past-present-future interweaving and copresent, and yet with the silent power of the future—what is not yet but is to be—as the persistent tug upon us pulling the spinning threads along.

Life is many days, day after day. But it is not, we hope, a mere succession of days. We long that these days shall somehow add up to a meaning or a drama that we can call a life. Unlike Wittgenstein's *Investigations*, which has no beginning, middle, or end, Heidegger's treatment of the everyday has an intensely dramatic, even melodramatic, structure. It has almost the elements of a plot or story about it. And this story, oddly enough in a work so austerely secular in tone, follows the outlines of the traditional religious tale of salvation. Heidegger tells us how our human being, thrown into the world, may lose itself there, and sink to a fallen state; but how through the encounter with conscience, anxiety, and death, it is called to and can become an authentic self. But if Heidegger follows the outlines of a religious parable of salvation, what he finally offers is at the farthest remove from the usual consolations of religion. The encounter with anxiety and death opens up no heavenly perspectives for the self. It discovers in that encounter only its own nothingness. Yet the discovery is liberating. In the light of this disclosure we can attain a resolve that frees us from the petty servitudes of the everyday. The fundamental human freedom is our freedom toward death. In the light of that freedom we can take upon ourselves, as authentic humans, whatever decisions and tasks fall to us in the ordinary course of life.

Anxiety and death are shocking matters to be thrown before philosophers who are engrossed in more formal and technical questions. A man must be something of a sensationalist, they think, to deal with such themes at all. The result is that these matters have bulked so large for commentators, both friendly and hostile, that they have obscured the more persistent theme that Heidegger was after from the start. Anxiety and death, to be sure, are integral parts of life, and the philosopher who wishes to understand our existence must come to terms with them. Death is a fearful thing against which the teachers of mankind in the past, including the ancient philosophers, have sought to bring consolations of one kind or another. But Heidegger does not enter the lists in order to bring some kind of modernized version of ancient stoicism that would teach us to face death with equanimity. His purpose is neither therapeutic nor moral; and if his effect is at all moral, it is so only incidentally, insofar as he enlightens our human condition. We interrogate death and anxiety for the light that they shed on the unique kind of being that is ours. But whence do these separate lights borrow their light?

And this, of course, is the question of truth itself—the question that lies behind the dramatic scenario of *Being and Time* and establishes the link between the earlier and later Heidegger, where some critics have seen only a drastic rupture.

II.

AFTERNOON

The question of truth, truth as such, is likely to strike most of us as rather remote and far-fetched, or alternately, depending on our mood, as gratuitous and unnecessary because the matter is so obvious. More often than not we can harbor both prejudices without any sense that they may be contradictory. In fact, they may even tend to reinforce each other. It is so obvious what truth is that we need not ask about it; and yet it is at the same time something remote and hard to grasp just because it is woven so closely into the texture of our experience. The things directly at one's feet are always the hardest to see.

But if we do take a look we may be in for some surprises. We may find that the source of our alienation lies hidden at the center of this apparently trivial question.

At first glance the philosophical tradition might seem to confirm our conviction that the whole matter is altogether obvious. Aristotle, that luminous master of the commonplace, begins it with a definition: Truth is the correspondence of our thought with what is actually the case. Aristotle said some other things on the subject too; but no matter, the tradition congealed around this, and the

Middle Ages codified it in the formula *Veritas est adaequatio intel-lectus et rei* (Truth consists in the agreement of our thought with reality). We are thinking truly when our thinking is in accord with the facts as they are. Who can doubt this? This is self-evident common sense, and we should not seek to becloud it with puzzles. Indeed, we don't in the least seek to doubt it. It is the truth about truth—as far as it goes. But it speaks at a level of abstractness of which common sense remains unconscious and which in the end begets all manner of puzzles.

These puzzles are quick to appear as soon as we enter the modern era in philosophy with Descartes' dualism of mind and matter, subject and object. Mind and matter are radically different kinds of things; how then can we compare an idea in the mind to a thing outside the mind? For us to make the comparison, the thing outside must somehow come inside the mind. The question of truth now becomes one of consistency between my idea and my perception—between two different contents of my consciousness. Thus arises the well-known coherence theory of truth, according to which truth is a matter of our ever-widening and self-integrating consciousness. This gets rid of one set of puzzles, but brings another in its place. We seem now imprisoned in the mind and haunted by the ghost of a subjectivism that has bedeviled even the greatest among the modern philosophers.

But let us leave such puzzles to the classroom and return to this day in the everyday to see if we can find truth there.

I sit here at my desk as the afternoon wanes, struggling to work, only now and then raising my eyes to stare absently around me. Same old room, same old objects. I do not take notice; my attention is on my work, and my eyes return to it. But I begin to be vaguely uneasy; something in the room is troubling me, but I do not even stop to think what it might be. A friend suddenly enters and says, "That picture is hanging askew," pointing to the painting that hangs on the wall directly across the room. And sure enough, that's what it is, that is what has been vaguely troubling me all this while: The picture has been hanging lopsided, and I was really seeing it but not noticing it. Now the hidden fact leaps out and stands clear. And I experience that feeling of momentary ease and satisfaction that always comes with the resolution of any problem, even when it is as slight as this one.

In this ridiculously commonplace incident we witness nothing less than the happening of truth. Forgive this suddenly portentous language; but we have to hold fast to this tiny situation as a whole or we shall never see what truth is. Usually, philosophers take one part of the situation and find it sufficient. Truth has occurred, they say, because a statement has been made, "That picture is hanging askew," and the statement turned out to be true. And it was true because it corresponded with the fact: the picture hanging there on the wall is really lopsided.

But is this what really happened? Do we really compare a proposition with a fact? If I want to compare two coins, I set them beside each other and see if they match. Each coin must be equally accessible to me. In general, if I want to compare any two things at all, each must be equally evident to me. The fact would have to be evident (true) to me before the proposition arrived to bring us its truth.[2]

Does anything happen like the following? I hear noises that somehow provoke the idea in my mind, "That picture is hanging askew"; I then exit quickly from the mind, garner a sense perception from the picture; return inside the mind and compare the perception with my idea. Decidedly, our whole picture of things here has gone very much askew! What we have done, as it were, is to take a great pair of scissors and cut the single proposition out of the concrete situation in which it functioned and did its work; and then on this dislocated fragment we have constructed a fantastic and meaningless structure to build it back into the whole.

Language works differently from a point-by-point matching. Suppose my friend had simply said, "Look!" while pointing at the picture. The exclamation could have disclosed the lopsided picture just as well. Does it therefore "correspond" to—resemble in any way—the fact? Yet it has done the same job as the full proposition: It has brought something hidden into the open. Suppose there had been a curtain draped over the wall and my friend had pulled it aside to uncover the picture hanging askew. His action takes place out there in the open; we wouldn't think of locating it in somebody's mind. Yet our language, which here performed the same job of uncovering a fact, seems somehow infected with the virus of the "mental," and we think it has to be pushed back out of the world into the mind. It is as if we were to carry on a conversation with each other inside our separate heads. We forget that the primary

[2] See note 2 at end of this chapter.

function of language, if we have something to say and are not merely babbling, is to uncover something within the world, to bring it into the open; and it can do this only because it itself transpires within the open world.

The old comic strips used to show us truth dawning on one of their characters as an electric bulb lighting up in the head. These cartoonists seem to have gone to school with Descartes. Nor should we smile in too easy superiority here, for we ourselves, so deeply embedded are these notions, more often than not may be unconsciously thinking according to the same pattern. Nevertheless we should keep the image of light; only it is not an electric bulb flashing in our head when truth happens, but some portion of the world that has become illuminated. If we go looking for truth inside the mind we shall only find the mind already outside of itself in the world. When a new truth arises to change our minds, as we commonly say, it does so only in that it changes some portion of the world for us. The world here is taken to include all the things of nature as well as of the life of humans in history.

The means and provenance of illumination may vary greatly. Statements may be the instruments of enlightenment, but not the only ones. As soon as we are freed from the notion of the single proposition as the ultimate locus of truth, which each proposition carrying its truth on its back like a rider on a saddle, we are also freed toward understanding other modes through which truth may be realized. In particular, we might begin at last to ask seriously in what way truth may be embodied in works of art. Instead of squabbling, as philosophers will do, about the trivial matter of how that picture is hanging on the wall, we might ask the more important question, What truth is present in it? For a great painting (of which this is a reproduction) can light up a whole historical chapter of the human spirit for us. If we had nothing from the eighteenth and nineteenth centuries but their music, the profound differences of the human horizons within these two epochs would be overwhelmingly evident and clear to us. We cannot understand these truths of art within the framework of strictly propositional truth. Nor is it any more possible to understand the truth of literature, which uses language as its medium, within that framework.

What we have said so far, particularly on the instrumental aspects of language, is obviously related to the controversy launched by the pragmatists William James and John Dewey in the first years of this century in their all-out attack upon the correspondence theory of truth. Bertrand Russell, who was among their adversaries, found the Americans unsophisticated and crude. From what we have since come to know about the constructive nature of scientific theory, it turns out to be the pragmatists (on this matter, Dewey particularly) who were the more sophisticated—sophisticated because more imaginative. The scientist may construct models for which it becomes gratuitous and empty to ask for a point-by-point correspondence with each item of fact. The theory is tested as a whole.

In retrospect, the main issues of the controversy can now be sorted out more clearly. The pragmatists insisted that if truth is not to be embedded within the human context, including the context of language (as the pragmatists insisted it is), then the alternative forced upon us is a doctrine of independently subsisting propositions, each of which has the rider of truth or falsity attached to it. Russell, then a Platonist, could embrace this position gladly, but it has not worn at all well. Nevertheless, the pragmatists could not shake off the correspondence view altogether; it clung to them like the can tied to the dog's tail, and they accepted it at key points—"in face-to-face verifications," namely, where we are facing the thing directly—because they did not yet have the phenomenological understanding that for a thing to be directly evident does not imply any correspondence.[3]

The Greek word we translate as "true" is *alethes* (literally, "unhidden"). This word does not speak of the correspondence between a statement and a fact, between a mental judgment and a thing, between an ideal content and the matter of perception. It speaks only of something that has emerged from the hidden into the open. The word came into being in the earliest days of the Greek language, we know not how or when or what thoughts may have accompanied its formation. It emerged before the Greeks had become literate and produced grammarians and logicians, and it remains closer to the primal sense and function of language than the subtlest analyses of later grammar and logic.

---

[3] In general, pragmatism deserves great credit for stressing that the locus of truth is not in the isolated proposition but the total human context. Whether it grasped this context widely and deeply enough remains in question. For example, it never developed any account of the specific mode of truth of art. The subject is conspicuously absent from Dewey's *Art and Experience*, and its absence is a serious deficiency in an otherwise very valuable book.

Nevertheless, Heidegger did not arrive at his understanding of truth through a piece of ancient etymology. That would be inverting the real order of events. On the contrary, he was able to see the meaning hidden in the Greek word only because he had already come to some fundamental philosophical insight of his own. His doctrine of truth came to him through prolonged reflection upon the theory of evidence that Husserl had first attempted in his early logical investigations and elaborated in later works. If the function of language is to make our ideas clearer, it can do so only by making the things themselves to which the ideas refer more evident; and Heidegger, accordingly, takes the bold and simple step of planting us directly before the things themselves.[4] And with this step he transforms the nature of phenomenology much more radically and decisively than by his spectacular analyses of anxiety and death. But having followed the path, we may then guard the Greek word as a talisman. As we shall see in a moment, it will also serve as a somber reminder of what remains hidden to us in all of our truth.

Notice we do not say: The Greek word for true is *alethes*. That would be to impose ourselves as the standard by which to measure them, and then add a little dash of etymology by way of color. The simple fact of the matter is more drastic: The Greeks did not have a word for "true." They had only a word that meant evident, manifest, open, present. Was this a deprivation on their part, a symptom of their relatively primitive state in comparison with ours? In fact, it was a distinct advantage. And if we follow them here, we shall not only learn to think a little more "Greekly," but we shall also be able to see where truth is to be found in our everyday. We have simply to look for *ta alethea*—the things evident and manifest that we encounter there.

And indeed truth was with us at every step in the long day's journey through the everyday. Not poked away in some odd corner or other, or popping its head up at some unexpected and unusual

---

[4] The point may be expressed in a simple paradigm. One man, A, says to another, B:

1. "You have made that matter clear to me."
Or he may say:
2. "You have made my ideas clear about that matter." If 2. means anything at all, it simply means what 1. does.

The whole of Heidegger's notion of Aletheia—and consequently his difference from Husserl—is contained in this simple paradigm case.

juncture of events, but persisting through and within this day in which you and I, reader, have still to be. From the moment we opened our eyes a world was disclosed to us. Familiar faces, houses, streets, cars, trains—all that stand out clearly to us. Wherever there is disclosure, there is truth. To be in a world—any world—is insofarforth to be in the truth. The world so disclosed may be a tiny and unprepossessing affair, but we must hold fast to it nonetheless. However far from it our theorizing may soar, it must take off from and return here. Even when we seek to go behind this world and dismantle it piece by piece as mere appearance, we would still have to borrow our initial language and meanings from it.

And this day itself? Has it not also been something manifest and evident in its presence? Yet we cannot grasp it like the things that came and went and were present within it. They are visible and tangible, and it is not; yet it has been with us as persistently and as unnoticed as our breathing. Can we grasp presence itself? Yet it is closer and more present to us than any of the things that came to be present within it.

But someone might say: Why make a mystery of it, it is only a day, a segment of time? Alas, we do not escape so easily. When we undertook a journey through the everyday, reader, it was *this* present day and not any other. "Twenty-four hours" is an abstraction that could be tomorrow or yesterday but not this day in its presence. Nor can we capture this presence by assigning a date: "Today *is* . . ."—and filling in the blank with its calendar date. For it is precisely the "is" in this sentence form that we wish to grasp, and tomorrow this date will not name the present.

Nor can we grasp this presence as the present instant of time. I look now at my watch and count off ten seconds. Ten jerky little jumps of the hand and ten "nows" have followed each other into and out of existence. Watch and ticking hand are things that are present. The counting also is done within this presence that envelops watch and ticking hand. The *now* thus becomes manifest only within and through presence, and therefore can never serve to define presence. Being, as presence, is manifest through time but can no more be captured under the forms of time than under the forms of space.

With this simple and enveloping fact of presence we have come upon being. Being manifests itself as presence. It is a reality neither remote nor abstract, but there all the time, pervading our day in the everyday throughout its most ordinary encounters. Whenever we said, "Here is . . . ," "There is . . . ," or "Today is . . . ," which are indispensable modes of ordinary expression, we were acknowledging presence. And within this presence we spoke of the ill-hanging picture. Even with such provisos constantly in mind, one takes up uncertainly this poor word "Being," which is freighted with so many distortions from history. I would prefer instead to speak of the IS, if this usage did not seem even more arbitrary and barbarous. We have here to do with a struggle with words that is not of our arbitrary and willful choosing. We have to speak of this IS, which is not in the least like any distinct entity or thing, which has no definite characteristics, qualities, or relations like a thing; and we are to speak of it in a language geared to things, qualities, relations. And yet it is only in the light of this IS that we can talk at all about things, qualities, and relations. We shall have to use all the resources of language to circumvent this obstacle—an obstacle without which, paradoxically, we would not have language at all.

At the heart of what should be the most luminous and evident of all things, truth itself, we come upon a mystery before which we are suddenly aliens and strangers. Or have we ourselves, out of our own freedom, chosen not to be at home with it?

III.

NIGHT

We may have aroused false expectations that we have more truth than we do. We say, for example, that the world through which we move is illuminated to some degree. And, further, whatever world might open around us would have to be illuminated and would in fact be illuminated to the degree that it lay open before us. Thus wherever there is being there is truth. That would seem to give us a universe more radiant than the one we know.

The philosophers of the Middle Ages had formulated as one of their principles: *Ens et verum convertuntur.* (Being and truth are convertible)—each implies the other. Whatever exists, to the degree that it exists, conforms to an idea of the divine mind. To the degree that it falls short of truth, it is accordingly deficient in its being. Here the universe overflows with the radiance of Christian theism.

It is a very different picture we are dealing with now. The world through which we move has to be illuminated in order for us to get around in it at all, but there are also vast patches, and even abysses, of darkness within it. The human animal is full of contradictions. Only a creature capable of truth is also capable of lying or deliberately deceiving himself. The gods gave men language and a tongue to tell lies with. Sham, deception, hypocrisy—these are distinctly human products as much as are the awesome bodies of knowledge that mankind has triumphantly built up for itself. Truth and untruth weave the seamless web of human nature, and history is the arena of their struggle.

The history of the Greeks tells us all we might want to know about these bizarre and contradictory human propensities for truth and untruth. The Greeks were the people of the light. The root for "light" runs through their verbs for speaking and saying: to utter something is to bring it into the light. The older poetic word for man is *phos:* a mortal creature of the light. The poet of their race, Homer, is characterized throughout, as Erich Auerbach has shown, by the desire to bring every detail of his story out of some hidden background into a clear, evenly lit foreground. The Greeks created the clarities of geometry, logical thinking, philosophy. Yet the history of this people is also shot through with the most glaring kind of darkness. Nowhere else do we find such spectacular, almost superhuman, qualities of guile, deceit, treachery, alongside the most powerful gifts of mind, as in a Pausanias or Themistocles. The Greeks knew very well then why the *Letheia* (hiddenness) was to be preserved within the same word for the luminous and evident.

Oedipus is the tragedy of the struggle between light and darkness. The hero wishes to see, he will have the truth at all costs; and when the light finally bursts upon him, he puts out his eyes so that he will never see again. As he had been blind in the bright days of his glory, now in the light of his wisdom he sinks into another darkness. So the dramatist would teach us that light and darkness, truth and untruth, always commingle.

But surely this is a mere matter of human pathology, someone might say, and therefore the business of the psychologist, not the philosopher. Our surrogate of Greek drama is now psychoanalysis. In a secular society it seems to be the only ritual left us. The patient is supposed to be in search of his Oedipus complex; I suggest he is re-enacting the Oedipus drama in a more fundamental sense—he is struggling for light against darkness. He wants, or ought to want, the truth about himself; but sometimes the more earnestly and energetically he sets about it, the more obstacles he puts in his own way. He is not yet free for the truth. All this is the well-known matter of "resistance," and the psychoanalysts tell us all about it; we have no need here for the philosopher.

Perhaps. But in the very moment you speak of "resistance" you use the word "freedom," and philosophy immediately begins to prick up its ears. Perhaps there is a more intimate relation between truth and freedom than we commonly think. We must be free for the truth; and conversely, to be able to be open toward the truth may be our deepest freedom as human creatures. The capacity for untruth is not a mere private matter of personal psychopathology. Truth harbors within itself the tragic possibilities for untruth because of its intrinsic connection with freedom.

Thus truth and untruth are inextricably mingled not only in the deeds of men of action, in tragic heroes, patients suffering through psychoanalysis, but also in our theoretical efforts to understand. The light of a new scientific theory blinds us for a while, and sometimes a long while, toward other things in our world. The greater and more spectacular the theory, the more likely it is to foster our indolent disposition to oversimplify: to twist all the ordinary matters of experience to fit into the new framework, and if they do not, to lop them off. Newton's *Principia* dazzled two centuries with its light and blinded them to explain all human matters, even our moral virtues and vices, within the framework of mechanics. Another *Principia*, also out of Cambridge, that of Russell and Whitehead, seemed for several decades of this century to offer the key to all philosophical questions. Freud had some fundamental insights about infantile sexuality, and now some of the more zealous partisans of psychohistory want to persuade us that the true history of this century has to be written in terms of what went on in the nursery. Marx grasped the economic factor in history more deeply than anyone before him; and Marxist criticism interprets Kafka as a tool of capitalism.

The examples could be multiplied: In each case we take a partial truth and make it total. We become totalitarians of the mind; but we ourselves are our own victims, for we have imprisoned ourselves in a total ideology beyond which we cannot see. We are no longer free to let things be what they are, but must twist them to fit into the framework we impose. Yet we ourselves have freely chosen to surrender this freedom. Why? Because, like children afraid of the dark, we cannot abide to stand within mystery, and so must have a truth that is total. It may be helpful, then, to remember that any portion of reality with which we deal stands always within the encompassing presence of all that is. No doubt we can draw no specific conclusion for research therefrom. But if we let this presence recede altogether, if we make ourselves so alien to it that we forget it entirely, then we are so much the more likely to succumb to the blindness of one ideology or another—not excluding, by the way, that peculiar ideology of skepticism.

Let us return to our trivial case of the picture hanging askew on the wall. This fact, through the efficacy of language, was made present to us within the presence of this room. But the room is part of the house; and beyond the house is the more enveloping presence of the out-of-doors with whatever objects may be found there. To be is to be within a world, the borders of which can be indefinitely extended. Those further borders may be remote from what is luminously present, but not always; and however remote, the background is also always present with the foreground.

We walk now into the out-of-doors, and it is night. Let us take up again, reader, our little fiction of a day in the everyday, with which this chapter began, and round it off now appropriately with the night that closes this day.

The cold winter evening immediately enfolds us in its presence, in which the stars too, sparkling and crisp, stand out as present. The faintest sliver of a moon seems almost to borrow its light from their shining presence. Ah, there *is* Orion, ancient hunter, looming in the southeast, while Sirius, the Dog, has just cleared the tall trees near the horizon. The two, the Hunter and his Dog, will go on marching toward the west, marking off the hours within this present night; and then night after night will loom farther west in the sky as they mark the progress of our world toward spring. Within the presence of this night these stars, like so many shining symbols, gather into themselves the procession of the seasons.

You and I know, of course, for the astronomers have told us, that these stars are almost unimaginably far away, and that their light now reaches us across the distance of years. Suppose one of these stars had already gone out; then what you and I are presently seeing is the star of several years back. This crisp clear night that envelops us harbors then its own deceptions. Here too, within this shining presence, there prevails as everywhere the everlasting conflict that the Greeks knew between appearance and reality, semblance and truth.

The deception, however, is there only if we jump too quickly to conclusions. The reality that hides itself behind this presence is also manifest through it. We have to reflect that it was within the presence of certain phenomena that scientists were led to draw their conclusions about the speed of light. With pencil on paper they made their calculations evident and present to one another. The readings on their instruments had to be present and visible to them in order that they might correct the reading of their naked eye about the stars overhead. And their results, past and present, were gathered together into language in which their thought, though physically they could have been continents apart and centuries distant, could be present to each other. Presence, always presence. Only by the light of one presence can we correct the deception that may be harbored within another.

The night is so clear that if you look sharp you can even make out the faint stars of Orion's sword as they curve away from his glittering belt. The mighty Hunter faces squarely the Bull in the opposite quarter of the heavens. These stars suddenly leap into life with the myths of mankind. Myths, the calculations of astronomers, the procession of centuries, are gathered within the presence of this night. The *now* of measured time, the tiny and jerky pause of the second hand in its sweep of the dial, is but a fragment within this presence; contained but not containing, and certainly never identical with presence. And if we reflect upon the long life of humankind upon this little planet of Earth, against this unfathomable background of the stars, we are suddenly thrust into the mystery. Why is there this world? Why is there a world at all?

The mystery may be put in various ways, each of them no doubt inadequate in its own fashion. Toward the end of the seventeenth century Leibniz uttered the mystery as a question: "Why is there anything at all rather than nothing?" For Wittgenstein in the twentieth century the mystery is no longer to be expressed as a question. It is neither a problem to be resolved scientifically, nor a puzzle to be discarded by unraveling our language; and yet it persists: "*That*

the world is," he exclaims, "is the mystical." Not how the world is;
for science, though its task there is endless, can describe the myriad
ways in which things are and are operant in relation to one another;
but the sheer fact that there is a world at all—this must forever
elude us. And there Wittgenstein stops and passes into silence. Leibniz, however, stays with his question, and we may accordingly
dwell there a moment with his answer.

Why is there anything rather than nothing? Why is there a
world at all? Existence may be a brute fact for which there is no ac-
counting. But if there is a reason at all that a world exists, then
Leibniz—in conformity with the tradition—gives the only possible
rational answer to his own question. There is a world, there is existence or being, because there is one being whose existence is necessary. The nature of that being entails its own existence; and if we
could intuit that nature we could grasp the necessity of this existence with the certainty and self-evidence with which we grasp an
analytic proposition in logic or mathematics. The necessary being,
of course, is God.

Such is the position of Western theism. Within this framework,
from the high Middle Ages down through the eighteenth century,
Western man experienced the meaning of beings and being. Or, following more Heideggerian language, it was always within his
framework that beings were present and manifest to mankind.

This traditional theism, however, does not abolish the mystery,
but only pushes it away into the distant and remote region of the
divine nature. The more men reflected upon this nature the more
absolutely incomprehensible it became to them. One could multiply
its attributes or names to nine and ninety but each in turn was as
verbally empty as the next. From the things of the world we could
borrow no notion at all of what a necessary being would be like.
Everything of which we have experience in this universe can be
imagined not to exist. "If I can think of something existing," Hume
said, "I can also think of it as not existing." A thing that necessarily
existed, whose existence was intrinsic to its nature, would then be
radically different from any kind of thing we know. And so radically different that we do not have any notion at all what sort of
thing it might be, despite all the ink that theologians once shed on
the subject. God is wholly other to us, and so other that He remains
utterly incomprehensible. The nine and ninety attributes merely
embroider a mystery.

Through the concrete practice of religion this theistic framework served to keep Western man somehow rooted to being. One existed, after all, within this whole scheme of things under the governance of God. And one's thoughts and feelings, one's life and death, had meaning ultimately in relation to this whole. But in pushing the mystery away from us into the remote and hidden region of the divine nature this theism may have done an immense damage to our Western consciousness. The mystery ceased to be enveloping and present. The universe passed into the disenchanted and secular aggregate of things. And now that this theistic framework has receded for us, when it is no longer the conscious or unconscious presupposition of our age, what becomes more and more questionable to our "alienated" age is whether we have not become rootless.

Heidegger would insist that we cannot push the mystery away from us since we are always within it. Its presence is presence itself. The mystery lurks in the nature of truth. Whether conscious of it or not, the Greeks hit upon something uncanny in their word for truth. They kept the privative or negative form—*A-letheia*, or unhiddenness—and did not, like other Indo-European languages, pass over into some directly positive word like our own "truth." The positive word suggests a state or condition that has divested itself of any reference to its hidden opposite. But in the light of the privative word of the Greeks we must think of truth as the deprivation, the wrenching, or tearing something out of hiddenness; and in such a way that the hidden mystery persists in and through and around what is disclosed. The most ordinary truths of our everyday stand within this riddle as well as our speculations about the farthest galaxies. To go back to that simple and trivial disclosure from which we started: "Look, the picture *is* hanging askew"; and with these words a fact became present within the presence of our room. Pursue this presence far enough, and we stand now under this engulfing presence of the night with its near and distant stars.

No future discovery by humans will ever alter this situation. Science proceeds from the known to the unknown; but both known and unknown are grasped within the enveloping fact of existence. Any future analysis may refine the language by which we elicit the mystery but will never abolish it. And if new gods or a new revelation were to arrive in this tired world, our hearts might be lifted up, our will exalted, and we might learn again to live in the presence of the holy. But in that new dispensation, whatever it might be, the mystery would still persist and be present. The mystery was there for the first humans conscious enough for it to become present to them, and it will be there for the last who draw their breath upon this planet.

But enough for this evening. Under the circling vault of these stars we have had enough meditation to hold onto. The mood is neither somber nor elated. There are no blurred edges of "the mystical" about it. You have simply to be there and the mystery will be there for you too. The schoolboy hears his name called and answers "Present!" Here we call *Present* and our call calls us into presence.

A sound stirs in the thicket nearby; some cautious animal moves softly there. In the distance an unlikely owl hoots. And we are suddenly moved to think of all those other creatures besides man upon this earth who are not tortured by this question. Humans alone, among all the animal species, respond to this mystery. Is it too great a burden for us to bear?

We come back thus to the question of alienation, with which this chapter began. We are strangers in the universe in a way that no other animal can be, for the mystery opens only to us. It is on this level that the ultimate alienation of man has to be faced. We may chatter about alienation as a cultural or social phenomenon, but all such talk falls short of the deepest dimension in which man is a stranger in his universe. And yet this dimension of strangeness is the peculiar home where he is drawn closest to all that is. Any utopian social arrangement, where what is facilely called "alienation" would cease, would make humankind most truly alienated from its own being. Creatures of a void without knowing it.

Humankind, conscious of its death, must also bear the burden of this mystery. Is it too great, amid our other anxieties, for us to carry? It makes us feel more homeless within the world than any animal can be. Yet is it altogether a burden? Is it not rather a gift too? It is given to us and to no other animal to stand within the mystery. It claims us as its own and we are at home there where no other animal can be. Tonight the stars shine overhead like old and reliable friends. This cosmos is ours to the degree that we are still able to be enthralled by its stupendous presence.

NOTES TO CHAPTER 8

1. The disappointment from reading this interview is not about particular facts that would incriminate Heidegger. The general picture of

events was already known, and he gives some further details to confirm it. In brief: After he had resigned as rector of Freiburg in 1934 he began to detach himself from the Nazis; and after 1935 it became clear that his thinking was at odds with the Nazi philosophy and he himself consequently was *persona non grata* to the Party officials. He also seeks to dispel the rumors that there was a break in his relationship with Husserl because the latter was a Jew. And there are facts cited, of his befriending of certain Jews, to indicate that Heidegger was in no way an anti-Semite, etc.

What then is our disappointment with this interview? One somehow wants more from a philosopher, in the way of a human and moral voice, than a cautious defense of himself before some imaginary Allied tribunal. What did he *feel* about Nazism in that brief period when he was a partisan of it? And what does he *feel* now in retrospect? After all, there were "idealistic" Nazis in the early years, and Heidegger might have given us some insight here on what he, like some of those others, saw in the movement at that time. But more than this, one would have hoped for some kind of personal reflection, looking backward on that whole awful chapter of history he had lived through and what meaning it now has for him with all its millions of victims.

But there is none of this. Perhaps the interviewer was at fault in not pushing his questions. But Heidegger himself should have pushed these matters forward, for they are what the world wanted to hear from him. Instead, after the recital of facts, he plunges into a discussion of his ideas about the history of Being and technology—which are interesting and powerful, but which he has written about elsewhere. He lives in those ideas, and he cannot really tear his gaze away from them, or not for very long. There is no doubt of his intellectual integrity or his commitment to his ideas, and that no political party could bend him away from his pursuit of them—from that consecrated meditation upon Being, that was his life's mission. Much as one admires this dedication to an intellectual vision, one feels there is a kind of Olympian detachment about it. There is an intellectual passion in Heidegger's writing, but not much sensitivity to the actual occasions of our human history and their moral import.

The reader would do well to bear these questions in mind when we come later to Chapter 12, "The Moral Will."

2. Modern logic has taken up the question of truth in the discipline of semantics, and it has been claimed by some that this "semantical concept of truth" resolves all the age-old questions of philosophers on this particular subject.

These claims are, I believe, illusory; and since they bear on our general theme of technique and philosophy—they are in fact one more expression of the wistful hope that technique can take over philosophy—it is worth taking brief notice of this semantical issue.

a. Semantics is in itself a highly interesting part of logical theory, and is useful for dealing with classical paradoxes like "The Liar." But it is not a philosophical exploration of the meaning of truth. This is made clear by Alfred Tarski in his beautiful essay of 1935, which virtually founded the discipline. Tarski tells us that he is taking for granted the classical Aristotelian conception of truth as "correspondence" with fact. A statement is true if and only if the fact is as the statement says it to be. The whole formal apparatus of semantics is erected entirely in the light of this conception.

But that does not prevent us from exposing this traditional concept to philosophical scrutiny and reflection.

b. The procedure of semantics is to *translate* the statements in a given language (called the object language) into statements in a metalanguage, and only in this latter can one speak about the truth of statements in the object language.

The "correspondence" in question is between the statement in the metalanguage and the fact signified by the statement in the object language. We are able therefore to certify the semantical assertion only if the fact itself is *evident*. (This being-evident thus turns out, as we have indicated in our chapter, to be a more basic notion than "correspondence.")

Thus it is no accident that Tarski begins his exposition by erecting a semantics for the simplest and most evident part of logic, the calculus of classes in its formal development by Schroeder.

Once again, in short, we face the general situation: To compare two things, A and B, to see if they correspond, both these things must be evident to us as what they are. Being-evident is the ultimate *sine qua non* of truth.

c. Semantics is really a theory of translation and not a theory of truth. This is no denigration of its value as a formal theory, for it calls our attention to the necessity of having accurate translations and of restricting our assertions of truth in relation to those translations so that we avoid contradictions. But in the end it tells us nothing about truth itself. When we are told that the sentence *Der Schnee ist weiss* is true if and only if it is the case that snow is white, our knowledge of German may have been extended but our understanding of truth is left exactly where it was.

Chapter 9

———◄◆►———

The Cash Value of Being

MOST OF US, AND MANY MORE THAN EVER PUT IT INTO WORDS, HAVE EX-
perienced the idea of Being at one time or another. We have only,
in a relaxed and unguarded moment, to let our thoughts stray to the
universe as a whole, and we are overcome by the awesome fact that
it is, that there is anything at all rather than nothing. But for the ordinary person this thought is quickly swept aside as he plunges back
into the cares of life and his preoccupation with the concrete things
around him. He does not have time to let the idea gather and deepen
within him. That is a job for the philosophers: Let them become the
sacrificial addicts of the enigma! If they exhaust their powers fruit-
lessly in its service, they will at least have discharged their professional duty to the rest of us by reminding us of the mystery that
dwarfs our human arrogance. But modern philosophers no longer
bring this sobering lesson to the rest of mankind: For the most part
they have let the idea of Being disappear from their thinking. More
than this: They would bar us from even entertaining the idea by
erecting barriers of language against it. Of course, one can understand why there should be an obstacle here, since human languages
have grown up around our preoccupation with the things and objects that have to do with our survival. But these philosophers
would refine on those natural obstacles; they would build the barriers higher by developing their own more restrictive forms of linguistic analysis. It is difficult enough as it is to talk about Being;
they would make it impossible.

In all of this, language seems to emerge as the particular enemy of

Being. But what if, turning the tables, we were to find out that language itself is not understandable apart from Being? And that every philosophy of language is incomplete until it grasps this?

William James brought the term "cash value" into philosophy under rather different circumstances. When pragmatism came to the attention of Europeans at the turn of the century, it was the first original voice in philosophy to be heard from the New World. And the response in certain quarters of the Old to the New World was to be predicted. Oxford and Cambridge turned up their venerable noses in disdain. What else could one expect from a raw and bustling country like America when it got around at last to produce a philosophy of its own? Naturally, that philosophy would reflect the narrow practicality of frontier life or the philistine practicality of the American businessman, or both. James took up the challenge without turning the other cheek. Rather than disguise the product he had to sell, he chose to flaunt its American style at his critics. They found this philosophy too American; very well, then, he would flaunt the American lingo in their face. So he came to speak of the "cash value" of an idea as the measure of its meaning: the requirement that somewhere along the line this idea must make a difference within our actual experience.

One would be foolish to try to match the dash and swagger of James' performance. But his example does serve to suggest that in philosophic controversy, instead of turning the other cheek, we have sometimes to engage the adversary on his own turf. The rejection of the idea of Being, in recent times, has been made by philosophies that turn one way or another around the analysis of language. Very well; we shall defend this idea by showing that it has a distinct "cash value," that it is in fact indispensable for our comprehension of language as a human phenomenon.

Despite his democratic and plain-spoken manner, William was in his own way as cosmopolitan and subtle a mind as his brother Henry James the novelist, and of course did not intend to confine the cash value of an idea to whatever narrow utility it might procure for us in the marketplace. Ideas make a difference for experience on different levels and in different contexts. An idea may serve us not so much as an instrument we use but as something into whose service we are called. Indeed, the ideas that matter most to people, those that make most difference in experience, are the ones that give experience itself its sense and meaning. The idea of "God," for example, once had a tremendous resonance for the will of mankind, and consequently an incomparable cash value in their experience. And it is on the level of such broader questions that the value of the idea of Being has ultimately to be explored and evaluated. Here, however, we have agreed to restrict ourselves to its usefulness for our understanding only, and specifically our understanding of the particular phenomenon of language.

But even on this level the question of cash value is not so easily decided. When is an idea really useful for our understanding? That leads to the more fundamental question: When is our intellectual account of any matter ever to be judged satisfactory or not? James addressed himself to this question in one of his greatest essays, "The Sentiment of Rationality," which seems to me even more remarkably applicable in its general conclusions today than when it was written. We have, I think, to admit with him—and with much more compelling reasons now in the light of developments in logic and the foundations of mathematics—that there is no neat, fixed, and formal criterion by which we can deem any of our explanations rationally satisfying or not. We take up a question when we have some sense of malaise or incompleteness in things as they confront us, and the inquiry is terminated satisfactorily when the original frustration ceases. So far as any philosophic account of our experience is concerned, we should have at least the feeling that the main facts of the matter have not been omitted from our reckoning. And what we shall be urging in the case of Being is precisely this: that our philosophical picture of language is incomplete without it. A philosophy may give the most copious and minute account of details in the foreground, but so long as Being is either dismissed or passed over, we feel a great emptiness in the background, and the words of the philosopher sound without depth or resonance. There is the nagging and unshakable sense that something is missing, which is just the sense from which our desires for explanation start in the first place. A philosophy that lacks any idea of Being appears to us then as itself deficient in being.

But these generalities need to be exhibited concretely in the case of a particular philosopher. The example of Wittgenstein already lies to our hand in this book; and in line with our present purpose we may now try to bring his thought and Heidegger's together in some kind of dialogue. The reader may find in the course of this that the meanings of both philosophers become clearer. At the least there will perhaps be the interest of novelty in the effort. Usually when Anglo-American philosophers of the "analytic" school take any glance at the philosophy of Being, it is by way of subjecting the latter to the restrictions of their own language; and the aim most often is not to secure dialogue but to voice disdain and rejection. We invert these linguistic priorities: We shall seek to embed Wittgenstein's language within Heidegger's, as within the deeper and wider context; and not to reject the former but to make its presuppositions more intelligible. Molière's bourgeois gentleman spoke prose all his life without knowing it. So the ordinary-language philosopher has an involvement with Being of which he is not aware.

I.

The presence of Being is acknowledged explicitly, or almost explicitly, only once by Wittgenstein. That occurs in the celebrated passage toward the end of the *Tractatus*, where he arrives at the "Mystical," which lies beyond the limits of language. "*That* the world is," he tells us, "is the Mystical." (He would have been nearer the mark if he had also italicized the "is," but let us not quarrel with any bone that a modern philosopher throws to us.) And here he passes over into silence: "Of that of which we cannot speak we must remain silent." We have come into the presence of Being, where names and descriptions fail us, for these must always be of specific beings.

But Being, after this momentary contact, seems to drop out of view for Wittgenstein. The single clap of thunder peals and as suddenly rolls away. Or, to paraphrase Robert Frost: "Being took the veil and withdrew." And yet, perhaps not; perhaps it is not so easily dispensed with. And indeed it does not vanish altogether, it only goes underground. It circulates from beginning to end through his later *Philosophical Investigations*, present but not announced—not even by way of a thunderous declaration of silence, as in the earlier work. To be sure, this is another aspect of Being than the cosmic one we express when we say that the world is. It is the aspect of Being Heidegger seeks to bring out in his doctrine of truth as *Aletheia*—Being as the open and illuminated presence within which we are able to speak at all. This presence runs through the whole of the *Investigations*, persistently between the lines, reached for but never explicitly grasped, as if Wittgenstein were perpetually circling around trying to get behind himself to seize his own tail. And only as we ourselves grasp this presence does the book become fully intelligible.

Language is the central datum of philosophy for Wittgenstein. Yet the philosopher does not explicate the nature of language since it itself is the medium in which all explications are carried out. He does, however, let it show itself for what it is insofar as he carries out his task of clarifying other things within language. And right here, at the beginning, one sniffs something peculiar about language; it is not a thing quite like other specific things whose nature we can dissect; and yet it is the medium within which other things are brought into the open and become clear and evident. And right here, too, we have our first hint of the peculiar kinship of language with Being, which itself is never a determinate thing or entity. Does Wittgenstein grasp this peculiar phenomenon of language—its simultaneously hidden and open character—at its full range and depth? That will be our question throughout.

The leap into ordinary language, which is Wittgenstein's step into philosophic maturity, does not come out of any philological passion for the idioms and locutions of our everyday speech. It is in no way an indulgence in a "cult of natural language," as some critics have claimed, though their accusation may not be without its point against some of Wittgenstein's followers. Ordinary language is hardly an immaculate vehicle. For the strict logician it is an untidy mess. For the historical philologist, who stands outside it and dissects it, this ordinary vernacular is like a vast archaeological midden from whose shards and fragments he would construct the whole life of a people. But the philosopher who makes this ordinary language his chosen medium does not stand outside it; he enters into it, not out of any philological curiosity for its odd turns of phrase, but because it marks off the region in which all explication must eventually take place. ("If you can't explain it to me in plain English, I don't believe you understand it yourself!") It is there in the realm of this language that things and our explanations of them either become or fail to become evident and clear. Thus the justification of this primary choice of our medium must be phenomenological: It has to do with the question of evidence. Wittgenstein does not give us this phenomenological justification; it is left implicit in his procedure throughout.

The choice of this philosophical vehicle carries other consequences with it. With Descartes' doctrine of the two worlds, the existence of an external world and of other minds became problems
for philosophers. Wittgenstein's entry into ordinary language is
meant to bypass these problems. They become artificial and vanish.
So far as we use ordinary language (and a language is nothing apart
from its use), anything like a proof of an external world and other
minds becomes as unnecessary as it is also bound to be circular.

At this point the figure of G. E. Moore must enter briefly into
our picture. Moore gives a famous argument for the existence of an
external world; and because his argument is linear and plodding
(unlike the swoops and darts of Wittgenstein's insight), we can
more clearly isolate in him the points we are after. Wittgenstein and
Moore were colleagues at Cambridge, and their joint influence was
such as to shift the direction of British philosophy away from the
dominance of Russell. As a Cartesian, Russell begins from a private
mind, with its private data, from which we have to construct a public world with objects and people in it. Naturally, a proof of an external world was called for under such conditions; and Russell
wavered back and forth on the possibility of giving such a proof.

In March 1912 Russell wrote about the matter to a friend. Since
this was just about the time that Wittgenstein enrolled in Cambridge, we get a vivid impression of the philosophic atmosphere he
encountered there from one part of this letter of Russell:

> In my lecture yesterday I changed my mind in the middle. I had
> gone to prove that there probably is an external world but the ar-
> gument seemed to me fallacious when I began to give it, so I
> proved to the class that there was no reason to think anything
> existed except myself—at least no *good* reason—no such reason as
> would influence a man in investing money, for instance. That was
> very sad, but it doesn't seem to matter much. It made a better lec-
> ture than if it had been more pat.

Here philosophy has become a playful exercise. This is the higher
frivolousness carried out with aristocratic *panache*. *Lord* Russell indeed! Perhaps only a nobleman can play philosophy as a mandarin's
pastime so nonchalantly. Moore and Wittgenstein were to play the
game more seriously and thereby change the rules. In 1939, as if in
reply to Russell, Moore delivered his celebrated lecture "Proof of
an External World" before the British Academy—a public and

worldly occasion, as befitted his theme. These two dates—1912 and 1939—can thus be taken to mark a full-circle turn in the dominant outlook of British philosophy.

Moore's "proof" is curiously circular, though that does not, to my mind, diminish its value. Anyone who has studied mathematics will know that there are no proofs in philosophy anyway. Philosophic arguments are a different kind of thing: They exhibit the ramifications, conditions, and codicils of an insight, and if they change our mind, as they sometimes do, it is because they make us see something in a new light. Moore could just as well have said to the assembled Academy, "Here I am, reading a paper to you, and that is sufficient proof of an external world, and what more could you possibly want anyway?"—and have sat down. In effect, that is just what he does say, though at greater length and with more complexity. "Here is a hand," he says, showing one; "and here is another," showing the other; and thus "there are at least two objects external to our minds, and you know it and I know it." And if there are at least these two, that is enough to establish an external world: one can repeat the argument wherever and whenever one pleases with whatever objects come to hand.

Now, it so happens that Heidegger has a discussion (in his *Being and Time*) of this problem of the external world, and on one point, but one point only, there is an interesting parallel between him and Moore: Both begin by quoting Kant, who had said: "It remains a scandal to philosophy that there is as yet no satisfactory proof of an external world." But immediately the two, Moore and Heidegger, diverge as sharply as possible. Moore proposes his own as a satisfactory proof to remedy this situation. Heidegger, on the other hand, declares that the real scandal is not the absence of such a proof but the fact that philosophers should demand one! Proof or disproof take place within the world. To prove the existence of any object (Moore raising his hand) is to show it as a thing within the world. You do not arrive at the fact of a world additively by way of piling up object after object into an aggregate—"Here is a hand, here is another one, etc." Each object in turn is exhibited only as an item within the world; and we have already to be in the world to make the addition. Our Being-in-the-world is a unitary phenomenon and not the total of separate components. Moore's approach is naïvely reductive; as a realist, he has an ontology only of things— there are hands, tables, chairs, teacups, and saucers, and so on and

on. But what of the *copresence* of himself as speaker and his audi-
tors around which his entire argument turns ("Here is a hand, and I
know it and you know it"), but which is not a thing like a hand at
all?

And what of language itself as the witness of this copresence?
Imagine someone who might look in at the window at the moment
Moore is raising his hand but who does not hear what is being said.
Moore could make his gestures very emphatic at times. "The professor is threatening his audience," might be the thought that passes
through that observer's mind. In the absence of language the behavior loses its meaning. Moore shows his hand physically, but his language makes clear what the *presence* of the hand means on that particular occasion. Nor would his words carry the meaning they do if
the particular historical context from Descartes to Kant and onward
were not present through them. This historical presence is also part
of our world; but it is not a thing like a hand.

In the last fragments he has left us Wittgenstein was wrestling
with this question, and he was not satisfied with Moore's answer.
The belief in an external world, he feels, is not like the belief in a
particular matter of fact within the framework of experience; it is a
part of the framework itself, without which our particular "form of
life" would not be what it is. Here Wittgenstein is edging toward
Heidegger's Being-in-the-world, but Wittgenstein is still too
chained—like all analytic philosophers—to an ontology of things.

II.

Wittgenstein's shift from a formal calculus to ordinary language
means a shift in the typical kind of situation in which one envisages
language at work. As a formal calculus, a language may be taken as
marks on paper that we manipulate according to certain rules. The
typical situation, however, in which ordinary language is alive and
at work is a human conversation. The whole of the *Philosophic Investigations* is a series of conversations, or, perhaps more accurately,
a single conversation interrupted and resumed and ramifying off
into various correlated subjects. The main speaker is Wittgenstein;
but the voice of the respondent is continuously present as Wittgenstein puts his questions, answers them, or devises questions that
should be asked by the respondent. Not enough has been made of
this conversational presence. If language is, as Wittgenstein tells us,

a form of life, then this conversational form is of the essence, and if we miss its presence we miss something essential. Philosophers ask, "What ontological commitments are involved in the use of ordinary language?" We should put the question more concretely: What understanding of Being must be present in order to carry on a conversation?

A talks to B. Nothing seems more transparent and simple to our ordinary understanding, and yet some philosophical theories make this situation almost impossible to grasp. For traditional dualism, for example, there is A's mind and A's body, and B's mind and B's body; and communication between A and B takes place as follows: A's body receives physical signals from the direction of B's body, and these signals are somehow transformed in A's mind into thoughts; he has consequently thoughts of his own that initiate bodily movements that B's bodily receptors will pick up; and the same process goes on from B's body to B's mind; and so back and forth. This is hardly a picture of a conversation. It might do perhaps as a picture of intergalactic communication where we receive physical signals from some source in outer space, then infer the minds and meanings of the transmitters, and send out our own signals in turn. The partners in an ordinary conversation may at times be quite cool to each other, but never that remote.

Does behaviorism do any better? Here the two minds go by the board; there is only A's body and its overt behavior (including the activity of his speech), and conversely B's body and its behavior. But the behaviorist cannot escape adding just this much of mind: There is A observing B's behavior, and similarly B observing A's. This is not so much a conversation as an experiment in behavioral psychology in which the experimental subject and the experimenter are constantly shifting roles.

This situation gets more complicated if we try to get a real conversation going. There is not only A observing B's behavior, but also observing B observing his. And the same for B. We begin to get all the fiendish complications of possible "bad faith" Sartre describes with a very different vocabulary: A conversation becomes an endless dialectical interplay between the observer who is observing the observed; and the other, who, in being observed, is also observing his observer. And both A and B are playing these roles simultaneously! This might describe a parley between a Soviet and an American diplomat under détente, each walking warily around the other, but it is hardly a picture of an ordinary conversation.

What we understand by a conversation is the situation in which two people are genuinely interested in a topic, become absorbed in exploring it, and are held together in the unity of their talk. The conversation, in short, is *between* A and B and *within* language. Notice we emphasize the prepositions here. If we are to take language seriously, we have to give the prepositions their due, for they are in fact indispensable. Without them we cannot assemble the isolated ingredients of minds and bodies into a conversation. That is why neither dualism nor behaviorism really permit us to talk as we do in life. A conversation does not take place inside each other's heads alternately, nor at the surfaces of our bodies in their overt behavior; it is really in the region between the speakers that the conversation takes place.

But someone might object that we are taking these prepositions too seriously. To be sure, a conversation does take place in language, but this "in" here is merely a metaphor. But are we so sure what is and what is not metaphorical in ordinary language? Is it incorrect to use the word "in" except when we want to denote the existence of a table in a room or an object in a box? Consider the question often asked: Do we think in language? Wittgenstein certainly must hold this, for everything in his text points that way. We do not grope for thoughts outside language and then, having fully formed them, seek to put them into language. That would be as ridiculous as saying that the composer fashions his musical idea and then puts it into notes. Our groping in thought is a groping within language for the particular language we shall want to use for our purpose.

But what peculiar kind of thing, then, is language that not only do we think in it but also that within it we may share the same thought with another?

III.

Consider it first in the category of a tool or instrument.

"Think of the tools in a tool box; there is a hammer, pliers, a saw, a screwdriver, a rule, a glue pot, glue, nails, and screws." Wittgenstein invites us thus to think of the words in language in their full and concrete materiality. He wants to call us away from the temptations of the Cartesian mind and its subjective ideas, on the one hand and of the Platonist with his subsistent universals on the other —the philosophy Russell was teaching when Wittgenstein first became his student. Well and good. But if we are to take words as tools, what then is the *being* of a tool? A tool points beyond itself, to the situations of its use, to interplay with other tools, to a world in which it enters and has its place. Tools are what we build with them. Give a box of tools to a man who cannot use his hands and it will end up in the attic or cellar as a mere heap of material objects. Give it to a carpenter and it opens up a whole world of possibilities to him.

Language opens into the world more abruptly and extensively than any set of tools. A tool has a certain opacity; any word in language is immediately transparent to the world beyond it. And its meanings always open beyond the narrow zone of their immediate application. This openness holds even for rather limited languages. Consider the game of chess and the notation we have for it. The notation is a language that enables us to describe a game. But here is another description of a chess game, from Vladimir Nabokov's novel *The Defense:*

> Luzhin settled down to play with particular care. At first it went softly, softly, like muted violins. The players occupied their positions cautiously, moving this and that up but doing it politely, without the slightest sign of a threat—and if there was any threat it was entirely conventional—more like a hint to his opponent that over there he would do well to build a cover, and the opponent would smile, as if all this were an insignificant joke. . . .
> Then, without the least warning, a chord sang out tenderly. This was one of Turati's forces occupying a diagonal line. But forthwith a trace of melody very softly manifested itself on Luzhin's side also. . . ."

It would be a mistake to take these words as merely peripheral and "poetical." The player himself, presented with Nabokov's description, might very well observe, "Yes, that's just how the game went." The chess notation and its literary description describe the same game, and you cannot bifurcate one from the other. Freud speaks of certain symbols in the psychic life as "overdetermined": They have several different meanings at once, and these meanings are to be taken together. Analogously, language always carries the density of its multiple references. The trained musician reading a score sees certain marks and hears a chord sing out tenderly. So the chess-player sees the notation R–R5 and winces at the sudden threat this move may pose. Neither the chess notation nor the literary description is *the* expression of the game; both translate back and forth into each other because both express the same game.

My point here is that language not only opens into an interconnected world, but back and forth from one possible region to another within that world. Metaphor, Robert Frost reminds us, is taking one thing for another. In this sense, all language is metaphorical, for it insistently connects one thing with another. A word, any word, perpetually sends out tentacles of connectedness everywhere. (Who would have thought that the simple article "the," seemingly the plainest and most self-effacing maidservant in the English language, could ever acquire the overtones it does as the last word of James Joyce's *Finnegans Wake*, as the final expiring sigh of this vast symphony of language?) Rudimentary languages thus turn out to be more difficult to construct than one thinks. Put them in use and they will not stay rudimentary long. Confine people to the eight hundred words or so of basic English, and it will not be long before the vocabulary begins to expand with inflections, compounds, and intonations.

Wittgenstein gives as an example of a rudimentary language one in which a foreman shouts "Slab!" and the workman brings him a building slab. But is this situation so rudimentary? Are the involvements within that world, of man with man, of man with things, of man with words, so elementary that the meaning of this command will not extend beyond the fetching of a block of stone? Is the workman merely a robot responding to a signal? From day to day the voice of the foreman may sound differently to his ears. The workman does not hear a sound but a voice; and in that voice the zone of authority that surrounds it. And over against that zone, there gradually begins to be defined another region of being that is occupied by himself and his fellows. Is that workman unionized? Someday he may hear in the shout "Slab!" not just an actual sound but also a possibility, a call to define himself and his fellows in some association.

So far I have been indicating the ways in which language opens out into the world; now I should like to turn about and indicate the way in which the situation where we use language gets closed off. We shall arrive at the same result in either case: namely, that language and our Being-in-the-world go hand in hand, that neither is explicable without the other.

One cardinal point in Wittgenstein's treatment of language is the identification, or at least close linking, of meaning with use. If you want to know the meaning of a word, he tells us, look to its use. Well, I want to know the meaning of a word, and I find out its uses from the dictionary. But I must understand these uses if they are to help me—that is, I must understand what they *mean*. Of course, I may be able to explain that meaning in turn by usage; and so we go on, our context ever widening. Where do we stop? "Explanation must stop somewhere," Wittgenstein remarks; and his statement here, at once platitudinous and profound, gives us the key to the matter if we but follow its lead. Where explanation stops may be an entirely practical matter—we have had enough of our conversation, or the subject is clear enough for the time being, or we have exhausted our powers of analysis. But wherever we stop, however far we go in explicating the meanings we use, we end within a context of meanings. We end, that is, in a world where some things are evident and some things hidden; some things in the light, others in the half light, some in the dark (the situation of truth, or *Aletheia*, which we tried to sketch in our last chapter). But that is also the world from which language starts in the first place. However far we travel during the day, and however much the landscape and its lights shift, we are still ringed at eventide by the horizon. Language speaks always within this finitude of the human condition; but it is able to speak at all only through the largesse of gifts that our Being-in-the-world provides. For example:

At the end of the Second World War, I was thrown into the company of a young Yugoslav soldier who had fought against the Germans until their surrender and was now in flight from Tito. We had no language in common, and yet it was necessary to communicate—more necessary for him, since he was running for his life and looked for my help. We would have to invent a language between us. It crossed my mind even then, and much more so later, on reflection, that we were faced with the problem for an answer to which, according to the philologist Jespersen, the learned academies of the eighteenth century used to give prizes: *How did man in his primitive condition come to invent language in the first place?*

Well, this Yugoslav and I somehow managed; it turned out after all that we had a world of language between us. And I imagine this might have been what happened among those primitives who first came together to talk, and out of their grunts and squeals began to fashion the nuances of vowels, consonants, and diphthongs. They could begin to make talk because they were already within language. Meanings are first and foremost not in the mind but in the world, in the linkings and interconnections of things we find there.

From time to time I wonder what became of that Yugoslav. Two days later I had sent him on his way to one of the Allied camps for refugees that were then forming (and where they were likely to have interpreters with whom he would be able to speak in less primordial fashion than with me). He was a lively and clever youth, and I like to think he made out in the end. *"Wir sind ein Gespräch"* (We are a conversation) declares the poet Hölderlin; and Heidegger quotes this as one of his principal keys to the nature of language and human existence. Well, we were only a conversation, that Yugoslav partisan and myself; but such as it was, such as we were, it stands out as one of my most human memories against the confusion of that war.

IV.

I hope that the peculiar kinship between language and Being begins to emerge from the hints I have given so far, but it might help now if we concluded by bringing these together into a more systematic unity. And it might help above all if we brought our discussion down from the abstract to the concrete; if instead of talking about language in general we came down to the specific and asked about a particular language—this English language that we all share. This is a language that linguistic philosophers do not really discuss. The "ordinary language" they talk about always strikes me as something remote, a peculiar abstraction that has not taken on actual flesh and bones. The English language, on the other hand, is a definite historical entity whose destiny is part and parcel of my actual life.

What is the English language? The question might seem pointless —just the silly kind of thing a philosopher would ask—since we all know very well what this language is in which we talk with one another and struggle to think. But we might remember here the case of St. Augustine on the question of time. "What is time?" Augustine asks; and he answers that if you do not ask him, he knows; but as soon as you ask him, he does not know. And if we put the same question about the English language to ourselves, we shall not find it pointless. We may find out, like Augustine on the subject of time, that the answer is far more difficult than we had imagined. None of the current "linguistic" philosophies succeed in answering this question. How can they, since they have never put it to themselves? They do not even have the categories that might point us in the direction where we might seek an answer.

To anticipate the general form of the difficulty here, we note that there seem to be two fundamental kinds of entities available for explaining what the English language is. On the one hand, there are the physical things that seem to constitute language: sounds spoken and phonetic marks on paper to indicate those sounds. On the other, there are the thoughts that people have in connection with those physical marks and sounds. Physical things and mental ideas—we seem caught perpetually in this dualistic schema. But language seems to elude us under either category. It lives its life between these opposed poles of subject and object, it is in fact the medium between them. And our difficulty in grasping it is exactly of the same order as our difficulty in grasping Being, which, like language, eludes and embraces both these categories at once.

Following Wittgenstein and some other analytic philosophers, let us avoid mental entities if we can, lest we appear to be resurrecting the Cartesian ghost in the machine. Besides, as we have already noted, if language is something mental in A's mind, and similarly in B's, we would have difficulty getting them together in a conversation. Well then, we seek to construe the English language in terms of things. Is it, to try to speak purely objectively, the aggregate of all sounds being made by English-speaking persons all over the world at this particular moment of history? As an aggregate or set, this one can hardly be constructed in any clear or intelligible way; in its sheer unwieldiness it boggles the mind. Clearly, nothing like this is ever effectively present to anyone who is trying to speak or write English.

The English language is historical. Like all things human, it runs its course in time, changes, and evolves. At a certain approximate point backward, we mark off its course and say Middle English; at a certain point forward someday perhaps it will have changed into what George Orwell called Newspeak. Meanwhile, in that long interregnum people have spoken, written, and tried to think in English. If we are to think of this language in purely physical terms, then it would be the aggregate of all the sounds, and the accompanying phonetic marks on paper, made by all those speakers of English over the centuries. Our original unwieldy aggregate becomes even more amorphous and impossible to consider seriously as the English we use.

But someone—a behaviorist, perhaps—might object that we are making the matter too complicated. Could we not regard our English as a selective class out of that immense aggregate? What we call correct or proper English has been set down in certain books, has been transmitted through the physical agency of teachers, and has left its deposit on my organism in the form of certain norms or inhibitions of my verbal behavior. This description may look at first glance like a strictly physical interpretation of the language I use, but in fact is far from it. At innumerable points in this long chain of causation that has conditioned me, there have been numerous conscious acts of creation, selection, and elimination at work.[1] Nevertheless, let us take the foregoing for as near a physical interpretation of our language as we can get. Our objection to it is as follows:

Like so many of the behavioristic accounts, which look hardheaded and factual at first glance, it proves remote and schematic when brought face-to-face with the concrete phenomenon it is supposed to depict. The question is how I experience the English language as something present and operative upon me. What is my living relationship to this language? A good part of me may be responding like a robot to the norms of speaking and writing that have been drilled into me. But I am also drawn forward by this language, I feel the pull of its possible resources upon me as I struggle from one sentence to the next. The actuality of this language is the presence of its possibilities of expression. Somewhere this English language may grant me, as I fumble forward, the grace of coming up with an illuminating sentence. Here in language we find that peculiar interlinking of the actual and possible that is the mark of human being as distinct from the being of things.

And indeed this point was already implicit in our previous example from chess. For the chess master the game is neither the physical

---

[1] A philosopher like Hegel would say that the English language is a concrete historical form of the spiritual life of a part of mankind; and he would be more nearly right; but we have agreed to rule out any reference to mind or spirit.

pieces nor the rules for manipulating them, but the possibilities of play that these open before him. The move of a piece on the board is not merely the translation of a physical body from place to place, but the sudden emergence—and that is what Nabokov's description catches—of a whole web of possibilities either immediately threatening or remotely looming. But the world of the English language is infinitely wider and infinitely closer to me than chess. I wake each day into the words that are waiting for me. I exist, I am what I am, within the world that language lays open to me. My language is a region of Being I inhabit. And here the comparison of language to a tool falls short. *I do not use English in the way I use a typewriter.* With this simple sentence the whole elaborate model of language as an instrument, and nothing but an instrument, crashes to the ground. Familiar as my typewriter may be, intimately as I may know the touch and feel of its keys, it still stands external to my life in a way that the English language does not. I shall soon replace this typewriter—its keys have begun to stick—and it will be forgotten. My last expiring thoughts, assuming I am still conscious, will be in English.

The presence of this English language is resonant with its past. The poet most of all makes us know this. Through his voice the language comes alive again as the language of a Shakespeare or a Wordsworth even while he is opening our ears to hear new things. In poetry the copresence of past, present, and future, unique to our human existence, comes overwhelmingly to the fore. And do not set this fact aside into some finical realm of the "poetical," especially if you call yourself a philosopher of ordinary language. For poetry is in fact ordinary language come fully alive; it is our common language when, to adapt a phrase of Wittgenstein's in another context, it is least idling.

And indeed this connection of language with time is a strict and literal consequence of Wittgenstein's nominalism, though I think the point has scarcely been noticed. The nominalist holds that the only things that exist are individuals; there are no Platonic universals to supply the connective thread of our discourse; and consequently if our speech is not to fall apart into disconnected and meaningless babble, then human memory must shoulder the burden. It is not usually emphasized, as I believe it should be, what a central role memory must always play for the nominalist, and Wittgenstein himself brings it out only in a very fleeting passage. He is arguing

with the Platonist who believes that meanings have a being independent of individual things or individual minds. The Platonist says:

> Something red can be destroyed, but red cannot be destroyed,
> and that is why the meaning of the word "red" is independent of
> the existence of a red thing.

And Wittgenstein responds:

> Don't clutch at the idea of our always being able to bring red be-
> fore our mind's eye even when there is nothing red any-
> more. . . . For suppose you cannot remember the color anymore.
>
> [I, 57]

Suppose there are no red things to look at, and you have forgotten
what red looks like; then the word "red" would have ceased to have
any meaning. (And, analogously, to revert to the topic of a previous chapter: If the human race were to forget how to count, those
sacred Platonic entities, the numbers, would cease to be.) Memory
is an essential condition that there be any meanings at all. *Every
word in our language is memory at work for us.*

Now put this point beside what Wittgenstein has to say about
memory (II, xiii). To remember is not to experience a subjective
mental state, a memory content, from which the past is inferred.
(*Erinnern hat keimen Erlebnisinhalt.*) A statement about yesterday
is a statement about yesterday, not about my mental content today.
The past, as direct referent, is preserved in my present language.
Language makes possible this copresence of past and present.

And what of the third of the three tenses, the future? In line with
Wittgenstein's generally pragmatic emphasis, language is to be
regarded as an activity, a "form of life," and therefore essentially
open-ended toward the future.

Language, then—to put all three together—is memory cutting a
path through the present toward the future, but in such a way that
it gathers the three together into itself.

But what kind of a being is it that can embrace time in this fashion? This is the kind of question that Wittgenstein does not ask, and
for an answer to which we have to turn to a philosopher like
Heidegger. Accordingly, what we have been trying to suggest

about the likeness of Being and language can be summed up in three points of the latter's doctrine:

1. The unique and radical character of human existence, according to Heidegger, is its temporality. This is not because our days, and we ourselves, pass away in time—so do the animals. This uniqueness has to do with the way in which man *ek-sists*, stands out within time and in relation to time. Man, it is commonly said, is the time-binding animal. But we can only join the parts of time—past, present, and future—because we stand out within a region of being that already embraces their disjunction. I can bind the rose branch to the trellis because both come within my grasp. It might be said that we have language only through this unique temporality of our existence. But it could be said just as well that it is because we are held within language that time can come to be as it is for us. Language and human being are thus coordinate.

2. This unique temporal character of ours makes us shift our thinking with regard to the traditional terms of actuality and possibility. The possible is not merely some isolated event lurking for us in the future and therefore external to our existence now. Possibility penetrates the actual and makes it what it is: We are what we are through the horizons that lie open to us. So too, the actuality of our language is given as the possibilities of expression it opens to us.

3. Both the above points involve us in thinking against our usual habits, which revolve willy-nilly around the dichotomy of things and thoughts. But that is just our usual difficulty in thinking of Being, which is neither a concrete thing, on the one hand, nor on the other a concept in the mind. It is the third that lies between and beyond them. Wittgenstein's emphasis is to get us away from the subjective and mentalistic, but he has no philosophical apparatus—no ontology—that allows him to grasp this dimension, which is neither thing nor mental entity, and within which our language circulates and lives. Yet Wittgenstein is plunged into that medium from the moment he ceases to be the technician of logic and turns to embrace the common language; for this latter language, as a "concrete form of life," lives and moves within the open region between subject and subject, subject and object, thing and idea. And it is there too that Wittgenstein's own exposition takes place, not inside his own or his hearers' heads. He has to bring out into the open, to show what he means by the unflagging ingenuity of ex-

amples, counterexamples, paradigms. To borrow Heidegger's term, the *Investigations* is a marvelous dance in the open clearing of *Aletheia*.

All that we have said will probably have little "cash value" for the technician of language. He looks through Being—it is so transparent —and does not see it; it is of no use to him, and so he ignores it. In the end, however, Being is what technical man cannot conquer, though our civilization may have to learn this at last only through catastrophe. But perhaps in this very uselessness lies the real "cash value" of the Idea of Being: In disclosing to us what is absolutely other than technical man and his interests, it points the way from which we may be able to comprehend the nature of technology as a whole. To which effort we now turn in our next chapter.

Chapter 10

———◆———

Technology as Human Destiny

THE IDEA OF WORLD HISTORY WAS BORN OF THE EUROPEAN MIND AT
a time when Europe itself was spreading its power to the four quarters of the globe. We, who are so used to it, forget how novel this
idea was and how late in its appearance. The voyages of the
fifteenth century, and the continued explorations and settlements
that followed, opened the whole world to European civilization.
Hitherto history had been local or tribal, limited to particular peoples or empires. By the eighteenth century the age of the enlightenment could envisage all humanity as the subject of one history
and the whole earth as the theater of a single drama.

It was only natural then that Europe, at this moment of expansive
power and in the self-assurance of its mission, should create the idea
of universal history after its own image and see itself as the center
of the historical process, natural too that it should read the meaning
of this history in the terms on which it prided its own civilization.

This exuberant and positive mood of the Enlightenment over-
flowed into the beginning of the nineteenth century. The younger
Hegel may be taken as an exemplary spokesman; he was the first
major philosopher to take world history as his explicit theme, and
he wrote out of a very vigorous sense that modernity was a great
step beyond the past. The modern age, as he saw it, was the flow-
ering of enlightenment out of the narrow other-worldliness of the
Middle Ages. Three great events had combined to usher in this
period—the Renaissance, the Reformation, and the development

of science. Each of these represented a broadening and liberalization
of the mind. This new era of mankind, then, seemed everywhere
destined for the confident expansion of human liberty and the
heightening of human self-consciousness. It is only natural thus that
Hegel should take these two as the themes and indeed the very
meaning of history itself.

But at this moment, when Europe was dispersing its power
throughout the world, it was also, unknown to itself, in the process
of self-dispersal and self-disintegration. Today Europe no longer
stands at the center of world power. It cannot so confidently
prescribe its own forms as a standard for history. Indeed, it has lost
sight of its own center and is unsure what these central forms may
be. Our task of finding a unity in history becomes more difficult
and tormented than it was for Hegel, for whom the figure in the
carpet was so patently there in the contemporary reflection of his
own ideals.

The Protestant Reformation, for example, can hardly be taken as
a central event in history by the Chinese. Europe has long since
ceased to be Christendom. It cannot hope to convert Asia and
Africa; indeed, it seems both unable and unwilling to reconvert itself to its own original Christian faith. From the point of view of a
post-Christian civilization, the Protestant Reformation would seem
then to be central to European history only as an event that marks
the beginning of the waning domination of Christian faith on the
lives of the Western nations; and for world history, memorable
therefore as one more step in the secularization of nature preparing
the way for our technical domination of the planet.

The glories of Renaissance art are still there for our enchantment.
But this art no longer provides the standard for judgment of all the
world's art. It is no longer even the strict canon within which our
contemporary Western artists operate. Ours is the period in which
the arts of all humankind, Western and Eastern, primitive and
civilized, have become accessible to and carry equal validity for
modern viewers. As far as contemporary artists themselves are concerned, the forms of the arts are in something of a crisis. Art, it is
said (and with considerable plausibility), has become peripheral in
modern life; and the future of art has consequently become problematic. The ideal of humanism that inspired the art of the Renaissance is something we can no longer aspire to and do not dare to

imagine for ourselves. For one breathtaking and luminous moment the Florentine humanists caught a vision of ideal humanity—of human nature redeemed and intact, radiant, strong, and yet tender—but the vision turned out only a passing dream of the European mind. Renaissance man would be a misfit in our specialized and fragmented society where, as Heidegger remarks, the man who does not wear the uniform of a particular calling looks out of place.

In either case, as against Reformation and Renaissance, the quieter emergence of modern science and technology now appears as the much more decisive event for world history. Science reaches into every area of our contemporary existence. Technology spans oceans and unites continents. Not only does it conquer space, but it also leaps over time to join the diverse strata of human evolution together. The vanishing remnants of Stone Age man in New Guinea look up and see airplanes and come to accept them as part of life; the Moslem *fellahidin* learn to cope with oil rigs and modern weapons; Micronesian tribes are moved from their island paradise to make way for an atomic explosion. Technology thus creates one world out of our planet for the first time since humans appeared upon it. In so doing, it transforms world history itself from an abstract and daring idea in the minds of philosophers and historians two centuries ago into an actual and pressing reality, full of promise but also freighted with catastrophic possibilities.

Consequently, we are led to look for a different key to our history from the one given us by earlier philosophers like Hegel. The fact of science-technology, in its sheer bulk and massiveness, thrusts itself in front of the more ideal concepts of liberal institutions and humanistic culture that engaged the attention of the Enlightenment. If we look at the Communist states, they do not confirm Hegel's idea that the direction of history is toward greater freedom. In the Western democracies, liberty has been extended in the direction of equality in ways that Hegel did not envisage and would not have approved. But if we note the popular culture of these societies, which constantly spreads and imposes its standards everywhere, we can hardly think that history moves toward heightened and deepened self-conciousness when we consider the passivity, pathos, and superficial knowledgeability of the mass mind. Technology and science, meanwhile, continue their march unabated. If we seek the central theme of our history, perhaps we should look there.

To begin with. What is this strange phenomenon we call modern science?

I.

Modern science has been on the scene now for three centuries, yet perhaps we still do not fully grasp its nature. This science is built upon the foundations of Greek science; that much we know and are sure of. Without Euclid, Archimedes, and Pappus, Newton would have been impossible. Yet our science is somehow different from that of the Greeks. Otherwise why do we so persistently call it "modern" science? Then too, we are more likely to couple it with technology, often in the hyphenated form "science-technology," as if we were referring to a unitary phenomenon. What is the force of this hyphen here? Is it only an accidental coupling, or does it signify some more essential bond between the two terms it unites?

A brilliant treatment of the subject has been given us by Whitehead in his *Science and the Modern World*, one of the assured philosophic classics of our century, a work of genius, copiously and delightfully so, abundant with darting and graceful insights, stimulating in the sweep and comprehensiveness of its theoretical scheme. Yet it does not altogether settle our questions. A comparison between Whitehead and Heidegger is illuminating on this question of modern science.

Whitehead begins by upsetting one of the clichés of conventional history. As schoolchildren, we are taught that the modern period began when men turned from the faith of the Middle Ages to a reliance on reason. The facts of the matter, so far as they concern the origin of science, are altogether different. The Middle Ages, in its theoretical life, was characterized by a sweeping and "unbridled rationalism." The modern period begins as a revolt against such rationalism, and turns instead to the "irreducible and stubborn facts" of experience. It is this thirst, according to Whitehead, for the irreducible and stubborn facts that sets the new science moving on its path.

There is a considerable grain of truth here, but not the whole truth. Consider the theories of Copernicus and Kepler, for example. They are as revolutionary as any theories can be, for they change the whole picture of the universe in which men live. The earth is no longer the center of the cosmos, and the heavenly bodies do not

move in the patterns that our immediate perception discloses. If you
are a persistent stargazer, reader, you will know that natural and
congenial sense of the heavenly bodies—sun, moon, stars, and
planets—wheeling in their circle around you as center. Walking in
the summer night, you become accustomed to that movement almost as an extension of the axes of your own body, as it takes its
direction from them. Greek science maintained this immediate
bond between ourselves and nature. The motto of this science—
Sozein ta Phainomena (To preserve things as they show themselves to be)—meant that the Greek scientist would preserve this
congruence between natural objects and our direct perception
of them.

What, then, do Copernicus and Kepler do? They do not alter
things by turning to stubborn and irreducible facts that had not
been known before. Instead, they construct intellectual models that
are contrary to the facts as these disclose themselves in immediate
experience. The phenomenological congruence between ourselves
and the things of nature is broken. These theories wrench men
away from the world in its apparent and simple immediacy.

The example of Galileo is both more simple and more striking.
The chief theoretical part of the new science was to be mechanics—
indeed, it was to continue as the central part of physics until the
end of the nineteenth century—and to establish mechanics mathe-
matically, it was necessary to have a decisive and clear-cut concept
of inertia as a fundamental characteristic of moving bodies. What
does Galileo do? He does not turn to the "irreducible and stubborn" facts; rather, he sets up a concept that could never be realized
in actual fact. Imagine, he says, a perfectly smooth and frictionless
plane; set a ball rolling upon this plane, and it will roll on to infinity
unless another body and force interpose to stop it. Well, experience
never presents us with perfectly frictionless surfaces nor with planes
infinite in extension. No matter; these conditions supply us with a
concept of inertia more fruitful for theory than any that would be
yielded by the "irreducible and stubborn" facts themselves.

Rationalism does not surrender itself here to the brute facts.
Rather, it sets itself over the facts in their haphazard sequence; it
takes the audacious step of positing conditions contrary to fact, and
it proceeds to measure the facts in the light of these contrafactual
conditions. Reason becomes "legislative of experience"—this was
the decisive point that Kant's genius perceived as the real revolution

of the new science and that he, consequently, proclaimed should become the revolution within future philosophy. Francis Bacon had already declared that the advancement of knowledge required us to cease following nature passively, and instead "put her to the rack to compel her to answer our questions." Bacon was a public-relations man for the new movement; but he had genius, and here made a lucky hit. Kant, however, comes after the fact; he has more than a century of the new science to reflect upon, and he is the first philosopher to understand what has happened. The whole of his *Critique of Pure Reason* is not primarily an attempt to set up a system of idealistic philosophy; it is the effort, stubborn and profound, to grasp the meaning of the new science and its consequences for human understanding generally. So read, it does not become merely a topical book, but rather gains even greater depth and significance.

What has emerged here—in the thinking of Copernicus, Kepler, and Galileo—are not merely some novel ideas, albeit brilliant, in the long succession that scholars call the history of ideas. What has happened is nothing less than the transformation of human reason itself, an event that consequently transforms all subsequent history. Reason takes up a new stand and posits new goals for itself in the face of all that is. The change reaches into every cranny of human existence. Religion, art, and culture acquire a different meaning and value in the epoch that follows. Even the political ideologies that hold sway in the modern world are different from those of antiquity, because they envisage man as the active master of nature who sets out to transform the whole of his social existence. The essential link between science and technology in modern times, which is left unexplained in an interpretation like Whitehead's, now becomes evident. The hyphen in the phrase "science-technology" indicates an essential bond. Technology embodies physically what science has already done in thought when science sets up its own conditions as a measure of nature. The new science is in its essence technological.

II.

The changes brought in by the revolution in science are so total that they cannot be described as a transformation of human reason alone. Reason is not an isolated faculty, but one mode in which man stands open to the things in his world. The transformation in reason, the change in its scope and powers, is nothing less than a change in the being of man himself. Henceforth he stands very differently within Being, and in a different relation to the beings that encompass him. The authentic history of our epoch has to be grasped at the level of Being rather than ideas.

Here Heidegger enters with his own particular philosophy of history, the only contemporary venture in this field that for its radical originality and scope can be set beside the philosophies of Hegel and Marx. *Prima facie,* Heidegger's would seem to have certain initial advantages over these older views. It is simpler and more comprehensive. It is phenomenologically more evident: It seeks to let the historical phenomena show themselves as they are without constructing any speculative hypothesis either that mind is more basic than matter (Hegel) or matter than mind (Marx). And it is much more in agreement, as we have seen, with the technical-scientific march of history since the deaths of those thinkers. It catches thus the fundamental character of technical civilization as it comes to dominate the life of modern societies, whether these call themselves socialist or capitalist.

Yet despite these recommendations, Heidegger's view of history is not likely to capture the imagination of the general public. It goes too much against the grain of our inveterate anthropocentric prejudices. It inverts the usual order of our thinking by displacing man from the center of the stage and putting Being there. We have to shift our sights to follow him here.

Yet his attempt is as simple as it is audacious. Being is the protagonist in the historical drama. Of course, Being is not an individual being, and cannot be an agent in any physical or human sense. Being never does or suffers anything. Being simply *is*. What else do you expect Being to do? Heidegger remarks in one fretful moment. Yet as its light waxes or wanes, it energizes the actions of men and marks out the lines along which the destiny of the particular epoch is played out, and so is more active than any mortal agent ever could be. It is a strange protagonist, to be sure, for almost always it wears disguises. It does not appear as itself but in the semblance of something else. For most men, it has long since vanished into the disguise. Yet, though hidden, it is all the while the presence that enables them to see the disguise in the first place. And only in this light do we as the human chorus sit down at the end of drama and seek to gather some wisdom from the epoch that has faded.

All this, of course, sounds like mere myth and metaphor. And indeed it is metaphorical, but only because the shorthand for any comprehensive idea is always metaphorical. Hegel sounded equally mythical when he first gave his ideas to the world. The Hegelian view, when compressed into the formula that history is the journey and struggle of the Idea through time, may seem fantastic and metaphorical when we first encounter it. The practice of subsequent historians has given substance to the metaphor by unraveling its compactness. A great many historians, whether they were aware of it or not, have written their histories in the shadow of Hegel and in corroboration of his thesis. The historical reality cannot be presented as this and that individual thinker, separate and discrete, harboring his private thoughts and then adding them like isolated grains to a sandhill. Rather, an idea takes over a whole period, holds men in its grip, serves and is served by them, as it runs its fateful course for good or evil. We have come to be at ease with this Hegelian way of seeing things. The history of ideas is now a respected field of historical research, and when we engage in it, we are surprised to find that ideas do have a quite dramatic life of their own. We no longer shudder at the supposed violence of metaphor in saying that an idea may have a historical career and destiny.

But if Hegel no longer sounds fantastic to us, if we take the history of ideas as genuine history, then we have only to take a short further step to arrive at Heidegger. We have simply to push a simple and radical question: What is an idea, after all, when we subject it to phenomenological scrutiny? What is it but the way in which a world is illumined for men and their projects? The particular way or ways in which Being emerges, takes hold of us, and claims us in its service? The history of ideas has to be understood in the end as a history of Being. Heidegger begins then to sound a bit more plausible.

In any case, the test of a general idea is the illumination it throws on the actual facts. Accordingly, we proceed now to sketch a "scenario"—if we may borrow this now popular word from the sociologists and futurologists—of Western history, as seen by Heideggerian eyes. We began this chapter from the fact of the scientific-technical revolution of the seventeenth century as the dominant fact for the modern world. We have now, in our little scenario, to take a step backward. To grasp the advent of technical civilization we have to situate the emergence of the new science within the larger

background of Western history. We have to begin at the beginnings of thought among the early Greeks. If our view seems thus
restricted to the West, and therefore somewhat parochial in nature,
we have to remember that it is this technical civilization of the
West that has now become dominant and drags the rest of the
world in its wake.

III.

The scenario is very simple in outline. One could imagine it indeed
as a program for presentation on television. The preliminary cam-
erawork immediately suggests itself. The opening shot is of dawn,
somewhere in the Greek world, perhaps Elea, the birthplace of Parmenides. The particular place does not matter; the camera must
concentrate upon the dawn itself and its light, the details of human
habitation or natural landscape relatively faint. The light itself is
here the camera's subject. Hold; the light gathering and growing.
Fade suddenly into the blinding flash and the puffball of smoke of
an atomic explosion. The screen goes dark. Hold. Then the narrator's voice begins.

Too pat, you say. Too melodramatically simple to be the unifying thread of human history? The reasoning behind these images,
however, is clear-cut. Without science there would be no atomic
bombs. But science itself developed out of philosophy. (Until the
close of the nineteenth century physics and chemistry were commonly referred to still as "natural philosophy.") Hence, if there
had not been those early Greek thinkers who created philosophy,
there would be no atomic bombs. No doubt, between the initial and
terminal point of this line there are great gaps—the turmoil, up-
heaval, and convulsions of mankind; ages of darkness and ages of
renewed creation—but nevertheless, without that beginning there
would not have been this culmination.

No such eruption of thought occurred in the ancient Orient.
China is the particular case in point that philosophers of history
need to reflect upon. The Chinese were a highly intelligent and
clever people. There is no indication that in intellectual capacity
they were in any way below the level of the Greeks. The Chinese
civilization was extraordinarily stable, and their population was
numerous. Considering the number of educated persons involved in
civilized pursuits, and the long stretch of time over which they

were so engaged, the "volume of civilization"—Whitehead's phrase
—was greater in China than anywhere else. Yet China did not produce science nor even the beginnings of science. Nor is there any
indication that left on its own, even as it came into the twentieth
century, it ever would. Indeed, the exquisite and balanced patterns
of this civilization set their bulwarks against that reckless adventure
of the mind that Westerners have come to call reason.

Why did this eruption of thought take place among the ancient
Greeks? Why did it take place at all? We are so ensconced in an
unconscious determinism that we tend automatically to fall into the
lazy habit of thinking that the events in history had to happen, and
indeed happen just the way they did. Faced with the fact of human
creation, this bland supposition falters. Causal reasoning proceeds
according to this schema: *Whenever* A happens, B follows. The
creative act, as new and unpredictable, cannot be fitted into this
scheme of uniformity. In the case of minor inventions, where a
whole framework of interrelated parts has come into existence, we
allow ourselves to say that the discovery had to happen. Given most
of the rudiments of the internal-combustion engine, somebody or
other was bound to come up with the idea of a carburetor. But
when the creation is a new vision that exceeds any previous framework, even this weaker necessity does not hold. The outburst of
light in ancient Greece that led to philosophy and from philosophy
into science need not ever have happened to the human race at
all. Humankind would have gone on in some fashion or other as it
had done for millennia before.

The birth of philosophy cannot be reckoned as the effect of a
cause. It *happened*. The word for a happening or event in German
is *Ereignis*. This has the root *Eigen* (one's *own*, what belongs to or
is appropriate to one). And there is the cognate verb *eignen* (to fit
and be appropriate together). The cluster of associations, directly
and clearly present in the German, and neither forced nor far-
fetched, is entirely suited to Heidegger's use of them. The birth of
philosophy, then, among the early Greeks is a *happening* in which
Being comes into its own and claims mortal minds as its own. There
is no split between subject and object here. "Thought and Being,"
as the sage Parmenides declares, "belong together in their unity."

Parmenides can be taken as the prime figure among these thinkers.
He begins from a radiant vision of Being as the whole, the All, that

calls to thought. Not only is there intellectual awe as the mind raises itself to the thought of all that is, the universe, the *eon;* but also we are seized by the marvel of the sheer fact that it *is, esti.* And the two—what-is and the *is* of all that is, the *eon* and the *esti*—must both be held inseparably in thought. To keep these two together, Parmenides tells us, is to follow the path of light and truth— *Aletheia* (unhiddenness). To let the two fall apart is to pass into the intellectual darkness of the senseless and unrelated many.

A century and a half separate Parmenides from Aristotle, who brings to completion and to its end the great age of Greek philosophy. Nowadays we complain of the dizzy speed of historical change, beside which all ages in the past seemed to move at a relatively leisurely gait. But this speed may be a deceptive matter. If it occurs in the grossly visible features of the common life, the vehicles we drive and the clothes we wear, it is more likely to capture our attention. Moreover, when certain bodies of knowledge, like the sciences, have once been set in motion, acceleration is easier and the curve of change ascends more steeply. It is an incomparably harder and more revolutionary thing to set the engine going in the first place. Seen in this light, the 150 years that Greek thought traverses from Parmenides to Aristotle are perhaps the period of the most breakneck and revolutionary acceleration in all of history.

Consider: The period opens with Parmenides' vision of Being as an intelligible whole within which human thought is to find its element. It closes, at the death of Aristotle, with the various and distinct realms of beings mapped out into the territories of different disciplines, much as we have them today. Aristotle has created logic, laid down the outline by which mathematics is to become a strictly deductive system; he has marked out the separate but interrelated regions of physics or natural science, biology, psychology; and in the sciences of man, there are ethics, politics, and economics. In some of these fields his contributions are already massive, in others more rudimentary, but in any case he has divided the terrain and laid it out for the future. Science as specialized research has now at long last sprung forth full-born, though it must still cling to the maternal apron strings of philosophy, without which it would not be intelligible to itself.

The one Being of Parmenides has vanished into the many kinds of individual beings that make up the world of Aristotle. In the process the meaning of Being that henceforth engages the attention of philosophers has become changed. To the question What is Being? Aristotle gives the simple and straightforward answer of the empirical mind. To be, according to him, is merely to be an individual entity of some definite kind; to exist is to be an individual instance of a species. This conception of Being has been determinative for all future Western philosophy right down to our own day. When Bertrand Russell, for example, asserts that the meaning of existence is to be a member of a class, or a value of a propositional function, he is merely giving us his logical variant on the original conception of Aristotle.

Let us recall our previous image of light and the dawn. If you get up in time, reader, to watch the dawn break, you will really be looking at the light. The objects in nature still lurk indistinctly in the dark so that they have not taken over your vision. It is the light itself you see, the drama of its dawning, as it gathers moment by moment, and then has disappeared because it is everywhere. In the full glare of noon you move among the things of your world and no longer are aware of the light as such. So the Greeks, creating philosophy, ceased to be aware of the light itself in which they saw. The history of Being, for Western thought, begins with the forgetting of Being.

Nevertheless, this schematized world of Aristotle is still pervaded with an inner unity that we moderns have lost. Physics and biology are not set off against each other because no dualism between mechanism and organism has as yet cleft them apart. Psychology is linked with biology, not because Aristotle has adopted a behavioristic psychology, but because the human psyche is inseparable in its functions from an organic living body. What we now call the behavioral sciences cannot be separated from questions of ethics and values, for these are a natural part of the life of men and women in society. The unity that pervades the Aristotelian world is the Greek sense of *Physis*, which we inadequately translate as "nature." If we read Aristotle's writings on nature as supercilious moderns, we may smile condescendingly at their various scientific lapses and gaffes. If we read them a little more intelligently, however, if we allow our imagination to dwell within them, we cannot help marvel at the coherent picture of the world of our perception that they give back to us. Stone, plant, animal, stars, and planets—all belong to the one cosmos in which man too draws his breath as a natural being. The cosmic alienation, from which we moderns suffer, had not entered the Greek spirit.

IV.

The immense labor of the early Middle Ages was to spread the Christian faith and civilize Europe. Once the faith was secure, they were ready to give nature its due. The intellectual achievement of the later Middle Ages was to elaborate the relative autonomy of reason and nature vis-à-vis faith and the supernatural. They were thus freed to develop their independent understanding of nature. This understanding was to come to them in the first place through the works of Aristotle as these arrived in Latin translation; but unfortunately in this process of assimilation the original Greek sense of *Physis,* or nature, is lost. Though the medieval followers of Aristotle might write diligent and copious commentaries on his natural writings, the organic and intimate Greek bond with the cosmos has receded for them. They see it, as it were, through a frosted glass— the frosted glass of their philosophical Latin, which no longer carried the resonant associations of the Greek.

In the Christian scheme of things, all of nature could be lumped together as *ens creatum* (created being). This realm of natural beings could be left to run on the momentum of its own laws except for those points where God chose to insert His miracles. The medievals did not go so far as to let it run on purely mechanical laws; it was left to Descartes to do that. Yet it would not have disturbed their faith if that picture of the world had been presented, so long as the governance of God, the provenance of miracles, and the operation of grace were still assured.

There was one great exception, however, among all the beings of nature, and that was man himself. The destiny of the Christian did not lie within nature but in the world beyond, and the traces of this destiny must be found in human nature itself. With considerable effort and ingenuity, the Christian Aristotelians had to superimpose upon the naturalistic psyche they had inherited from Aristotle the notion of an otherworldly Christian soul. In this way they prepared the way for Descartes in the seventeenth century and his view of the mind as in a peculiar and precarious relation to its body. The notion of an otherworldly soul foreshadows the "worldless" consciousness of Cartesian philosophy—a consciousness essentially outside of its world but tangent to it just enough to secure its own power.

v.

Descartes separates mind and body, subject and object. Such is the usual formula for describing the Cartesian philosophy, and this description is perfectly correct as far as it goes. But the formula does not enlighten us on the motive or goal of this separation; and consequently it leaves in the dark the premise on which this separation is built: the act of the mind that is required to establish the separateness of these two items in the first place.

What do we mean, for example, when we speak of separating mind from the objects external to it?

Consider the grapes and cherries in the fruit basket there on the table. They are very distinct in color, and different enough in shape, for me to separate them easily. I have only to sort them out, for they are already given as separate and distinct. But the dualist's separation of mind and external objects, whatever else it may be, is not a simple sorting out of items already given as separate and distinct, like the grapes and cherries in that basket. The primary fact about our "natural consciousness," to use Husserl's apt term, is how inseparably it is embedded in the same stream of our life as the objects around us. My thinking, in ordinary life, is constantly engaged with the things about me; and it is intelligible at all only as it moves within the same medium with them. To separate itself from things, thinking has first to *establish* itself as separate. It requires an elaborate chain of reasoning for the dualist to arrive at that result. Descartes sweats and strains to get there. In so doing, thought establishes a rift between itself and external things.

The familiar things of my experience do not appear as objects set over against me. As familiar, they enter into and are extensions of my own life. These things are not objects, in the sense of the philosopher. Ob-ject, from the Latin, signifies what lies over against, what stands in opposition to one. Even when a particular thing unexpectedly frustrates me or resists my handling, it does not reveal itself as metaphysically different from mind. Its "otherness" consists in the fact that it now sticks out obtrusively within the context of other things. It is not alien to the mind, but for the moment alien to the setting of other things within which it normally functions.

How and why, then, does Descartes separate subject and object as he does? Why should this great thinker, at a certain moment of history, decide that it is of crucial importance to wrench mankind away from the simplicity of its "natural consciousness"?

The answer, of course, lies in the great adventure of the new science. Descartes transfers into philosophy the procedures on which science had already embarked, and he proposes that these be extended to all domains of human enquiry. When Galileo set up his concept of inertia, he did not reproduce passively a fact in external nature. He sets up an artificial concept, one that the mind does not find in nature but in itself, and he sets this up over against nature as the measure of it. The mind, out of its own powers, provides its own standards of exactness.

Thus in the subject-object pairing of Cartesian dualism the two terms are not left on the same level; it is the first term, the subject, that has, or rather asserts, its priority. The quest for certainty leads Descartes to affirm the existence of the conscious Ego (*ego cogitans*) as the central certainty. The conscious Ego would then extend this initial certainty over the object, which it proceeds to reduce to mere extended stuff in space. It impoverishes the object of all qualities except those relevant to its own purposes. It considers in the object only what is measurable, numerable, and calculable. In this way it guarantees the certainty and exactness of its own thought. The subject separates itself from the object in order to ensure its own mastery over it. Dualism is man's self-assertion in the face of nature.

Here in outline is the metaphysics that lies behind the technological era. It is not the philosophy that popular criticism usually attributes to a "materialistic" society. The spirit of technology is not to be characterized as a simpleminded and crass materialism, an inordinate lust for material commodities and gadgets in every shape and form. The philosophical design that has brought about our age belongs to another order of mind. In comparison with all our indolent and bloated "consumerism," the originating design has at least a certain grandeur of bleakness about it.

Nevertheless, grand or not, it exacts a heavy toll. Through it our human bond with the cosmos has vanished. And not vanished on its own; we ourselves have banished it. The mind now confronts a nature that has become alien to it through its own conceptions: a realm of objects whose objectivity consists precisely in those quantifiable aspects that fit into our calculation and control. Nature sinks to the level of mere material for exploitation, and man towers as the master over it.

All this is in germ in Descartes; what is needed to make it explicit is only a philosophy of the will, with which the Germans proceeded to supply him.

VI.

THE PHILOSOPHY OF THE WILL

We are likely today to be very poor judges of German philosophy. Two world wars gave the German character a bad reputation in the eyes of the world, and we are inclined to read that character out of their earlier culture. That the philosophy of the will is almost exclusively a German product seems to confirm these prejudices. What else could you expect from the Germans when they came to develop their own philosophy at the high tide of the modern period? This people, whose legendary hero was Faust, celebrant of the titanic and striving will, would naturally produce a doctrine that would serve to glorify the drives to imperialism and conquest. After the horror of the Nazis, we ourselves tend to become racists against the racists.

Our own philosophers, American and English, have mostly abetted us in this adverse judgment. Santayana and Dewey condemned idealism as an expression of German egotism, a self-inflated mixture of romanticism and extravagant system-building. In England the attack by Bertrand Russell and G. E. Moore, though more moderate in tone, was no less destructive in intent. It is even more devastating in intellectual controversy to show that your opponent is speaking nonsense than to castigate his morals. Russell and Moore virtually launch twentieth-century philosophy, at least for the English-speaking peoples, as the refutation of idealism—to use the title of one of Moore's early essays. And such it has largely continued to be. The history of philosophy in the first part of this century could be written in terms of its successive withdrawals, in almost all areas, from the position that idealistic philosophy had once occupied. Whether this represents an advance in truth may be left to the future to decide. On some important points we have already had to inch back, however altered our language, to positions not unlike those of the idealists. And the last quarter of this century may very well turn out to be a period when we have to rethink the problems on which German philosophy lavished its speculative energies.

The historical facts, in any case, appear quite different from what the conventional prejudice alleges. The doctrine of the will is not the expression of an age of imperialism and conquest, but stems much more from the peculiar moral earnestness of the German at an earlier period. A people with a Lutheran consciousness plunged into modern philosophy at the high tide of the Enlightenment. The moral earnestness, whose previous outlet had been in religious worship, turned itself into a passion for knowledge and reflection. Reason and enlightenment could not be left to the witty persiflage of the French *philosophes* but must be exhibited as the labor and achievement of the morally striving subject. Learning would be their passion, and the Germans flung themselves with moral fervor at the library. Moral earnestness, however, like every human quality, can be an ambiguous gift. When it later fell foul of industrial civilization and the nation-state, as Germany became unified and passed into the modern technological world, this earnestness could be transformed to feed the nationalist frenzy for empire and domination. But all of this is a later phenomenon, almost a countermovement to the older philosophy, part of the period that has been described as "the collapse of idealism." And let us not forget that the last in the line of the great philosophers of the will, Friedrich Nietzsche, could find no words adequate to express his contempt for this nationalistic furor.

With these prejudices aside, German philosophy in its development from Kant through Nietzsche, however speculative and remote its language sometimes strikes us, emerges for what it truly was: one of the very great chapters in human thought. Not only does it gather together the deepest themes of the modern age, but it is also prophetic of the problems we are living through now. In thought, though in more than thought with Nietzsche, it lives through the death of the Christian God. Cumulative and massive in its progress, it has the dimensions of a great drama. The will itself is the hero of this play. We watch this hero as he goes through his various adventures and radical transformations, until he reaches for the heights and tumbles into the void. Beginning as a Christian character in Kant, the will becomes progressively more secularized and naturalistic, until it ends as the demoniacal anti-Christ of Nietzsche.

Perhaps comparison with a musical composition would be more

appropriate, since the development of tonal music, one of the greatest of human arts, was the parallel and comparable achievement of the Germans in this era. The progress, then, step-by-step from Kant through Fichte, Schelling, Hegel, and Schopenhauer to Nietzsche, can be imagined as a great symphony. But alas, this one does not end in the rousing harmonies of a Beethoven, but in cacophony and discord, like the nervous collapse that breaks off Stravinsky's *Rite of Spring* or the eerie sounds of some of our more fragmented atonal music. That Nietzsche's collapse suggests the kind of music we actually do have today is a sign of how much his questions are with us and still remain unanswered.

Kant—to begin with him—is the last great philosopher of Christian theism. With him the philosophy of the will begins its fateful adventures as a strictly *moral* will. It is submissive rather than self-assertive. It kneels before its moral imperative as before an inner altar. This will, moreover, is the center of our strictly human and personal reality. Our intellect knows phenomena, the aspects of things seen from the outside, but does not grasp things in themselves, the Noumena. But in our moral life we are in touch with the real from within, as we ourselves experience the pinch of life in this or that urgent decision. Notice that Kant does not speak of the will as some metaphysical stuff that constitutes the inner core of things. That is the gross transformation of his doctrine that will come later. Nevertheless, this moral will in its act and exercise does incline us to believe certain things about the ultimate scheme of things. The righteous man acts as if there is a God and immortality. Let the heavens crumble, he must still do what is right even if it means his destruction; like Luther exclaiming as he rejects the papal edict, "I cannot do otherwise." Yet this will to righteousness, though ethically valid in itself, would not be ultimately rational if there were not some moral and providential order in the universe that rewards good and punishes evil. Thus the mere existence of the moral will in us points toward what we can never prove but only believe on faith: a theistic God and human immortality. As finite individuals our existence at its core is ethical-religious. Though Kant supplied dynamite against traditional theology and its proofs of the existence of God, his moral will still bravely carries the banner of Christianity. Thereafter this Christian content becomes progressively diluted in his followers.

Fichte preaches Kant with oratorical fervor, summoning nation and folk to the cause of moral idealism. But the addition of oratory to any doctrine never leaves it altogether unchanged. The moral imperative that, with Kant, had spoken as a still, small voice *in foro interno* (in the inner chamber of conscience), now goes forth into the world and preaches at the top of its lungs to the multitudes. In the process the will now becomes more aggressive, striving, and dynamic. We applaud spirit that goes out into the world and seeks to do the world's work rather than remain a cloistered virtue. But the moral idealism that runs too eagerly and vociferously into the marketplace may be compensating for the loss of its faith. We are reminded of those churches which, unsure of any doctrinal content, seek to justify themselves by social and secular crusades. Religion becomes merely a form of enlightened and idealistic activity within the community.

Schelling takes the momentous step of transforming the moral will into a metaphyscial entity. "The will is primal being (Ur-Sein)." What had been a strictly ethical-religious organ in Kant becomes here a natural fact—indeed, the basic fact underlying all the facts of nature. We have not yet arrived, but we are on the way to Schopenhauer's thoroughly naturalistic conception of the will as a force that works throughout nature in the sheer urge to persist and reproduce itself. And here in Schopenhauer the will has become so far transformed from its original moral role in Kant that it has become amoral and even antimoral in its operations, as it drives humans like helpless pawns and victims. The pessimism of Schopenhauer is the first warning voice in which the Modern Age begins to doubt itself and its great historical mission.

Hegel, the tireless synthesizer, seeks to gather together all the threads of idealism into one last modern effort toward a complete philosophical system. The effort fails. After him the nineteenth century becomes, as Heidegger correctly remarks, a series of isolated movements and countermovements—including the supreme countermovement of Nietzsche.

The difficulties of Hegel's text are legendary. It helps a little, however, if we keep in mind some of the ordinary connotations of the German words that he uses—particularly the words that we translate as "self-conscious" and "self-consciousness." When we speak in our ordinary English of a self-conscious person, we usually mean someone who is timid, unsure of himself, shy and shrinking before the public. The corresponding German word, *Selbstbewusst,* denotes a person who is self-assured and confident before the world. Hegel proceeds to give this ordinary resonance of the word philosophic dimensions. To realize itself, the human spirit must go forth into the world and make this world its own. But we are not yet at the Nietzschean stage of naked self-assertion, for in seeking to appropriate the world to itself, spirit has in the end to submit to the tribunal of world reason. Since it seeks the Absolute, the human spirit wills that the various contemporary expressions of itself in its culture—whether social and political forms, its art, its systems of thought—should aspire to be total and all-encompassing, but they in turn must perish because they are one-sided and incomplete. In the long run, and in the larger view, what perishes deserves to perish. The redeeming presence of Christian providence has deserted Hegel's universe, but its place is taken by a stern moral justice, a kind of Greek *Themis*, which presides over the workings of the world. History is both Greek and Shakespearean tragedy at once. The hero, the human spirit in its self-assertion, transgresses the due limits imposed by the gods and must perish to affirm the eternal norm, the dialectical balance of things. Or, as in Shakespearean tragedy, the good are corrupted and perish along with the evil who destroy themselves, too, but always that some wider good may come. The new actors enter the scene, like Fortinbras in the last act arriving at the shambles of Elsinore, to restore some order amid the chaos of destruction; the new historical epoch takes upon itself the burdens of spirit in its never-ending task of self-affirmation. History is a tragedy with a happy ending, which becomes its own tragedy in turn, and so on and on world without end. Whether this scheme of things be viewed as optimistic or pessimistic depends on where you happen to be sitting on the turn of fortune's and history's wheel.

Nietzsche brings the whole chapter to an explosive end. He leaps back over the movement to its source; he is more truly Kantian than Kant's other followers—but a Kantian in reverse. The Protestant conscience here turns against itself. Nietzsche admired the classical moralists of French literature, but his own earnestness made him incapable of their cynical and catholic adjustment to life. The Kantian conscience had taken its own existence as a sign pointing toward the existence of God. Deny the existence of God, and this same moral conscience, if it is to be morally truthful about itself, must confess that it is groundless. Only an uncompromising honesty can tell the truth about the will to truth—that it has no absolute ground, and under certain circumstances a beautiful illusion or lie may have a higher value for life. To prove he is serious, Nietzsche must mock at the seriousness of morality and assume the motley of the jester and buffoon.

With Descartes, the bond between mind and nature had become tenuous, but there was God in the background to guarantee some residual link between them. With God gone, this last link is broken. Nietzsche's famous statement "God is dead" is not directed only against the anthropomorphic God of religious worship, it is also meant to dismiss the notion of a "higher world," a "true world," the "thing in itself," or any other notion that philosophers have clung to as a ground for the world of appearance. There is only this world, and it *floats*—it is without a ground. The alienation, which entered modern philosophy with Descartes, here reaches its peak. Henceforth humankind, without God or gods, stands before an alien and meaningless universe and must assert itself in the face of this cosmic emptiness. This self-assertion, however, cannot become the mere dragging and tired acquiescence to Schopenhauer's will to live, that slothful and stupid persistence in one's own superfetation, or we would all die of boredom; it has to become the energetic and triumphant will to power—a will to extend and enhance one's own vitality and that of the race. Every affirmation of a value is the assertion of this will.

But what is this will to power? It would be a mistake to think of it as a drive to secure some stable state of power, in which we would then squat contentedly. In this universe of flux and endless becoming there is nothing static. To be in a position of power is continuously to exercise power. Power itself is the discharge of power. And toward what end? Toward further power. Power, then, is the will to power in act, willing itself toward further power, and so on endlessly. The will to power is a will to will. It wills itself endlessly in a void from which the very notion of "the true world"—of which earlier philosophers dreamed—is denied it, and which it in turn defiantly denies.

This picture is not cheering; and it would be a mistake to think Nietzsche gloats over it, however charged and exciting his language becomes. Even in the matter of religion, which he so often attacks and scorns, he has the painful sense of the vacuum that its departure will leave. Throughout Nietzsche's pages there sounds the heartrending cry that modern life may become meaningless, trivial, despairing. Toward the end, the problem of nihilism obsesses him more and more, and he sees in it the question that will afflict our coming century. The last sentence of his *Genealogy of Morals* has thus to be read as a somber warning to us today: "Mankind will will the void, rather than be void of will." Rather than drag on in a vacuum without goals, humankind will pursue destruction for its own sake. This is not a bad prophecy of a good deal that has already happened in our century and of the aimless violence that still goes on all around us. It may even turn out prophetic of the ultimate *Götterdämmerung* when one of the world powers, out of frustration and emptiness, cries out with the will to destruction, "What difference does it make? Let us all perish together, ourselves and the enemy!"—and presses the button to release the bombs.

VII.

This scenario is brief and stark. It could be plentifully confirmed, however, by innumerable details from the large sweep of history it encompasses. The important thing here, though, is that we not lose the forest for the trees, that we keep the main outline clear, so that we know at least the shape of the thing that engulfs us. The era of technology has been long, very long, in preparation; but it has come with such a rush of acceleration in our lifetime that we are apt to be swamped in its details anyway. To the extent that we are unaware of the fullness of this past, we are not likely to gauge the extent to which the phenomenon of technology now gathers our human destiny into its hands.

With Nietzsche the history of Western metaphysics comes to its close. We have arrived at the end of philosophy. This conclusion of Heidegger may seem at first glance too drastic to be entirely plausible. Nietzsche's language, too, so charged and personal, may put us off, inclining us to believe we are dealing only with an expression of individual temperament. But if we set aside the satanic antimoralist and consider Nietzsche only as a straightforward metaphysician, we shall find that he is simply following out the options that Western thought has brought us to. The immense labor of philosophy was to bring science into being; to establish the world of objects over which the subject, mankind, has now to assert its mastery. We already exist *de facto* in the Nietzschean framework. The "higher world" is gone for us; and as citizens we are joined in the organization of modern societies to control this earth.

Philosophy has gone on, of course, and still goes on in the hands of its academic practitioners. But it is mainly the elaboration of detail within this framework, beyond which it offers our thought no new options. And this is true even when the philosophies in question have exerted their force outside the academy. The two major modern movements of Marxism and Positivism, for example, still exist within the premises of the technical era, though these premises remain hidden to them.

Marxism uses the most sweeping populist and egalitarian slogans as instruments of its will to *come* to power. But once in power and stable, the Marxist regime establishes the strictest degrees of rank in the administration of the state apparatus. The whole populace is marshaled in a planned economy in order to subdue nature and wrest their human sustenance from it. Marx's challenge—"Philosophers have hitherto reflected on the world; they must now seek to change it"—speaks from the same metaphysics of power as Nietzsche. Nature becomes the merely exploitable realm for human purposes; and the mastery of nature requires the mastery of man over man in the technically organized society. Nietzsche spoke ironically of Christianity as Platonism for the people. We might say, and even more accurately, that Marxism is the metaphysics of Nietzsche for the masses—and, of course, disguised, for it evades the eventual questions he asks. In the end, though, it may not be able to escape. One imagines some further stage of the Marxist state, its economic goals achieved, the people materially satisfied; and then the ghost of Nietzsche reappears in the unasked and unanswered question of nihilism: Why? What is it for? What is the meaning of it all?

As for Positivism, it seeks to drag out the death rattle of philosophy as a series of annotations upon science. The positivist exists so completely in the era of technology that he must strive to justify himself by imitating the technician. The Positivist indulges in a kind of philosophical technology as empty as it is unnecessary. Science, begotten of philosophy, no longer has need of philosophy—certainly not this kind of philosophy—to explain its own techniques to it. Mathematical logic, to take a case in point, has by now passed into a particular discipline within mathematics, and it is better handled by mathematicians than by philosophers.

"Philosophy is finished." This statement is not a petulant outburst against the triviality of our philosophic journals or the transactions of our philosophy congresses, however much they seem to labor at times to deserve this judgment. Heidegger's words here have rather the solemn consummatory tone of an *Ite, missa est* (Go, your mission has been accomplished). To see this judgment in proper perspective we have only to bear in mind these simple and massive historic outlines: that the great age of philosophy among the Greeks created the outlines of science; and that, further, the great period of the seventeenth century gave these outlines the definite shape that we know as modern science; but now the sciences have been securely established and go their way independently of philosophy, so that the latter, having lost its great historical mission, begins to flounder about without direction. Meanwhile, science and technology have not merely arrived on paper, they have also been at work in the world; and their dominating presence has brought mankind to a new and unique level of its historic existence, behind which the imagination of most philosophers still lags. What would be the kind of thinking commensurate with this momentous epoch of the world in which we now stand? We do not know; but we feel that it should be as different from what is now current as the thinking of the early Greeks was from the consciousness that preceded them, or as the seventeenth century from the early Middle Ages—so different indeed, Heidegger remarks, that it might not even be called "philosophy." So far as philosophers remain within their present patterns of thought, they can only embroider the old framework with the details of technique, which in the end become trivial and pointless.

But what looks like a dead end may offer the chance of a new turning. A great chapter of human history—twenty-five hundred years long, from the beginnings of rational thought among the Greeks to the present—has come to an end. But the end of a chapter is not the end of the book. So the statement that philosophy is finished is not a pessimistic foreclosure on our human future, but calls us toward some other dimension of thinking of which we can catch now and then perhaps only glimmers.

And it is precisely here that the question of freedom presents itself on another level and with a fresh virulence. We may become no longer free for the kind of thinking that would redeem us from the world we ourselves have created. We may have made ourselves incapable of such thinking.

The danger already shows in the superficiality of our complaints against the technical world. We rail at technology when it gets too noisy, pollutes our air, or is about to drive a new superhighway through our living room. For the rest, we are content to consume its products unquestioningly. So long as we can negotiate the triumph of technology successfully, we are unconcerned to ask what the presuppositions of this technical world are and how they bind us to its framework. Already these presuppositions are so much the invisible medium of our actual life that we have become unconscious of them. We may eventually become so enclosed in them that we cannot even imagine any other way of thought but technical thinking. That is the point at which we shall have turned all our questions over to the think tanks as problems of human engineering. We seem already on the way there.

Chapter 11

———◆———

"Utopia or Oblivion"

IS THE HISTORY OF OUR AGE REALLY THE ENACTMENT OF A META-
physics? Our immediate impulse is to answer "No." We have been
taught, or have taught ourselves, to look elsewhere for the decisive
factors in history: in determinate social and material forces, in comparison with which the questions of metaphysics would seem like an
odd pursuit by a few rarefied minds. Such history, we tell ourselves,
is more "scientific," but we forget that this concept of science, as
well as the mode of history we prefer in its name, is itself the consequence of a distinct metaphysical position. And if metaphysical beliefs are to be so historically trivial, it is surely an odd fact that at
the present moment of history one particular metaphysics, and a
very dogmatic one at that, Marxism, appears about to take over the
world.

Whatever else one may think of Heidegger, one has to admire his
great passion for the history of philosophy, and his ability to communicate to us a vivid sense of that historical life. Philosophy, he
tells us and truly, is one of the very great things man has achieved.
The history of philosophy, then, far from being a succession of curious opinions, is an integral part of the whole life of humanity; it is
indeed this life come to its fullest intellectual expression. It would
be strange therefore if it did not cut deeply into the actual life of
mankind and reveal the issues around which, sometimes unknown to
ourselves, our history turns. And surprisingly enough, despite our
positivistic affectations, the modern age is one in which philosophy
has played a more than usually powerful role. Aristotle's meta-

physics expressed a general scheme of ideas about the world that was shared by a relatively few minds of his time. These ideas did not re-enter history until the Middle Ages, when they became a central part of Christian theology. The philosophy elaborated in the seventeenth century, on the other hand, was promptly codified in a body of science, around which our modern civilization turns. Ours is then, in a very distinct sense, an age of metaphysics. Far from being a remote doctrine, this metaphysics is the expression of the ultimate presuppositions of our epoch.

Nevertheless, there seems to be something of a gap between the philosophic generality of our last chapter and the concrete social realities that would embody it. Heidegger's scheme, in outline, was quite simple: To a pervasive scheme of Cartesian thought there has been annexed the philosophy of the will to power. We have now to give some indications how this general scheme is to be translated into the details of social fact.

I.

This translation must sometimes look past the surface. If we take the American businessman, for example, as a representative figure of our age, he hardly strikes us an incarnation of the Nietzschean will to power. We are hard put to imagine him as the audacious and fire-breathing superman that Nietzsche's more excited rhetoric sometimes invokes. On the contrary, everything in this businessman's makeup tends to suggest a cautious and conservative temperament. It is good business that he should so impress us; we are supposed to believe that he is steady and reliable. Hegel took the figure of Napoleon on horseback as a historical embodiment of his *Weltgeist*, or World-spirit. Napoleon really looked the part; he was ready for casting. But the American businessman of our time—at first glance, anyway—seems not to fit the role he is supposed to play in our metaphysical scheme.

For one thing, if we follow statistical probability, he is more likely to be a corporate executive rather than the lone buccaneer or robber baron of legend. He will therefore exhibit those more desirable qualities of the American middle class that are likely to ensure his rise in the corporate ranks. The chances are he may be a regular churchgoer. Some church affiliation at least would not count against him in the long and arduous chain of his various promotions. (Notice, though, that it is rather characteristic of our time that a man's faith should become a matter of a "religious affiliation" to be entered on his dossier—one among the other objective items of fact by which we classify him.) This corporate executive may not have any personal philosophy he is aware of beyond the beliefs that come with his class and status. If he reflects at all on the ultimate aim of his work, he probably thinks of himself as a servant of the public, and therefore in his own way a benefactor of mankind. The idea of himself as conscious subject seeking domination over the object, nature, has probably never entered his mind. How then can we ungratefully pretend to take him as an embodiment of the Nietzschean will to power?

But perhaps this will operates in a more devious and circuitous fashion, and to see it at work we have to watch our executive as he sets about his tasks.

He is charged—let us suppose—to build a new factory in the company's chain of plants. Nothing in the least philosophical enters his thoughts, which are confined strictly to the practical matters at hand. Nevertheless, this restriction to the merely "practical," or objective, features of the problem represents a level of abstraction to which men of another or earlier culture could not aspire. Every civilization operates on a level of abstraction that it comes to take as second nature and so forgets the prodigious intellectual ancestry needed to establish that level. Thus in the present case, when our businessman calculates men and materials as so many units to be added and balanced against each other, there is nothing of the diabolical or Machiavellian plotter about him. He is simply proceeding in the "natural," objective way to manage a problem. Nature enters his plans only as a site selected for its nearness to raw materials, transportation, and markets. The natural terrain may have to be altered: bulldozers appear, and earth is leveled and moved. The site is changed forever, and roads cover what was once a wooded hill. The momentum of technology, once launched, does not stop there. There will have to be "housing units" for workers (the poet Rilke took it as a most doleful portent of our time that the word "home" should pass into "housing unit"); a shopping center will be needed, and consequently roads to and from this center. Nor can the momentum stop locally: The products of the new plant will enter a market that in turn has to be calculated in relation to other products from other regions and countries. The network of technology, as it spreads and involves our businessman, becomes total and global.

Though this interlocking chain of events is a commonplace of our industrial life, our thinking still falls short of grasping it as a whole. We fall back instead on clichés and declaim against the evils of capitalism or the faceless corporation. In fact, the capitalist is not imposing his will upon the rest of us. He is doing our will as much as following out his own, for we consume his products and want more of them. And here we have to insist once again, lest our position not be understood, how sharply we separate ourselves from a certain sentimental and facile rejection of technology that has become current among some circles. Man is the problematic animal; and it is not to be expected that so essential a part of his existence as his technology should not also be problematic, whatever immense advantages come with it. To see this problematic character in its true depth and perspective is the philosophic task, which can only be beclouded by the sentimentalism of wholesale rejection. We need all the resources of technical organization in order to maintain the population now alive on this planet. And we should not forget, on those occasions when we are railing against it, that only through capitalistic organization have we been able in this country in less than a century to raise 50 per cent of our people to a standard of living once enjoyed by only 1 per cent.

Marxist planners are caught within this technological web as completely as their capitalistic counterparts. Indeed, the Marxist planners can impose its will more directly and brutally upon a people with utter disregard of adverse public opinion. The human differences between the two regimes are of course immense; and on the matters of human rights and individual liberty the balance is incomparably in favor of capitalist society. These political and civil aspects do not enter Heidegger's scenario of history. They are not necessarily excluded from it; nor does he preclude our valuing them, though he himself simply looks past them. His view is theoretically indifferent to them to the degree that the technical order itself can be indifferent to the human qualities it may promote. Whether this indifference points to something really lacking in his theory as a whole is a question we shall have to take up in a later chapter. All that we wish to insist on for the present is that Marxism, just as distinctly as capitalism, is the offspring of the technical era, and has to be understood within that context.

Who is exercising the will to power in the technical framework? Who is master? Who is servant? As the structure becomes more complex and interlocking, these questions are more difficult to answer. To denote this framework, Heidegger uses the ordinary German word *Gestell*, which nevertheless carries a cluster of associations that are significant for him. The verb *stellen* means to lay down or posit something, to assert it as real; and since Kant this verb has had a peculiar resonance in German philosophy. There is no intrinsic difference, according to Kant, between our idea of a thing as merely possible and our idea of the same thing as actually existing. One hundred possible dollars is the same amount of money as one hundred real dollars. The difference lies not in the concept itself but in the judgment of existence by which we posit the second. The reality of the thing, so far as our judgment is concerned, proceeds from the act of will that establishes it as real. Thus in this simple word *Gestell* there is a link with the whole philosophy of the will.

But the unpretentious first syllable also awakens some interesting associations. The German word for mountain is *Berg*, and for a mountain range, *Gebirge*. Accordingly, we are to think of the technical framework, *Gestell*, as a chain of wills taken as a single entity. And as in a mountain range the separate heights may merge and grade off into each other, depending on where we stand, so in the technical framework the separate wills in the interlocking chain shift and shade off into each other. And, again, as we cannot always tell where one hill in the range leaves off and another begins, so we may not be able to tell where the domain of power exercised by one will in the technical chain is subject to or master over another. A garbageman seems pretty low on the scale of power; but if the garbagemen strike, they may paralyze a whole metropolis.

Does the apparatus as a whole have a will of its own? Perhaps we had better call it the *framework*, keeping Heidegger's meaning in mind, for the word "apparatus" may be too closely tied down to the sheer mass of physical machinery. The framework is more than that—more even than the collective organization of humans using those machines. To apply Heidegger's earlier terminology from *Being and Time*, the framework does not belong to the world of "ontic" fact but of "ontological" possibility. It is a project into which humankind has entered step by step and to which it is now committed. It is a design and a possibility for the mastery of the globe and its resources into which mankind is now called strictly as a matter of survival. The actual configurations of peoples, powers, and economic organization take place more and more against the background of this framework. No one therefore strictly controls it. It seems thus to have a will of its own. And here we begin to encounter something uncanny: The framework is historically the supreme expression of man's will to power in coping with nature; and yet it is something that begins to elude his will. It seems to live a life of its own, and yet in one way it is nothing but ourselves in our collective life.

Clearly, then, it would be silly for anyone to announce that he is "against" technology, whatever that might mean. We should have to be against ourselves in our present historical existence. We have now become dependent upon the increasingly complex and interlocking network of production for our barest necessities. More than this, our modes of communication and expression take place within the framework and are increasingly shaped by it. It lays down the horizon within which our human future has to be planned. Almost invisibly it becomes our mode of Being in this historical epoch. The question looms whether we shall shortly be able to see around it or through it to grasp any other mode of Being. The task of philosophy in this situation becomes neither the meaningless rejection nor the equally meaningless affirmation of technology, but to try to see where technical and technological thinking, with no other principle but itself, must lead us; and whether some countervailing mode of thought may not be called for.

II.

Buckminster Fuller might seem to be the last person to go to for such countervailing insight. He is the exuberant and cheerful technicrat *par excellence*, who seems never to entertain doubts that our salvation lies in technology. Part of his cosmic optimism may come to him by inheritance from his great aunt Margaret Fuller, the New Engand transcendentalist. Something of the mystic strain in him may derive from that same source too, though his mysticism takes the form mainly of a vision of tetrahedrons sprouting everywhere throughout nature. In private conversation his enthusiasm is so contagious and captivating that he is the only nonstop talker I have ever known who was not irritating. Only when you come away from being so beguiled do you begin to doubt the vision he harbors for us. While some of our more ardent planners appear intent on paving

us under, he seems to aspire in the other dimension: to roof us over
—with Fuller domes, of course—from sea to shining sea.

Yet he has his somber moments too, if only in passing, and some
of them appeared in the book *Utopia or Oblivion*, which came out
a few years back but did not attract as much attention as it de-
served. Fuller's general thesis was simple enough, though it tended
to get lost, as usually happens with him, in a great mass of incidental
detail. The gist of his thesis was this: Technology at its imperfect
and incomplete stages poses problems, sometimes very grave ones,
that did not exist before and have now to be solved; and we are
consequently pushed to extend and perfect our technology. Each
step creates an imbalance, and we are compelled to take a further
step toward a more comprehensive technology in order to rectify
that imbalance. There is thus a drive toward totality inherent in
technology itself. We are compelled to aim at utopia—in the sense
of completing and perfecting the technical apparatus—or this civilization will collapse from the technological problems it will have
failed to solve.

Utopia or oblivion! Fuller impales us on this frightful dilemma
while he himself, nothing daunted, is confidently on the wing to
utopia. What we more plodding mortals would wish above all is
that technology were not so total a matter that it forces these dire
alternatives upon us. We want survival, certainly; but the oblivion
we want to avoid is something more than mere survival. We would
like some signficance to persist in our lives that we in turn may be
able to pass on to the generations after us. With life become empty
and sterile, even while mechanically perfect, we might very well
find that utopia and oblivion coincide.

To tell the truth, the idea of utopia in any of its versions hardly
inspires us anymore. The prospect of life without any frictions or
imperfections, either to be overcome or courageously borne, must
strike us as an empty and insipid ideal. Spared the struggle against
evils, we are also denied the zest of battle and the satisfaction of our
partial victories. Utopia would bring such a rupture with the whole
human past that we would lose the inheritance of history, particularly in the arts. Tolstoi remarks at the beginning of *Anna Karenina*
that happy families are all alike, but each unhappy family is
unhappy in its own way. The rub of imperfection brings out the
singular and individual. How could you write a story about two

people whose life together was an uninterrupted happiness? They were happy happy happy. . . . Their private utopia would in fact be the empty monotony of oblivion. Condemned to utopia, mankind would have to go through the spiritual agony of re-creating a religion to give itself meaning.

But utopia may be only a rhetorical flourish on Fuller's part that we ought not to take too seriously. What it seems to mean in practical terms is that a technical civilization must reach some state of homeostatic equilibrium with regard to its sources of energy so that it is not menaced by the catastrophe of perishable fuels. And in the midst of the present threatening energy crisis this is indeed a very serious challenge. Whatever the solution to this *particular* problem, however, we still face the more *general* question in Fuller's stark alternatives: Is the drive to totality locked into modern technology as such? If each step commits us to the next step, where do we stop? Can we stop? *Assuming—and it is a big assumption—that our civilization does not destroy itself, then our present technology is only at its beginning.* We must hold fast to this premise if our thinking is to be adequate to the phenomenon that will shortly be upon us. Sensitive souls in the nineteenth century complained about their new technology, which now seems primitive to us; and ours in turn will seem primitive to the future—if there should be a future. It is with the possible totality of these technical conditions that our thinking must be engaged.

In the late 1940s, which already begin to appear technically archaic to us, Norbert Wiener, who had done much to develop the use of computers, made a very simple and unambiguous statement that still hangs over our heads:

> We have modified our environment so radically that we must now modify ourselves in order to exist in this new environment.

Behaviorists like Skinner must be given credit at least for attempting to do something about this situation. What is the point of building the New Jerusalem, so far as the material environment is concerned, if the mankind you drag into it still carries the same old Adam with it? If you are to engineer everything else, why leave human beings out? But this technology of behavior leads to the demand for a further and more drastic engineering of humans. If the people you turn over to the behaviorist for conditioning have bad genes to start with, why not attack the problem at the root? The final and logical step would be genetic engineering that would transform the biological stock of humankind itself.

And with this matter of genetic engineering we are no longer in a purely speculative state, as witness recent controversies over experiments in recombinant DNA. Geneticists themselves are divided over the danger of these attempts to tamper with genetic materials. Here the thirst for knowledge seems to make use of human foibles and passions: Some older scientists, who already have their Nobel prizes, are against the experiments, while the younger scientists, who are eager for the project, seem to be clamoring for their chance to earn a laureateship for themselves. In a controversy like this I have to side with the party of youth. The pursuit of knowledge must ever bring with it some aspect of danger or risk, from which only the halfhearted or timorous would turn away. There was once, we are told, a popular grumbling, "If God intended us to fly, he would have given us wings." Well, God gave us the brains and hands with which to build airplanes, so that the fact of human flight seems to have been part of His providential designs. In the same vein we might ask ourselves to what end life has gone through aeons of laborious evolution in order to produce intelligence if this intelligence is not itself to intervene in the processes of life. The question is—and this is the real danger—whether it will intervene intelligently.

"The essence of technology is danger," says Heidegger. The danger he has in mind is not that the test tubes in the Harvard lab will suddenly foam over, like an incident out of science fiction, and the froth spill out into the streets of Cambridge to start a plague. That is the kind of danger which, if the experimenters are responsible, they should be technically competent to prevent. It falls within the purview of technical thinking. But the danger Heidegger has in mind is of another order: It is that technology, when it becomes total, lifts mankind to a level where it confronts problems with which technical thinking is not prepared to cope. Suppose the experimentation has been done successfully, and we have arrived safely at the point where we have in our hands the powers of genetic manipulation. What then do we do with them? What kind of life do we foster? What human traits do we seek to engender? The first section of this book suggested that technique by itself cannot determine a philosophy; accordingly, the powers of genetic manipulation, were they all at our disposal, would not provide the wisdom for using them. That must come from another kind of thinking, for which a technical civilization might have become incompetent through sheer lack of practice.

III.

But here someone might object: "Very well; you have pointed to the objectifying tendencies of the modern era. The technical organization of life reduces people to so many items of fact that have to be calculated within its plans. This is all quite familiar, and indeed old hat. But you were to exhibit this process in relation to the metaphysics of Descartes, which starts from the split between subject and object; and so far you have given us only half the picture. Where is the subject that Descartes had set in opposition to the object? If our age is the enactment of that metaphysics, then we ought to find subjectivism rampant amid the current forms of our cultural life."

The point would be well taken. A dualism that separates two aspects of experience must end by unduly accentuating both. The emphasis thrown upon one of the opposites ends by heightening the other in compensation. It is a law of psychic life that when one extreme is pushed too far its opposite is galvanized into an extraordinary and sometimes overexaggerated form of its own. German philosophy was such a response of subjectivity to the objectifying tendencies set loose by Descartes and modern science. But where do we find any such compensating subjectivity in the forms of contemporary life?

To a casual glance it might seem that human subjectivity has become so inconspicuous that it has virtually disappeared. Our life-styles—a horrible term, which is itself part of the general objectifying phenomenon—go in the direction of extroversion, of the most mindless and aimless sort. The television talk show replaces conversation; the information bulletin supplants serious and detailed journalism; and the weekly news digest crowds out the older reflective periodical. One could go on almost endlessly merely on these prevailing modes of communication that tend to rivet us more and more to the quick, casual, efficient, but also thoroughly external snapshot of reality. Subjectivity of any kind seems to have become a fugitive and alien thing.

Fugitive and alien! These words point to where the subject in the subject-object pair has gone: It has not vanished, it is present in its overwhelming alienation. And here we have to grasp the phenomenon of alienation in its more diffuse and crude manifestations. Human subjectivity is not an absolute; it differs in its shadings, degrees, and kinds. The subjectivism that haunts the machine age has nothing to do with the difficult and highly conscious subjectivity of the single person, the *I* that struggles for its passionate inwardness in the writings of a Kierkegaard. Rather, it is the subjectiveness of the "we," all of us together in our loneliness as "the lonely crowd." This phrase of David Riesman's a few years back had a considerable vogue because people could recognize the omnipresent fact it pointed to. Without divesting it of its sociological applications I propose we appropriate it for philosophy. "The lonely crowd," then, denotes the kind of subjectivism that haunts the mass in the technical era, and by extension a mode of being that haunts each of us in our own separate existences. Think of the rapidly dwindling crowds around Times Square in the small hours of New Year's day, after the celebrations are over and the loudspeakers and songs have gone silent, as they drift apart into little islands of emptiness. Or think of the subway, not at the rush hour when people ferociously jostle one another, but on some quieter afternoon when everyone is seated: We stare vacantly at those who stare vacantly back at us, unnoticing; none of us is there, each lost in his own absence.

Metaphysically speaking, humankind has become "the lonely crowd" adrift in a cosmos from which its traditional ties have been severed. This is the ghost that haunts all science fiction. Comb through the pages of this bleak genre and you will be hard put to find anywhere a reassuring picture of the human future. And I do not refer particularly to accomplished writers like E. M. Forster, Aldous Huxley, or George Orwell, who set out deliberately to do a destructive job on technology and the future. The ordinary science-fiction hack, who would like to accent the positive and give a rosy view of the millennium, ends by being just as depressing. This future mankind, who have solved their material problems and live amid the almost unimaginable magic of their gadgets, are just "the lonely crowd" lost in the universe. The astronauts on their star treks have changed their costumes, but they are still the leather-jacketed youths roaming town in the dark searching for adventure. Saturday night way off there in Alpha Centauri, and what do you do for a blast? Cosmic space has become the empty city square through which they drift.

The modern metropolis, itself a unique product of the technical

era, is haunted by the lonely subject. Baudelaire, who is often celebrated as the first truly "modern" poet, is also the founder of a new
genre of "urban" poetry. The swarming city—*fourmillante cité*—
washes up its estranged waifs at the odd corners of alleys and
faubourgs; and the poet himself in his garret, as pure observing consciousness, is more estranged and outside of it than any of the
specters he encounters in the streets. Baudelaire's city has the grotesque but still very human touches of nineteenth-century Paris. But
in one poem, *Rêve Parisien,* he dreams of a futuristic Babel that
brings him closer to us: He imagines a city from which trees,
shrubs, and everything vegetal have been removed until there is
only the "monotony of metal and marble." Well, we have less marble nowadays; but concrete, steel, glass, and aluminum may serve
just as well to produce that inhuman effect Baudelaire dreamed of.
One looks up at night at the enormous façades of apartment houses
ablaze with lights, each a beacon from its own sealed and comfortable cell; and thinking of the separate lives there, one remembers
T. S. Eliot's lines at the end of *The Waste Land:*

> I have heard the key
> Turn in the door once and turn once only
> We think of the key, each in his prison
> Thinking of the key, each confirms a prison . . .

Eliot is in fact the continuator of Baudelaire, and Eliot's *Waste
Land* is the greatest monument of "urban" poetry. The poem has
grown so familiar to us that we tend to forget how shocking and
hypermodern were its techniques. The quick shuttling of images
parallels the montage of the cinema, the art *par excellence* of our
technical age. The voices that float in and out of it are like a sound
track of the modern metropolis that is always there in the background. And what is the final note that is struck? Through all the
flickering images and voices, the poem is the chant of a fragmented
and despairing alienation, ending with the cry of the isolated subject
we have just quoted.

Eliot's note on this passage is even more to our literal-minded
purpose. It is simply a quotation, with no further comment by the
poet, from the philosopher F. H. Bradley, whom Eliot had studied
at Harvard:

My external sensations are no less private to myself than are my
thoughts or my feelings. In either case my experience falls within
my own circle, a circle closed on the outside; and with all its elements alike, every sphere is opaque to the others which surround
it. . . . In brief, regarded as an existence which appears in a soul,
the whole world is peculiar and private to that soul.

This is but a beautiful and elegant condensation of Descartes. Consciousness has become so intrinsically private and subjective that it
is like a sphere hermetically sealed off from the world without.
Eliot's metropolitan ghosts carry this Cartesian self within them as
they wander the streets of the modern city.

Hegel, who was a very shrewd historian in these matters, cele-
brates the art of the modern age as a triumph of subjectivity. He
was speaking of the earlier and more heroic stage when the inwardness of a Shakespeare or a Rembrandt stood fully open to its
world. Yet Hegel also had time to see a less favorable development
of this modern subjectivity. He noticed in the art of his time a
greater freedom of imagination, the pursuit of art for art's sake, and
the consequent proliferation of new and varied styles. But all this
splendid variety and freedom was paid for by a detachment of the
artist from the real life of mankind. Art became a more peripheral
and marginal affair to the actual concerns of its society. Since he
wrote, of course, this isolation of the artist has proceeded apace. It
has become a staple topic of critics, and by this time we are all more
or less bored by the subject of alienation; yet it is doubtful whether
criticism has really gotten to the bottom of the matter. Critics with
a leaning toward politics have tended to see this alienation as a form
of social protest. Baudelaire and Flaubert, with their hatred of the
bourgeois world, are held up as typical cases in point. Yet what
both hated about the bourgeois was that he seemed the embodiment
of the rational, calculative, and technical side of modern society;
and neither would have been appeased in spirit by a planned socialism that exhibited the same features. The malaise of these writers
was a spiritual yearning they could not satisfy within their own
time and place.

The great Russian novelists of the nineteenth century stand out in
sharp contrast to Flaubert. Where he tends to be negative, destructive, and almost inhuman in his detachment, they breathe a spirit of
affirmation and faith. The Russians had the great advantage for the

writer of coming from a technically "backward" country. (It is an advantage that Irish writers have enjoyed in this century.) Russia was going through profound social changes, to be sure; and the writers were often uncomfortable amid these upheavals. Yet it was a country in which the great bulk of its peasantry was still in live contact with the earth and in possession of their pristine Christian faith. And those Russian writers who were able to identify with the people could find spiritual sustenance there. In the West the spirit of science and technology had become too widely dispersed, and Flaubert was acutely and bitterly aware that he was living with the legacy of rationalism left by the French Revolution. At bottom, the phenomenon of alienation is a religious one.

Flaubert in himself is almost an epitome of the whole history of the novel in its tension between objective and subjective claims. He flagellates himself to be mercilessly objective in his art, and loathes the masterpiece, *Madame Bovary*, that results from it. Meanwhile his spirit aspires after the faith of the Middle Ages and St. Julien the Hospitaler.

The novel as we know it is not found in antiquity or the Middle Ages; it is the distinctive literary form of the modern age. Accordingly, it shows the deepest traits of the Cartesian epoch: Its history is a long tug-of-war between the subjective and objective poles of experience. It begins as a simple narrative, a comic epic that amuses by the episodes it recounts. It has thus the direct and unprogrammatic objectivity that the teller of a tale has toward his story and his audience. Quickly, however, it begins to take upon itself the program of depicting manners and society, and thus—in the hands of a Balzac, for example—strives toward the objectivity of science. On the other hand, as the most flexible of literary forms, the novel permits the author the greatest amount of exploratory comment upon his characters. It has the capacity beyond all other genres to delve into human psychology. So it turns inward; and we get novels that show us the external world only as reflected in the characters' minds. Character is dissolved into its complexes, the hero turns into an antihero, the self disintegrates into the fragments of an uncapturable self. But the pendulum is always ready to swing. After the extremities of Proust and the psychological novel, French writers in the 1940s were ready to seek renewal in the simple and brutal objectivity of the American novel.

We could document our theme abundantly, if space permitted,

from the other arts, where the same tension of opposites has been at play. Painting is a particularly striking case, since vision is the sense that ordinarily attaches us most to the external world, and yet modern painters have systematically detached the visual image from objective representation. Still, every once in a while there will be countermovements, "The New Realism" or *Die Neue Sachlichkeit*, usually advancing some very *self-conscious* program for restoring the objective world to painting. It is as if, like Descartes, one approaches the external world only from a subjective program. This intensely programmatic character of the movements within modern art is indeed one of its most significant characteristics for the philosophic historian. It is a symptom of the self-consciousness that infects our whole attitude toward art, and the enjoyment of art, within the modern epoch. The appreciation of art has become a self-conscious part of human "culture." It was not until the eighteenth century—well on into our Cartesian period—that "aesthetic experience," as a distinct mode of subjective consciousness, came into being. Nobody had aesthetic experiences before that time, yet art somehow managed to survive and flourish.

This programmatic character of modern art, with its constant jostling of movements and countermovements, has reached something of a peak in this country. In the late 1940s and in the 1950s, abstract expressionism emerged as a major style, which worked deeply and originally enough within the traditional resources of painting that it might have permitted considerable development for some time. Ordinarily a significant style in the history of art is one in which artists can settle down and produce "more of the same" in a way that we find fresh and rewarding. But whether it was our American restlessness, or the pressure of the commercial market, or both, that period of consolidation did not happen here; instead, there followed the quick succession of op, pop, minimal art, and other quasimovements. Each artist, it seemed, was struggling to come up with a new gimmick in order to establish his credentials for genuine originality. This is the situation behind Harold Rosenberg's book *Tradition of the New*, whose title we should ponder carefully—perhaps a little more carefully than the author himself. If art styles vary so incessantly, there ceases to be a viable tradition that the artist is carrying on. What is established instead is a tradition of perpetual novelty. Art becomes the ceaseless fabrication of new models. We go to the galleries each season as we go to the salesrooms of the automobile companies—to see what new lines have been developed. Art styles become obsolete like the old models of cars. Art and the artist become assimilated to the production lines of the technical order.

IV.

To sum up: The human subject lurking in the subject-object dualism that has shaped our modern epoch has not disappeared. Technical requirements have led us to quantify and calculate a great many more parts of life; but preoccupied as we may be with objects and data, the human subject is still there, restless and unappeased, haunting the edges of the technical world. In its lower manifestations, this subjectivism is the malaise of the mass, "the lonely crowd" of the modern city—a malaise diffuse and inchoate, but sometimes desperately restless in its boredom. In its higher manifestations it is the subjectivity captured by modern art, complex and subtle, but also high-strung and alienated.

Of course, any sketch of modern culture so brief as the foregoing is bound to appear disparaging. We hasten to add, though it should be unnecessary, that no disparagement is intended of the greatness of the very great works of art that have been produced in our period. These works formed us in our youth, and we would not forego them in old age. Nevertheless, we begin to feel a little bit uncomfortable in their presence. The suspicion is abroad that the great period in modern art is coming to an end, if indeed it has not already done so. Questions about the peculiar marginal condition of art become more persistent. Former periods may have wondered from time to time what were the possible connections between genius and madness, or why poets often seemed to display an irritable temperament; but in our time the theme of "art and neurosis" becomes more clinical and insistent—too insistent to leave us altogether comfortable. Walter Pater remarked prophetically of Coleridge that one could hear in him "that inexhaustible discontent, languor, and homesickness, the chords of which ring all through our modern literature." Pater was speaking of a certain condition that had first found expression in the Romantic poets, but by his time had spread through the nineteenth century; and accordingly his language has some of the Romantic resonance about it. We today might use different language, but the phenomenon to be described is the same. For anyone who has been exposed to modern literature and art, "loss of Being" will not appear as an empty and remote term borrowed from a philosopher like Heidegger. It is a condition against which poet or artist, beyond the wrestle with his craft, has to struggle in order to find a foothold somewhere, to draw a breath, and to stand in some relation to life and nature that permits him to be what he is.

Modern civilization has raised the material level of millions of people beyond the expectations of the past. Has it succeeded in making people any happier? To judge by the bulk of modern literature, we would have to answer "No"; and in some aspects we might even have to say it has accomplished the reverse. Of course, all literature—even comedy—deals with the troubles of humankind. If a character is not in trouble of some sort, there is no situation to develop, no plot to unravel, and consequently no story to tell. But when we have allowed for this universal fact, there still remains a very distinctive and pervasive unhappiness throughout modern literature that we cannot pretend to look away from.

Certainly we cannot ignore it when we set about constructing our technological utopias. The utopians usually arrive at their pictures of the future by simple projection: Extend the curve of technical power and beneficence onward and upward and you automatically diminish the evils of the human condition. But if we are to proceed by such simple extrapolation, we might just as well extend the curve of our present malaise and anxiety continuously downward. I do not recommend either procedure as sound method; the future is too complex and difficult a matter to be calculated so simply; and in the end we shall have to let it make of itself what it will be. Meanwhile, we can draw one prosaic and sensible conclusion, that technological advance in itself is not sufficient to secure the happiness of mankind. The sources of that happiness seem to lie elsewhere.

Conclusion to Part II

The picture we have drawn in our last two chapters may be somber, but is not intended to be pessimistic. Radical pessimism must always be deterministic; it enunciates a curve of decline and fall from which there is no escape. If it does not shut the doors of hope upon mankind, its pessimism is less than complete. But the scenario we have sketched, following Heidegger, leaves us still with an opening of freedom; indeed, it challenges us to seek that opening. We would no longer be dealing with history if freedom were not involved. History arose out of prehistory to widen the possibilities of our freedom; and if freedom were to disappear in the further advance of civilization, humankind would sink to a level of routine more grim than the anonymity of prehistorical man. The technological framework, the *Gestell*, is itself a creation of freedom—the form in which our human freedom finds its global expression in this epoch. Our picture is somber only because it warns us that the very power and success of the technological structure may stultify us for other and more basic modes of freedom.

Thus our argument in this book has moved in two complementary directions. In Part I we sought to indicate some limitations of technique in its own terms. Human creativity exceeds the mechanisms it invents, and is required even for their intelligent direction. Quite literally and simply, *technique presupposes freedom for its own meaning*. We had to do there with the formal and internal aspects of the technical question; Part II has dealt with technique as it is factually and concretely embodied in our actual technology. And this latter appears to violate all the formal cautions we had suggested. The technical order, in the flush of its success and in its infiltration into every cranny of our life, seems to brook no inherent limitations to technique. The consequent danger is not that we become slaves to the machine, as an older and simpler imagination represented the future to us. On the contrary, we can imagine the technical order operating at maximal and humane efficiency such that abundant and pleasant leisure would be at the disposal of all—and the danger would still be there. The system would enclose us within it all too comfortably and, alas, all too completely. The open spaces become fewer in which we can draw breath and see beyond the enclosing framework itself. A certain poetic dimension of life shrivels. We do not walk the earth and look up at the stars; we prefer to see them on photographic plates. And as for freedom itself, we tend to confuse it with the will to power and our frenzied manipulation of objects.

This last is not a fanciful or remote premonition; the details of the phenomenon are already recognizable everywhere about us. They are brilliantly presented and dissected by psychoanalyst Leslie Farber, who concludes after thirty years spent observing patients that ours has become the age of "the disordered will." Farber notes that we live amid a constant bombardment of solicitations toward such willfulness:

> Day in, day out, every citizen is instructed by the public media that there is no portion of his life that is not wholly within his control or . . . wholly subject to his will. If life is difficult for you, an evening of television watching will teach you how to dispel your miseries through aspirin, deodorants, mouthwash, dance lessons, laxatives, vitamins, hair lotions, and edifying panel programs.[1]

And he rightly traces the phenomenon back to the omnipresence of technology, to which effect he quotes a young student:

> Everything else in this world is being turned on and off—lights, television sets, refrigerators, stoves, fans, phonographs, vacuum cleaners, and so on—so why shouldn't we want to be turned on too?[2]

---

[1] Leslie H. Farber, *Lying, despair, etc.* (New York: Basic Books, 1976), p. 7.

[2] Ibid., p. 9.

But if the details have already become recognizable, the outlines of our picture may be too simple. Of course, all thought aims at simplifying experience in some way; but it has always to take the next step of questioning its own simplifications. So far we have followed Heidegger; and though we have improvised freely, where necessary, to fill out his meaning where he had left it schematic, we have nevertheless remained pretty well within the confines of his thought. We have now to question what may be lacking to the grand simplifications of his general scheme.

The simplicity of any pattern of thought is not in itself an objection. The greatest philosophers always leave us with some simple residual pattern of insight. But it is one thing to seek a pattern within the flux of recurrent experience, and another to seek it in that unique and unrepeatable chunk of becoming that is human history. The philosophy of history is the one field where the sheer human element—the irregularities and contingencies of human nature—come into full play. The "march of history" may look like that when mapped on a large scale; but seen up close, it is really the continuous flow of events back and forth amid the shoals of human contingencies. Historical tendencies do not push forward in a straight line toward some ultimate consolidation; they go only so far, and then meet reversal, either through internal conflict or through a contrary impulse that thrusts them back or shunts them to one side. Empires do not last forever; they collapse and dwindle into fragments of themselves. Such might happen to the empire of technology. The technical framework, the *Gestell*, is depicted by Heidegger in his more mournful moments as if it were a process that would expand inexorably, logically, and devouringly. Today we are all too aware what accidents might halt this process. The disappearance of readily available sources of energy could throw the whole technical structure into panic. Decentralization in one form or another might come about; and we might settle for a less opulent but more resilient technology. And the most dire possibility of all: A thermonuclear war between the superpowers would leave civilization a shambles. The humankind that survived would crawl along at a level of technology that would be aboriginal.

This last possibility serves indeed to show how the question of technology is at bottom a political one. Were the political turmoil of the world to subside, were some general regime of liberty and enlightenment to set in, then the whole business of technology would not seem as threatening as it does. Indeed, the pressing question at this moment in history is not the technical question per se, but the survival of human liberty. A good many of the popular and sentimental jeremiads against technology really seek to evade this issue. In some cases they are even a subterfuge for depriving the United States of its chief advantage in its present struggle for survival. But the issue cannot finally be obscured: The question for our generation, or the one just coming up, is whether or not mankind will decide for liberty or sink under some modern form of tyranny. And this decision is in the end a moral matter; for some individuals, as events are now moving, it may well be a matter of moral sacrifice and moral heroism. But of this moral dimension of history, Heidegger says nothing; the moral individual, as such, does not lie at the center of his thinking.

There is, I believe, a certain spiritual kinship between the late Heidegger and his fellow Suebian, Hegel. To be sure, they do not correspond at all in points of doctrine; and the feelings communicated by their philosophies are very different. Despite Hegel's very shrewd eye for the "negative" aspects of the human condition, his thought still belonged to the Enlightenment and was saturated with its optimism. Heidegger distinctly belongs to the post-Enlightenment. He would not be of our time if he did not; for the achievement of the twentieth century is to have absorbed the counter-Enlightenment into its own culture, so that it looks with a skeptical and suspicious eye on the assumption of progress. The similarity lies in the preoccupation of each thinker with the sweep of history as the main matter of his thought. The vision becomes so sweeping indeed that we feel that consideration of the actual and concrete individual gets lost within it. So Kierkegaard the rebel arose to assert the claims of the existing individual against Hegel and his panorama of world history. A similar corrective may be needed in the case of Heidegger. He begins as the analyst of human existence; but in his later thought our individual being seems to become absorbed into the stages in the history of Being. We have to go in search of the individual again.

Two themes are dominant in this later Heidegger: the question of poetry and the question of technology. Poet and technician confront each other as antithetical figures, and the philosopher's thinking revolves around their confrontation. Let us not underestimate the depth or the seriousness of this opposition. We do not deal with poetry here as a mere adornment of culture. It is not an elegant concoction of words to provide us with an "aesthetic experience"—that latter-day construction of philosophic aestheticians that removes art to the periphery of our common life. Heidegger is struggling to recall poetry to its primal dwelling among us on this earth and under this sky. If poetry does not touch the daily round of our existence somewhere or other, then we ourselves have become homeless on this earth. The figure of the poet thus represents a dimension of our human being, the loss of which would leave civilized man an emotional cripple. What is the difference between poet and technician? The poet walking in the woods loses himself in the rapture of its presence; the technician calculates the bulldozers that will be needed to level it. At some point in our life we have to follow the poet in that "wise passiveness," to learn to let be, or we remain forever caught in the nervous clutch of our willfulness.

But this antithesis between poet and technician is not the only one that confronts us in a technical civilization. Between the passivity toward Being and the drive to power is there not another area of life in which we are called on to exercise our will and its freedom? Not the will to power indeed, but the moral will, which is something very different? This is the question to which we now turn. Freedom is the real, the positive subject of our quest. And if we have spent so much time on technique and technology, that is only because these loom nowadays as the negative and opposing face to freedom. To have argued for their limits, and even to have succeeded in showing them would not be enough to establish a positive conception of freedom. And without this positive sense of freedom we shall not be responding to the question that originally set us going.

Part III

―――――◆―――――

Freedom

Chapter 12

The Moral Will

"WHEN ARE YOU GOING TO WRITE AN ETHICS?" THE QUESTION WAS asked of Heidegger by a young friend shortly after the publication of *Being and Time* in 1927. Heidegger himself recalls the incident twenty years later. The question must touch a sensitive spot—one his critics had made sensitive—that he should remember it long afterward. The thinker must be allowed in the end to deliver judgment upon himself, even if indirectly. For there is a judgment implied here since he touches on the question that remains unanswered in the whole philosophy. Heidegger did not go on to write that ethics. That in itself would signify little; philosophers whose thought is morally saturated from beginning to end—William James would be an example—never bowed to the labor of producing an ethical treatise, and we are not the least troubled thereby. But this absence in Heidegger strikes us as more serious: It is not the incidental fact that he did not write an ethics that is troubling, but the doubt that he could write one and remain within the confines of his thought.

This may seem a strange accusation against a thinker whose effort, now that we are able to see it as a whole, was nothing less than a preparation to enter anew the sphere of religious existence. But all the preparation, so scrupulously and patiently carried on over the years, cannot reach its goal: It cannot enter the religious because it does not arrive at the ethical. To reach the ethical would require a leap to another level, a *metabasis eis allo genos* (a step into another region of existence).

This criticism might be fatal to another philosopher, but it does not, nor is it meant to, demolish Heidegger. It indicates, rather, the limits within which we have to measure his value to us. And right now such limits are particularly important to establish because in some circles Heidegger's name threatens to become the password of a cult, and his works the object of a pious scholasticism—which is all to the good so far as it helps disseminate his doctrine and serves to counteract certain narrower philosophic tendencies of the moment. The danger is that the scholastic pieties, oversensitive to any criticism, lead us eventually to believe that the philosophy accomplishes more than it actually does. Heidegger himself has stressed that the great philosophers of the past were always consumed by a single vision. They had only one thought, he tells us, which they were struggling to utter and which nevertheless remains unsaid or ill said through all they have written. We may allow his own beautiful words to be applied to himself: "To think is to confine oneself to a single thought that one day stands still like a star in the world's sky." He is the thinker of only one idea, Being, but this single star of his shines with a surprising radiance. We read the history of philosophy, and so history itself, differently now by its light. His thought undermines the subjectivistic constructions of modern aesthetics, and so enables us to think of a poem or work of art in at once a newer and more ancient manner. But rich as the bearing of his thought may be elsewhere, with the matter of ethics itself Heidegger does not come to grips.

This is not to imply that his thinking is somehow unethical or nihilistic; that was an impression carried away by his earlier critics, because his themes often seemed so austere and chilling. Here was a philosopher who took nothingness seriously and wrote about it openly; and surely that must hint at some strange and morbid trait in the man himself. A response like this is itself but the reflex of a superficial and socially acceptable nihilism that recoils from anything negative in our existence. And Heidegger is surely right that until we think through the "nihil" (nothing) in nihilism we only continue to drift from one bogus "affirmation" to another. No; the reason the ethical does not appear within the scope of Heidegger's thinking is not to be sought in these imaginary twists of his temperament. It lies much more fundamentally in the subject of ethics itself, and the obstacles that subject seems to place before him.

From its very beginnings, in the hands of Aristotle, ethics has taken the will as its central fact. The will is "deliberative desire," the place in our psychic landscape where reason and appetite meet; where our wishes and emotions submit to reason, and reason in turn is activated by desire; hence the central pivot of the human being as a practical agent. The tradition has remained virtually unbroken ever since. Kant, the most systematic moralist after Aristotle, internalizes but remains fully within this tradition when he takes the moral will to be the center of the human person.

But in the fateful course of modern thought (as we saw in Chapter 10), this essentially moral will was to become transformed into something else: the will to self-assertion and dominance; the will to power. Reason, under its sway, is pronounced legislative of phenomena, and eventually becomes technical reason. Nietzsche, because he consented to it and willed it as his own will, was able to probe this will in its tragic and demoniacal dimensions. In much less conscious but far more blatant manifestations, this will is everywhere around us in the modern marketplace. The Nazis had proclaimed their own vulgarization of the German philosophy of the will as the voice of national resurgence. Leni Riefenstahl's documentary on the rise of the Nazi movement, still extolled by *cineasts* as a model of its kind, was entitled *The Triumph of the Will*. If the matter of ethics is inseparably involved with the will, and the will has been compromised and even polluted at its source, how can one go ahead and write an ethics?

Yet freedom holds a central place in Heidegger's thought, and that would seem to have something to do with the will. Traditionally the question of freedom has been discussed by philosophers as the freedom of the will. To be sure, Heidegger's conception of freedom is detached from the will to action. Freedom is the condition of truth itself, for unless we are free to let be, to let things show themselves as what they are, we will only force our willful distortions upon them. But is not this detachment from willfulness a condition of the will itself? And is it not a moral state, since we praise people for it and attach blame to the opposite willfulness? Perhaps then there is another sense of the will, hidden in Heidegger's own pages, beyond that dissonant and self-assertive sense of the will he is seeking to avoid—a sense that we have to bring out into the clear. Perhaps we have to reach back beyond post-Kantian German philosophy to an older meaning of the will: to the meaning that *voluntas* had for some medieval philosophers, which goes back to St. Augustine and beyond him to the *Eros* of Plato. Perhaps the will, at its deepest, does not connote self-assertion and dominance, but love and acquiescence; not the will to power but the will to prayer.

In raising such questions, of course, we look beyond Heidegger to the whole of modern culture. To try to restore the moral will to a central and primary role in the human personality is bound to appear as an effort against the mainstream of this culture. After all, modernism began as a revolt against Victorianism, particularly the cramping moral code of the Victorians; and modernism has continued ever since in its goal of self-liberation. The great literature of the modern movement, on which we were raised, takes the side of Dionysian instinct against the moralist. "Nothing is more characteristic of modern literature," Lionel Trilling puts it very aptly, "than its discovery and canonization of the primal, nonethical energies." Freud and psychoanalysis were another powerful current flowing into the same mainstream. Whether it meant to or not, the psychoanalytic movement hardly strengthened the force of traditional morality. By dethroning the sovereignty of consciousness, by showing its weakness before the unconscious, it left people less able to believe in their moral freedom. When the conscious mind loses its potency, the will ceases to be a central governing agency. Our moral vocabulary was superseded by a psychoanalytic one. Instead of talking about the virtues and vices, people thought it much more profound and "scientific" to talk about neuroses and complexes. The moral component of experience, no longer taken as primary and irreducible, was left at best the peripheral status of a social policeman. In trying to reassert the claims of the moral will against such formidable influences, one starts with an apologetic sense that one may be taken as a prig or a hypocrite.

Yet in all this disparagement of the moral will there remains one glaring discrepancy between this culture and our actual life; or, to bring the point closer to home, between ourselves as partisans of this culture and ourselves in the ordinary course of our private lives. We still go about our everyday business guided by this moral will, and we still discriminate in its terms. We do distinguish the people we know by their virtues and vices, and deal with them accordingly. We forgive an old friend who is sometimes odd and tedious by saying that, after all, she is a "very dear person" and "a good soul." And with a brilliant and neurotic friend, on the other hand, for whom we have made psychoanalytic excuses over the years, if the friendship reaches the breaking point, we usually give up then all the jargon of the neuroses and declare simply that he has become so perverse, inconsiderate, and selfish that we do not care to see him again. It clears the air sometimes to say of someone that he is a stinker, period, as if coming out of the psychological clouds we were at last touching solid ground. In short, without being aware of it, we do follow Kant's view that the moral will is the center of the personality. And yet, amazingly enough, modern philosophers have yet to come to terms with this fact.

                                   I.

In attempting to disengage these points both within and against Heidegger, I am aware of a great deal of personal experience hovering in the background, and perhaps it will make matters clearer if I were here and now to avow this aspect of my enterprise. The late W. H. Auden once remarked that an important book is one that reads us, not the reverse. In this sense, I have been read by Heidegger for many years, and his response to my needs has varied. His German was simple and well within my ken, and so I was easily admitted past that barrier. The points on which I was rejected were particular obstacles of my own philosophical background, beyond which I had gradually to see my way. There followed a good many years of growing acceptance, closeness, and attachment. And this closeness was further heightened by the experience of teaching him, of putting him across over the resistances of students, having to re-create his meanings for them when they had, and perhaps fortunately in some ways, no English translation available. Nothing brings one closer to a thinker than to share his meanings with other people.

It was above all this experience of teaching him that added a vivid and adventurous note to our relationship. Over the years one found sympathetic students, and here for a philosophy text I had a singularly adventurous work to share with them. *Being and Time* had a dramatic story and a hero, Dasein, who went through some very powerful and moving experiences. "Dasein" is Heidegger's word for human being—the being that each of us is in his or her own separate fashion. Since the word has such powerful connotations in German, we did not translate it, and in time used it as easily as if we were speaking of a familiar character in a novel. Dasein's story is this: He is thrown into the world, and loses himself in its various external trivia; but through the encounter with death, in the light of his own extreme possibility that death discloses to him, he may rise to the level of an authentic existence. He may even become aware of the unique and authentic sense in which his existence is historical, and so play a free and authentic part in the historical mission of his time. Since the class was in philosophy, it was not enough to follow this story; one also had to contrive and explore situations not in the text. "What would Dasein do in such-and-such a case?" "How does Dasein feel about so-and-so?" There were jokes attempted and made, of course, but our purpose was not flippant; we were talking in an easy and familiar way about someone who seemed to have become, in our imagination at least, a mutual friend. And so I continued in this happy state of companionship with the author and his character for a number of years.

And then I woke up one morning with a very disturbing feeling that there was, after all, something strangely empty about this Dasein. I did not try at first to wrestle intellectually with this feeling; the words that expressed it came spontaneously and forced themselves upon me, and they were these: "Dasein has no soul." To some philosophic sophisticates this may seem a simpleminded, or should we say simplehearted, reaction; but even now I find no more concise and compelling way in which to put my judgment. Nor was the feeling dispelled by the fact that I knew, and had known long since, the formal reasons against it: Heidegger's analysis is not intended to give us the actual person but only the structure of possibilities within which each of us has to enact his own finite and mortal drama of enlightenment. Even with allowance made for that self-imposed limitation, the same sense of a final emptiness seemed to stare back at me from Heidegger's text. Nor did it help that I chose to keep this feeling to myself before the class. They would have been confused, and I felt I could not then spell out for them clearly enough the source of my uneasiness. My task, after all, was to enlist their sympathy in the philosopher so that they might extract whatever insight they could from his text. To have placed this grave doubt, and one so inchoately formulated at that, before them would have immediately abolished every willing suspension of their disbelief and seriously undermined the rest of my pedagogical efforts. I chose therefore to hug my guilty secret to myself.

So I come at last to disburden myself of it here, and with the premonitory misgiving that I shall not probably produce any clearer statement than those instinctive words with which it originally forced itself upon me. For myself, I would prefer to leave it at that—that Dasein has no soul—trusting that there are still some uncorrupted readers around who will find such a judgment perfectly understandable. But philosophers distrust such instinctive responses; we are trained to distrust them, and so well sometimes that we lose, alas, the capacity for them. And so, in this professional capacity, the rest of this chapter will struggle to find reasons for a response that came spontaneously and will probably persist spontaneously whatever the reasons I shall give.

II.

We may as well begin with the theme of death, since we have already alluded to this, and it also happens that some of Heidegger's boldest and most powerful pages are on this subject.

Philosophically, the key ideas here are those of actuality and potentiality. From an impersonal and public point of view, death is an actual event that happens every day in the world. We read about it in obituaries: It is something that happens to other people. To be sure, in the course of things it will happen to me, but not yet. As an actual event, or an event that will be actual sometime in the future, it is thus external to my existence now. But everything is changed if we shift our gaze from actuality to potentiality. My death will never be an actual event within my world; I will not be there to read my own obituary. This death, *my* death, the death that haunts me is the possibility that I shall lose that world. And as such an internal possibility, it pervades my existence now and at every moment. To be sure, it is the most extreme and absolute possibility, because it cancels all other possibilities. Yet if we do not turn away in panic, this vision of our radical finitude brings its own liberation. Free for our death, we are freed from the tyranny of petty worries and diversions, and thus open to the authentic self that beckons to us.

The thinking is straightforward, powerful, and cogent; and yet we get the feeling that something essential has been left out. What? It is not unusual to teach this part of Heidegger side by side with Tolstoi's great story *The Death of Ivan Ilyich*. Heidegger himself had learned from Tolstoi, and gives a footnote of approval to the latter for describing the breakdown of those impersonal structures with which we and society conceal the truth of death from ourselves. Placed side by side, Tolstoi's story and Heidegger's dissection form a powerful and corroborative parallel—up to a point; for in the end there is a whole world of difference between them. And this difference is not merely the greater immediacy of the artist's language, for Heidegger's existential analysis has a potent expressiveness of its own. The difference is the absence of the moral dimension from Heidegger's account. What, after all, is the transforming experience of death for Ivan Ilyich apart from the moral revulsion that assails him for the life he has led? That life, which had seemed "normal" and acceptable to himself and his social peers, now shows itself to have been selfish, empty, vain, and therefore meaningless; and with this there comes also the vision of another and very different way in which men ought to live. That is the truth, the disclosure, the *Aletheia,* that the imminence of death brings with it. Heidegger's existential analysis makes explicit an ontological structure implicit in Tolstoi's story, but leaves out the moral message at its center. What we get is the anatomical skeleton of an organism without its beating heart.

To be free toward one's death! That is easier said than done. For the man who loves life, death looms as the supreme injustice. To submit to this injustice out of a sullen and stubborn stoicism is one thing; admirable perhaps, but not a reconciliation. To become genuinely reconciled, to assent to death as no longer unjust, is an infinitely farther step. That requires a leap as great as the medieval assent to Dante's inscription over the gate of Hell, "Divine Love made me." To be free toward one's death would require a conversion of the whole person, a transformation of heart and will. It could hardly be accomplished by the intellectual shift to viewing death as an internal possibility rather than an external actuality.

Tolstoi's is the case of the passionately religious mind struggling to make sense of the reality of death. But even for the passionately irreligious, where the confrontation with death is defiant, the moral will plays a central role. The nihilist or criminal, who sets his life at a pin's fee, is able to carry his pride and courage with him to the end only because he has taken up a certain stance toward life. He has established his style and he is morally bound to its gestures. He will play out his role to the end. Damning his executioners, he goes defiantly to the guillotine, like the antihero of Camus in *The*

Stranger. The encounter with death remains the supreme adventure to test the moral will. No man dies freely save in affirmation of the values he attaches to life.

III.

If we are liberated at all by death, it is in virtue of the light that it sheds on our human situation. Heidegger's theme throughout, as we have already said, is this drama of truth and untruth, for which the pathos of our human lot only supplies the occasions. Indeed, his doctrine of truth—of the intrinsic connection of truth with Being, in the sense of evident presence—is his great and original contribution to philosophy. Yet even here, in the phenomenon of truth itself, do we find the will altogether absent? Let us see.

Freedom, he tells us, is the essence of truth. This does not, of course, mean that our will is free to legislate arbitrarily what is true or false. "Essence" here signifies the ground—the condition that makes a particular phenomenon possible. We have to be free to let the things in question show themselves as they are. But of course, we say, everyone knows this; and so this thesis, which first struck us as paradoxical, might seem to be an idle platitude.

But viewed historically, far from being an innocuous commonplace, Heidegger's point is in fact an ambitious impeachment of the modern age and its doctrine of truth by conquest and rape. Francis Bacon proclaimed the coming time when mankind would put nature to the rack in order to compel her to answer our questions. Yet, however we twist her, we would still have to be free to listen to the answers that poor tortured nature gives us. And if we follow Kant, who says the same thing as Bacon in more gentle and reasonable words—that knowledge must organize our experience within the framework of certain categories and concepts—we have still to let experience, so organized, speak for what it is. More than this: We have to take the step backward and let that framework itself be seen for what it is.

This last step is one of the most difficult things to do, and scientists in this respect are as humanly imperfect as the rest of us. The history of science abounds in cases of scientists who cling tenaciously to their pet theory, refuse to be dislodged from it, twist facts to fit into it, or remain resolutely blind to whatever facts resist such twisting. The pet theory has become such an ingrained part of their vision of things that they cannot see it for what it is because they are always seeing everything else through it.

We suffer from the same willfulness in our ordinary life. Our traffic with other human beings is an endless tale of the obstacles we set before our seeing things as they are. We are all capable of a quite devastating perversity of will in distorting the situations we encounter daily. A man may go through life side by side with people whom he never sees truthfully and whose real relationship to himself remains hidden. He believes he loves when he really hates, hates when he loves, and alternately makes too much or too little of either. So we go on in our blindness, twisting and distorting and obscuring what is so palpably there if we could only give up our hysterical meddling.

We begin to tread here on the familiar terrain of the psychoanalyst, to whom we may leave his own particular means of curing the cancer. Without intruding on the details of the clinic, we would only note in passing that whatever cure comes—and perhaps we should better say improvement, for our mortal condition never permits us to be totally cured of untruth—it does not come through the patient's acquisition of psychoanalytic theory. He could just as well have stayed home, read books, and spared himself the considerable expense of psychoanalysis. No; the significant changes come deeper down, though our intellectual views may also change in consequence. The patient comes to feel differently about the world, about himself and other people, and as a consequence he will see things differently.

No doubt, our vocabulary must be halting when we try to get close to this central region of the self where the great transformations occur; and we have learned little from Heidegger if we were merely to fall back upon some stock antithesis of will and intellect. The will—this volitional part of ourselves—is not to be understood as a mere organ of drives and blind desires. On the contrary, the will carries in itself its own enlightenment or darkness, as the case may be; and we move within this light and darkness in the most ordinary traffic of daily life. Freedom is not to be sought as a localized property that inhabits the will the way strength resides in our muscles. It does not show itself in some singular and violent leap, like an extraordinary feat of strength. Our freedom is the way in which we are able to let the world open before us and ourselves stand open within it. Our loves and hates disclose or conceal the world in this or that way. Far from being blind "affects," to which the intellect alone adds its light, they carry their own light within themselves. But this will is also a moral will; and not in the sense that we tack on "values" and "imperatives" that are extraneous to it; it is a moral will at its very source, in and of itself, for in its light we are called upon to bear ourselves thus and so within the world.

Clearly, the most important thing for us at this stage of history, according to the gospel of Heidegger, is to learn to let be. His word for this condition is *Gelassenheit*, which he uses also as a title of a slight but beautifully evocative dialogue that he devotes to this subject. How to translate *Gelassenheit?* Release, deliverance, self-surrender, the peace that passeth understanding? Perhaps we might remember Eliot's line,

> Teach me to care and not to care,

to express the consummation of the self in selflessness that Heidegger's word intends. But however we translate it, *Gelassenheit* is central to the whole of the later Heidegger, and our natural human inclination is to ask how we may achieve it. We have to be will-less, but we cannot will to be will-less. And Heidegger leaves the matter at that.

But we cannot leave it at that. For we would be left with the quite paradoxical position that the human will, as willfulness, leads us into untruth; yet we cannot say that the will, in its positive and opposed sense, is in any way the source of truth. If we cannot will to be will-less, at least there should be something we can *do* about our willful condition. Otherwise we are left the helpless prisoners of our own perverse will to power.

We are caught in the old theological puzzle of grace and freedom. We cannot will the advent of grace, for we have to surrender the will if grace is to come at all; but how can we surrender this obstinate and perverse will unless grace itself enables us to do so? Perhaps we cannot penetrate farther into this mystery than the old theologians did, but at least we should go as far—we should not fall below their level. The traditional religions come to our aid with their ritual practices or codes of behavior that might possibly prepare the will for deliverance. For, contrary to many philosophers, Wittgenstein included, we can set about changing our will, and sometimes succeed, through the roundabout course of action. In any case, no workable religion can send us away empty-handed; there must always be something, humanly speaking, that we can do, though success (grace) is not assured. But this realm of the pragmatic does not concern Heidegger; the connection between Being and doing is not a central preoccupation, and attracts his attention chiefly in those situations where our frantic doing involves a loss of Being. The self-surrender, the *Gelassenheit*, that interests him is not the peace that might attend us as we set about an ordinary moral task—in the doing of which sometimes indeed the release of love may be born. He is drawn instead to the exalted rapture that may come to us in a walk through the woods or over a country path, and which, if we were poets, we could turn into a lyric poem.

What emerges here is the distinction between our ethical and our aesthetic existence, and the voice of Kierkegaard warning us against the aesthete suddenly sounds in the background. I do not wish to urge that distinction as Kierkegaard made it—I am not sure it is altogether satisfactory as he does make it—but I believe his point cannot be evaded. In the end, these two—Kierkegaard and Heidegger—are the ultimate antagonists.[1]

IV.

To be sure, the concern with poetry is not an "aesthetic" luxury to Heidegger, but a necessary and fulfilling step in his philosophic thought. In the technical era, when everything becomes an instrument at the service of the will, language is manipulated as a calculus. Poetry resists this will and thereby reveals a more fundamental dimension of language. Before the poem one must lay down one's self-assertion; one has to surrender oneself and enter the same circle of Being where poem and poet dwell. Thus the date 1936, when he published the first of his essays on the poet Hölderlin, is taken to mark the celebrated "turn" in Heidegger's thinking, though this turn is not so much a reversal as a fulfillment, a direct step into what lay behind his earlier analyses of human existence.

We can understand then why poetry should be so central a subject for Heidegger. But why has he made Hölderlin his chosen poet? Heidegger himself voices the question. Why has he not chosen to explore the nature of poetry through some other more famous poet, Homer or Sophocles, Virgil or Dante, Shakespeare or

---

[1] See notes at end of this chapter.

Goethe? The immediate answer he gives is that Hölderlin writes about the poetic calling itself—poetizes about the nature of poetry —and we may therefore gather that nature more directly from him. But the deeper and the real reason for the choice follows a little later: Hölderlin is a prophet of our time, the "time of need," when the old gods have fled and the new god has not arrived. Standing between two worlds, he is the poet who speaks out of this void, and therefore Heidegger finds in him his spiritual kin.

All the same, he is a strange affinity, this Hölderlin, one of the greatest and loneliest of poets. Born in 1770—the birthdate, as it happens, of Beethoven and Hegel—Hölderlin was part of the most brilliant and productive generation of Germans, but also was to undergo a sadder fate than any of his contemporaries. Toward the year 1802, when he was only thirty-two, he began to show signs of derangement, and by the end of 1804 had become incurably insane. The last thirty-six years of his life he spent as an amiable and harmless lunatic, being cared for in the household of a local carpenter and doing odd jobs as a gardener. Until we know enough about schizophrenia to settle such questions, we may continue to wonder in these cases of genius, as with Nietzsche too, whether the vision provoked the madness or was merely a consequence of it. With Hölderlin, in any case, the illness and the vision seem to go side by side. As the shadow darkens over the poet, the poems themselves become more daring, disconnected, schizoid—more "modernist" in manner, as one critic aptly puts it. The great hymns are like magnificent and shining blocks of ice that detach themselves from a continent and float off into an empty sea.

And so our question persists: What if Heidegger had chosen another figure, a Dante or Shakespeare, as the paradigm poet from which to explicate the nature of poetry? Would not poetry itself look different to us then, and the will emerge as one of its themes? "Hölderlin and the Essence of Poetry" was the first Heidegger I ever read, more than thirty years ago, and the question has never since left my mind. Why not Shakespeare or Dante indeed? With them the human person does not vanish into an empty presence. Here are real human agents, embodiments of the will in its sublime as well as its atrocious shapes—not the technical will, to be sure, but the moral will for good and evil. The antithesis to Hölderlin is, of course, Dante, and *The Divine Comedy* can be read as the great poem of the will in its various stages: the congealed will, fixed in its perversity, of the *Inferno;* the laboring and yearning will of the *Purgatorio;* and in the *Paradiso* the consummation of the will in prayer. In Hölderlin the voice of prayer sounds from beginning to end, but it is prayer that, finding no effective relation to the will, drifts off like a cloud thinning out into the void. For myself, I find Dante's Hell less terrifying than the alpine air of some of Hölderlin's poems. At least the damned are intensely alive in their perverted will, while Hölderlin's world rarefies off into the frightening and thin air of holy schizophrenia.

But Heidegger is able to look past these human aspects of Hölderlin and his poems that disquiet us. Is Heidegger humanly insensitive here? In any case, he is protected by the detachment of his philosophic calling. Intent on the single theme of Being, he has to look past our human pathology. He is guarded and protected by the thought he patiently builds. "Poet and thinker are near akin," Heidegger tells us; and perhaps they are, in the themes that preoccupy them, but in this particular case they are very different individuals with very different spiritual needs. One compares the philosopher going on into his seventh and eight decades, serenely elaborating his meditation, with the youthful poet who succumbed in his early thirties. Heidegger writing about nothingness is the lucid and detached phenomenologist analyzing a datum. Hölderlin sounds a different note when he laments the fate of mankind that has lost its gods and is caught

> In the grip of that Nothing which rules over us, who are thoroughly aware that we are born for Nothing, believe in Nothing, work ourselves to the bone for Nothing, until we gradually dissolve into Nothing . . .

This is the voice of the actual man, not merely observing but also living through an anguish for which he must find a more sovereign remedy than philosophic meditation.

Is Being enough? Hölderlin evidently did not think so. Though he was caught in its grip and utters its encompassing presence more purely, if thinly, than any other poet, it could not sustain him. In search of the holy, he set off on the track of the fugitive god. Since the Christian god was no longer able to work for him, he sought to raise the antique gods to life again—an impossible task, as the Greeks themselves might have told him. After his first breakdown, which was brought on by overexposure to the sun on a trip through the South of France, he wrote to a friend that he had been stricken by the shafts of Apollo. It was really the absence of Apollo that finally struck him down.

The enchantment with Hellas has been one of the most profound but also one of the most questionable features of the German spirit since the eighteenth century. The German interpreters of the Greeks number among them some of their greatest figures— Winckelmann, Goethe, Lessing, Schiller, Hölderlin, Nietzsche; and now Heidegger himself must be allowed to enter that august circle. We do not doubt the greatness of these interpreters; what we question is how much of this infatuation with Hellas has been prompted by romantic longing, by a nostalgia for a simpler and more vital stage of the human spirit; and how much of it, in consequence, tends to an "aestheticizing" of the Greeks. We lose their reality for the dazzling image of them we would erect. But of all these German interpreters of the Greeks, Heidegger tells us, the greatest was Hölderlin. Why? Because he alone tried to take the gods of the Greeks seriously. But what is it then to take a god seriously?

I sat once on one of the stone seats of the theater of Dionysos at Athens, the relentless blue sky overhead and the sacred hill of the city beyond me, and tried to imagine myself two millennia earlier sitting as a spectator before a drama of Aeschylus or Sophocles. What was the response of the ordinary citizen of Athens to these plays? As I sat there, I began to have a sense of identity with that unknown whose place I now held. He is the forgotten man among all the interpretations, brilliant and varied as they have been, that we moderns have concocted of Greek drama. We have had the youthful Nietzsche expounding them in terms of Schopenhauer's metaphysics; Freudian interpretations under the leading idea of the Oedipus complex; and latterly Heideggerian readings of the Greek plays as the drama of revelation (*Aletheia*) and hiddenness. However stimulating to us, these interpretations inevitably pass that ordinary spectator by. As moderns, we come to the drama as literature and thus as part of our intellectual and aesthetic culture. But the city that put Socrates to death on suspicion that he taught against the gods would not have dug into the public till to sponsor performances that explore the intellectual themes that interest *us*. These dramas are "morality plays," as directly and completely so as the medieval morality plays, though the morality they teach, to be sure, is very different from the Christian one. Sophocles and Aeschylus are partisans of the gods, perpetually warning their audience that the power and prescience of the god is not to be discounted even when the course of events in the play seems to be eluding his prophecy. The long "theological" debate that rounds out Aeschylus' cycle of the *Oresteia* strikes us on our first reading as prosaic, tedious, and altogether "undramatic"; and it takes on life for us only as we acquire a scholarly interest in Greek religion. To the Athenian contemporary, however, these theological debates were supremely dramatic, since on their successful resolution depended the preservation of the city and its laws, and consequently the well-being of the citizens themselves.

The religious morality of the Greek bound him to the cosmos in its actual and local presence, to his city and region (*Polis* and *Chora*) in a way that Jewish and Christian faith were to terminate. If we sigh for these Greek gods, it is the dream of alienated men hankering to come home. We begin then to fancy that to the Greek his religion was only an aesthetic affair of beautiful images fashioned by sculptors and poets. When they are alive, however, these gods create *obligations*. They bind the moral will of the worshiper to their service.

Our era is the night of the world, Heidegger mournfully echoes Hölderlin, when the old gods have fled but the new god has not yet arrived. Perhaps. But what are we supposed to *do* during this sullen interregnum? In his interview with the magazine *Der Spiegel*, published only after his death, Heidegger declared against us and our civilization, "Only a God will save you." He too seems to have come around at last to believe that Being is not enough. But do we merely wait around until this unknown god strikes us like a bolt from the blue? This is to surrender too much to a kind of historicism, in the manner of Hegel, as if the prevailing climate of opinion were to decide our possible salvation. The individual who needs God will seek Him out, whatever the fashion of his age.

Heidegger is too great and restless a mind to remain chained to the mechanical rhetoric of "the death of God." He grumbles against the critics of his godlessness: Perhaps his "godless thinking" is closer to the divine God than is philosophic theism, and he castigates the aridity and abstractness of the philosophic deity:

Man can neither pray nor sacrifice to this god. Before the *causa sui*, man can neither fall to his knees in awe, nor play music nor dance.

Three centuries earlier, Pascal made a similar point: "Not the God of the philosophers," he cried, "but the God of Abraham, Isaac, and Jacob." But what a world of difference here from Heidegger, for this God of the Jews does not come to us through "thinking"—not even that "piety of thought" that Heidegger, mixing religious and intellectual vocabularies, recommends to us. We come to Him in faith, by a surrender of the will. And this God is perhaps more tenacious of life than Heidegger's historical scheme imagines. As the deity of a nomad people, He is not confined to his local shrines and natural sites, like the gods of the Greeks, but may still hunt us down in our modern homelessness. There are still those who pray through the Psalms of David; I know of no one who worships through a choral ode of Sophocles or Aeschylus. If I worship by means of a psalm, it has been something much less and much more than a poem. The living God binds me morally in my flesh and spirit. The ode of Aeschylus remains alive to me, through aesthetic appropriation, only as a great poem. Hölderlin knew he had come too late for those antique gods and he expired in the emptiness of his vision.

v.

We come back to the moral will as the center of the human person. But in the history of thought, as in life, we never come back exactly to the point where we were and find ourselves unchanged. We are different as we return, and part of that difference has been made by Heidegger.

The moral will as our human center! How disappointing a message this must sound to our modern ears! How odd and simpleminded it seems against all the complex and sophisticated currents of modernity that have run the other way! But above all, how tame a cause this is to argue, how prosaic and stodgy, how positively hackneyed and old-hat! Ours has been an age of sensational discoveries, and if anyone is to bring us a message, we expect it to be revolutionary and spectacular, something that sets all our previous world by its ears. Intellectually we seem to have developed a fear of the commonplace and the truth that may reside there. So the very modesty of the message we seek may be after all a sign of its importance for us. And we have to insist on this modesty if we are to keep this moral will clear of the seductions of the will to power in any of its numerous disguises. The pervasiveness of this will to power throughout modern thought and modern life is one great lesson from Heidegger—so that he serves, even if he has avoided the matter of ethics, as something of a moral teacher after all. Whatever dominance we come to have over beings, we have in the end to bow before the mystery of Being. There, if at no other point, we have to learn to let be or else the tyrant will becomes its own slave. This saving grain of acquiescence is needed to preserve the moral will from the demon of its own earnestness, to restrain it from becoming overassertive of its own claims, so that it does not succumb to the temptations of hypocrisy or priggishness. In its modesty it will have enough to do in the days to come simply to keep alive the elementary decencies without which human civilization relapses into the jungle and human beings lose their meaning.

And perhaps it is just in this resistance to power in the world today that this moral will may bring a central message for our time. What else is the burden of Solzhenitsyn's life and writings? We may read his books as political reportage on the Soviet Union or to satisfy our sociological curiosity about the strange hierarchies of survival in the prison camps. But their deeper story is something else. They are above all moral documents—the story of a whole population struggling against the corruption forced upon them by a political regime. To survive under that regime is to practice continual duplicity, treachery toward one's neighbor, and to develop a brutal callousness toward life generally. And the miracle is that the moral will still survives in this people; that there are individuals who carry on the struggle for no more heroic reason than to stay decent—above all, "not to become a scoundrel." If dictatorship should become the wave of the future, then the doctrine of the moral will may not be so tame a thing after all; it might in fact have a genuine revolutionary content.

Our return to the moral will, however, is not a mechanical return to the doctrine of Kant. We have to burrow into the foundations that Kant, unknown to himself, really took for granted. He sought to make the sphere of the moral an autonomous and purely rational affair. The principles of ethics were to be certified on their intrinsic formal grounds alone. But are they really autonomous? Here Kant juggles in most legalistic fashion: yes and no. The laws of ethics are formally complete in themselves, but somehow he must tack on the assumptions of God and immortality. Practical reason, he tells us, if it is to be completely rational, must add the postulates of God and immortality. In short, it would be silly to practice the Kantian morality of duty if you did not also have faith in God or immortality. It required very little of Nietzsche to turn this about, and quite logically to point out that if you disbelieved in God and the immortality of the soul, then on purely rational grounds you would develop a different morality altogether. No; the moral will is not an autonomous function reigning in splendid and sovereign isolation. Man is a being in the world, if we remember our Heidegger; and each part of our being is caught up in our other multiple involvements with the world. For Kant these were the theism of his time and place. The Christian will, and its faith, has been there from the start in Kant's thinking. It is not the case in the Kantian system, as is commonly said, that "Reason has to make room for faith," as if the latter, once a place was made for it, slipped in independently. That faith is present and operant throughout the whole of the moral edifice that Kant constructs. Unknown to him, child of the Age of Reason that he was, he is as much a case of *fides quaerens intellectum* (faith seeking to elaborate itself intellectually), as the medieval St. Anselm, who coined that saying. And behind Anselm lies Augustine, as he also lies at a farther and less recognized distance behind Kant. The Kantian good will, which wills to submit itself to the moral law, is a descendant of the *voluntas*, the will in St. Augustine, which is restless until it rests in God.

Does our moral life then rest on a faith of some kind? Or to put the matter more pointedly, could we as existing individuals have the strength and courage to persist in our moral striving if we did not have a faith of some kind? And what kind of a faith, at the least, would it have to be? These are the ultimate questions to which the problem of freedom leads us; and to follow them we turn now to the company of another modern philosopher very different in style and outlook from both Wittgenstein and Heidegger.

NOTES TO CHAPTER 12

1. Kierkegaard makes the distinction between the aesthetic and ethical stages turn on the key notions of actuality and possibility, and the relative roles these play in our life.

The aesthete is in thrall to the lures of the possible. The actual person

or situation with which he has to deal interests him only to the extent
that his imagination can invest it with poetical possibilities. And if he
is driven to move on restlessly, like Don Juan, from one woman to
another, it is because he is in pursuit of the image of the Ideal Woman,
a possibility that actual possession can never supply. In a less gross form,
the aesthete emerges as the detached intellectual who seeks to contemplate actual existence as a purely aesthetic spectacle. The existing individual case, for this purely contemplative mind, is interesting only as it
may be an instance of some possible universal or law.

The ethical man, on the contrary, is wedded to the individual and
actual. The gritty, the humdrum, the ordinary reality of life are what
he takes upon himself to live with and redeem if he can. And if he does
find redemption, it is as this actual individual—this body, this flesh and
blood, this spirit—who he is.

Now, on its surface, Heidegger's analysis of human existence might
seem deeply ethical. His key terms are ones that normally have ethical
connotations: care, solicitude, conscience, guilt, resolve, authenticity, and
inauthenticity. Yet he himself has warned us against taking these in any
explicit moral sense. His warning, however, seems to have fallen on deaf
ears in the case of some avid but naïve Heideggerians who persist in trying to read *Being and Time* as if it were a moral tract. One would think
that after the counter-culture of the 1960s it should be sufficiently clear
to almost everyone that terms like "authentic" and "inauthentic" have
no definite moral content at all.

The fact is that if we try to read *Being and Time* as an ethical work,
we only come up with a parody of the ethical—a parody, moreover, that
reveals itself as transparently aesthetic, in Kierkegaard's pejorative sense
of that word.

Consider, for example, the matter of conscience:

Heidegger deals with this subject only as it illustrates the way in which
Being and Nonbeing are woven inseparably together into the fabric
of our human reality. He projects before us the instance of human being
lost in the anonymity of its public and external roles, for whom somehow, and from somewhere, amid this drift of impersonality, the voice
of conscience sounds. Who speaks in this call of conscience, and to
whom? A self that is *not yet*, a more authentic self that is to be, calls
to a self that, in its sheer diffuseness and anonymity, does not properly
exist. A negativity calls to a negativity. And yet something significant
has happened, for we become different in our being insofar as a new
and different *possibility* of being beckons to us.

As a strictly ontological dissection of the peculiar enmeshment of
possibility and actuality, of nonbeing and being, that we are, Heidegger's
analysis here is both powerful and acute. But let us consider a living
instance in its specifically *moral* aspect:

I have done something wrong: I have thoughtlessly hurt someone I love. (I am in fact thinking of an actual incident, which even now, twenty years later, still rankles.) What overwhelms me here is the sheer particularity of the situation itself and my deed: that it was *I*, and no one else, who did *that* particular thing to *that* particular individual; and the grief and pain on the face of the beloved one whom I have wounded becomes my own pain in turn. No doubt, I shall resolve not to do anything like this again; and in that respect I am already differently oriented toward the future. But if I rush to such generalization; and if I take my juggling with concepts to convey the heart of what I have been through, then I have hardly felt very deeply at all. Unless I have been transfixed, as by a spear, by the particularity of that act, of the particular wrong I have done to that actual individual, then I still remain as humanly and morally insensitive and callous as, unsuspected by myself, I had been before my treachery.

Now, let us imagine some young man, who, crammed to the full of Heidegger, has gone through such an experience and attempts to assay it in the master's terms. (Yes, I was almost, but thankfully not quite, that young man.) He is smitten by conscience, but what does this voice of conscience tell him? It speaks of the authentic self that may issue from this troubled incident. But what meaning has such authenticity if he has not been stung by the sheer moral wrongness of his act? The pain and suffering of the other person vanish before this narcissistic self-absorption in the self that he may become. I think we should find this young man's posture both offensive and ludicrous at once—the posture of the aesthete who stands at a distance from the actual experience and contemplates it simply as a stage in his self-development. And I think we should have to say too that so far as moral feelings are concerned, his conscience has really remained untouched after all.

With these matters of moral sensibility, with conscience as a strictly moral phenomenon, Heidegger does not deal. His analysis moves in another and different dimension altogether; and to attempt to read *Being and Time* as a phenomenology of the moral consciousness is to produce something grotesque and monstrous.

2.   *Being and Time* begins with a deliberate and audacious reversal of the whole Western tradition on the relation of the actual and possible: "*Possibility is higher than actuality.*" It is important to see why and how far this reversal can be carried through.

The Western tradition, from the first, grasped Being in terms of actuality and reality. What is, after all, is what is the case: what is real and actual. The German word for actuality, *Wirklichkeit*, connotes also that which is efficacious and urgent. Thus, Being is taken to signify what is real, actual, and urgent, in contrast to what is fictitious, merely possible, or of indifferent efficacy. But "real" comes from the Latin *res*, which means "thing"; and, accordingly, this Western understanding of Being had become too exclusively confined to the being of things.

And whether the things in question were taken as objects or subjects, depending on whether one was a materialist or idealist, Being was still understood as thing-being: the being of a thing.

It was against this exclusive notion of Being that Heidegger set out on his philosophic journey. Our human being, our ordinary concrete existence, cannot be grasped as the simple being of a thing. The axiom of traditional metaphysics had been: Actuality is prior to potentiality. The knife—to use Aristotle's example—has the potentiality of cutting because of its actual characteristics of hardness and sharpness. The thing is what it is; its actual properties are what they are, and its potentialities derive therefrom. But that very peculiar being, the human being, is not a simple utensil or thing like a knife. Possibility and actuality are woven more intimately within the web of our human being. We are what we are through the horizon of possibilities that lies open to us. And Heidegger went on to make brilliant use of this insight to illumine the human condition in the light of certain regions of being in which we dwell or from which we are shut off.

But the thinker who challenges the tradition is bound to lose in the end. If he is great enough, however, his victory will have been to modify the tradition before it rolls back over him to correct his own one-sided emphasis and strike a new balance. After Heidegger, the notions of the actual and possible cannot be universally invoked again with the same simplicity as when they are applied to things like utensils and tools. Nevertheless, his own formula "Possibility is higher than actuality" belongs to his earlier thinking; and he never returned to qualify it in the light of his later themes. And now, having learned from him to acknowledge "the silent power of the possible," we have to come back in the end to give actuality its due priority.

In an earlier chapter we traversed a day in the Everyday, in the company of Heidegger. We noted that the presence of this day, in which you and I are now, cannot be reduced to the things and objects encountered within it. But if this day opens as a field of possibility, it also encloses us within its definite horizon. It is *this* day and no other—a day that may call me to some decision or action that I cannot postpone. And if I lose it, I have lost part of my life forever. "*Temps le pressant,*" James Joyce puns: "Time the pressing." And he is right: The present is also the pressing.

Finally, it is with question of cosmic Being that the issue of actuality becomes most crucial. The existence of the universe itself is the ultimate actuality with which thinking has to be engaged. That the world is, that there is anything at all rather than nothing—this is the supreme miracle and mystery, and also the supreme actuality within which our own existence has been cast. Here we face the fact of the All, the One, the unique and singular existent, as it was confronted by the ancient Parmenides; and the question of Being becomes perforce cosmological in its sweep. Heidegger brings us only to the threshold but does not enter into this cosmic question of Being.

Since Heidegger's thinking deliberately moves in certain ways parallel to Kant's, comparison with the latter becomes particularly relevant here. Thus Heidegger has writen two books on Kant, as if checking his own progress at each stage by a backward look at the master; and each book, in turn, mirrors his own preoccupations at that step in his development. But these two books take us only through the first two parts of Kant's *Critique of Pure Reason:* the transcendental Aesthetic and the Analytic. There is no third book on the third and consummating part of the Kantian work, the Transcendental Dialectic, in which Kant deals with the enigmas to which cosmic Being gives rise: questions about the universe as a whole and the existence of God. Heidegger does not deal explicitly with these questions; at best there are two or three pages in his late essay *Identity and Difference* that touch on the question of the One, and that may be why he considered this little work the most important step in his thinking since *Being and Time*. But these few pages are only a faint beginning. Thus the absence of a third book on Kant corresponds to a real gap in Heidegger's thought.

And this gap consequently appears in his description of human existence, and particularly the moral aspect of our human condition. For these ultimate questions about the cosmos and God, as Kant rightly insists, are a part of our human nature that we cannot escape. We exist within these questions that reason cannot answer; and indeed the deepest part of our existence is involved with them. The man who says, "I am going to die, and what meaning, then, has my life?" is asking in the same breath: "What meaning has this world, this cosmos, in which I came to be?"

In short, the question of God remains unasked in Heidegger, however he may prepare *us* to set about asking the question anew. And for those who believe, with Kant, that our moral existence is inseparable from this question, this absence in Heidegger is one more reason for finding that his thought never finally arrives at the ethical after all.

Chapter 13

The Will to Believe

WHAT STRIKES US IN READING WILLIAM JAMES NOW IS AT ONCE HOW distant and yet how close to us he is. Some of his most famous essays, particularly on determinism and freedom of the will, were written almost a century ago. Their philosophic idiom is not our current one, and they speak out of a different historical and human ambience from ours. In point of actual chronology he can be squeezed into our century only in its first decade, though in those years he did produce some of his most decisive philosophical statements. Yet he belongs to our time, he is our contemporary in the twentieth century, for deeper reasons than this narrow and literal-minded appeal to chronology can show. He speaks to us now, I believe, more forcefully than at any time since his death in 1910.

Even the great differences in the intellectual and spiritual milieu from which he wrote, and which at this distance we can discern more clearly, have a more immediate meaning and use for us now. By contrast they help to reveal what our own very different situation is. In America in the latter part of the nineteenth century, and certainly in New England, God was very far from dead. The new tremors of agnosticism were stirring, of course, like the advance waves of an earthquake. Scientific materialism seemed by this time to be incorporated into the body of physics itself; and the shock of the theory of evolution altered not only our picture of the origin of mankind but also our perspective on its possible destiny. But these matters disturbed the intellectuals mostly. The faithful, if troubled at all, were quick and ingenious with the responses of their will to believe. New England and Boston particularly buzzed with their varied circles of spirituality and spiritualism.

We get some sense of part of this background against which William James philosophized from his brother Henry's novel *The Bostonians*. We get here too a lively sense of the difference between the two brothers. Henry is the adopted European, the artist, and the aristocrat; and he takes consequently a very negative view of the spiritual seething in and around Boston. He finds the people engaged in it mostly shabby and seedy—"The great irregular army of nostrum-mongers, domiciled in humanitary Bohemia." It was *The Bostonians* that gave Henry James the most trouble with his audience; and, significantly, for readers today it is one of the novels most favored in the whole Jamesian canon. It seems to us one of the most prophetic and "modernist" in spirit. It gave Henry James trouble in other ways, too, besides its public reception, so that he did not rewrite it to be incorporated in the later New York edition. For us that is also one of its attractions; it seems to us more pungent in the earlier style, and therefore more modern too in its spirit of dissent.

William was inclined to be more democratically tolerant of all these odd manifestations of the human spirit. Where there was moral earnestness abroad one should appreciate it no matter what peculiar expression it might take. Besides, all these dealings in the occult aroused his curiosity as a psychologist. Nor was the time spent in such study wasted, for he carried away from it his lifelong sensitivity to the hidden and subliminal sources of the human mind that gives him a breadth and profundity that more cerebral philosophers lack. But most of all there was in the atmosphere a general will to believe, and this he could appeal to and mobilize. Liberal religion was then at the height of its vogue. Confident in itself and its virtues, it enjoyed the best of both worlds. It had assimilated the Enlightenment, banished superstition, yet still seemed to preserve the religious values that were worthwhile. By contrast, how different our own period emerges. Faith or the lack of faith seems hardly a live option anymore—at least among intellectuals. To raise the religious question in certain circles would be an embarrassing *gaucherie*. And so far as the public at large is concerned, there prevails alternately a flaccidity or frenzy of the will; apathy or violence; cynicism or a ranting fanaticism over the momentary ideology. Nihilism has become the matter-of-fact state of mind of our period. And as happens when a state of mind becomes so pervading, it becomes for the most part unconscious of itself.

Yet James speaks to us over all these differences of time and circumstance, and it is a mark of both his genius and his unique intellectual power that he is able to do so. It is important for us now, in the midst of what might be called a James revival, that we be under no misunderstandings as heretofore on the quality of mind that makes up this power.

Part of his genius, which even his detractors have admitted, was his remarkable sensitivity to the actualities of life. It took quite an unusual eye to pick up from the newspapers of his day the kind of odd and sensational cases that he sometimes used to press home his point. He was able too to comb through some of the most bathetic literature of religious conversion to come up with some unforgettable if rough-cut gems of the human soul speaking *in extremis*. "That adorable genius, William James," Whitehead says of him, having in mind this captivating and lively sense of the actual, and particularly James' grasp of feeling as the central fact for any human life. And it was from him that Whitehead borrowed the phrase "concreteness and adequacy" as the goal toward which philosophic thinking should strive. But once this gift for the actual—this capacity for concreteness and adequacy—is acknowledged, disparagement is likely to set in among some critics, though Whitehead is emphatically not of their number. James is considered to be woolly minded, intellectually impressionistic, too subjective and emotional in his approach to qualify as a really rigorous thinker.

This was a prevalent attitude during the decades when Bertrand Russell and Russellian logic dominated philosophy. Russell himself, as one of the sharpest critics of pragmatism, has helped propagate a general disdain for what appeared to be its sloppy thinking generally. In retrospect, there is one very large irony in Russell's being associated with this disparagement, since at one point in his career, when he sought desperately to get beyond the Cartesian impasse with its split between mind and matter, he had to turn back to some suggestion about the nature of consciousness that James had advanced twenty years earlier. The supposedly impressionistic thinker was here supplying the logician with his intellectual capital.

Two changes in the philosophical climate during recent decades combine to alter this disparaging judgment of James. The first is the widespread influence of Ludwig Wittgenstein's later thought, which considerably undermines the imperial claims of Russellian logic. Wittgenstein in fact pursues a fundamentally pragmatic analysis of language to far more drastic lengths than any of the pragmatists. Logic is no longer the pre-existing and procrustean framework into which the activities of discourse have to be fit. The forms of logic are eventual; they come out of our use of language and the decisions that we have to make in the course of that use. The logician and mathematician must perpetually stand open to the possibility that he will come to a point where he will have to ask: Now what decision must I make so that such and such an undesirable situation will not arise in the way I use my symbols? Where a language has interesting things to say, precision is never perfect. The second change in intellectual climate has been the advent of existentialism as a major movement of contemporary thought. In the wake of the existentialist thinkers we are much less disposed to find fault with James for philosophizing in a personal and emotional mode. If philosophy is to say something that matters to us, it will have to touch upon that personal core of experience which after all is the center of being for all of us. And whatever else existentialism may have contributed by this time, I think it has at least succeeded in establishing some major revaluations in our judgments of past reputations: Kierkegaard and Nietzsche, for example, who philosophized in a most personal and passionate mode, now loom as two of the most powerful minds of the nineteenth century. We are less likely therefore to condemn William James out of hand for his personal style.

The fact is that he is at the very farthest remove from being woolly minded. He is not a raconteur of cases, not an artist or novelist manqué, but a thinker of very great force. He wrote in a vivid and often colloquial style, and in trying to communicate to a wide audience sometimes affected a popular jauntiness of expression. Only a pedant or prig would be put off by these qualities. What matters is the intellectual power that lies behind or within this direct and vigorous appropriation of the vernacular. James has the great power of going for the gut issue in any question. Rarely if ever does he get lost in the aimless byways that often capture other philosophers. Half of the business of thinking is to know what one is after in the first place. A question may fascinate us as an intellectual puzzle that we can play with for our own amusement; but when it becomes a real problem it presses us toward some decision.

And what we ask of a thinker is that he sift through the great mass
of incidental and obscuring details in order to lay bare the main
structure within which the decision has to be made.

Nowhere does James show this power more effectively than in
his treatment of the problem of freedom.

I.

I remember my disappointment as a young student years ago when
I first read the classic essay "The Dilemma of Determinism." The
title led me to expect some objective and logical refutation that
would once and for all impale the determinist on its prongs and
leave him squirming there forever. I expected, I think, some new
and surprising facts or some new logical relation of the facts that
would finally settle the question in favor of freedom. Instead, James
seemed to hurry past the objective question in order to get to the
moral issues involved, and I was disappointed to find the bulk of the
essay, as it seemed to me then, a moral appeal to the reader. For the
dilemma of the determinist, as James presents it, is essentially a
moral and not a metaphysical one. The objective question between
freedom and determinism was thus left open and inconclusive as it
had always been, and my young mind still felt dreadfully unsettled.

But of course this is where the question has to be left, and James
is entirely right to hew to the line that he does. In this matter he is
following the position of Kant a century before him. The fire-
breathers of determinism, like B. F. Skinner, who enter the dialectical fray convinced that they have seen the proof of determinism in
their laboratory results last week, are greatly mistaken. The case for
or against free will still stands where Kant left it. We have introduced all kinds of changes and refinements in terminology, but the
objective merits of the case remain unaltered. Anything like a decisive proof for free will or determinism is unavailable. And where
the matter is thus logically inconclusive, practical concerns enter. It
makes a great deal of difference, practically speaking, if we do believe in freedom. We are more likely to improve our character if
we believe that the power to do so lies in the exertion of our will.
Determinism, if really followed in practice, would tend to close off
the will toward such striving. Thus it is to our practical advantage
to believe that we are free beings, and our subjective decision in the
matter does have objective consequences in our life. Faith in free-

dom produces future facts that confirm it—at least in its practical efficacy if not its ultimate metaphysical truth.

Freedom on such terms would seem to be a bald practical transaction, a cool *quid pro quo*. But what we have in the above summation is half, and less than half, of the Jamesian position. For if the belief in freedom is a moral choice on our part, it is ultimately for James also a religious act. Our moral life in the end makes sense only as an affirmation of some religious attitude toward the universe. Many of his pragmatist followers have sought to dilute this position; but it is nonetheless James', persistently though sometimes waveringly held throughout the body of his writings. To disengage this view, and present it more sharply, is the main burden of what we have to say in this chapter.

Still, there may be some rumblings of the old controversy over determinism that have to be dealt with. The reader may wonder whether there are new facts that enter the picture which would cause us to reassess the objective merits of the case for or against determinism. Has science, which changes so rapidly in our time, not brought forth new discoveries which would bring us some conclusive decision one way or the other? The trouble is that the voices of the scientists, when they speak apart from their special fields, are likely to be part of the disunified clamor of our period. The public pronouncements of some of our physicists sound at times like dithyrambs for a universe of such indeterminacy and utter chaos that often after reading them we wonder how the ordinary world can possibly go about its way even as uniformly as it does. The psychologists, on the other hand, fresh from some new conditioning experiment, are eager to tell us how they have the techniques to engraft an ironbound necessity upon our behavior. Clearly, we get no unanimity of illumination from science. In view of the perennial and shifting area of debate between philosophy and science, it may be worthwhile to ask why on this particular question matters must stand inconclusive; and for this purpose we may pause to take a brief look at the logical structure of the old controversy.

What is it that the determinist really claims? However he may put it, his claim must be a total one. British philosopher C. D. Broad gives us a succinct and accurate formulation as follows:

> What determinism asserts is that given the totality of all antecedent conditions in the universe that lead to the present occasion (in

which we are to choose or act), one and only one future can follow.

The distinction between soft and hard determinism, already familiar
to James, does not mitigate the totality of these claims. The soft determinist seems to sugarcoat the bitter pill of fatalism by telling us
that our own desires and choices are among the conditions of our
act, and that we therefore play a part in shaping our fate. There
need not then be any strict antithesis between freedom and determinism. That we may be autonomous and free individuals is perfectly consistent with a strict causal determinism.

But this promise of respite is only an illusion. The soft determinist might be more aptly called the lucky determinist. If we are
lucky, our desires and choices fit fluently and smoothly into the
web of our life, and we act with all the harmonious appurtenances
of freedom. We do what we want, and we are satisfied with the
kinds of things we want. But for the unlucky man cursed with odi-
ous and self-destructive desires, there is not the least bit of solace
here. Tell him that his own will is part of the conditions of his act
and you leave him still groaning in travail. His own desires may be
the most monstrous obstacle in his path against which he struggles
to no avail. What formed these desires? Previous conditions in the
chain of events. We are led backward to the youth that ruined man-
hood, to the childhood that blighted youth; to the role of parents,
society, the historical situation into which he was born. The total
claims of determinism begin to reassert themselves. If a man's will
has been blighted from the start, and confirmed by circumstances
bit by bit into its monstrous obsessions, you have not given him one
bit of freedom by naming that will among the conditions that spin
out his fate. Unless there is a break somewhere in the deterministic chain, you have not made him master of his own destiny but
simply labeled him as the helpless instrument of his own doom.
From the strictly logical point of view, there is only one determinism, and that is the position of hard determinism.

We come back thus to the simple and sweeping thesis that the determinist must strictly insist upon: Given the totality of all conditions that make up the present state of the world, one and only one
future can issue therefrom.

This is, admittedly, an extraordinary proposition, and we would
do well to pause for a moment to contemplate it. Is it an analytic

statement, like the propositions of logic, or an empirical hypothesis about matters of fact?

Clearly, it is not analytic. One can imagine that the route of the universe could be just what it is up to the present, and two or indeed many more different futures could follow from that past. There is at least no logical contradiction involved in conceiving alternative futures. And in the case of a truly analytic proposition, its denial leads us forthwith to a self-contradiction.

The thesis of determinism must then be an empirical proposition. And indeed it does appear to talk about events, human acts, and the condition of the world generally. But if it is an empirical statement about matters of fact, it has to be accounted a very strange one. No scientific hypothesis is ever put so sweepingly. A legitimate hypothesis for science is a restricted form that enables us to specify the conditions or the definite observations under which it could be proved false. But the determinist thesis—and this, I think, is its most significant peculiarity—is not a proposition that is ever falsifiable. Whatever cases one may try to present against it, the determinist can always respond that we do not know the antecedent circumstances in their totality. I say to the determinist, "Look, I choose to raise my arm and now I shall proceed to do it." I then raise my arm and ask, "Why isn't that a free act?" I only elicit a tolerant smile from him, for I have been silly: if I really knew all the conditions—absolutely all—that led to my words and my act, then it would be clear that at just that particular moment in the evolution of the cosmos I was fated to say and do just what I did.

Of course, neither he nor I can ever know all these conditions. The determinist has secured an unassailable position for himself at the expense of making it empty. I say that I believe in freedom, and that this belief makes a difference in my experience; for I then have greater faith that I can make an effort, and I therefore struggle harder than I would were I without this belief. The determinist smiles again, and remarks that it was fated in the course of things that I should believe in freedom. Whatever we try to point out in the foreground of experience, the determinist can always evade by taking recourse to what lies—or must lie—behind the scenes.

And so the dialectical game can be played back and forth as endless as it is inconclusive.

Yet surely there is more substance than this to the dispute between free will and determinism. A controversy that has drawn the

energies and anguish of so many great intellects over the centuries
cannot be reduced to a mere idle dialectical joust. Nor is it simply
to be assigned to the past, for it is vigorously alive and troubling
today. It lies behind the latest and boldest programs of behaviorists
for reshaping human nature. And the same old question of freedom
and necessity, though it remains unanswered, is lived through in the
tortuous transactions day by day between psychoanalysts and their
patients. Surely the question here is not merely academic but also
touches real life. And it is precisely when we have seen the point at
which it touches life itself that we are given the true sense of the
problem, as well as the indication of its solution.

II.

To begin with, we should recognize a peculiar kind of unreality
that infects the way in which the problem of free will is presented
in our philosophic classrooms. We present it as a puzzle to tease the
student into thinking. It serves this purpose somewhat like the antinomies of logic, and like the latter is indeterminate of solution unless further specifications are added. In the interest of being logical
and objective we present the problem with a certain detachment.
And here is the source of unreality to the problem: *we are really
talking about an agent who is in fact a spectator at his own life.*

The medieval schoolmen, partly out of their own sense of amused
detachment, invented the famous illustration of Buridan's ass. Imagine a poor donkey who is equally hungry and thirsty and is placed
equidistant from hay and water. What will the poor beast do? Will
he not remain equally and indifferently suspended between the two
desires and so perish of hunger and thirst simultaneously?

No contemporary philosopher would appear to take Buridan's ass
seriously. The case is a caricature at best. We have created a thoroughly artificial and unreal donkey—a beast who is suspended and
hovers indifferently above his own poor animal existence. But do
not philosophers create an equally unreal human agent in their own
discussion of freedom? And I do not mean only those objective philosophers who go on endlessly chewing the logical cud until the
juice has run out of it. I cannot read Sartre on freedom without
sensing the ghost of Buridan's donkey hovering in the wings. On
the surface everything looks different, of course: The Sartrian
agent is possessed by a complex consciousness—too complex, per-

haps—and a freedom so absolute that Descartes—as Sartre himself notes—reserved it only for God. But this "total" freedom of which Sartre talks—does it not project before us a human being in suspension above his own existence? From there he can leap into any indifferent and absurd path that takes him out of the normal and prosaic rut. True, this freedom is dizzying, and we are haunted by anguish in being exposed to it. The *angoisse* gives an existentialist coloring to the whole account, but in fact the Sartrian agent is as detached from actual existence as Buridan's imaginary ass.

Freedom becomes a reality to us in much more mundane and humiliating situations. We know it in its harshness as a lack and a struggle rather than a superfluity of powers. The alcoholic struggling against his body shivering for that next drink knows what freedom means. Freedom becomes fully real to us in those situations when it is literally a matter of life and death. We are *in extremis*; we have fallen into a black pit and we are gasping for breath as we struggle to crawl forward. Freedom is no longer an academic debate or the dizzying luxury of an indifferent choice between alternatives. The question of freedom has turned into a cry for help.

James knew this need in the only way in which it can be known —by direct personal experience. In 1870, when he was twenty-eight, he had a severe crisis that left him in a state of acute and paralyzed melancholy. We do not know exactly what circumstances may have precipitated this crisis. James' personality, despite his open and expansive manner, is shrouded in considerably more mystery than is commonly thought. He has left us an anonymous case in *The Varieties of Religious Experience* that is now taken to be largely a description of his own experience. Why this refuge in anonymity? Would it have seemed too mawkish and unmanly, too unashamedly personal, to make public confession of something so intimate? In any case, the passage describes the kind of experience around which much of his philosophizing turns; long as it is, we need to give it in full:

> Whilst in this state of philosophic pessimism and general depression of spirits about my prospects, I went one evening into a dressing room in the twilight to procure some article that was there; when suddenly there fell upon me without warning, just as if it came out of darkness, a horrible fear of my own existence. Simultaneously there arose in my mind the image of an epileptic patient whom I had seen in the asylum, a black-haired youth with

greenish skin, entirely idiotic, who used to sit all day on one of the benches, or rather shelves, against the wall, with his knees drawn up against his chin, and the coarse grey undershirt, which was his only garment, drawn over him, enclosing his entire figure. He sat there like a sort of sculptured Egyptian cat or Peruvian mummy, moving nothing but his black eyes and looking absolutely nonhuman. This image and my fear entered into a species of combination with each other. *That shape am I,* I felt, potentially. Nothing that I possess can defend me against that fate, if the hour for it should strike for me as it struck for him. There was such a horror of him, that it was as if something solid within my breast gave way entirely, and I became a mass of quivering fear. After this the universe was changed for me altogether. I awoke morning after morning with a horrible dread at the pit of my stomach, and with a sense of insecurity the like of which I never knew before, and that I have never felt since. It was like a revelation; and although the immediate feelings passed away, the experience has made me sympathetic with the morbid feelings of others ever since. It gradually faded, but for months I was unable to go out in the dark alone.

We witness here such a convulsion and seizure by the unconscious that consciousness and its ideas would seem by comparison to exert only a feeble and peripheral force. Yet, on closer look, ideas play more of a role in this crisis than might first appear. It is hard for us today to recapture in imagination the stark and frightening power that the determinism embedded in physics had for the nineteenth-century imagination. "The molecules blindly run," the poet sang in his distress; and those molecules blindly moving would spin out our fate as they would, whatever we appeared to will in the matter. That idiot will be me, and there is nothing I can do, if the particles are already irreversibly spinning in that direction. The imagination cowered before this prospect like a Calvinist shivering at the conviction of eternal damnation. And if this philosophical idea does not of itself beget the attack of acute depression, it nevertheless intensifies that depression because any way out seems to be barred beforehand. Ideas, as we see here, can have a most potent connection with the will, in this case a negative and frustrating one.

James was to find a more positive idea to help his will out of the impasse. In the spring of 1870 a turning point seems to come and he records in his diary:

I think that yesterday was a crisis in my life. I finished the first part of Renouvier's second *Essais* and see no reason why his definition of free will—"the sustaining of a thought *because I choose to* when I might have other thoughts"—need be the definition of an illusion. At any rate, I will assume for the present—until next year—that it is no illusion. My first act of free will shall be to believe in free will.

In comparison with the murky and subterranean atmosphere of the previous excerpt, we are here in the daylight world of the mind and its ideas. Perhaps too daylight; perhaps the note here is too selectively intellectual, and there were other subliminal and more obscure forces at work floating James past his blockage. We have, however, to follow him to the letter: It is an idea—in this case the idea of free will—that opens the door out of his darkness. Yet James knows—though he had not yet written his great chapters on habit in the *Psychology*—that the idea by itself is not enough; that the links between idea and will, and between will and action, must be quickly and firmly established. He proceeds therefore to put the idea immediately into action:

> For the remainder of the year, I will abstain from the mere speculation and contemplative *Grublei* in which my nature takes most delight, and voluntarily cultivate the feeling of moral freedom, by reading books favorable to it, as well as by acting. After the first of January, my callow skin being somewhat fledged, I may perhaps return to metaphysical study and skepticism without danger to my powers of action. For the present then remember: care little for speculation; much for the form of my action; recollect that only when habits of order are formed can we advance to really interesting fields of action—and consequently accumulate grain on grain of willful choice like a very miser; never forgetting how one link dropped undoes an indefinite number. . . .
>
> Hitherto, when I have felt like taking a free initiative like daring to act originally, without waiting for contemplation of the external world to determine all for me, suicide seemed the most manly form to put my daring into; now, I will go a step further with my will, not only act with it, but believe as well; believe in my individual reality and creative power. My belief, to be sure, *can't* be optimistic—but I will posit life (the real, the good) in the self-governing *resistance* of the ego to the world. Life shall be built in doing and suffering and creating.

We have dwelt on this crisis of 1870 because it gives us the human and philosophic center around which James' life was to turn. In view of the extraordinarily productive and vigorous career that was to follow this breakdown, we could rate his as one of the prime cases of a victory over neurosis. Yet we do not conquer a neurosis unless we have learned from it and in some measure preserve within us the message it had to impart in the first place. For the rest of his days James remained sensitive to the desperation that lurks always at the core of even the best regulated lives. He could understand the "sick soul" and its morbid temperament because he himself was one of the morbid. He who has once had a terrifying vision will never doubt the existence of evil in this universe of ours. The torments of the sick soul, James tells us, if viewed objectively would be less than an adequate response to the abominable and loathsome things that take place in the world. Consequently James thereafter could never accept any idealistic philosophy that would make evil disappear through some ingenious feat of dialectic. All of which gives James a sense of actuality which makes him seem close to us.

More than this. The brief entries quoted from the journal for 1870 give us in compact outline the whole of the Jamesian philosophy that was to follow. The philosophy of *The Will to Believe*, twenty-seven years later, is already summed up in a single paragraph from the diary. Everything he was to write comes in some way out of the datum he had grasped in the crossing of this valley of the shadow. He was to become a moral philosopher essentially; but a moralist preoccupied with the scope, power, and above all the source of our moral will. Even a major work like his *Psychology* fits into this large design. For what James, coming from his studies in physiology, saw in the neural impulses was that consciousness is primarily connected with the discharge of energy, with action; and that motivation must therefore be a prime factor in human conduct. Happy the thinker who knows his direction so early.

"My first act of freedom will be to believe in freedom." How cheerful and courageous this note sounds after the discord and stress of his crisis. This simple utterance of the moment is the gist of the position later taken in *The Will to Believe*. Since freedom of the will is not ruled out on strictly logical grounds, one is therefore free to believe in it. But this belief, which is not itself a strict consequence of logic, nevertheless has distinct consequences in action. To believe in one's freedom has the advantages that it liberates the will and fosters action. Faith in freedom creates its own future facts, and thus confirms itself in action.

The argument is exactly the same, but in this later context James introduced an example from an altogether more extrovert and heroic domain of human effort than the one he had known in his crisis. Let us imagine, he tells us, a mountain climber who is caught in an impasse where he has to leap across an abyss to save himself. His way is barred behind; he must go forward or perish where he is. The jump is not too long that he cannot possibly make it; yet it is long enough that there is a chance he could fall short. Which then shall he believe? That he can make the leap or that it lies beyond his powers? If he believes he can do it, James argues, then his energies will be bolstered by that very faith, and he is much more likely to succeed in his leap. And afterward, when he stands safe on the other peak, his belief will have yielded confirmation of its truth.

This example, drawn from the daredevil and adventurous life of the out-of-doors, seems a far cry from the situation of James a quarter-century earlier sitting paralyzed and despondent in his father's house in Cambridge. But perhaps the two situations are not so different as they appear at first glance. The melancholic, to get past his despondency, has to make a leap as heroic and total in its own way as the mountaineer's jump from precipice to precipice. Only it is not done all at once, but day by day. That makes it more difficult, and should we not therefore say more heroic? There must be the slow and dragging accumulation of what James here calls "willful choice" until the sufferer emerges at last into the open air. And in both cases the choice is forced upon us: it is a matter of life and death, of individual salvation.

Ironically enough, the question of free will, in becoming real to us, has changed its nature. It becomes real to us when it becomes urgent, and ultimately urgent when it becomes a question of our survival. The question then does not leave us hovering in indifferent doubt over various alternatives, each of which might be equally possible to pursue. We are no longer spectators at our own life, dizzied by the gratuitous possibilities it affords. We are stuck in it up to our necks, the choice we have to make for survival is beyond doubt, and the only question is whether we can make that choice and go on at all. The question is no longer the choice between A and B. A is life, and B death, or its moral equivalent. Everything in us cries out desperately for the choice of A, but do we have the will to make it? *The problem of free will thus becomes, more fundamentally, the problem of the will itself.* And thus plunges us into the ultimate question: Why?

Consider the case of the patient who is told by his doctor, "Drinking has become a very grave health hazard for you, and you must find some way to give it up." If this man, looking down the long corridor of the years ahead without the consolations of alcohol, finds the prospect meaningless and bleak, he may very well ask, "Why make the effort? What point would that life have, anyway?" And he will not be able of course to free himself of the habit. His freedom depends on the strength of his motivation. We tend too often to think of motivation as a *vis a tergo,* a blind force pushing us from behind; but in fact motivation and meaning go hand in hand. If we are not motivated at all toward a certain prospect in life, it will seem meaningless to us; and vice versa. If, on the other hand, the desire for life is strong enough, if he finds it meaningful and worthwhile on any terms, then he will be free to find or make his own way out of the habit. And of course such cases of freedom are a fact: People have to change, and they do sometimes change. It is not up to the philosopher, by the way, to prove that freedom exists; he simply notes, describes, and analyzes the ways in which it does occur. In any case, the important thing to note here is that any serious situation of choice brings with it the ultimate question, What is the point to living, anyway?

Now imagine the somewhat different case of a patient in depression who is told by his psychoanalyst, "You have lost your motivation, you must find some way of getting it back." Of course, if the man had lost all motivation, he would not have any motive to try to get it back. He would not even have enough motive to take the trouble to come to a psychiatrist. What the analyst means is something more restricted: "Your motivation has fallen much below your ordinary level; or you cease to have it for the things you once did." And the course of therapy is to marshal what motivation is there so that in the course of things energy may flow back into the usual channels of the patient's life. But "motivation" is the kind of imposing scientific-sounding word that may becloud the fact that it is supposed to report. To lose motivation is to cease to find meaning in the life one has been leading. One finds no reason for continuing as one has. The sense of meaning is the primary fact in motivation.

But we need not go to these particular cases of pathology; nor need we invoke James' extreme situations—whether of the heroic mountain climber in his writings or of the desperate melancholic of his own life—to see that the will is always haunted by this ultimate question, Why? We need only turn to the routines of ordinary life and the heavy load we must carry every day. A man in some idle and reflective moment—a normal man, let us say, without the specific afflictions of drink or depression—catches a glimpse of his whole life to come, the limited place that is assigned to his ambitions, the limited satisfactions he will have, and the burdens he must carry for them—all terminated by death. And he begins to wonder. He has at the time some painful choice to make, and for a moment he loses heart. Why go to the trouble? What is the point of it all? But then the questions pass from his mind, habit takes over, and he shoulders his burden once again. The nameless voice in Samuel Beckett intones: "You must go on, I can't go on, I'll go on." If you listen, you can always hear it as your own voice, deep within you, behind the acceptable façade you present to the world. And at those moments too, if habit altogether deserts us, the will must assemble all its reasons for living. The problem of the will thus becomes the problem of nihilism itself. And we are present here at what, underneath all the formal trappings of philosophy, must remain for most of us its fundamental questions: Why live? Why go on? What meaning does it all have?

James died before the virus of nihilism had passed from a few intellectuals into the democratic mass at large and became the epidemic of our time; and the one powerful statement of the question available to him, that of Nietzsche, he found distasteful and shied away from. Yet his sensitivity was such that the question is always there in the background for him, and that is another reason why he speaks to us at the present time.

The question of nihilism immediately places us on the terrain of the religious, whether or not we decide for or against religion. The philosophic naturalist, who rejects religion, must nevertheless take up the questions that both the nihilist and the religious raise. Whether we believe the naturalist's philosophy or not, he is not likely to convince us as a man unless we feel he too has known those troubled depths from which religion originally sprang. And some temperaments, of course, will always feel that for this reason the naturalistic attitude leaves them unsatisfied. To attempt to give meaning to life in terms of a positive balance of satisfactions over pains will seem to them woefully inadequate in the face of all our actual experience. "Apart from the religious vision," says White-head, who was on the whole a very cheerful person, "human life is a flash of occasional enjoyments lighting up a mass of pain and misery, a bagatelle of transient experience." The utilitarian and nat-uralistic answers seem thin and pallid beside the experiences that provoked our questioning in the first place. Answer and question seem to pass each other by. Our will clamors for some deeper an-swer when its longing for freedom is indeed a *prayer*—whether we actually voice that prayer or not. The question of morality becomes a religious question, and the moral will a religious one, or one that must seek its completion in religion. So James, deciding at an early age to turn his intellectual energy henceforth to what he calls "the moral impulse," was in fact committing himself to becoming a reli-gious thinker.

Chapter 14

The Faith to Will

LIFE IS AND HAS TO BE A MORAL STRUGGLE IF WE ARE NOT TO COLLAPSE into the passivity of defeat; and this struggle in turn must reach out toward some religious aspirations or faith to sustain it. Such is James' position, and he has consequently to be reckoned as a religious thinker. The interest in religion is not an adventitious curiosity attached to his pragmatism; it is in fact central to his view of things, just as he believed the religious concern to be central to life itself. To attempt any critical judgment of him as a whole we have to turn now to ask how well he has dealt with the phenomenon of religion.

There is a peculiar paradox about any expression of the religious attitude. It seeks to express a subject matter that is perennial, and yet the mode of its expression must always be borrowed from its time and place. And indeed the more powerful its expression the more likely it is to borrow all the coloration of time and place. Lacking these, it speaks to us only vacuously. *The Varieties of Religious Experience* improves as a classic with each rereading. A classic, it has been said, is a book capable of being reborn with each generation. The rebirth is nonetheless vital if it also provokes rebellion. In the case of religious experience there is the further peculiarity that we are dealing with what cannot ultimately be put into language. Any expression of it will therefore be alive to the extent that it provokes us to attempt our own halting and ineffectual effort to restate the unstatable. The *Varieties* lives with us in this provocative and appealing way. At the same time, one must feel a guilty sense of ingratitude at taking up an adversary position toward the book, for our rebellion has been nourished by the source it would attack.

"Better to be hanged for a sheep than a lamb," runs the old adage. James has been belabored by secular-minded pragmatists for leaning too far in the direction of religion. To attempt to make religious belief in any way intellectually possible or even plausible is bound to incur the dissatisfaction of some philosophic minds. Why make the effort then? James' period could believe in such persuasion because the audience as a whole stood within the atmosphere of religion. America at the turn of the century persisted in a state of innocence. Between that time and ourselves the whole of what we know as modern culture has burst like a great tidal wave of negation. Its labor and its triumphs have been everywhere to strip us of our illusions one by one. We cannot speak as if we still stood within the warmth of a period when religious liberalism—that strange combination of the Enlightenment and moral idealism—seemed to offer the promise of the future. We have been through greater negations and require greater affirmations. Only if we are aware that we approach the subject of religion as desperate men can we hope to be at all convincing. And rest assured, whatever tiny lamb we try to appropriate for ourselves from the religious fold will inevitably seem like a gigantic and monstrous sheep to those who find religion unpalatable in any shape or form.

I.

To begin with, we shall have to insist on a proposition that may seem startling and scandalous to some but is nevertheless borne out by all his writings. The proposition is this: Among all the things that James says about religion he never speaks from within faith. I do not mean by this the absence of any particular dogma or church to which he subscribes. I mean that he does not speak, nor does he profess to speak, from within the attitude of faith. To be sure, he is often the lay preacher exhorting us to the moral life and the possibility and efficacy of religious belief. But the lay preacher—or in this case the professor favorably disposed—is talking *about* religious faith and not struggling to communicate with us from *within* the faith.

Thus the difference between James and his archfoe, the agnostic W. K. Clifford, may not seem as great to us as to their contemporaries. Clifford is the intellectual puritan among agnostics: He insists that on no conditions will he ever lend his assent to any belief for which the evidence is not absolutely compelling. It would, in fact, be a mortal sin against one's reason to do so. James argues against him that this attitude is unduly rigid and indeed unreasonable, and that in the ordinary exigencies of life we are compelled to adopt more flexible and less absolute standards for believing. From the point of view of philosophy generally, and epistemology specifically, there is a great difference between Clifford and James; and today we would be inclined to think that James is surely right to speak against such narrow notions of certainty and belief. But from the point of view of the believer, the difference between the two may seem less striking than their similarity.

This assertion will, again, seem paradoxical, and we need to clarify it by a simple example. Two men stand outside a building. Let us call the building religious faith. The two men, James and Clifford, discuss the merits of the building and the possibility of their entering it. One, Clifford, says that on no conditions will he ever enter the building; it would be morally wrong to do so, a sin against the probity of one's reason, when the evidence is not absolutely compelling. The other man, James, says, "I don't know; the building isn't so bad; it has its points; and under certain circumstances it might be perfectly all right to go inside." But notice this, and it is the important point: Both stand outside the building; neither speaks from within it.

James knew this of himself; and in this connection we cannot ponder often enough the remark in one of his letters: "Although religion is the great interest of my life, I am rather hopelessly nonevangelical, and take the whole thing too impersonally."

From the point of view of the believer, in fact, an attitude like Clifford's may in the long run be more likely to lead to conversion. The shock of events may swing him around from one extreme state of mind to its opposite. The philosopher favorably inclined to religion as a human *phenomenon* is more likely to dwell in this twilight zone all his life long.

The danger for a philosopher trying to show that religious belief is not so implausible as might seem is that he will be led to dilute its

content in the process. At the end of the *Varieties* James boils down
all the multifarious and wayward tenets of religious belief to three
crucial propositions:

> 1. The visible world is part of a more spiritual universe from
> which it draws its chief significance.
> 2. A union or harmonious relation with that higher universe is
> our true end.
> 3. Communion with the spirit thereof is a process wherein
> work is really done; spiritual energy flows in and produces effects
> in the phenomenal world.

Considering the vast scope of the *Varieties*, the immense amount of
disparate materials that it covers, we have to agree that this digest is
an admirable effort toward comprehensive summation of its subject.
But, to speak pragmatically, does this summation work? Does it really give us religious help?

A story may help us here. The late Cardinal Cushing of Boston
used to tell it, and it gained some of its appeal from the harsh yet
amiable croak of that admirable churchman. A man is run over by
an automobile, and lies in the street apparently dying. A priest de-
taches himself from the onlookers and, having ascertained that the
man is a Catholic, proceeds to hear his last confession before it may
be too late. "Do you believe in God the Father, in Jesus Christ the
Son, and in the Holy Ghost?" At which the victim opens his eyes
and exclaims: "Father, I'm dying, and you ask me riddles!"

The Trinity is Christianity's most exuberant adventure in the incomprehensible. God by himself is an unfathomable and abysmal
mystery to the human understanding. To complicate this mystery
by adorning it with the intricate figures of the three persons-in-one
was a baroque feat of the Western imagination. To propose this
enigma within an enigma to a dying man only serves to illustrate the
chasm that can come between the concreteness of life and the abstractness of belief. To dilute the mystery might seem to offer us
something more credible and less taxing on our powers of assent.
But would it really help if we were to substitute the apparently
more plausible three articles of belief that James gives us?

We ask the dying man: Do you believe that the visible world is
part of a more spiritual universe? etc. I can imagine the man opening his eyes and exclaiming: "William James, I'm dying and you ask
me riddles!"

I am not here setting up dogmatic theology against liberal religion. Matters of theology can be of great significance if they make some live connection with our will. But I doubt if this generation is ready for such questions; it hardly has enough faith to seek to articulate it in dogma; we have to re-enter religion, if we do at all, by the basement door. What I have against the liberal attempt to make religion more plausible is that it tends to make the question of beliefs the central religious phenomenon. We ask whether the hypotheses religion offers—and notice that the word "hypotheses" is already a speculative and detached word—are at all likely or plausible, and to what degree. We get caught up in questions of the cognitive status of beliefs, and pretty soon we are on the slippery turf of epistemology. We become the captives of our ideas and in turn surrender the living fact of religion to them. As a professor of philosophy, James had to carry on his trade in the philosophical language, and amid the philosophical currents, of his day. But as a pragmatist he should have held fast to the fact that doing is more basic than belief, and that in the domain of religion the doing that is fundamental is the act of prayer. That, after all, is what is involved in our discovery of freedom as a cry for help, an invocation, a prayer. And praying may take place without articulate beliefs, or in deliberately shunning the questions of beliefs.

II.

Abetissez-vous, Pascal said, addressing himself to the exigencies of the doubter. "Stupefy yourself; take holy water." That sounds ominous and crude to us, as it did to James. To bring in the whole ecclesiastical machinery to abet one's devotions, as if grace were piped from one part of the apparatus to another, offends James' deeply Protestant sympathies. But Pascal, who had one of the most subtle minds in history, is not likely to be crude on any matter so central to his religious thinking. If his language is blunt and sounds cynical here, that is part of his deliberate intention to shock us and make us reflect. Beneath the hard-boiled rhetoric, there is a very profound point about the relation of doing and believing and the primacy of one to the other.

Holy water, no doubt, may look too much like an institutionally prepackaged item; and, besides, it may not be always at hand for one. Consider instead a simple gesture like crossing oneself, which is always available. Forgive me if I seem to bring in what might look like a bit of sectarian ritual here. I would like in the present discussion, at any rate, to avoid sectarianisms of any kind. The gesture does not come back to me now from my remembrances of church but of the more truant days of boyhood and particularly of those companions of my adventures in whom the gesture would spring out at the last moment before they dove into the waters of the East River from one of the higher piers. They were older, bigger, and more criminally audacious than I, and some of them might have gone on into the Mafia. I doubt whether their gesture was preceded or followed by any reflection on the status of the belief that may or may not have accompanied it. It was simply called forth, like a reflex, at the moment of extremity. It comes back to me now so strongly at an older age because I have come to look on any moment as possibly one of extremity. Who knows when we may not have to make that dive into the waters below? We have need then of this or any similar gesture you might prefer. The advantage of the gesture is that it can be wordless. We are not trapped within the labyrinth of words and all the inherited ideas that fester there. We need not abuse ourselves in the doubts of epistemology. The gesture is pure invocation, pure prayer. And is not belief itself—in this religious sphere—a form of doing? The performance of a prayer?

"I believe X." This is the propositional form that holds the center of attention for the philosopher, and which he therefore tends to push forward as the very center of the religious phenomenon. He cannot help doing so, for his professional concern is with the status of beliefs. X will consist of some statement or statements about the evidence for which he proceeds to inquire. In James' case, the X is made up of the three statements previously cited. The evidence for them is inconclusive; on the other hand, there is no conclusive evidence against them that would make it rationally impossible for us to believe them. As in the case of free will, we have the freedom to believe, if we so choose. In the then current parlance, these are called overbeliefs—a term, by the way, that should have immediately suggested to James that we are not dealing here with beliefs in the ordinary sense at all.

Indeed, this notion of "overbeliefs" immediately suggests the kind of image under which James is thinking. We are to imagine our beliefs situated along a spectrum, ranging from those nearer and more evident to those more remote and problematic. For things near at

hand the evidence is close to me and within my grasp. Farther
along, I believe in such things as, "The sun is ninety-three million
miles away." Here the evidence does not lie to my hand, though I
know the ways in which it is gathered, and have confidence in the
body of scientists who have asserted this belief. Farther out, however, science itself may be unsure what may be happening at the
edge of the galaxies. Some steps farther, or maybe only one step,
and we get to something like the belief in God. We have stepped
over the edge and are in the invisible part of the spectrum. We have
arrived at "overbeliefs."

Or to vary the image slightly: We stretch the elastic of belief farther and farther; it gets thinner and thinner, the beliefs more tenuous; and finally the elastic snaps. We have then arrived at "overbeliefs," like the belief in God. But if the elastic has snapped, in
what sense are we really dealing with beliefs at all?

These images break down as soon as we stop to remember that
the matter of religion is not the most distant but the nearest to us.

An illustration out of Wittgenstein, though his context is a
different one, may be helpful here. Toward the end of his life, still
worrying at the old bone of the certainty of our ordinary beliefs, he
raises the question about belief in one's own name. "Do I know for
certain that my name is L.W.?" (Substitute your own name,
reader.) This is a peculiar situation in which to invoke the idea of
belief. If I have been dazed by a blow, or have taken some halluci-
nating drug, and someone asks me, "Do you believe your name is
. . . ?" the question is appropriate, for it asks after a definite item
of information: whether I have come back now to my senses and
am aware who I am. But if we are asked this question in the ordinary course of things, we should find it very odd and unnatural. My
relation to my name is not that of belief. It has neither the objectivity nor the distance from me of the kinds of things I normally
say that I believe. I live this relationship, I live within it; I am constantly renewing and re-creating it. You ask me to pretend to step
back from it and look at it as something different from what it is.

Now imagine a man of faith, some peasant out of Tolstoi or
Unamuno, who is suddenly accosted with the question, "Do you believe in God?" (Or, to make our point plainer, we might put the
question in an even more artificial manner: "Do you believe that the
religious hypothesis is a plausible one?") He might very well stare
at you uncomprehendingly. The question will seem just as odd as to

ask him whether he believes in his own name. His relation to the faith in which he lives is not an epistemological relation to a proposition. The question you put to him belongs to the discourse of philosophers but not to the actuality of his own life. You ask him to step out of that life, to look at it from a distance that would destroy it; to see something he lives as one objective item of fact among others in a class of beliefs. His relationship to God is not like that at all: He lives and re-creates and is re-created by this relationship every day. Thus when James talks, as he so often does, of "the religious hypothesis," he is playing the wrong language game.

What I am trying to call attention to here is not only our uncertainty about the X in the formula "I believe X," but, that we are also uncertain about the first two words, "I believe." The Catholic existentialist Gabriel Marcel has remarked somewhere, *"Je ne sais pas ce que je crois"* (I do not know what I believe); and I would like to push his words a little farther and more literally than he seems to do. Not only do I not know what I believe, but also I cannot know for sure that I believe. How can I define precisely what my attitude is toward something it cannot conceivably grasp? Can I be said to be in the relation of "belief," in any usual sense of that term, toward something that I cheerfully and readily acknowledge to be absolutely incomprehensible to me?

The whole of the religious tradition confirms the uncertainty of this "I believe." And quite apart from any questions of theological doctrine, the psychological perceptiveness of this tradition, with its long experience of human self-deception, ought to be convincing to us. No man, we are told, can be sure that he is in the faith; and we can say of no man with certainty that he has or does not have faith. The Gospels nailed this point down once and for all in the cry of the doubter: "Lord, I believe, help thou my unbelief." For the literal-minded rationalist, this statement is a logical contradiction: if the man believes, as he himself says, then how can he have unbelief? But the Gospel pins down here, with canonical accuracy, the essentially dialectical nature of faith. Not only does it always carry its opposite uncertainty within itself, but also this faith is never a static condition that is *had*, but a movement toward . . . And toward what? In the nature of the case we cannot state this "what." We cannot make a flat assertion about our faith like a simple assertion that we have blue eyes or are six feet tall. More than this, the affirmation of our faith can never be made in the simple indicative mood at all. The statement "I believe" can only be uttered as a prayer. In the beginning was the prayer.

But in throwing so much emphasis upon *practice*, by outpragmatizing the pragmatism of James, do we not fall into that ritual Machiavellianism of which he accused Pascal? You perform the ritual gesture, someone asks me, but do you believe in it? Here the demon of sincerity raises its head. The whole of French literature from Montaigne to Proust should be testimony enough against the claims of this demon. In that system within system, that unsortable mélange of what is mine and not mine that I call "I," how can I be sure what real motives lurk at bottom? If you torture yourself with the claims of this demon, it will eat away at you like a cancer, and in the end only make you . . . more insincere. The people who insist most loudly on their sincerity are always the most insincere. Do you doubt, then, the ritual gesture you have performed? What recourse have you but to perform the gesture again? I cross myself. You ask me if I believe in what I've done. I can only cross myself again; and again . . . I establish my conviction in the only way I can—by multiplying the occasions of life in which I put it into practice.

In the end you will come to trust in this gesture more than in any of your ideas.[1]

In any case, the ritual will provide you with a discipline, a regimen, so that your life will no longer seem meaningless. Life has meaning to us only to the degree that we expend ourselves in some such *askesis*. The runner does not doubt of the race, even if he is behind the pack, so long as he continues to strain every nerve and muscle in the effort. If he eases up for a moment, he is likely to see the whole thing for what it is—an absurd and useless display, not worth the effort. Years ago, when I attended track meets, I used to find ridiculous those poor fellows in the distance events who, lapped by the entire field, nevertheless continued to torture themselves to keep going and lumbered on to the finish line long after the crowd had already spent its cheers for the winner. I have changed my mind: I find them now more admirable than the victor whom we crown. Consider the extraordinary number of entrants each year in the Boston Marathon. The list of finishers, as given in the news-

---

[1] Again, we must emphasize, there is no sectarian pleading here. The reader is free to find his own ritual gesture.

papers, is always far far from complete. Usually it stops when we get just to the beginning of the pack. But my imagination is captured by those who run not merely in the pack but behind the pack. And not those toward the end, but a single, solitary, and unique individual at the end. Just think of it: Every year among the many hundreds who enter that race there will be someone who finishes last. My imagination and my heart go out to him. I see him stumbling onward, gasping, never quitting. It will be dark—long after dark, perhaps—when he gets toward the end. The people, the cameras, the judges will have all gone home. Perhaps it will be too dark for him to see the finish line. He will not know if he has crossed it. Perhaps there is no finish line at all. You already have the situation of a Kafka story. If there is no finish line, there never was a race to begin with. The officials who organized it are invisible and an illusion. Perhaps in the dark he has run altogether off course. Yet he keeps running. There "simply cannot" be a question of his quitting. An image of the man of faith.

In that very "simply cannot," says Kafka, lies the insane power of faith.

"But," someone will object, "this religious figure you construct— this individual unsure of the objects of his belief, unsure of belief itself—is surely a needy and threadbare case. You have already assigned him to be last in the race." I agree. But it is precisely that point in myself and in others—that point where the popular language in its unconscious wisdom describes us as having "nothing but a prayer"—that I seek out as the fulcrum or turning point. We might indicate the religious task of our time in the following way: how to let prayer re-enter the world of Samuel Becket, (which is where modernity leads us finally).

In an early and rare public appearance, before he had written the work that has made him famous, Beckett described the situation of a certain kind of artist, the artist who interested him: "Having nothing to express, nothing with which to express, together with the need to express."

We might transpose these words to the situation of faith as follows: "Having nothing to which to pray, nothing with which to pray, together with the unquenchable need to pray."

And in the mood of Beckett one would imagine a bit of dialogue. Two men, A and B. A asks B, "Do you believe?" and B responds in a bellow of annoyance, "Stop bothering me with these questions about belief. Can't you see I'm busy praying?"

And this need is no pallid matter of genteel piety; it has the fe-
rocity of a hunger. Even if my life is the monotonous playing out
of the end game in which checkmate is already certain, the more I
realize that my position is lost, and the more impossible it becomes
at each step, the more this voice cries out in me. I am obliged to
pray. I shall never be silent. Never.

"Even if God did not exist," Dostoevski said, "Jesus would still
be divine." One may add beside Jesus the other great religious
figures. If materialism were true, and all religious hopes absurd,
these human figures would be the only ones that give meaning and
resonance to the long, tortuous record of human history. Even if
there were no ear for them but the void, our prayers would be the
only things that sanctify our existence. He who has reached this
point is long past putting the question of the credibility of beliefs at
the center of religion.

Having acknowledged the poverty of our condition, we may
cease at last to strike poses—particularly the pose of superior courage affected by the nonbeliever. The young Camus, still in his ab-
surdist phase, declared his resolution "to live with what I know, and
only with what I know." The words come nobly from his lips.
Camus had the grace, rare among moderns, of moving with a simple
nobility as if he had stepped out of some older Mediterranean civilization. Yet there is something of an aesthetic stance about this attitude. He will live lucidly and self-reliantly; he will be the dupe neither of any ideology nor of any person. The noble Roman folds his
toga imperturbably about him. But if one examines his words, they
do not hold up. To live only with what you know! If you were to
try this, you would collapse on the instant. At every moment of
every day of our lives, we are involved in a continuous and living
transaction with the unknown. This being the case, what then shall
be my strategy? It is this: to multiply my points of contact with
this unknown wherever I can let it work to my advantage; to deny
myself none of the privileges that its unbounded resources might
offer. We need all the help we can get, and I propose to forego
none of it for the sake of striking some statuesque but self-castrat-
ing pose that will only serve to foster the illusion of my superior
courage.

Let us, in short, have the audacity once and for all to admit we
are chicken. I like in this connection the declaration of his faith by
Jewish writer Isaac Bashevis Singer: "Whenever I am in trouble, I

pray. And since I'm always in trouble, I pray a lot. Even when you see me eat and drink, while I do this, I pray."

It is surprising, in view of the wide scope of the *Varieties*, that James does not deal with the subject of Orthodox Judaism. All the more surprising on the part of a pragmatist, since here we have one of mankind's most successful religions. The gods of Greece and Rome lorded it over this tiny and stubborn nation. Those gods, once beautiful and glittering presences, have vanished completely among the dead antiquities of mankind. Judaism survives. If pragmatism means anything, it is surely an attempt to call our attention to the element of *practice* that constitutes our experience far more than we commonly realize. And here is a religion whose maximum emphasis is put upon faithful, stubborn, unwavering *practice*. What would the world be like without that perseverance? I sometimes tease my Jewish friends that if Orthodox Judaism were to disappear, Jews all over the world would collapse. And the rest of us? Can we even begin to guess how much we too would be shaken?

III.

The famous phrase "The Will to Believe," if we scrutinize it by itself, has some misleading implications. It smacks a little too much of a muscular YMCA kind of Christianity. James is exhorting us to make an effort, which is normally admirable counsel; but in this case the goal of the effort is not something we can arrive at by sheer force of will. Earlier we criticized Heidegger for leaving no room for the will, but now we must say against James that he would accord it too much place. Apparently then, the two views could not be more opposed; and yet both are in accord in this: that they cannot do justice to the middle ground between them—to the self-surrender in the ritual gesture of prayer, about which we are here speaking. In Heidegger the notion of *Gelassenheit* remains poetical and aesthetic: there is no notion of our self-surrender in *doing*. James, on the other hand, has no adequate notion of self-surrender at all. To surrender oneself in the ritual gesture is not a deliberate means toward some end external to the doing: toward "belief," for example, as some special state of mind which would crown our effort with success. If you stop the gesture at any point to ask yourself whether it is promoting something called "belief," you have killed it at once. To surrender yourself in the ritual act is a gesture of your humility and ignorance, helplessness and hopefulness, of which the epistemological intellect is quite incapable. James somehow conjures up the image of muscular strain and tension to produce out of oneself something that is not there to begin with. One thinks, ridiculously, of an infant straining and straining and finally whining, "Mommy, I can't *do* anything." In those moments when we are at the end of our tether we may not be able to summon up a will for anything—much less so difficult and intangible a matter as belief, with all its self-analyzing and self-accusing byways.

The phrase, in short, suggests the following crude image: We stand on one side of an abyss that has to be crossed, and on the other side is belief and everything positive that follows from it. On one side, belief; on the other side, our will, naked of all belief. We are to tense all our muscles and leap. But where is the will to fetch its strength for that leap? Is a will naked of belief capable of willing at all?

The difficulty may be seen better if we substitute "faith" for "believe" in James' famous phrase. It then becomes "the will to faith." The will to faith, indeed! Can we reasonably ask anyone to produce a faith as if we were dealing with an object that could be commandeered at will? Pascal is right: We can reasonably ask people only to perform acts that lie clearly and openly within the public domain. In the visitation of faith we are more the recipient of a gift than performer of a deed.

James, of course, knew this as well as any man. A great part of the *Varieties* deals with the kinds of religious experience in which the individual is, as it were, passive; those occasions when the will is not the agent who commandeers, but the vessel that is mysteriously flooded by energies and powers that the subject did not know were there at all. James has dealt with all these varied phenomena of conversion as copiously and sensitively as any writer on the subject. Yet this part of his thinking stands opposed to the dominant idea and tone of *The Will to Believe*. Or, at least, he has not put these two parts of his thought together. Can we attempt now to do it for him?

To begin with, we cannot split the situation of willing and believing apart, as if there were two distinct things—the will on one side, and belief on the other. The will by itself, naked of faith, is no will at all. We should speak then more correctly not of "the will to believe" but of "the faith to will," for it is a faith that enables us to will anything at all. Not, again, as if this faith stood opposite to the will and then passed into it. Faith is not affirmation of a proposition independent of the will; it is the act of will in its prayer.

IV.

The essay "Is Life Worth Living?" was delivered by James as an address to the Young Men's Christian Association at Harvard in 1895. It will be illuminating to dwell on this occasion itself—the time, place, and audience—in order to gauge the force of the question itself. Many anthologies of James' writings do not include this essay, perhaps because it seems too "popular" in tone. Yet it is one of his more eloquent performances, and deals with a problem that is not only central to his own thought but also to philosophy itself. And its "popular" tone, which is quite typical with James, is in fact a theoretical advantage, for he seems to be so close to his audience that he shares with them both the question as they face it and the expectations of the kind of answer they want.

The intent of a question, Wittgenstein observed, is formed by our expectation of the kind of answer that would satisfy us. We have no particular information about that audience, but we may easily imagine them within the costumes and climate of their period. Certainly, the YMCA at Harvard in 1895 belonged to a different world from what we know today. This audience would have been troubled perhaps by the doubts of the nineteenth century; but however much they might have shared in the "free thinking" of the time, they probably still persisted within the moral earnestness of their Christianity. They knew nothing—James himself knew nothing—of Kierkegaard and his devastating question, "Who then is really Christian?" They thought of theirs as a Christian age still, as well as a period of unexampled progress and the harbinger of an even more progressive time to come that would still preserve the benefits of religion, though in more enlightened and purified form. We, looking back, see them rather in the midst of something that was coming to an end and would leave us, who have had more of that progress than they ever imagined, now pacing the somber corridors of our more secular and violent time.

This audience, then, did not go to James' lecture without their having some sense what their answer to its question would be. They did not expect that the lecturer would come forward with facts or reasons that would change their mind from No to Yes. But if they

came to be confirmed in what they already believed, that did not
make the work of the lecturer pointless. However affirmative we
may feel about life, we can always do with a little bucking up. A
cynic like Schopenhauer might claim that this need of ours is only
another sign that our affirmation itself is hypocritical. In fact,
though, it is part of the conditions that the peculiar logic of this
question imposes.

And James does not disappoint their expectations. He sounds
a ringing paean to the value of life as a moral struggle; to the excitement and stir of doing battle in a good cause, the thrill at partial
victories, and the courage to stand defeat in the confident faith that
others, after us, will rally around the fallen standards. And he concludes, as he usually does, by suggesting that all this striving of ours,
reaching out as it does toward the religious, may in the end, who
knows, find its consummation there.

Suppose, however, there had been a real doubter in James' audience. We do not mean some worried soul who may question this or
that particular proposition in ethics or religion while he still remains
securely within their framework. The doubter we have in mind
stands so completely within his doubt that he moves perpetually on
the brink of suicide, on the razor's edge between death or life. We
would be more accurate to call him the nihilist, since doubt implies
a merely intellectual attitude toward certain propositions; and this
nihilist, on the contrary, lives within his own negative conviction.
At any moment he could pull the trigger; he knows that in the long
run it will be a matter indifferent to the world. If he does not do so,
it is only out of some lassitude or inertia, or perhaps some lingering
curiosity to turn the matter over once more in his mind. Since he
pursues above all a lucidity of mind, he knows that what really
holds him to life is the same blind instinct that keeps the rat struggling in its trap; and that this is what really keeps the rest of the
human race alive, however they may disguise it. The difference between him and the rat is that he *knows* what keeps him alive, and
knows too that it cannot be intellectually justified.

Confronted with this kind of doubter, can we ever present him
with convincing reasons why he should live? As soon as we place it
in this context, the original question whether life is worth living
takes on a quite different complexion. We are led beyond the
framework of discourse where rational arguments are expected to
prevail.

At this point the naturalistic philosopher, a very different kind of nonbeliever, is likely to be impatient; and we can imagine him breaking in: "What is all this nonsense that the meaning of life can't be stated? Suppose you are in good health; that the work you are engaged in is interesting and rewarding; and that your personal relationships are both happy and fulfilling. Don't all these things make life meaningful and worth living? What more can you possibly want in the way of reasons?"

Such is the naturalistic temperament that came by and large to prevail among American pragmatists after James. And if these newer pragmatists still honor his name, it is rather as an old and odd grandfather whose brilliance may be admitted but whose eccentricities in certain directions have to be condoned. The naturalist has never had any doubts on the subject of religion; he has rejected it as an illusion that his own energetic and happy constitution has never felt the need of. As for a reason for living, a rational utilitarianism is sufficient to justify life as a successful balance of pleasures over pains. The position of the naturalist is clear-cut; so too is that of the nihilist; but when we try to situate James in relation to both we see how richly ambiguous his position really is.

The arguments that seem so convincing to the naturalist do not work with the nihilist. He has been through it all, he has seen through those reasons. Indeed mankind itself, which has lived through it all, has seen through them. The great religions—Buddhism, Judaism, Christianity—simply record the experience of the race in finding the human condition unsatisfactory and empty. The nihilist accepts their verdict; but he does not, or cannot, take the step into religious faith or religious discipline.

The naturalist may say impatiently that the nihilist is sick; and that if he would only hang on, recovery would set in and he would come to find life, in all the variety of its interests, to be worth living after all. The nihilist can only smile; if we wish to call what he is suffering from a sickness, then we are playing the game of labels, and what we name sickness is nothing more than the fact that he does not agree with us and find life worthwhile. We might just as well label the naturalist's attitude as the sickness of insensitivity, or of lack of imagination, or of self-deception about the quality of his own achievements and pleasures. And as for the nihilist's "recovery" from his sickness, by that we mean simply that he would have changed his mind and come to agree with us that life is worth living.

It is odd that James himself, who elsewhere warns us copiously against it, should have fallen at one point into this game of labels—odder still that he should have done so in discussing the towering figure of Tolstoi. Of course, common opinion would like to shelter itself from the nihilistic question by seeing it merely as a symptom of weakness or pathology: We are alleged to raise the question at all only because we are frustrated, or in the midst of personal disintegration, or out of disappointment at not being successful. In fact, however, it requires strength, courage, and clear-headedness to push the nihilistic question to its conclusion; and Tolstoi is the great case in point. In the full vigor of health, with all his powers of mind and incomparable gifts as a writer, and both rich and famous to boot, Tolstoi nevertheless felt assailed by the sense that life was empty and meaningless; and he flung himself at the nihilistic question with his characteristic passion. And how does James react to this? Tolstoi's, he says, is a case of "the anhedonia" of middle age. Which is exactly like saying that opium puts you to sleep because of "its dormitive power," the kind of conversion of a label into an explanation at which James guffawed in other contexts. Why does he fall prey here to the psychologist's fallacy and seek to pin the pathological label upon what is the inevitable and most normal self-questioning the human mind can address to itself? The fact is that he does not grasp the nihilistic position as such; he sees it only under the trappings of "the sick soul." It is this failure that really compromises James' whole treatment of religion. Between the religious man and the nihilist there is a kinship, which separates them both from the naturalist. After all, if the nihilist did not grasp the truth about life, what need would there be for religion? James wavers at times; but on the whole he treats the natural life as sufficient, and religion an added bonus, whose democratic *right* to exist—but no more than that—he passionately defends.

There is no exit from this circle in which dialogue between the nihilist and his opponents seems to, but does not really take place. And that circle lies in the logic of the question itself. Every question draws a line across the world dividing it between the answers Yes and No. With most questions one can move intellectually back and forth across the line, gathering reasons Yes or No, trying to strike a balance until coming to rest on one side or the other. But the question "Is life worth living?"—at least when seriously asked —is different: You answer it as already standing on one side of the line or the other, and you can only find reasons for those who stand there with you. It is idle to tot up the good things in life as sufficient to persuade those across the line, so long as they believe that the total you arrive at is still without meaning. We meet here another application of Kant's principle that the part presupposes the whole: like attempting to constitute time as a series of moments when the notion of a moment already presupposes time. To the nihilist, the attempt to establish the value of life by adding up its valuable increments is like counting the paper stock of a company that is already bankrupt. If anyone crosses that line dividing No from Yes, it will be for other "reasons" than the rational arguments a naturalist can adduce.

Dialogue fails here between the two sides because the motive to live—the motive behind all motives—is in the domain of the incommunicable. There at the center of the will—where the decision to live or not to live takes place—we are below the level of articulate reasons and rational persuasion.

The region where language fails and silence takes over Wittgenstein called "the mystical." But the mystical phenomenon we encounter now is not at the limits of the world—not in the encompassing mystery that a universe exists at all—but at the very center of ourselves. Are the two unrelated?

We come back thus to the question of mystery and mysticism, which seems to wind like an inevitable thread through the fabric of our investigations.

v.

MYSTICISM

It is something of a shock to learn that James did not find mysticism or mystical experience at all congenial. With his flair, his psychological sensitivity, his capacity to project himself into the inner feeling of others, one might have expected him to revel in the mystical material. But his disclaimer here, blunt and unambiguous, shows us very clearly the limit of his own religious capacities:

> Whether my treatment of mystical states will shed more light or darkness, I do not know, for my own constitution shuts me out from their enjoyment almost entirely, and I can speak of them at second hand.

He makes no such statement, we notice, in his discussions of the sick soul or of the divided self, for of these he had experience at first hand. Moreover, he could approach these matters with his professional expertise as a psychologist. He had studied briefly at the first clinics in psychiatry on the Continent (which also produced Freud), and James never ceased to feel a lively interest in that particular branch of psychology. But with mysticism he does not have the sense either of personal or professional expertise; and he cannot quite find the handle with which to grasp it. One feels that he would have liked to annex it, if he possibly could, to the domain of abnormal psychology.

Yet though he stands outside of it, he does not dogmatize against mysticism. The mystic has a right to be heard even though we are not compelled to believe him. James sums up his position in two admirable propositions:

1. Mystical states, or the revelations therefrom, have no binding authority on those who stand outside them.

2. On the other hand, the rationalist cannot dismiss the existence of these states out of hand. They break down the dogmatism of the rationalistic consciousness that would assert its own exclusive validity as the only legitimate form of consciousness.

Once again, James would leave us with that intellectually open situation that he favored in the questions of free will and God. Lacking decisive proof for or against, we are free to believe if we so choose. The mystic might point out against James—who is so hung up on this matter of "beliefs"—that he is not offering us any definite belief like that in free will, but simply urging on us that we develop the sense of our union with all that is. But even if we should agree with James that the general logic of their credibility is the same, there is a marked difference in the importance he accords to mysticism as compared with the questions of free will and God. The latter two become for him existentially central; we need to call upon them as we struggle on the moral battlefields of life. But as for mysticism, he is willing to leave that a quite peripheral matter indeed.

Yet on practical grounds alone, it would seem unwise to leave mysticism so marginal a matter. James had argued that if you remain in theoretical suspension forever on the question of free will, you have in effect decided against it, for you lose the resources in action that a positive belief in our freedom brings with it. An analogous argument could be offered in behalf of the mystical attitude. To be sure, this attitude does not come to a head in the singular and urgent action—the leap from precipice to precipice, in James' illustration—where our belief in our freedom actually furthers our strength to make the leap. But if we consider our life over a longer span, and particularly our life in its most banal and humdrum aspects, then mysticism claims to open channels of awareness and energy that would not otherwise be available to us. To suspend your judgment here is in effect to answer No, and thereby to deny yourself one further possible resource in this painful pilgrimage from darkness into darkness that is our life.

James' treatment of the mystic really proceeds from a misunderstanding—a misunderstanding, however, not peculiar to him, but one that prevails throughout our whole culture. We think of the mystic as one who has entry to some special sphere of reality, and brings us back bulletins of information from there. We ordinary mortals do not have access to that special world, but out of democratic tolerance we cannot reject the mystic's reports of it out of hand: He may be telling the truth, for all we know. Still, since these reports come from such a different world, they do not affect our life here, and we can go about our concerns as if mystic and mysticism never existed. But of course, existentially speaking, this is a rejection of mysticism quite as thoroughgoing as any by the most dogmatic rationalist or positivist.

No doubt, this widespread misunderstanding may be due in good part to the mystics themselves. They speak to us out of their time and place, and from a great variety of creeds—there have been Hindu, Buddhist, Taoist, Jewish, Christian, and Muslim mystics; and since they must clutch at any mode of expression available, they make use of the particular theological or religious structure at their disposal. Yet there is always the insistence on the provisional and makeshift nature of this apparatus—whence the mystic, however pious, is so often suspect by ecclesiastical authorities. Some mystics too have seen visions, in the sense of extraordinary images or prophetic fantasies that are not given to normal people. But this visionary gift has to be separated very clearly from the issue of mysticism, which can remain quite free from any auxiliary visions. Indeed, we have to remember here the common emphasis upon "the detachment from images" as part of the mystic discipline. And throughout history there been various "mystical" sects that have pursued these special states of consciousness by means of drugs, hallucinogens, or some particular techniques to induce trancelike states of being. Against this mania for pursuing the various distortions of consciousness, we might remember the majestic words of one great mystic, the sage Hui-neng, who became the great patriarch of Zen Buddhism: "The *Tao* [the truth] is your ordinary mind." The most ordinary thing in experience—a grain of sand or a blade of grass—will do for the mystic.

All of this motley external history has filtered down into our current confusions on the matter. What, then, is the common misunderstanding of myticism? The word is possibly one of the vaguest and most abused in the language. The mystical is whatever is mysterious or occult; paranormal phenomena and extrasensory perception; mediums and seances; ghosts and the survival of consciousness after death; trances and demoniacal perception—in short, a kind of grab bag of all the items of speculation and superstition that lie outside the boundaries of the normal and that, lately, seem to have become popular with the movies. It would be unfair to saddle James with this vast, buzzing confusion, but it is also true that he has not sufficiently detached the meaning of mysticism from this popular amalgam. The empirical bent of his temperament, indeed, led him in this popular direction. If any phenomenon interested him, it was as a channel to some possibly new *information* on reality. Ever the empiricist avid for new facts, he was passionately interested in the investigation of occult psychological phenomena, and actively championed the Society for Psychical Research against any dogmatism that would foreclose on these issues beforehand. But this researcher's mentality is precisely what is likely to miss the whole point about mysticism. *The mystic is not a purveyor of new information at all.* Why should he seek to multiply the items of the Many for a people who have lost sight of the One? He does not bring forward any new beliefs about particular occult matters of fact. He is simply a witness to Being, and its mystery, within which he seeks continuously to stand.

That, however, is the last thing the world at large is ready to be interested in. We can be interested in all kinds of spooky phenomena because they may gratify our curiosity for facts. Men get lost in beings, as Heidegger observes, and turn their backs on Being. We will poke into any hole and corner of particular mysteries for which the psychic researcher may set up some apparatus of testing, but we ignore that open and compelling mystery that envelops every son and daughter of humankind. But that is the mystery that engages the mystic, and once we ourselves turn our eyes there, we cannot be satisfied with James' conclusions. The message of the mystic is binding upon us as a call to open ourselves to that mystery.

Indeed, there may be no more important task for our culture than to rediscover the sense of the mystics. For some time now we have been told that man has become cut off from nature; and sometimes this is put in more imposing terms, that he suffers from the loss of "cosmic consciousness." These descriptions are nonetheless true for being banal by this time. But the way out, or the way back, may require from us a kind of discipline and patience that we had not suspected. If you sit down and brood on large abstractions like "cosmic consciousness," you are not likely to remedy your situation. Better to turn your attention to things nearer at hand. In that simple and unself-conscious relation you have established with your dog or cat you have already affirmed a bond with the great unconscious life of nature. You have already taken a step beyond the prison of a narrow and excessive humanism. Boxed in a city apartment, you may begin to discover a curious kinship growing between you and the plant that you water daily. You and it, after all, are partners in the same pilgrimage: you share the one life together on this earth. Dwell in that bond and let your thinking start there.

The bond that attaches us to the life outside ourselves is the same bond that holds us to our own life. James' question "Is life worth living?" can only be answered from this center. In the end, it is through instinct that we cling to life; left to corrosive reason alone, we would not be able to get through the day. Were some universal disease to afflict the hypothalamus and limbic systems in the brain, which regulate our emotions, mankind as a whole might go the way of suicide—whatever elegantly abstract reasons for living philosophy had concocted. Let us grant biological materialism its clear possession of half the truth. In the meantime, while these systems are normal and at work for us, let us lavish our loves wisely. The mystic reclaims and redeems this instinctual source of life for us. We live from the same instinct that keeps the rat struggling in his trap. But who is to say that the struggle of the rat is not holy? Mysticism is instinct lifted to the level of faith and love. The mystic represents that point in evolution where consciousness, a perilous offshoot of the whole process, rejoins and affirms the great flood of life that has produced it.

For purely practical reasons, then, the mystical appears as one of the most valuable of all religious phenomena; and we are all the more surprised that James, the pragmatist, could not come closer to its spirit.

VI.

Why should James' temperament, as he himself confesses, have shut him out from any kind of mysticism? One is tempted to say that he has therefore missed the center of religion itself. At one point, for example, he states quite flatly: "Faith-state and mystic state are practically convertible terms." If this be so—if the assent to life in faith and the assent in mysticism are one and the same—then indeed James does stand outside of the whole religious life that he so copiously and sensitively describes. To fall back on our earlier image: He talks about the building from the outside.

On deeper consideration of the man himself we should not be surprised that the mystic would be someone alien to him. James is first and last the strenuous moralist. The meaning of life lies in its moral struggle. The whole of his background—the New England inheritance and the activist urge in American life at the time— conspires to reinforce this emphasis upon doing over Being. To tell the truth, James as a philosopher does not have a very strong sense of Being at all.

Of course, he does admonish us in one place of the necessity of taking what he calls "moral holidays." On these occasions we are urged to let the cares of the world go hang while we abandon our-selves to the voluptuousness of Being. We are to lose ourselves in the joy of nature or in the mass of mankind in the manner of Walt Whitman. We need such respites from the tension of the will in its perpetual seriousness and striving.

Yet this recognition, even in the way it is put, is too scanty a con-cession to Being over doing. We are to take a "holiday"—that is, a period of departure from what is the urgent and serious business of our lives—to which we shall then return with our energies renewed for the real tasks that give our life meaning. Being is at most an oc-casional interlude in the doing that really makes the drama of our lives.

James himself was too driven and self-driving a person to let him-

self ever rest. Even up to the end of his life he was obsessed with
the problem of "the energies of men"—the thoroughly American-
problem of how to get the most out of yourself. His ultimate and
simple justification of religion is by the pragmatic principle, "By
their fruits ye shall know them," but the fruits he is most likely to
acknowledge are those of action and doing. Mysticism may be
remote from his temperament, but he can admire nevertheless those
mystics who, in their practical lives, were prodigies of energy.
Pragmatism must always emphasize the future tense, and in human
affairs generally this attitude is a healthy one; but in the case of
religion James overdoes this emphasis. Consider, he tells us, all the
facts that make up the past of the world; the "religious hypothesis"
—and notice again the word "hypothesis," as if we were dealing
with the language game of explanatory theories—could be true or
false, and it would make no difference to those facts. It does, however, have a bearing upon future facts, since it sustains and drives
our will to act, and our consequent behavior changes our world.
But to hold that religious faith pays off only in the future is surely a
cruel judgment on all those generations of the dead, whose future—
in this world, at any rate—has already been closed, but whose
religion must have made a difference somewhere in their actual life.
The confusion here is to assimilate religion to the condition of an
explanatory hypothesis. The verification of a hypothesis always
looks to the future, but religion somewhere along the line must give
redemption in the present—not the feeling of some endlessly progressive future, onward and upward, but the sense of eternity in the
moment.

If, among modern philosophers, the reading of Heidegger makes
us long for a compensating voice like James', it is also true that the
latter makes us return to the thought of Heidegger. Perhaps this is as
it should be: The truth of human life must perpetually lie in the
tension between Being and doing. We can never resolve the question exclusively in favor of one or the other side. All our doing
must take place within the context of Being, with its mystery present and alive to us. Otherwise we are simply scurrying around
aimlessly in the mazes of our own contrivance. On the other hand,
to seek absorption in Being, as an escape from the tasks of ordinary
life, can only lead to quiescence and boring repetition. Man is the
creature who must live in perpetual tension between these opposites.
He *is* their tension and copresence.

Part IV

The Shape
of the Future?

Chapter 15

------◀◆▶------

The Shape of the Future:
American Version

THE BEST ARGUMENT FOR FREEDOM IS THE HORROR OF THE WORLD
without it. One way in which our century may have advanced the
age-old debate about free will is by putting determinism into practice. Formerly determinists argued for a metaphysical reality that
remained invisible behind the scenes; in our century they have not
only brought it onto the scene, but also made it dominate the action,
as they seek to shape society by its light. And this is as it must be,
for the metaphysical and political aspects of freedom are in the end
inseparable. Freedom is indeed indivisible in this respect too: If you
believe in determinism, then you will want a society that submits its
citizens to the maximum of planned conditioning. The Soviet Union
has been doing this for the past fifty years; and now the Chinese,
though starting later, from all accounts have made even more rapid
strides toward building the human anthill. The results are already
visible enough for us to form a judgment of the philosophy that
sponsored them.

Fortunately for us, the American version of the determinist society still lies in the future and in the imagination of our behavioral
scientists, whose most popular and aggressive spokesman is Professor
B. F. Skinner of Harvard. Some friends tell me that I attach too
much importance to Skinner, that his views are extreme and not
shared by other behavioral scientists. Perhaps. But his general popu-
larity and sales are not to be overlooked; his *Walden II* is assigned
reading in our secondary schools; and he is particularly persuasive
for the simple-minded and half-educated, whose numbers con-

stantly increase in our society. And more significantly: With regard to behavioral scientists generally, I think I shall be reassured about them when they come up with some positive doctrine of freedom of their own. Until then, I shall continue to believe that Professor Skinner may be more naïve than some of his colleagues, but that he has also been more forthright and point-blank in uttering the philosophy that lies behind their theoretical efforts.

To be sure, there is a great difference in coloration between Professor Skinner's imaginary utopia, as portrayed in *Walden II,* and the grimness of Communist reality. His ideal community is so bland and pleasant that the sympathetic narrator has to compare it at one point to a "big summer hotel." Indeed, in its innocence about human beings, its bland and gregarious good will, and its amiable love of gadgets, this utopia has an almost unbeatable combination for winning over a large section of the American audience. (One feels that Professor Skinner might have made a great career for himself in advertising or public relations.) Our country was founded in good part with varied utopian notions and enthusiasms, and these still linger deeply in the national psyche. The community of *Walden II* is pastoral and idyllic enough to satisfy some of the longings that went into Brook Farm. It has the features of decentralization and deindustrialization that will be agreeable to all of us who are appalled by the shrillness of the modern urban environment. But in fairness to Professor Skinner, the difference between his community and the Communist regimes is not merely one of coloration but of principle too. At one point he expressly separates himself from the Soviet experiment by abjuring power, and insisting on persuasion (reinforcing conditioning, in his terms) over coercion. The carrot, he believes, works better on the donkey than the stick. And the carrot, moreover, will be sufficient: When positive conditioning has been thoroughgoing, all will become sweetness and light. And what could be more thoroughly in the American grain than this optimistic faith that human nature will impose no recalcitrant obstacle if we but apply the right knowhow?

Yet the comparison with Communist regimes must be made because Skinner's society is a *totalitarian* one. The individual is to be shaped from cradle to grave. And not only is it in fact totalitarian, but also it has to be so in principle; for if the conditioning were incomplete or faulty at any point, the whole structure might come apart at the seams. A link untended anywhere in the sequence of causation and the whole chain might break apart. In the world that the determinist constructs there can be no loose ends. The minimal cause may trigger a maximal effect.

Thus Professor Skinner comes before his general audience as a political and social ideologist, and he has to be judged on this basis. It is a role to which he brings considerable skills as a propagandist. One of his ploys—and it may be one of his most effective for a good many readers—is to enlist our sympathies for him as an underdog. He is, he tells us, attacking the Establishment; and any plea against the Establishment these days is likely to have our antecedent sympathy. But in fact Skinner is very much part of an Establishment of his own. The behavioral scientists are not a negligible part of our society, and in terms of their influence upon certain key areas of our culture—in the matter of educational testing, practices, and curricula, for example—they wield an extraordinary amount of power. Their opponents, if they ever rise to so belligerent a condition as to declare themselves such, are a handful of humanists within the academic community, who in terms of grants and funding are usually beggars by comparison. And despite Skinner's beleaguered tone, the notion of the dignity and freedom of the individual, which is the central object of his attack, is not now as dominant an ideal as it once was. In our general climate of opinion this particular idea has been in retreat for some time.

But the propagandist in this case is a social ideologist in substance too, for he comes before us with a program. And it is not a program like any run-of-the-mill recommendation to change this or that particular feature within our society or social environment. Skinner's thinking, if not totalitarian, is always total; and his program is a total one—a proposal that we submit ourselves completely to the "technology of behavior" and so change ourselves and our society from the ground up.

Before going into the detail of this proposal, we can't help noticing a curious ambiguity at the very outset. The determinist, when he gives up the passivity of fatalism, comes before us as an activist with a social program. Now, a program, in any understandable sense of the word, is something on which, after due deliberation, we are to make our choice. Here is one of the dilemmas of determinism that Willliam James never explored, perhaps because the program of determinism had never been advanced as social policy in his time. The donkey, once inside the shafts of the cart, is not to be driven forward by kicks and blows, but lured by the perpetual carrot. But what is to get him between the shafts? Even if we try to seduce him into the shafts by another carrot (and Skinner seems to think that the idyllic picture of *Walden II* will do for such a carrot), the human donkey can refuse to submit to the seduction. The factor of choice never gets eliminated from the picture after all. Since power and coercion have been ruled out, those who enter the behaviorist's utopia will do so voluntarily—that is, of their own free will.

I.

We have at least to agree wholeheartedly with Professor Skinner's point of departure—his dissatisfaction with the modern world as it now stands. And we agree with him too when he finds modern technology the source of much of this dissatisfaction. The great achievements in the physical sciences, and the techniques that have come with those achievements, have not solved our social problems, but in a very disturbing way have exacerbated old problems and introduced new ones. We need not repeat his particular illustrations; we have already brought them forward in an earlier chapter. What then is to be done? Some people might think that we ought to take a step back for a moment and reflect on the fundamental nature of technique, its possible completeness and sufficiency, and whether we have not expected too much from it in the first place. But Skinner does not like the qualified answer; his thinking is always linear and simple. If technology has brought problems with it, that is due to our use of it; and to cure the latter we simply need more technology, but applied now to the users. Hitherto we have applied our technical skills to physical nature; we have now to add to those skills the new "technology of behavior." The cure is not just a hair of the dog who has bitten you, but also to eat the whole dog.

Before we can ever put this human technology to use, however, we shall have to get rid of the antiquated notion of "the free and autonomous individual" with which tradition has encumbered us. Hence Skinner's long diatribe against this ideal in *Beyond Freedom and Dignity*. Etymologically, "autonomous" means an individual who is a "law unto himself"—and in this sense, of course, the term is forbidding. One imagines some impossibly musclebound Stoic, a law unto himself, floating in a void free from all conditioning. But that would be an absurd caricature of what the term actually intends. The autonomous individual is simply the responsible person—one who is capable—in certain significant areas, at least—of directing and governing his own behavior. Nobody, however responsible he be, is ever free altogether from the force of conditions and circumstances. The notion of the autonomous individual is an ideal only imperfectly realized in practice; yet it provides a norm or standard, like certain ideal conceptions in the sciences, without which we could not get along in practice. In our own hit-and-miss ways, without the blessings of behaviorism, most of us try to raise our children to become autonomous persons. They will be on their own in any case and will have to make their own decisions. And what else, one asks, can be the end of all the conditioning that Skinner would put his human subjects through except to turn them out as responsible persons? If they have at every turn to run back to the psychologist's apron strings, the conditioning would have been very inadequate indeed.

There is nothing in the idea of a free and responsible individual that implies the absence of conditioning, though behaviorists talk as if this were so. We are all creatures of habit, and habits are the deposits that conditioning—including our own self-conditioning—has left with us. The preponderant role of habit in human behavior is not a new perception. Pascal in the seventeenth century acknowledged as an old and accepted maxim that habit is second nature. And William James, in his celebrated chapter on the subject, quotes with approval the Duke of Wellington's remark, "Habit second nature! It is ten times nature!" But there is a great difference between humans and the animals passively subject to conditioning in the behaviorist's laboratory: We can devise and set up circumstances for our own conditioning. We can provide our own carrot and stick, whereas the donkey has to accept what the master offers. Powerful as the grip of habits may be on our behavior, people do often succeed in changing old habits and setting up new ones, and *on their own initiative*.

It is really quite surprising, when one asks around, to find out how many people do succeed in giving up habits of smoking, drinking, or in radically changing their diets. We may hear more about the failures and backsliders, and there may in fact be more of them. But if there were only one successful case of this self-initiated change, the behaviorist would have to alter his theory. And one of the most powerful levers we can have for changing ourselves is this very idea of the autonomy of the individual person.

The example of the writer Dashiell Hammett is particularly illuminating in this connection. Hammett, a heavy drinker for many years, had reached an advanced stage of alcoholism accompanied by delirium tremens. His doctor told him he would be dead in a month if he continued drinking. Hammett said he would go on the wagon; but the doctor told Lillian Hellman, Hammett's good friend, "He can't and he won't." But Hammett did go on the wagon and stayed there. Five or six years later, when Miss Hellman told him what the doctor had said to her, Hammett looked puzzled and observed, "But I gave the man my word that day."

"I gave my word." Hammett lived by his own code of personal honor and integrity, and in this particular instance it had the power of salvation for him. "I gave my word." That is the free and autonomous individual speaking who determines that he will make a promise and keep it. No doubt, Hammett's image of himself as a man of honor, an autonomous individual in the matter of keeping his word, was built up by a lifetime of conditioning, and thus had the efficacy it did in this particular situation. But the point is that he himself participated in the conditioning and actively built up the image. To create oneself, however partially, in the image of an autonomous individual does amass a great deal of capital, in the way of moral and psychic energy, that can be expended in times of stress. It is surely harmful, particularly in our present climate of opinion, to deprive people altogether of the notion of moral autonomy. To the degree that this idea departs from their daily consciousness, by so much are they weakened for the graver situations where they have to choose and act. The consequences of behaviorist teaching can be morally debilitating.

In the long run too they would be damaging to our status as individuals before the law. That the criminal is not really responsible for his act is taken by some people as the height of wisdom in jurisprudence. This view, so it is held, leads to leniency and understanding in our treatment of the criminal, and most of us would prefer to err on the side of compassion than severity. But this promise of greater leniency could be quite illusory. We have only to imagine the treatment of the criminal in a society built upon strictly determinist conceptions and with less liberal sympathies than ours. The

criminal—the person who exhibits antisocial behavior—is held to
be the product of conditioning that somewhere went wrong and his
punishment is to be considered as additional conditioning that may
change his behavior. Suppose, however, that he is judged to be
past changing; or that the resources of the society are too limited to
be spent on the prolonged treatment of him and others like him.
The philosophy of this society regards him not as a person but as an
object, an unfortunate and cancerous growth upon the social body;
and as with a malignant growth, the practical decision could be to
wield the scalpel promptly and eliminate it. Thus the disappearance
of the notion of the autonomous person would in this case lead not
to greater leniency than our law now exhibits but to a much more
drastic severity. And the severity would be likely to become greater
as people became more and more callous in their feelings.

The ideal of the autonomous person stands thus as a protective
and reasonable mean between two aberrant extremes: on the one
hand, a slipshod leniency administered without guiding line or
rule; and on the other hand, a draconian harshness in the interests of
sheer social utility, which in the end would be determined by some
tyrannical bureaucracy. It is in nobody's interest then, much less the
criminal's, that this ideal should die out.

We can have other motives for seeking to change our habits besides our feeling that they have become dangerous for our health or
destructive of our moral autonomy. Curiosity and the sense of adventure, for example. We may be bored with the old self and its ha-
bitual ways of being and doing, and want to see what the world is
like through some different set of habits. The French poet Paul
Valéry observed that we sometimes reach a point in our life where,
"*Il n'y a qu'une chose à faire—c'est à se faire.*" (There is only one
thing to do—to redo oneself.) Valéry himself was tempted by his
own demon of lucidity to think that consciousness might remake
the self almost out of whole cloth—as if Descartes' formula—I
think, therefore I am—were to be translated into a statement of
causal efficacy. But we need not take his observation in that total
sense. There are limits to what we can make of ourselves, and indeed
stricter ones than the behaviorist would accept; but we may also
find that within these limits there are more resources for change
than we had imagined. In any case, there is the interest and excitement of the adventure itself. In the course of it you may be surprised to learn that consciousness is not such a feeble reed after all.

You will be amazed at the wealth of stratagems and devices it can invent to assist you.

I myself have given up drinking while writing this book. The motives were various. There was the sheer practical one of finding out how much more energy was available when even "moderate social drinking"—which, as everyone knows, is sometimes not moderate at all—was given up. There was too a kind of experimental curiosity, since I was dealing with the question of freedom, and this motive may have been abetted considerably by a sense of rebellion against Skinner and the behaviorists. We can never be sure how much our freedom may be fueled by the sense of rebellion. Dostoevski made the point as powerfully and unpleasantly in his *Notes from the Underground* that one would think the behaviorist, if he had ever read him, would not have forgotten it. Thrown into the determinists' community, where our conditioning has all been pre-programmed, some of us might set about breaking laws simply out of a sense of rebellion. Very shortly too, I found that the motive of sheer self-denial became attractive. The ascetic impulse is a much stronger impulse than we think, and forms a not inconsiderable part of our sense of discipline, without which life would cease to have very much meaning. Yet almost everything in our culture, except perhaps the example of a few of our athletes, seems to conspire to discredit and weaken this impulse, and give us back the image of ourselves as passive consumers.

For a moment I am almost tempted to write a manual *How to Give Up Drinking*, but I am immediately checked from such a brash undertaking by the realization that there is no automatic technique that would be valid for everyone. What works for one person may not work for another. In the business of changing ourselves, each of us is ultimately on his own; and that can be one of the attractions in striking out on a new path. We touch again on our old question of the relation of technique to the individual and problematic situations with which experience confronts us. Skinner and his fellow behaviorists would be practicing a great deceit on those who submitted to their "technology of behavior," expecting that it would equip them for all the exigencies of life. The poor subject steps out of the conditioning box into a world where he is at a loss when he finds out he must often improvise as he goes along.

Yet this absence of a rigid technique is not a sign of the poverty of consciousness but of its richness. Consciousness is much richer and more fecund, as we learned earlier, than any of the techiques it devises. For every computer that the mind creates it can devise a problem that this computer cannot solve. One has thus to throw oneself on the resources of consciousness and let it invent all manner of associations to strengthen your self-denial and make it more attractive. Soon the absence of the habit may become more interesting than the habit you have discarded.

I was surprised to find that I was not involved in a day-by-day grinding repetition of denial, with teeth clenched, until the conditioning wore in. The difficult thing is the beginning, and the effort of concentration needed to change your whole attitude. Notice it is this change of *mental* attitude that is more important than the repetition of isolated bits of behavior. Once that attitude has been changed, you have turned a corridor and your path becomes easier. Behaviorists think of the life of the mind in an oversimple and linear fashion: A, then B, then C—condition A, response B, reinforcing reward C; and *da capo* over and over again until the conditioning has worn its groove. But the ingenuity of consciousness in shaping ourselves is more complex than any simple linear pattern can indicate. If you are going to compare the mind to the computer—and there is no objection so long as you realize it is a metaphor, within its metaphorical limits—then you had best make the comparison in a productive rather than a reductive way. Thus the mind may be regarded as an immense memory bank in which one can surprisingly retrieve day by day new items, or invent new combinations of those items, to further our determination. One drags up, for example, the occasions when, having drunk too much, one made more of a fool of oneself than usual. Self-mortification can be good for the soul as well as a reinforcement for our abandoning a habit. Or explore in imagination this paltry sensation that has had you in its grip. Sip mentally a glass of scotch, savoring it drop by drop. Like Proust exploring in imagination a defunct love, you may find the exploration more interesting than the actual possession. Scotch whisky tastes better this way, as Albertine remembered was more interesting than in the flesh. And the craving ceases as you lose its illusions. Proust's vast novel, by the way, is the greatest manual of asceticism since the sutras of the Buddha.

The personal example I have just given, it suddenly occurs to me, is hardly more than a hint in documentation of an old and simple statement by Aristotle that sums up, I think, the whole issue of freedom. The mind, Aristotle says, is a source of movement; consciousness can intervene in the world and change things. We become aware in a certain situation that something needs to be done or is desirable to be done, and we set about taking steps to do it. Sometimes the obstacles, both within and without, are too great, our will falters, and our efforts fall short. But very often, and in the most ordinary ways, people do succeed in doing what they intended —and thus the fact of freedom is confirmed around us every day. Why then has human freedom become so entangled a matter that behaviorists are led to deny the fact itself? I suggest it is because they have formed some antecedent conception of mind, contrary to ordinary experience, that allows it no leverage in things at all. But if consciousness is not to have that leverage—if it is not, in Aristotle's words, to be a source of change—whatever sense are you going to make then of the whole structure of science, which is a product of the human mind if anything is and has also transformed the entire fabric of our social existence?

II.

Most of the unfortunate consequences of technology as applied to physical nature, which Skinner like the rest of us deplores, have come from side effects that could not be calculated beforehand. What might the uncalculated effects be from the wholesale application of the technology of behavior to humans? This is a question that never seems to bother Skinner, and yet it is the one that poses the ultimate and gravest danger to his program, for we ourselves would be the victims of our own miscalculated techniques. Of course, one cannot tell what those effects would be until the program is put into actual operation; but that only enhances the danger, since we might find ourselves entrapped in a system from which we would have made ourselves incapable of escaping. All that, you may say, is hypothetical and belongs to the future; yet even now I think we may gather from Professor Skinner's tidy utopia some glimmers of what those possible side effects may be, however hidden behind its idyllic surface.

Expecting something grim and oppressive, like George Orwell's *1984*, I was surprised on my first reading of *Walden II* to find myself engulfed in the bland and amiable atmosphere of a "big summer hotel," as the narrator correctly describes it. The surprise gave way quickly to a disturbing sense of *déjà vu*—a feeling that I had actually encountered this whole phenomenon somewhere previously, if not in actual life at least in my reading, though I could not at the moment lay my finger on it. It was only after I had finished the book and put it down that the exact memory came back to me, and I turned to a passage in William James, recounting his own experience of an earlier and similar commune, to find perfectly expressed my own uneasiness before this later behaviorist Eden.

James visited the summer colony at Chautauqua, New York, in the late 1890s. This institution, I understand, still exists, though it has faded into obscurity. It belonged distinctly to an America of an earlier and vanished period. In its idealism and innocence, it was an expression of our middle class's aspiration toward culture and the good life, but this class has since become more sophisticated and its aspirations take other forms. James recites the impressive achievements of the community:

> You have magnificent music—a chorus of seven hundred voices, with possibly the most perfect open-air auditorium in the world. You have every sort of athletic exercise from sailing, rowing, swimming, bicycling, to the ball-field and the more artificial doings which the gymnasium affords. You have kindergartens and model secondary schools. . . . You have the best of company and no effort. You have no zymotic diseases, no poverty, no drunkenness, no crime, no police. You have culture, you have kindness, you have cheapness, you have equality, you have the best fruits of what mankind has fought and bled and striven for under the name of civilization for centuries. You have, in short, a foretaste of what human society might be, were it all in the light, and with no suffering and no dark corners.

At first he was altogether spellbound, as he himself confesses, by this "middle-class paradise, without a sin, without a victim, without a blot, without a tear." Yet his recoil from it was prompt and unequivocal, and when James is expressing himself in a moment of passion, one had best allow him his own words:

> And yet what was my own astonishment, on emerging into the dark and wicked world again, to catch myself quite unexpectedly and involuntarily saying: "Ouf! what a relief!" This order is too tame, this culture too second-rate, this goodness too uninspiring.

This human drama without a villain or a pang; this community so refined that ice-cream soda-water is the utmost offering it can make to the brute animal in man; this atrocious harmlessness of all things—I cannot abide with them. Let me take my chances again in the big outside worldly wilderness with all its sins and sufferings. There are the heights and depths, the precipices and steep ideals, the gleams of the awful and infinite; and there is more hope and help a thousand times than in this dead level and quintessence of every mediocrity.

And after this first explosion, when James found time to reflect, he thought that what this idyllic community principally lacked was

the element of precipitousness, so to call it, of strength and strenuousness, intensity and danger. . . . In this unspeakable Chautauqua there was no potentiality of death in sight anywhere and no point of the compass visible from which danger might possibly appear. The ideal so completely victorious already that no sign of any previous battle remained, the place just resting on its oars. But what our human emotions seem to require is the sight of the struggle going on. The moment the fruits are being merely eaten, things become merely ignoble. Sweat and effort, human nature strained to its uttermost and on the rack, yet getting through alive, and then turning its back on its success to pursue another more rare and arduous still—this is the sort of thing the presence of which inspires us, and the reality of which it seems to be the function of all the higher forms of literature and fine art to bring home to us and suggest.

In their objective details the two communities are quite different, but James' remarks about Chautauqua could be transcribed directly and totally to apply to Walden II.

Professor Skinner might reply, as he has actually done to similar criticisms in the past, that what James objects to would not disturb the members of Walden since they have grown up in this community and are conditioned to be satisfied with what they get. These people won't know any better, and what they don't know won't hurt them! When we put the matter so bluntly, the veil falls, and the attitude of the behavioral scientist stands out for the callous cynicism that it is. But leaving aside the question of cynicism, we have to ask whether this imaginary community, as it is set up, could in fact produce the level of culture that Skinner assures us it enjoys.

If the community is to maintain and enjoy the activities of culture, as it seems to, then it will have to put up with certain tensions that it is not at all built to absorb.

"As you may imagine, art flourishes here," says the leader-guide Frazier, and the visitor-narrator dutifully observes paintings on the wall, "surprisingly vigorous and fresh, in many styles, and almost without exception competently handled. I had seen many professional shows less interesting from a technical point of view and certainly much less exciting." In view of the quality of some of the current exhibitions in the New York galleries, this last observation may not be quite the compliment that Skinner intends. Some of the Waldenites, evidently, are Sunday painters and do well at it. But as soon as a person paints competently, he may not be able to rest with that; he may be captured by the medium and its possibilities, and want to explore these. Consumed then by the passion to paint, he will find it extremely irksome to spare even those few hours of unrelated labors that the colony will require from him.

The visitors, in passing, notice some of the colonists playing chess. What would happen if a Bobby Fischer were suddenly to emerge in Walden II? Someone not content to play chess merely for relaxation but who wanted to excel? The proper conditioning, you say, would have removed this kind of competitiveness from the Waldenites. It might turn out, however, a more difficult job than this community can handle to remove the competitive streak from the human animal, and perhaps not a desirable goal in the long run. But leaving the competitive aspect aside, consider only the case of someone who becomes attracted by the combinatorial possibilities of chess, and is drawn to give all his time to exploring them. Here competitiveness is not at issue, but only the passion of the mind for a particular subject matter and its exciting possibilities.

Creativity is inseparable from a certain restlessness of mind. If something has already been done, it is pointless merely to repeat it mechanically and competently. If a particular mode of expression does not present fresh possibilities, it becomes boring—like a closed system in logic or mathematics. The more talented the artist the more he labors to keep the medium open. Such labor takes its toll of an entire life—it is not a dabbling in leisure hours. One thinks of Cézanne, whose life consisted of painting and nothing but painting, writing in a letter three days before his death: "I begin at last to see my way clear." Art is a tyrannical mistress, but in the bland utopia

of Walden II everything seems to come easy and without its price—
American style.

There is also music to be heard in Walden II—the narrator at-
tends a performance of Bach's B Minor Mass and remarks on its excellence. Now, this particular work of Bach can be listened to as a
formal pattern of sounds up to a point, but sooner or later the
hearer is bound to ask, of the vocal parts, what all those words are
about. The Mass is a celebration of sacrifice, suffering, and death as
the means of human redemption. What possible meaning could such
ideas have for a community that has been raised to understand life
only as a process of tension-free adaptation through successful conditioning?

Literature would become an even more questionable art to keep
going here, for what could you write about in a community where
no one ever suffers? If you take literature in a broad sense—and as a
part of human culture you can take it in no lesser sense—then you
cannot exclude from it the great monuments of historical writing
that have come down to us from the past; and literature too, since it
incorporates the critical function, has to bring out its relation to the
past more explicitly and consciously than do the other arts. But it is
not clear what awareness of history, if any, this commune will have.
At one point Frazier, its leader, makes a slighting remark about history, not quite so blunt or candid as Henry Ford's obiter "History
is the bunk," though it comes to the same effect. The Waldenites,
however, are not to be barbarians, and we are constantly being
reminded of their considerable degree of cultivation. But how can
they maintain this cultivation without some lively sense of the past
and their own human tie with it? Presumably, as cultivated beings,
they will have read the great literary works of the tradition. But
what possible sense could a person raised from childhood in this
utopia make of these books? What could he possibly think of
Oedipus or Hamlet? Two cases of very badly bungled conditioning.

Nevertheless, the guide does not falter as he reassures the visitors
that *naturally* there is art in this utopia since there is leisure—as if
leisure by itself were a sufficient condition for the production of
any kind of culture worth taking seriously. Yet we may seriously
doubt whether there would in fact be so much leisure available in a
community like this. Anyone who has worked on a farm for even a
short spell will be dubious that a self-subsisting commune can survive on four hours of labor a day from its members. One would like

a cost-accounting sheet for a community like this. The whole thing, as one reads, sounds very much like a project sponsored by some foundation or endowment that is never mentioned but is there in the background ready to pick up the bill. This particular commune is in fact parasitic upon the larger industrial community, from which it derives its materials and implements. Eventually, so the plan goes, communes like this will multiply, people will drop out of the larger society, and Walden II, as a network of communities, will have come to power without ever exerting power. But this eventuality would make the economics of the whole project altogether more fragile and destroy any prospect of leisure at all: With each community required to be self-sufficient in the way of producing its own energy, materials, and implements, anything like economic solvency—or, more bluntly, bare subsistence—would demand far more than four hours of labor a day from its inmates.

These economic considerations are very directly relevant to our central theme, which is freedom, because they bring up the question of whether a community that is so completely controlled will not require the expensive overhead of numerous managers. Since this particular community intends to shape human personalities, the managers take over the very extensive functions of psychologists. And just on this point occurs the great deception in Professor Skinner's fairy tale, for though we are made aware of psychologists constantly at work in the background, we do not meet them and find out what concretely they do. There is a passing mention that "our psychologists keep in close touch with all personal problems"; and when a member is functioning poorly, we are further told, he "would be sent to one of our psychologists." Now, what kinds of "malfunctioning" warrant being sent to the psychologist? When a member is unhappy or depressed? To "keep in close touch with all personal problems" takes a lot of time, even for a relatively small community. Do these psychologists put in the time at community chores required of every other member? If not, they are already a class set apart from the rest, and that could be politically troublesome. And if the psychologists do share the communal labors, you are going to need quite a few of them to "keep in close touch with all personal problems." Remember the behaviorist's own laws of conditioning: If a member goes to the psychologist, and the consultation makes the member feel better, he is likely to return to the psychologist and pretty soon build up a habit. I have just put pencil

to paper—I will spare the reader the figures, he can try out his own
calculations—and computed that, allowing our own usual workload,
there would be required a minimum—and it would be a bare
minimum—of ten doctors for a community of one hundred
members. In any case, you come up with a relatively large bureaucracy of psychologists, who in actual fact would have dictatorial
powers.

III.

Still, one feels a certain pang at puncturing any utopian dream,
however simpleminded, since it represents, after all, one more dream
of mankind for a better world. Younger readers—students, particularly—are sometimes attracted to Skinner out of this sheer desperate longing for a future better than the present. They are not
gullible enough to accept Skinner *in toto,* but they are almost
willing to try any method that might better the wretched state of
things as they are. One has to tell these students that one shares their
longings, but that the quickest way to move backward may be to
hurl oneself blindly at the future. The notion of progress itself has
become a tricky and uncertain one by this time. And if one reaches
agreement on the areas where progress is definitely ascertainable—as
in science, or the improvement of the material conditions of life for
a greater number of people than in the past—one has to raise an
equally important question: How was this advance made? And the
answer to this latter question, if we look at history, is not so difficult
as it might seem, though it flies in the face of Skinner and the
behavioral scientists.

Any ascertainable advance in the human condition that we can
observe has been the product of individual invention and creation—
the labor of free individuals working on their own or freely together in groups. The method—which is no method, really—may
seem hit-and-miss, but there does not seem to be any other way for
the human species in its struggle for survival. Nature has the inex-
pugnable tendency to produce individuals who are not all cut from
the same die like the objects turned out by a mechanical assembly
line. This profligate disregard of uniformity sometimes has its social
embarrassments, and is always annoying to the behavioral scientist.
But it has the overwhelming value to the rest of mankind that
among the unusual and different individuals born some have inven-

tive and creative gifts that work for the benefit of the race. We can establish conditions that may assist such gifts when they appear, but we cannot program them into being. The creativity of freedom is precisely what cannot be programmed beforehand. It may seem an irregular, uncertain, and circuitous path toward the improvement of the human lot, but there is no other that we can trust.

While we are on the subject of personal idiosyncrasy, it may be interesting and enlightening to recall how Professor Skinner himself came into psychology. As a student he had taken a course in creative writing, and was told by his instructor that he did have a definite talent for writing but that his stories showed little understanding of people. This is the kind of disheartening comment that aspiring writers have often to meet; and the immediate impulse in response varies with the individual—rush into an affair, go off to sea, take a motorcycle trip across country, or some other gesture equally childish and unreflective. But Professor Skinner did nothing so foolish, or else it was altogether more foolish—depending on what one considers a writer's understanding of people ought to be. He immediately decided to take a course in psychology, enrolled, and has been there ever since. The response was altogether in character, typical of the resolutely simplistic way of going at things from which Skinner has never swerved. The irony, however, is that he should have directed himself to that part of psychology where the understanding of people plays no part and where a researcher may spend all his time dealing with animals, and animals not in their natural habitat but in specially contrived laboratory conditions. One wonders whether the instructor who unwittingly launched him on his career, were he to cast an eye on all Professor Skinner's writings since, might not have to repeat his original comment.

Since we have already cited liberally from William James for prophetic comment upon the utopia of Walden II, we may round off our conclusion by drawing once again from James a passage that could hardly be improved upon as a general admonition not only to Skinner but also to all behavioral scientists:

> Man's chief difference from the brutes lies in the exuberant excess of his subjective propensities—his pre-eminence over them simply and solely in the number and in the fantastic and unnecessary character of his wants, physical, moral, aesthetic, and intellectual. Had his whole life not been a quest for the superfluous, he would

never have established himself as inexpugnably as he has done in
the necessary . . . Prune down his extravagance, sober him, and
you undo him.

There is a deeper and more symbolic reason, besides the extraordinary appositeness of his comments, in pitting James against
Skinner. James was a professor of psychology at Harvard a little
less than a century before Skinner occupied the same post. Now,
the world has changed a good deal in the meantime, and Harvard
with it; but in one respect Harvard has not changed at all—and that
is in the position of a certain pre-eminence we still accord it in the
intellectual life of the nation. In this symbolic role Harvard is taken
to represent what is most valid and significant in the whole intellectual part of our culture; and it is fair thus to consider this institution, at different stages, as a measuring stick of the change in that
culture itself. The comparison of two individuals like James and
Skinner, it might be said, is a violent one: The two men are so
different in their gifts, sensitivity, imagination, and general flexibility of mind. But if we consider them in their institutional role,
then the violence of the comparison is not ours but Harvard's; and
beyond that, taking Harvard itself in its representative role, we
should have to say that the violence of the comparison is one forced
upon us by our culture itself—and perhaps only by holding these
two individuals concretely before our imagination, at the same time
mindful that they are representative men in the full Emersonian
sense of this term, that our complacency may be shaken and we
begin to be aware of the thing that has overtaken us. James was in
his own way a kind of forerunner of behaviorism: He championed
the extension of the methods of the laboratory to psychology, and
he always insisted on the essentially behavioral nature of consciousness. But throughout his varied scientific interests, James
never—and this is the point to be stressed—never lost sight of the
fact of the human person, in all its complexity and concreteness, as
the ultimate subject and center of psychological research. The
difference between James and Skinner, then, seen in its proper context, is a sign how far our culture, or one very influential segment
of it, has moved toward the reduction of human personality.

I suggest that this is no trifling bit of *academica*, to be noted
curiously for a moment and then passed over. It is something to fill
us with apprehension and foreboding. Intellectually, we have

drifted much closer to the totalitarian attitude of mind than we are aware. And, accordingly, we turn now in the next chapter to the Marxist world, where that attitude has been more fully and frankly embodied.

Chapter 16

―――――◆▸―――――

The Shape of the Future:
Russian Version

"THE ESSENCE OF MARXISM LIES IN THE CLASS STRUGGLE!"

This was the axiom drilled into me during my years as a young Marxist. My mentors were warning me, against my own temptations of mind, not to get lost in the subtleties of theory to the point that I lose sight of the human center of the whole doctrine. And this center, plain enough for the downtrodden and uneducated to understand, was the war between the haves and the have-nots. To hold fast to this basic principle, to see all history at bottom as a struggle between economic classes, also provided one a much more militant stance at the time. In the 1930s, with the Depression hanging heavily over the nation, communism still had a considerable proselytizing force, and to insist on the priority of the class struggle provided a good buttress against criticisms of the Soviet Union; for in that climate, with its overwhelming sympathy for the have-nots, only a reactionary would harp on whatever imperfections still lingered in the first socialist society.

A decade later, the same axiom was drilled into me time and again by the late Philip Rahv. He was older and much more experienced in politics, and I therefore listened to him avidly. I was new on the staff of *Partisan Review;* the older editors were by this time altogether familiar with his harangues; and he needed no other invitation than a fresh and willing ear in order to launch himself into the full flood of his eloquence. He had at that time considerable reputation as a literary critic and editor, but in our private conversations he talked most frequently of politics. Rahv had a thoroughly concrete turn of mind, for which I also admired him, all the more since I was at the time struggling against my own abstractness. I was also beginning to have some theoretical doubts about Marxism as a whole. Rahv would break through these in his blunt way with the old insistence: "The essence of Marxism lies in the class struggle!" The word "existential" had entered his vocabulary at about that time, and he had become quite fond of it. Forget about the dialectic, he would tell me, the labor theory of value, and all those other abstractions; the "existential core" of Marxism was the class struggle, and I must hold fast to that. Since I had fallen into the role of pupil, in the end I was disposed to agree with my teacher. We could still cling to our Marxism because its ultimate meaning and justification was that it expressed the aspirations toward justice of the poor and oppressed against their oppressing classes.

What strikes me now is the peculiar historical irony of those conversations. We were operating on the political tags of our childhood and adolescence that had already become obsolete. For us as children of the thirties the existence of the Soviet Union as the first socialist state still seemed a fragile and unlikely miracle; and we tended to look on the problems of Marxist socialism as those of coming to power, of a movement on the make. The abominations of Stalinism had seemed to us an accidental excrescence on the true nature of socialism. Yet these conversations with Philip Rahv took place in the late 1940s; the Soviet Union had successfully survived the war, and there was now no question of the stability of the regime; it was not only secure within its own borders but also was now dominating the whole of Eastern Europe. In fact, Rahv's insistence that the essential part of Marxism lay in the class struggle would sometimes be sandwiched between outbursts in which he would become almost apoplectic in denouncing the way Stalin was being allowed by the Allied powers to push his influence into Europe. As a nation, the Soviet Union certainly looked more like a have than a have-not. Yet when our talk became general, Marxism was still to be sanctified by the slogans that had accompanied its aspirations to power. So we continued to think of ourselves as Marxists—though always with the careful qualification that we were liberal Marxists.

I introduce this bit of reminiscence not for any adventitious personal color it may add but because we were, on these matters at least, typical intellectuals of our generation with the misunderstandings that the period fostered. Subsequent developments permit us now, if we no longer choose to be blind, to detach the phenomenon of Marxism from those earlier illusions and see it in a larger and more significant perspective. I myself believe it can be understood only if placed within the very large perspective of the whole Era of Technique, as we have earlier described the last three centuries (Chapter 10). To develop this interpretation in detail would be a further and separate study; but a more compressed version of our view is pertinent here because Marxism, as perhaps nothing else in our century, sheds light on the key theme of the present work: freedom and the spiritual integrity of the individual.

To begin with, if we are to comprehend Marxism as a historical reality now at the end of the 1970s, we shall have to start from very different premises from those of an earlier generation. We can scarcely overlook the fact that this ideology has been in power now for more than half a century. If the class struggle is the core of Marxism, then presumably in the Marxist state, when classes are abolished, Marxism itself would have withered away and be without any political or social content whatsoever. "By their fruits ye shall know them." We have to apply the pragmatic principle that the meaning of an idea is to be judged by its consequences in action. It is idle to go on with hypothetical questions about what Marx may have intended by this or that statement independent of the history that has been made in the light of those statements. Indeed, the emphasis has to be put the other way around: We are much more likely to gauge the significance of his writings insofar as they have become ingredients in the actual society that cites them. It is one thing, for example, to entertain materialism as an abstract philosophical hypothesis; quite another thing to gauge its significance when it is translated into state power and deals with human individuals as objects.

Above all, we cannot start with any premise that the essence of Marxism lies in the abolition of classes when after half a century of the Marxist state we are able to see that it has its own very distinct processes of class formation.

I.

The class struggle was hardly a discovery by Marx. It was a fact of political life familiar for centuries to the Greeks, and Plato and Aristotle have left us some searching analyses of it. The Greeks were in a fortunate position to study political behavior. Within the smaller and more observable world of their city-states they could observe the class struggle in the clearest light—sometimes as a contest where the antagonists might all be personally known to each other. In the Fifth Book of his *Politics* Aristotle gives a masterly account of the causes and varieties of revolutions as they had appeared throughout the history of the Greek world. In all cases he indicates that these revolutions arise from or involve a fundamental conflict between social classes. Aristotle's account can hardly be improved upon for its dispassion. He is free from the sentimentality about the masses that drips from modern leftists; nor does he have any romantic adulation of the upper classes that crops up in the aristocratic nostalgia of some modern conservatives.

Why then should the class struggle be counted as such a distinctive and essential feature of Marxism? The answer is that the notion of revolution itself has become transformed in the modern era. Modern revolutions become more ambitious, total, utopian.

The revolutions among the Greek city-states were more candid and limited affairs. They were contests in which one group or class sought to take over the reins of power from another group. Some changes in the general social fabric might ensue; but none of these revolutions was ever so insane as to proclaim that a new era for mankind would begin with its success. The whole of mankind, indeed, was something quite foreign to the rooted and localized sense of their own being that the Greeks enjoyed. And as for transforming world history, they were blessedly exempt from that theatrical nightmare under which modern revolutionaries labor. No doubt, these revolutions among the Greeks were not pretty affairs. Deceit, treachery, personal violence, and sordid passions accompanied them. Still, even in its most discreditable moments, one cannot help admiring these people, who lived in the light and the clear sense of limits it defined. Their minds were not befogged with the clouds of ideological abstractions. A revolution was a revolution, not a debut on the stage of world history.

The French Revolution is the first full outbreak of the modern megalomania. Like all neurotics, it must insist on being absolutely different: It will not resemble those ancient revolts among the Greeks. Its goals will not be limited but total. Far from representing a circulation of ruling groups, it would seek, first, to transform the whole of human life from top to bottom, and, second, would thereby mark a decisive turning point in history and the beginning of an altogether new era for mankind.

The pattern is followed by subsequent revolutions. The Bolshevik Revolution of 1917, in fact, went farther because it felt that it had the real key to achieve the total aspirations of the earlier revolution. The French Revolution, product of the bourgeois epoch, still thought in terms of the abstractions of political and legal structures. Marxist materialism, however, would go to the root of the matter. To transform social life one had to transform the economic relations that held among men. Political and legal structures—the so-called superstructure—would be consequent upon these changes in basic economic structure. The revolutionary aspirations to transform human life totally had found at last their proper philosophy in Marxist materialism. Only under the guidance of that philosophy could a totally new chapter begin for mankind.

(In view of these total aspirations, some of our intellectuals may find it more difficult than they had thought to determine at what point the totalitarianism of a Stalin was an aberration from, or the necessarily harsh implementation of socialist goals.)

What we have said here has become commonplace among historians. The philosopher, however, has to push his questioning farther. He has to ask: What are the presuppositions that underlie these total claims of modern revolutionaries? What is their philosophical ground? What makes it possible for men rationally to aspire after this total transformation of their life when such aspirations are absent from the great classical civilizations? Or, since the dominant ideas of a period only express the way in which Being has emerged and taken hold of man's mind, we have to ask more fundamentally: What has happened in the being of man within the modern epoch that he should now feel himself in a position to dominate and transform his history totally?

It is one of the more remarkable symmetries of history that the French Revolution should have occurred in the country of Descartes and that the metric system, an indispensable tool for mathematical physics, should have been one of its principal legacies to the future. We use the name of Descartes here, as we have previously done, to characterize a whole epoch. Accordingly, the rest of this chapter will have to repeat some points in our description of the Cartesian Era, as we have given it in earlier chapters. But the repetition in this case will not be idle; it will at once add new items of

confirmation for that earlier scheme and at the same time impart to
the scheme itself a further depth and dimension of meaning, particularly in relation to the prospects of freedom for our world today.

It is method, and the dominance of method, that marks the chief
difference between modern science and that of the ancients. This
method is universal: Faithfully pursued, it will unlock the secrets in
all fields of research. It posits a framework—to recur to Heidegger's
term—within which all that is, nature as well as man, is to be placed
and understood. Greek science, even at its height and perhaps most
of all at its height, remained relatively pluralistic. It still harbored at
its core the notion of surrender to phenomena rather than their coercion. The various realms of all that is—stars and earthly objects,
plants and animals, man with his history and politics—present themselves to us as they are with their distinct and specific structures.
The universal of science is not imposed on but emerges from the
flow of becoming. The word for knowledge or science, *episteme*,
refers to what comes to take a stand, and in so doing stands out
from, as well as constant within, this disorderly rout of experience.
The Greek commentator on Aristotle's *Physics* explains the aim of
this science as *Sozein to phainomena* (to preserve the phenomena).
The phrase has an entirely different meaning from the positivistic
interpretation given it by the physicist-historian Duhem in his classic history of science, *Le Systeme du Monde*. "Phenomena" has
nothing to do here with the "phenomenal" in the subjectivistic sense
of modern philosophy. The *phainomena*, for the Greeks, are the
most "objective" things that there can be. They are the things that
become overwhelmingly present to us so that, in their presence,
they establish themselves as evident and true (unhidden). As such,
they are opposed to what merely seems to be, *ta dokounta*.[1]

By contrast, modern science is characterized by its pursuit and
resolute employment of method, as we explained in Chapter 10—a

---

[1] The passage from Thucydides I, 32, 13–16, seems to me decisive here. The
envoys of Corcyra are pleading for help from the Athenians. Corcyra had
hitherto followed a policy of isolation, which had seemed (*dokousa*) prudent;
but now in the course of events what has emerged into the open and shown
itself to be overwhelmingly evident (*phainomene*) is that this policy was folly
and weakness.

The two words—*dokousa* and *phenomene*—are opposed to each other as appearance (in our sense of "mere appearance") vs. reality.

The passage is all the more decisive in that Thucydides is not a philosopher
speaking with some special lingo. He is using "ordinary language," as it would
be understood by the intelligent and educated Greek of his time.

method that looks past the phenomena, in the Greek sense, so that it may attain mastery over nature by its own instruments.

Modern revolutions may be considered as translations from theory into practice of this concept of method at the heart of modern science. In fact, however, theory and practice already converge within the new science. The knower no longer is the pure beholder of what is; he sets the conditions under which he asks his questions and elicits his answers. The meanings of question and answer themselves become less and less separable from the experimental conditions that the scientist has fabricated. We are mistaken if we think of technology merely as an extraneous and incidental application of science, for technology abides at the very heart of the new science.

Let us consider now this scientific-technical version of human reason extended into the social sphere. Marx spoke of the conquest of nature as the essential humanistic goal. Conquest implies war, and this particular war has to be total in order to satisfy human needs. All citizens must be organized effectively within the ranks of this struggle. Everything that exists—man as well as natural resources— is to be placed within the framework of technical-scientific planning. Human beings, as they fall within this framework, become calculable objects for management. Economics does indeed emerge here, as Marxists had wanted it, as basic to every social reality. And what is economics but efficient technical management? Here we have entered the era of technology—and at full blast.

What happens to the class struggle in all this? It belongs to the prehistory of Marxism, to the rhetoric of the passions that Marxism could use so effectively while it was a movement on the make. It is fuel to the flame that will destroy the old order. But when the new order has settled down to some kind of stability, what we observe instead is a new class stratification arising among technicians on the basis of technical skill and expertise.

Even among the victims of the society, technicians are given a preferred status. The monolithic state is nothing if not thoroughgoing in the application of basic principle. When Solzhenitsyn out of some quirk of curiosity listed himself as an atomic physicist on one of the prison rosters, he was promptly transferred to a much less uncomfortable penal camp. As in the older theology, even in Hell there are very strict gradations of rank.

Marxist theorists not only acknowledge but also justify this newer class structure. Jurgen Habermas, leader of the Frankfurt school, argues that science and technology have become the decisive productive forces in society and accordingly must command a central social role. One's rank in the technical-scientific hierarchy establishes one's place in society. Czech philosopher Radovan Richta agrees that this is the basis of a new class structure. Even Soviet sociologists now proclaim "the scientific-technical revolution" as the major feature of modern society. What has happened to the toiling masses of the old Marxist songs and slogans?

However these neo-Marxists may differ in their language, they sound a virtual chorus of agreement on the new society coming into being. Elsewhere on the Continent, Marxists call "the rational society" of the near present and future "the programmed society." The word suggests inevitably the programming of a computer. Notice that the word "rational" in "the rational society" is understood in a thoroughgoing technical and technological sense that has long since become the fundamental drive of the modern age. Indeed, the language of these sociologists begins to converge with Heidegger's: Their program is his framework, within which all entities are to be effectively calculated and managed. What happens to the individual's existence in the programmed society? To be is to be an item within the program of management.

II.

Earlier Marxists did not think in these terms. Without knowing it, they had absolutized their ideology, placed it beyond time and becoming. What has happened in recent history is merely that tragicomic reversal that, according to Hegel, must happen to every idea when it enters the world. Marx is supposed to have stood Hegel on his head, and in the minds of Marxists completely superseded the master. The Idea, for the Marxist, is nothing but the expression of the material conditions of human society. But what we have just noted in the foregoing is the gradual submission of Marxism to the sovereign Idea that made its original appearance possible. It could conceive of a revolution different from those of antiquity because it arose in a climate of ideas, the age of the new science, that permitted the dream of a technological transformation of the planet.

In the long history of the human mind—the only really interesting history of this perverse animal—Marxism is only one more episode. To be sure, it happens to be the most powerful ideology of the modern age. But in being so, it is also stamped, shaped, and limited by the deepest impulses of that age. If we turn the Hegelian vision back upon Marxism, we see now the latter for the finite and one-sided expression of a particular *Zeitgeist* that it is. Hegel, were he to come back to life now, would have the last laugh on his deviating disciple.

Indeed, the Marxist state produces in itself its own antithesis. In its actual working it itself is the refutation of its own metaphysics. The history of Western metaphysics since the seventeenth century can be summed up as a continuing struggle between the rival claims of mind and matter. Marxism, as a materialism, begins as the rejection of all idealisms. The idea is nothing but the expression of matter and material circumstances; mind is a subordinate and derivative reality from matter. Yet the irony of Marxism to date, both in its triumphs and still continuing burdens, is that its history is a continuous affirmation of the priority of mind to matter, of the power of the idea over empirical fact.

In its triumphs first: Its victories over its adversaries so far have been through individual leaders in the fanatical grip of an idea. Nothing is more compelling, and more dangerous, than the idea that is all-embracing, unqualified, and so simple that it appears to settle all doubts. Our century has already seen the collapse of such ideas in physics, in logic and in mathematics, in psychology. In every case reality has proved more recalcitrant and complex than our initial suppositions. With regard to nature, we are ready at long last to accept the verdict of British scientist J. B. S. Haldane after a lifetime of research: "Nature is not only stranger than we imagine; it is stranger than we can possibly imagine." But with regard to politics, no. There the simple idea lays hold upon our primal will to power and releases the passions of anger and resentment against centuries of misery. No religious zealot was ever more a fanatic than Lenin. A recent debunking biography raises the question whether Lenin was not a more sinister and evil figure than Hitler. The judgment on individual morality is here beside the point. Hitler's ideology was an antiquated cry to a tribal past, an invocation of the ancient Teutonic gods, and therefore of necessity circumscribed and ethnic in its appeal. Lenin's invokes all humanity and the pseudogods of the Enlightenment. It is more dangerous because it speaks with the power of the abstractions that prevail in the modern age.

The United States, despite the tremendous advantages in its material conditions, has been steadily losing ground in its struggle with world communism. This country, which has a tradition of anti-intellectualism, finds itself ill at ease in a contest of ideas. In its innocence it cannot grasp that an ideology is taken so seriously and practiced with such duplicity by the adversary. America cannot grasp the passion of an idea . . . or its malignancy. Belatedly it begins to acknowledge the role of ideas in this struggle, and would try to enter into dialogue with the so-called Third World. What would America have to offer in such a dialogue? Facts, cautiously qualified arguments, the balancing of good and bad, tentative conclusions. The semiliterate demagogues of the Third World have already embraced an ideology that spares them the tedious business of cautious thinking.

Yet despite such advantages in the struggle for ideas, the Communist countries still carry the heavy burden of subduing the human mind. This is the supreme irony of the Marxist state. Materialism can pay no greater tribute to mind than in the extraordinary lengths to which it goes in curbing the mind.

And these extraordinary lengths are pursued even when they take a drastic toll of material resources. Stalin's purges disrupted the productive forces of the Soviet Union for years. We have grown so inured to the gigantic scope of these oppressions that we are still surprised by the petty and almost comic steps that censorship must take. A short while back the New York *Times* reported about a small group of Muscovites who had attempted to exhibit their paintings one Sunday on a vacant lot in the outskirts of Moscow. Bulldozers promptly appeared, and these aspiring artists were hustled off the scene. This episode would be amusing if it were not also so gruesome. Did a regime controlling so many troops and guns feel itself threatened by this little handful of Sunday painters? Was the Kremlin about to totter because of these few pathetic efforts at self-expression? Freedom must indeed be indivisible if the merest little groping toward it, and even in a sphere where politics is not an issue, must be stamped out like a germ that might start a raging epidemic.

One is prepared by this time for a certain amount of suppression in a dictatorship. But why this inordinate need, and these impractical lengths to which a state apparatus feels it must go in order to shape and control the minds of its subjects? The answer falls into two parts—empirical and metaphysical; and in the course of things, as usually happens, the two mingle and the latter becomes dominant.

Empirically, first, the socialist states cannot produce the utopias they inevitably lead their subjects to expect. Attack utopian socialism as he did, Marx's own brand is nevertheless colored everywhere by utopian elements. An ideology that makes total claims cannot but awaken total aspirations. Socialist rhetoric had battened upon the image of the evil capitalist. The more you inflate this evil, the more you siphon off all other human evils into this one monstrous figure, the more your hearers become convinced that its mere disappearance must lead to some paradisiacal state. The emotion takes on the form of economic fantasy: You have but to abolish the parasitic capitalists, marshal all the energies of the entire population in a "rational" program of production, and surely milk and honey will flow. Alas, milk and honey do not flow that easily. The ruling class of bureaucrats, planners, and policemen consume far more surplus value than the greedy capitalist ever could appropriate for himself. "In the sweat of your brow you shall eat your bread," the Bible tells us. And if the Bible is not enough for you, there is Darwin. Nature never intended any of its species to be comfortably and indolently affluent—despite the pipe dreams of some of our own economists. The struggle for survival goes on implacably.

Alienation is the one reality where these empirical and metaphysical difficulties of Marxism converge. To deliver humankind from alienation was one of the great promises that Marxism had made. According to its doctrine, this alienation was the product of capitalist society, and therefore would disappear with it. Let the means of production belong to the worker, let him have his fair share of the products of his toil, and surely labor would become fulfilling and joyful. Alas, most labor is not so easily redeemed; for only a tiny fraction of humankind can one's labor be one's fulfillment, and then at the cost of personal agony of another kind. One has again to return to the Bible: "In the sweat of your brow you shall eat your bread." Modern instruments of production do not abolish this harsh truth, but only alter the conditions of its application. In the "programmed society," to use the phrase of recent Marxists (in the "framework of planning," in Heidegger's terms), the individual as one programmed item among others will feel his work dispiriting and empty however you attach the fiction of collective ownership to him and his fellows.

To overcome alienation and disaffection, the state finds itself now plunged in the business of producing happiness. It is not enough that the dictator has the antecedent right over our body; he must also pry open our jaws and pour the slop of his happiness down our gullets. The rapist is not satisfied unless he exacts a smile from his victim. We may content ourselves, however, with the thought that here Marxism has fallen into the most utopian of its illusions and has reached the point where it is at war with the human condition itself. Happiness is the bluebird that flies away. For a moment we are content, and then the crab of desire sticks its claws into our heart; the tentacles of the mind stir uneasily. Either stagnate or be restless—that is the curse of consciousness. Marxists would have done better to study Buddhism and Christianity simply for their factual descriptions of the misery of the human condition. A government attempts the impossible when it undertakes to guarantee the happiness of its citizens; at the most it can secure enough social tranquillity to leave us free to bear our own private crosses.

The state that makes total claims is forced to take upon itself total burdens—including those once assumed by religion. It must heal us of the trauma of having been born. It becomes engaged in the business of saving souls. Read Koestler's old novel *Darkness at Noon* in the light of *Gulag*. The interrogator is not satisfied to exact a confession; he has become a confessor of souls and must bring about contrition and a genuine change of heart, even when he already knows the victim will be shot. So Torquemada, even as he tortured his victim, would pray for the salvation of his soul. The Russians are cursed with a great literature that seems always to revolve about that point where the character awakens one day to ask himself: Why? Why live? What is the meaning of it all? The commissar, who does not believe in the soul, must nevertheless protect the soul against such questions. A new style of grand inquisitor is reborn on the soil of unholy Russia.

The Chinese are unhampered by the traditions of Christianity and Russian literature. They are more pliable and patient, and there are so many more of them for building the human anthill in which the individual will at last be totally absorbed into the group. Those Americans who have had one of those smiling guided tours through China should read the amazing document *Prisoner of Mao*, by the French Chinese Bao Ryo-wang, who lived through the Chinese labor camps. Here we get the staggering picture of an entire population zealously engaged in mutual surveillance, mutual denunciation, and endless self-correction sessions. From an economist's point of view that represents an awesome number of man-hours consumed. Well, China has enough people to spare. Bao worked out a seven hundred-page statement of his sins with his interrogator (confessor). Seven hundred pages! Long enough for a Victorian novel of sin and redemption. But only such prolixity could attest to its author's repentance and to his awakened ardor for the regime. The Communist state will not be satisfied to produce a society like Orwell's in *1984*, which holds captive its obedient but sullen population. The New Jerusalem will be made up only of true believers who compete with each other in the ardor of their faith. They will be minds so completely absorbed in their social reality that doubts of it can never arise. The idea of freedom, and the troubling questions it raises, will long since have disappeared. Nietzsche's tormented questions would have become as obsolete as the cross of Christ.

The materialist society must thus describe its ultimate victory in terms of a certain evolution of the human mind. Philosophically, that is a victory for the idealist. A Pyrrhic victory, alas; he will not be around to see it, for he will long since have become extinct.

William James held that freedom was the one fact in human life where belief in the thing and the reality of the thing coincided. If we believe ourselves to be free, this belief works in us, marshals our energies, and thus makes a demonstrable difference in our lives. It is sometimes thought that this view is unduly optimistic; it places freedom in our grasp for the asking; we have only to believe in it for it to become a reality. We have pointed out in an earlier section that the belief, to be effective, must be thoroughgoing and does not come that easily. In any case, the totalitarians have shown us another darker and more pessimistic side to James' view. If freedom follows from the belief in freedom, then we have only to make the belief disappear to produce unfreedom. James was speaking of metaphysical freedom, not political freedom. But the two converge at the point where we seek their destruction: A regime that would strive to extinguish political freedom completely is compelled to remove any vestige of the idea of metaphysical freedom. And in this the totalitarians have a shrewd instinct for the jugular. Load mankind as you will with chains, you have not completed your job until you have also changed their minds. Humankind will cease finally to be free only when it has lost the idea itself of freedom.

Epilogue

Nihilism, Faith, Freedom

Everything that exists participates in a religious essence.

—E. M. Cioran

WHAT DO I BELIEVE? AS A PHILOSOPHER, I WOULD SEEM ESPECIALLY equipped to give an answer here, and yet my profession may be just the thing that screens me off from the human intent that lies behind the question. A philosopher may be able to reel off his ideas by the yard and yet remain blind to the things that really keep him going in life. What, then, do I live by?—that is the question, and in its grip every one of us stands on the same ground, forced to be truthful about himself and face the day that opens before him. Looking back, what fragments have I saved out of my life to shore up its meaning? What rituals, charms, incantations, or loves help me forward? In the end these may be more real to us than any of our imposing and grandiose ideas.

Time itself forces the question upon you. Whatever your temperament, you reach that stage of life where you are compelled to think of death more insistently. In his novel *A Passage to India*, E. M. Forster tells us of an old lady, Mrs. Moore, who has suddenly fallen into the abyss of nihilism:

> She had come to that state where the horror of the universe and its smallness are both visible at the same time—the twilight of the double vision in which so many elderly people are involved.

I am yet far from being there; the lusts and rages of the living still dance their attendance upon me. I tell myself I shall never be there, that I shall see more in the universe than smallness and horror, whatever the failure of my body. But this confidence too may be but another illusion that time will strip away like so many others. Meanwhile I note that a few older friends have unexpectedly died, and I begin to be aware of death stalking all of us, to gather us together into *our* generation. The future that opens before me no longer seems boundless, and the horizons within which I move seem more closed than they were.

Freedom no longer spreads its gorgeous array of alternatives before me. If I assert that freedom now, it is but to affirm the narrow corridors within which my life will henceforth run. The rails have been laid down, the train will move in its appointed direction—more or less. At any rate, the rails cannot be ripped up at this late date, and a new line laid out, for me to strike out toward another quarter of the compass. Yet the idea of freedom becomes more central to me than ever. This freedom embraces the monotony of existence to which I henceforth condemn myself. "The galley slave sticks to his oars," says Samuel Beckett. It is precisely there where its conditions are minimal that the significance of freedom becomes maximal. Freedom emerges as the zest that transfigures what might look to the external glance like mere monotony. You rise each morning to the gift of life as if this day were a new beginning.

A far cry indeed from Forster's frightful words about his elderly character. Yet I am forced to keep Mrs. Moore and her condition in mind. What happens to her is something very dreadful, for which as readers we are not quite prepared. She comes upon us as an entirely sympathetic person, enlightened and wise, with a religious sensitivity left as the residue of Christian faith. Yet it is not strong enough to withstand the shock of India, the heat, the weariness of old age, and the tedious troubles of the young over which she is supposed to preside. In his discreet and quiet way Forster is nevertheless a "modern"—he sounds the typically modern note of desperation. Two centuries ago, a century ago, men thought of themselves as the masters of history; today we are more likely to think of ourselves as its victims. The literature of the twentieth century is largely a lamentation for ourselves as victims. And in nothing are we more victims than in this: that we have to cope with the same life as humankind in the past but without its most potent means of doing so. We cannot will back a faith that has been lost. We shall have to live back into that way of being in whose ambience the religious once drew breath. We shall have to find ourselves within nature before God is able to find us.

There, in any case, my own *Itinerarium mentis in Deum*, the journey toward God, has already begun.

I.

"Nature is in tatters," Merleau-Ponty once remarked to Sartre. The remark occurred during a conversation in the days before their friendship was broken, as happened so often between Sartre and his peers. Sartre himself reports the incident, and he tells us that Merleau-Ponty was quoting Whitehead. The remark sticks in one's mind, particularly as coming from Sartre. It is strange to hear him mention the name of Whitehead, whose thinking belongs to another region of discourse from his own; strange even to hear him mention nature at all since it plays so little part in his thought. Merleau-Ponty, however, was traveling a different road. He had discovered in the painting of Cézanne the stubborn struggle to stand within the presence of the earth. Seeking his own philosophic footing there, he was curious enough to explore Whitehead and be caught by the latter's observation of the "tatters"—the fragmentation—to which the philosophy of the last three centuries had reduced nature. Quite characteristically, Sartre merely notes his former friend's remark in passing, but does not pause to comment or reflect on it. It does not seem to trouble his thinking at all.

To be fair to him, he is not untypical here. The idea of nature has played a small part in contemporary philosophy. Bergson once remarked that most philosophers seem to philosophize as if they were sealed in the privacy of their study and did not live on a planet surrounded by the vast organic world of animals, plants, insects, and protozoa, with whom their own life is linked in a single history. Indeed, only two major philosophers of the century, Bergson and Whitehead, have taken the idea of nature as their central theme; and both are largely unappreciated today. Bergson is almost a forgotten name; Whitehead was never taken up by the English after he had left them to settle in America; and among the younger generation of American philosophers, he remains almost unread.

Bergson and Whitehead provide certain nuclear images of nature against which one's thinking about freedom must proceed. It is a great mistake to forget the role of imagination in supplying the background against which all thinking, however abstract, must find its place and meaning. Human freedom may be unique in the ways in which it becomes manifest, but it does have its roots in nature, and we have to be able to imagine the cosmos in a fashion that is congruent with that freedom.

Bergson, for example, invites us to see ourselves and our human questions against the background of the evolution of life on this planet. The earth, according to some recent estimates, is five billion years old. Its history, however, is a chapter in the life of our sun, a small star, paying out its energy into space during all that time. According to the law of thermodynamics, as energy is radiated out into space it spreads itself out more thinly until finally the whole universe reaches the same dead level. This is the famous heat death of the universe that stood like a solemn *memento mori* inscribed over the intellectual portals of the end of the nineteenth century. It was a somber perspective to fit the mechanistic and pessimistic mood of the time, and not a few literary imaginations were shaken by it.

Against this picture of cosmic death Bergson raises the complementary image of life. During the five billion years our sun has been dissipating its energy in space, slowly burning itself out, life has appeared and managed to survive on this earth. And not merely survived at some marginal and inertial level, but also rushed onward into ever higher and more varied forms. One estimate by biologists that I have seen numbers five billion organic species on this earth. Allowing for those forms of life that may have appeared or vanished, we might have to set the number much higher. No matter. For convenience and symmetry, let us say five billion species in five billion years. A species a year. A stupendous effort of creation, in which we are a part. If the universe exhibits processes of running down, it also contains those of building up. While our sun has been dissipating itself into space, in a contrary process this energy has been collected, stored, and gathered into higher and more complex levels of life, until, with the advent of man, life gives energy back to nature in the manner of its own source. Our nuclear devices create energy out of matter in imitation of the sun itself.

Is this merely an optimistic picture to be set against the nineteenth century's prospect of the universal heat death? The obsession with optimism and pessimism is like the bad habit of a reader who skims the book to find out how it comes out in the end. It is the drama from page to page that we have to live. Whether, untold millennia hence, the outcome will be dismal or happy will not get you through your day any better. But the image of life building itself up, stubbornly, lavishly, and recklessly, out of fragments of dissipated energy from the sun can make a difference to us here and now because it conveys the spectacular process of which we are a part and whose dynamism we share. In the light of this image we cease to think of our own life as a mechanical iteration of what has been. Life, any life, no matter how tiny, appears then as a more miraculous event than any mechanism can imagine.

Whitehead does not dwell on the sheer fact of life's evolution on this planet. Yet his single notion of "organism" is more radical and sweeping in restoring to us a live rather than a dead universe. For the past three centuries, since Descartes, we have been in the grip of a metaphysics of death that Whitehead calls "scientific materialism." We understand the phenomena of life only as an assemblage of the lifeless. The mechanical and routine are taken as the underlying reality of nature. We take the abstractions of our technical calculation to be ultimately concrete. Beneath our preoccupation with technique and apparatus there is the prevalent metaphysical disposition to see things ultimately resolved into bits of brute matter pervading space, "in a flux of configurations, senseless, valueless, purposeless."

Suppose, however, we were to invert this whole scheme; reverse the order in which it assigns abstract and concrete. What is central to our experience, then, need not be peripheral to nature. This sunset now, for example, caught within the network of bare winter branches, seems like a moment of benediction in which the whole of nature collaborates. Why should not these colors and these charging banners of light be as much a part of the universe as the atoms and molecules that make them up? If they were only "in my mind," then I and my mind would no longer be a part of nature. Why should the pulse of life toward beauty and value not be a part of things? Following this path, we do not vainly seek to assemble the living out of configurations of dead stuff, but we descend downward from more complex to simpler grades of the organic. From humans to trees to rocks; from "higher grade" to "lower grade" organisms. In the universe of energy, any individual thing is a pattern of activity within the flux, and thereby an organism at some level.

II.

Rocks and trees. I have grown to know them particularly this winter; they have accompanied me on my walks, or rather I have learned to enter into their company. Winter trees are more beautiful than under the fat and heavy foliage of summer. Now they lay bare their secret structure, the naked and living line of branch and bough, the supple harshness of their enduring struggle with the elements. Oak, maple, ash, chestnut, beech—these are now without their telltale leaves, and I have had to learn to read them by their barks, each as individual as fingerprints. With some I have come to know the particular curves and twists of their branches like the individual features of friends.

The rocks are no less individuals. Whoever thinks matter is mere inert stuff has not looked long at rocks. They do not lie inert; they thrust forward, or crouch back in quiet, self-gathered power. Like a cat sitting so still that his tail has ceased twitching. Only Cézanne, among artists, did rocks properly, painting them into the canvas as alive as the trees against which he sets them. In the gray light of winter they come alive in their color too—smoke-gray or blue-gray, molded and subtle in their shading that shifts as the gray light shifts. The living rock! More than an idle phrase. Out of the living rock the waters of spirit.

For the moment I have passed outside the world of man. Yet I am in no remote wilderness. This is only a strip of woods stretching for several miles along the Hudson; yet at the times I walk there I am able to be alone—at least from other humans. The broad river, glimpsed now and then through the lattice of boughs, and an occasional gull riding high and motionless on the furrows of the air—these are enough for background. For the rest, I am content to be in the company of trees and stones. Usually it takes a mile to begin to be free. The important thing is to find freedom in the movement of your body first, let the mind be what it will. By the second mile I am set free in the body, the havoc of the mind and the idiocy of its ideas recede. I am no longer homeless. I am there. The trees are there too, and the rocks; I have come into this stringent but secretly lavish life of winter.

Even about a fallen and dead tree there is something noble. That great oak over there, which was rooted in too shallow a lip of soil, was blown down last fall, and its dirt-browned roots gouged out a great hole in the earth. It lies now with the nobility of some dead king in the dignity of its death. I touch one of the roots as reverently as if it were a bier. Animal life, by superficial contrast so much more vivid, is more degraded and ignoble in death. Not long ago I stumbled on a dead raccoon in the bushes: This little animal, so pretty and captivating in life, had turned into an ugly carcass that stank disgustingly. Nature's law of opposites is at work here too: The more nervous and mobile in life, the more squalid and abject in death. A rotting tree re-enters the scheme of things more unobtrusively and with greater dignity.

I can understand why earlier mankind could worship trees. Perhaps I already do so myself. My ancestors were Druids, after all, and perhaps I am only rounding out the cycle by returning to their fold. Certainly, the more I learn of the biology of trees the more I am moved to awe and wonder. I am delighted to think of the intricate means by which that tall ash there draws water from the soil and lifts it to its topmost branches more than seventy feet in the air. The tiny cells of the xylem live only a few seconds because they are of no use while alive, but dead they form little hollow tubes to suck the water up by capillary action. They live only to die, and they die for the greater life. Steadfast striving, effortless effort.

Nature worship! Mysticism! The tags are ready that would consign one's experience to an old banality. We are a culture consumed by verbalism, and the effect of our words is to place a screen between us and things. Nothing exists until we have assigned it its name; and then, once named, its life becomes that of a word that begets more words in endless argument, debate, sophistry. Here among my rocks and trees I have passed beyond the needs of such labels. That does not mean that my mind has become some kind of nameless and inchoate blur. On the contrary, mind and eye are alert to read the texture of bark or the shape of a stone. I told a friend, who wondered why I spent so much time in these woods, that I was no different from a boy scout brushing up on his woodlore. My friend demurred; he would have liked me to use the word "mysticism." We forget that what we call mysticism was once a natural condition of mankind, and could be again if we let ourselves enter it. The mysticism that matters is one that has no need of the word. The same with Being. Another word. We are most within Being when we do not use the word and have ceased to grapple with its idea. These words are notations at a distance for something that up close does not require them.

What I have just written may be only one more expression of the classic doctrine of "No Mind" in Zen Buddhism. One has to pass beyond the prison of concepts to be directly and fully there, wherever one is. Twenty years ago, in a book in collaboration with the late D. T. Suzuki, I played a small part in introducing Zen to this country, and I have not always been happy with the results. American youth acquired another vocabulary to throw around. The "mindlessness" that Zen recommended was pursued by the young in the haze of marijuana and drugs. They forgot, if they had ever learned, the prosaic and magnificent saying of the sage Hui-Neng: "The Tao [the truth] is your ordinary mind." In recent years I have let myself forget all about Zen, and probably have been nearer to its spirit. Stick to your ordinary mind, reader, and forget the tabs. Find your own rocks and trees.

III.

But is it not mere self-indulgence to prattle on thus about a walk in the woods? How can I draw any philosophical lessons from what, as I myself insist, cannot be put into words?

Still, the question of the will, of avoiding the dreaded collapse into nihilism, involves every resource of the spirit that may help us. If I could not draw my breath in this stretch of woods, could not stand in this open clearing, I feel the balance of my sanity would be less steady for the tasks life imposes. In the end, the question of motivation is the crucial one. If I could not draw sustenance here, the strength of my motives for other things would certainly wither.

For philosophic sanction, though it is not needed, we might turn to Kant. In his old age, in the last of his three great works, *The Critique of Judgment*, Kant proceeded to develop a view of man in his concrete and sensuous relation to nature. Hegel and Schelling, otherwise sharp critics, hailed this as the greatest of the three great critiques. Their judgment is not to be taken lightly; they were the next generation, and closer to Kant's questions than the later tight-lipped Neo-Kantians who sought to force him into the straitjacket of epistemology. In this last work, in fact, Kant advances to meet the problem that had been waiting in the wings for him. He had dealt with man as a skeleton—an abstract knower, and an abstract moral agent—but now he must deal with him as a creature of the senses in his immediate perceptions of nature. Here the freedom of man must be encountered, not as an abstract moral postulate, but in his concrete being within nature. In the experience of the Sublime and the Beautiful, Kant tells us, we experience an unknown and unknowable harmony between ourselves and the nature we behold. No particular item within our perception can account for the depth surrounding that perception. What vibrates through it points to something beyond it that we can never grasp as a particular item of fact within it. There is a resonance that is sounded between the unknown depth in the self and the unknowable depth in the nature of things. Deep calls to deep. Here the distress of alienation ends. We are at home in a mystery that suggests some meaning of which we are a part, though we cannot know it in any precise conceptual way. And given any kind of meaning, we are thus given one more motive to sustain us in our solitary journey as mortal beings through this world. Thus in the end Kant comes back to himself as a moralist. The sublimity and beauty of nature are the sensory symbols of our high moral destiny.

It is as good a statement of the unstatable as any ever made. Yet no better than any of the others. We end, in any case, in the dumb and inarticulate presence from which Kant starts. That is the truth more important than any of the attempts to express it. We would be mistaken if we thought that Kant was merely developing some intellectual inference from the ideas of the sublime and the beautiful. He is merely fumbling, like any other mortal, though in the more elaborate and formal fashion of his philosophy, to give words to that wordless feeling that is ours in the presence of nature.

In fact, the ideas of the sublime and the beautiful are a makeshift that we learn to dispense with. They are our human perspectives; and if we stick too tightly within them, we are likely to stand in an "aesthetic" detachment from nature. That is why no photograph, however impressive, can have the power over us of our actual presence within a natural scene. The closer one comes to nature the less one seeks to dichotomize beauty and ugliness. That great ash over there, with its enormous bole more than fifteen feet around, seemed comely and beautiful under the drapery of summer. When it shed its leaves, I laughed to discover its upper boughs emerge as squat and homely. But if I stand now under it and look up, the great rippling torso soars over me with the muscular grace of a dancer; and I smile apologetically at having judged it ugly. As our perspectives change, beautiful and ugly shift with them. In time one learns not to pick apart beauty from the whole. Everywhere, in my wintry mood, I find beauty mingled with the harsh and painful. I remember the stabbing vision of a swan in the river at Zurich, at night under the cold and falling rain, asleep, rocked in the rippling water, its long neck folded back on its body. I cannot, even now, remember a more beautiful sight; yet it was also an image of anguish, cradled there on the cold swell. One cannot remain within the detachment of the aesthetic even here. These trees and rocks are companions with me in suffering.

Kant, trembling in the presence of the nature that enveloped him, was too quick to find in it the confirmation of his moral sensibilities. The romantics who followed him persisted in this humanistic framework. The landscape they loved gave them back their human image. So Wordsworth sings all too patly:

> One impulse from a vernal wood
> Can teach us more of moral evil and of good. . . .

Trees and rocks do not indulge in the impertinence of foisting lessons upon us. Their method of instruction is more circuitous and indirect, but perhaps all the more potent for that. Their first lesson is to draw us outside the narrow and presumptuous horizons of our humanism. They help restore the balance of our sanity without which we would be less free for the moral tasks required of us.

And then, suddenly, last week they had put up a fence that shuts off the far part of my walk! Today I've found a way to get around the fence, and so for the time being I am at peace again.

But not entirely. It is the next fence after this that I fear—and the fence after that. I dream of that last fence that humans will someday erect to seal themselves effectively from any world beyond man. The triumph of "humanism" at last! It is then that we may have most to fear about the human future. The species might go mad, or slide listlessly into the empty nihilism of science fiction.

IV.

One re-enters the human world nonetheless. There I have the usual quota of attachments, with its accompanying complement of loves, rages, and disillusions. I do not pursue detachment. Even if it were possible, it would be empty; and it is in fact impossible. The marvelous images from Taoism and Zen Buddhism, which seduce us into the quietude of Being, cannot be a permanent halting place for the Westerner. Between myself and them are interposed the Bible and the Russian novel, from whose grip I can never free myself.

As soon as we are born we are hurled into the question of first and last things. The secret of the Russian writers is that their characters are plunged irremediably into these questions, even in their most trifling actions. The shabby and frivolous characters of Gogol would not loom as monumental as Shakespeare's without that religious mania that eats away at their author. In the end, that religious obsession destroyed Gogol as an artist, but without it he could not have written as incomparably as he did. That is but another paradox of creation—and, we might add, of freedom.

As soon as we are born we breathe the air of a religion: We are alive, and so we must die. Amid all the definitions proposed for man the most truthful would in fact be that he is the religious animal. He created religions long before the Greeks created reason. And now that he lives at last in the world of science and the computer, new religions sprout all over the map. It would be folly to think that this religious part of him was an accidental excrescence terminated by the French Revolution. The fanaticism of subsequent history has shown that mankind simply displaced its religious passions into the world; and the results have been more terrifying than any religious inquisition.

A secular-minded psychoanalysis now encounters everywhere among its patients a sense of meaninglessness against which it is helpless. Religion may very well be an illusion, as Freud said, but then man himself is that illusion. It is the human animal, no one else, who is displayed in the history of his religions. Their evils and excesses are his, as much as whatever is poignant and sublime in that history. The frenzies of asceticism, which may seem mere aberration and abnormality to our secular minds, are in fact the inevitable means to which the human animal is driven to give meaning to his existence. Rather than be meaningless, we shall find ourselves seeking out devices of our own that are equally extreme. We create by denying ourselves. So long as we drive ourselves in the toils of some discipline, we cannot believe that our life is meaningless. In the tensions of the will—the simultaneous striving and surrender—the ghost of nihilism departs.

According to the old platitude, the most important thing a land-lady should know about a prospective tenant is his philosophy. The most important—perhaps as a matter of social utility; but hardly the deepest. A philosophy is only that part of ourselves that we can ar-ticulate before the public. The deepest part of any of us is our religion—that uncertain center of yearning, acceptance and rebel-lion, simultaneous despair and aspiration—out of which anything philosophically vital comes. When that center has not been touched, the philosophy rings hollow.

Each day when I enter my garret of a study I make the sign of the cross over myself as I pass the threshold. Do not ask me what it means. It is a gesture they taught me as a child, I had forgotten it, but it comes back to me now. It helps to keep me from thinking. In silence, performing it, I am not trapped in words and their cun-ning. Perhaps some other gesture might do, but it would come to the same thing. It would be the same gesture for me. I have become part of an invisible church of one. I am ready to accept whatever rituals or charms that can now sustain and quicken me within this mystery that is given me to live. "Stupefy yourself, take holy water," Pascal said. His injunction no longer seems outrageous to me. We will do the equivalent in any case so long as we continue to live. And some of our means may not be so harmless. Imagine a Communist—there must be one somewhere—who is afflicted with doubts. I see him at the moment when the thought crosses his mind that the whole idea that governs his life may be a ghastly mistake, that even in the mundane matter of economic efficiency the system shows itself to be bungling and inept. Yet for this single idea the whole of mankind and its future may have to be sacrificed. He sits dumfounded for a moment, then shakes himself as he rushes for his own stoup of holy water; and the doubts recede as he plunges into Party discipline and Party demonstrations.

We are all members of an invisible church of one—and everyone. On the stairway, in the half dark, I encounter the great yearning eyes of my dog. She looks at me as if aggrieved that I no longer take her on my walks. She is too old, and the distance tires her too much. She is aging rapidly and will soon be dead, and I shall lose the companionship of those eyes. I should like to tell her that I shall not forget her. We share the fact of mortality—it looks at me now out of her eyes—but we cannot share it in speech. That is the unique gift that humans have above all the other animals: They can share their death with each other. The fundamental cult in all religions is the funeral rite. Gathered together in its observance, we can make the sign of the cross—or whatever other ritual gesture you wish—not so much over the dead as over ourselves, the living, in compassion for one another. And thereby begin to live.

The psychiatrist Harry Stack Sullivan once had a patient who constantly threatened to commit suicide. One day, after one of these tirades, the analyst asked very softly, "Why don't you?" The patient, caught short, was suddenly speechless. Thereafter (so the anecdote goes) he ceased the threats against his own life. Once you have been put to the challenge and recoiled, you have made the great act of faith. You have made the primary affirmation beyond which any verbal eulogy of life is pallid.

It would be a good spiritual exercise for each of us to enact this situation for ourselves. We are then both patient and analyst, and put Sullivan's question to ourself. (It is wiser to practice this exercise, though, when we are calm of mind; it will build our strength against the moments of panic that come our way.) We let the mind have a free hand and range as it will. It will show me that my reasons for living are mere pretexts: that my pleasures are mediocre, my talents uncertain, and my virtues negligible. But even as I let the mind range and devour my substance, something stronger than reason takes over. If I project this paltry life of mine against the possibility of not being at all, then this gift of Being floods through me like a tide. To exist at all is to be happy. Dostoevski, in his startling and unpredictable way, chose to put his supreme truth in the mouth of the half-crazed Kirillov: "We are all happy if we but knew it." Against the void of nonexistence, any fragment of existence, however paltry, becomes a supreme miracle. My God, I am happy! This freedom as galley slave here in this garret is inexhaustible.

So each day I pass judgment and sentence myself to remain among the living. Condemned to live, I must then ceaselessly create reasons for living. The judgment is not so severe, nor the task so difficult, as we imagine. We have only to be open to the world and it will pour its riches at our feet. Before this winter I had not known that the bark of a tree, caught in yellow sunlight, could be enough to restore a life.

Index

Absolute, the, 196. *See also* God(s)
Abstract expressionism, 217
Adventure, sense of, 303–4
Aeschylus, 244, 245
Aesthetics, 240, 247–48, 251, 281. *See also* Heidegger, Martin
Agnosticism, 253, 273. *See also* specific thinkers
Airport (film), 133–34
Alcohol (and alcoholism, drinking), 262, 267, 302
  author gives up, 304–5
Aletheia (alethes), 144–45, 160, 169, 176, 187, 236, 243
Alienation, 133–56, 212ff., 327
Alienus, 133
Ambivalence, 97
Americans. *See* United States and Americans
Analysis of Mind, 10–11
Analytic philosophy, xvi, 59, 73, 160, 251. *See also* specific philosophers, theories
Angelus Silesius, 31
Animals, 154, 301
  author's dog, 129, 344–45
  and death, 339, 344
Anna Karenina, 209
Anselm, St., 247
Antinomies. *See* Paradoxes

Anxiety, 129, 139–40
Appearance, 124, 126. *See also* Bracketing; Phenomenology; Two Worlds
Archimedes, 180
Aristotle (Aristotelians), 37, 116, 128, 130, 156, 187–89, 203–4, 230, 231, 322
  and class struggle, 319, 320
  definition of truth, 140
  example of knife in metaphysics, 250
  statement on mind and consciousness, 305–6
Arithmetic, 12n, 19, 66. *See also* New Math
  with frills, 82–89
Art, 19, 64, 143, 178–79, 215–16, 230. *See also* specific artists, media
  in Soviet Union, 326
  and Walden II, 309–11
Art and Experience, 144n
Asceticism, 4, 304–5, 343
Ash Wednesday, 74
Astronauts, 213. *See also* Space: flight
Athens and Athenians, 135, 243–44, 322n
Athletes, 304
Atomic (nuclear) bombs, 185, 198. *See also* Thermonuclear war

Atomism, logical, 32–50
Atonal music, 29, 64, 194
Auden, W. H., 233
Auerbach, Erich, 148
Augustine, St., 74, 170–71, 231, 247
Austen, Jane, 70
Austria. *See also* Vienna
   Wittgenstein in, 27–32, 59–61
"Autonomous individual," 300–1ff.
Axiomatization, 82, 89–94ff.

Bach's B Minor Mass, 310
Bacon, Francis, 182, 237
Balzac, Honoré de, 216
Bao Ryo-wang, 328–29
Baseball, 65
Baudelaire, Charles, 214, 215
Beckett, Samuel, 268, 280, 334
Beethoven, Ludwig van, 194, 241
Behavioral scientists, behaviorism,
   xi–xiiiff., 69–70ff., 101, 103ff., 121,
   171, 188, 210–11. *See also*
   Determinism; Marxism; Skinner,
   B. F.
   in American future, 297–315
   and conversation, 165
Being, 12, 51, 107–225, 291, 293, 294,
   339–40, 343. *See also* Heidegger,
   Martin; Mysticism
   and alienation (homelessness),
   133–56
   cash value of, 157–76
   and technology as human destiny,
   177–201
   and Two Worlds, 109–31. *See also*
   Two Worlds
   and "utopia or oblivion," 203–19
Being and Time, 130, 136, 140, 207,
   229, 248, 249
   "Dasein" in, 233–35
Belief. *See also* Faith
   will to believe, 253–69
Bell Laboratories, 103
Berg, 207
Bergson, Henri, 335–36
Beyond Freedom and Dignity,
   xii–xiii, 300
Bible, 327, 343

New Testament (Gospels), 30, 31,
   278
Biology, 115, 188
Blake, William, xiv–xv
Blood, circulation of the, 111
Body, the, 68ff., 110, 112. *See also*
   Behavioral scientists, behaviorism;
   Two Worlds
   and freedom of movement, 338
Bolshevik Revolution, 321
Bombs, nuclear (atomic), 185, 198.
   See also Thermonuclear war
Boston, 254
Bostonians, The, 254
Boston Marathon, 279–80
Bourgeois Gentilhomme, Le
   (Molière), 160
Bourgeoisie, 215, 321
Bracketing, 116–17, 118, 126, 129. *See*
   also Phenomenology
Bradley, F. H., 214–15
Brains, 110
Brentano, Franz, 118
British, the (Anglo-Americans,
   England and the English), 2ff.,
   118, 160, 162–63, 192. *See also*
   Cambridge; specific writers
British Academy, 162–63
Broad, C. D., 258–59
Brook Farm, 298
Brothers Karamazov, The, 29
Brouwer, Wittgenstein and, 10n, 79ff.
Buddha, Buddhism, 99–100, 286, 328
   Zen Buddhism, 291, 340, 343
Buridan's ass, 261, 262

Calculus, 98. *See also* Mathematics
   and mathematical logic
   of classes. *See* Classes
   of Sentences, 48
Cambridge (England), 1–2ff., 31, 59,
   61, 79, 149, 162
   disdain of pragmatism, 158
Cambridge, Mass., 266
Camus, Albert, 236–37, 281
Candide, 23
Capitalism, 206, 327. *See also* United
   States and Americans

Caracteristica universalis, 5, 11
Carnap, and *The Logical Structure of the World*, 36
Cartesian Meditations (Husserl), 124
Cartesian philosophy. *See* Descartes, René, and Cartesian philosophy
Case law, 97
"Cash value" of being, 157–76
Catholicism. *See* Religion; specific writers
Cauchy, Augustin Louis, Baron, 66
Causation (causal relations), 36–37. *See also* specific philosophers, theories
Cézanne, Paul, 62, 64, 309, 335, 338
Chautauqua, N.Y., 307–8
Chemical fertilizers, 21
Chemistry, 185
Chess, 65, 167–68, 172–73, 309
Children, 59
  and New Math, 80–81, 95
China and the Chinese, 185–86, 297, 328–29
Choice. *See* Freedom
Christians and Christianity, 147, 178, 189, 193, 194, 196, 199, 204, 242, 244, 247, 274ff., 286, 328, 334. *See also* God(s); Religion; specific philosophers
  Wittgenstein's family background, 28
Church (logician), 91
Church, the. *See* Religion
Cigarettes
  as rewards to headhunters, 85
  smoking, 74–75
Cioran, E. M., 333
Circle, π and, 93–94
Circulation of the blood, 111
City (metropolis), 213–14, 218
Classes, 86, 87, 156. *See also* Class struggle
Class struggle, 317ff.
Clifford, W. K., 273
Closed/open systems, 48ff. *See also* Behavioral scientists, behaviorism; specific philosophers
Cogito, ergo sum, 113

Coleridge, Samuel, 218
Communes. *See* Walden II
Communication, 169–70. *See also* Language
Communists and communism, 105, 179, 298, 344. *See also* specific countries
  and shape of future, 317–29
Computers, 48, 49, 102–3, 104, 305, 324
Conditioning. *See* Behavioral scientists, behaviorism
Conscience, 196, 248–49
Consciousness (mind), 70ff., 189ff., 215, 232, 261–62, 303–5, 328. *See also* Self-consciousness; specific philosophers
  and mysticism. *See* Mysticism
  and Two Worlds, 110ff. *See also* Two Worlds
  and visions, 290–91
Consistency, 91
Contradiction, 97, 100
Conventionalism, 94–100
Conversation, 165–66
Copernicus, 180–81
Corcyra, 322n
Correspondence, 156
Creativity (creation), 19, 186, 221, 312–13. *See also* Art
  and Walden II, 309–11
Criminals, 76, 236–37, 302–3
Critics, 215
Critique of Judgment, 340–42
Critique of Pure Reason, 182, 251
Cross, sign of the. *See* Ritual, gesture
Curiosity, 303
Cushing, Richard Cardinal, 274

Dante Alighieri, 236, 241–42
Darkness, 148, 149. *See also* Light; Night
Darkness at Noon, 328
Darwin, Charles, 327
"Dasein," 233–35
Day (everyday), 136–54, 250
Death, 129, 139–40, 235–37, 262, 268, 333–34, 337, 339, 344–45. *See also* Suicide

Chautauqua and, 308
"Dasein" and, 234
of God, 193, 244
of universe, 336–37
Death of Ivan Ilyich, The, 235–36
Decidability/undecidability, 91ff.,
    102–3
Decimal system, 96
Decision procedure, 19
Dedekind's "cut," 9n, 83, 94n
Defense, The (Nabokov), 167, 173
Depression, economic (1930s), 317
Depression, emotional, 262–65ff.
Descartes, René, and Cartesian
    philosophy, 22, 46, 47, 69, 71,
    110–16, 124ff., 141, 162, 164, 167,
    171, 189, 190–92, 197, 204, 212,
    215ff., 262, 303, 321, 337. See also
    specific followers
Determinism, xiv, 253, 257–61ff. *See
    also* Behavioral scientists;
    behaviorism; Free will
Dewey, John, 5, 66, 144, 192
Dichten, 57
Dictatorship. *See* Communists and
    communism; Totalitarianism
"Dilemma of Determinism, The," 257
Dionysian instinct, 232
Dionysos, theater of, 243
Discipline, 304
Divine Comedy, The, 241–42
Division, long, 19
DNA, 211
Dog, author's, 129, 344–45
Dokousa, 322n
Don Juan, 248
Donkey and carrot, 299–300, 301
Dostoevski, Fyodor, 29, 31, 61–62, 70,
    73, 281, 304, 345
Doubt, 112, 126ff. *See also* Faith;
    specific philosophers
Drama, Greek, 243–44
Drinking. *See* Alcohol
Drugs, 291, 340
Druids, 339
Dualism, 165. *See also* Descartes,
    René, and Cartesian philosophy;
    Two Worlds

Duham (physicist-historian), 322
Dumas, Alexandre, 138

Earth, the, 336
Eastern bloc, 104–5
East River, diving into, 276
Eddington, Sir Arthur, 109
Ego, 191
Eigen, 186
Elea, 185
Eliot, T. S., 74, 214–15, 239
Energy, 210, 336ff.
Engelmann, Paul, 52n
English, the. *See* British, the; specific
    philosophers
English language, 6, 170–73. *See also*
    specific works
Enlightenment, the, 177, 179, 224, 272,
    325
Environment, 21
Epoche, 117. *See also* Bracketing
Ereignis, 186
Eros, Plato and, 231
Essence, essentialism, 127–28, 237
Ethics, 43, 53–54, 55, 188, 229–51. *See
    also* specific philosophers
Euclid, 180
Europe, 177–78. *See also* specific
    countries, philosophers
Everyday. *See* Day
Evil Demon, 112–13
Evolution, 253, 336
Excluded middle, law of the, 94
Existence. *See* Being; Existentialism
Existentialism, xvii, 127, 138. *See also*
    specific philosophers
Experience. *See* Consciousness
"Extensive Abstraction," 9n
External world. *See* Being; Two
    Worlds

Faith. *See also* Belief
    freedom, nihilism, and, 333–45
    to will, 271–94
Farber, Leslie, 222
Farbigkeit, 82
Fertilizers, chemical, 21
Fichte, Johann Gottlieb, 194–95

Ficker (publisher), 52
Finnegans Wake, 168
Fischer, Bobby, 65
Flaubert, Gustave, 215, 216
Florentines, 179
Football, 65
Ford, Henry, 310
Formalism, 49, 80. *See also* Logic;
    Mathematics and mathematical
    logic; specific philosophers
Forster, E. M., 213, 333–34
Framework, 207–8, 221, 223, 237, 322
France. *See* French
Frankenstein's monster, 20
Frankfurt school, 323–24
Freedom (liberty), xiii–xv, 44–45,
    49–50, 92–93, 101ff., 149–50, 221,
    224, 225, 227–94, 305–6, 329. *See
    also* Behaviorial scientists,
    behaviorism; Will; specific
    philosophers
  and death, 139
  and faith to will, 271–94
  and future. *See* Future
  and moral will, 229–51
  nihilism, faith, and, 333–45
  and technology. *See* Technology
  and will to believe, 253–69
Free will, xiii–xiv, 257–69. *See also*
    Behavioral scientists, behaviorism;
    Determinism; Future; Will
Frege (philosopher), 79, 85
French, 193, 196. *See also* specific
    writers
  language, 18
  literature (writers), 216, 279. *See
    also* specific writers
  Revolution, xv, 216, 320–21, 343
Freud, Sigmund, 149, 167, 232, 289,
    343
Friends, 232–33
Frost, Robert, 160, 168
Fuel, 210
Fuller, Buckminster, 208–10
Fuller, Margaret, 208
Funerals, 345
Future, 295–329. *See also* Day;
    Determinism

  American version, 297–315
  Russian version, 317–29

Galileo Galilei, 72n–73n, 111, 181, 191
Games. *See also* specific games
  "language," 65, 67
Gebirge, 207
Gelassenheit, 239, 240, 282
Genealogy of Morals, 198
Genetic engineering, 210–12
Genius, 19, 241
Geometry, 19, 98
Germany and Germans, 113, 192ff.,
    212, 231. *See also* Nazism; specific
    philosophers
  language, 18, 136. *See also* specific
    words, works
Gestell, 207. *See also* Framework
Gesture, ritual, 275–76, 279, 282–83,
    344, 345
God(s), xvii–xviii, 12, 34, 39, 53, 94,
    115, 116, 152, 153, 158–59, 189,
    193, 194, 196, 211, 242, 244, 247,
    251, 253, 262, 274, 277–78ff., 282,
    335
  "death of God," 193, 244
Gödel (mathematician), 84, 91, 92
Goethe, Johann Wolfgang von, 243
Gogol, Nikolai, 343
Gospels, the. *See* New Testament
Grace, 239–40, 275. *See also* Salvation
"Great Wall of China, The"
    (Kafka), 122
Greece and the Greeks, 20, 22, 37, 66,
    114, 121, 144–45, 148, 151, 153,
    180, 181, 185–89, 196, 200, 242–45,
    282, 322. *See also* specific
    philosophers, terms
  and class struggle, 319–20
  Heidegger and temple, 134
Gulag Archipelago, xii–xiii, 328
Gulliver's Travels, 92

Habermas, Jurgen, 323–24
Habit, 301–2ff. *See also* Behaviorial
    scientists, behaviorism
Haldane, J. B. S., 325
Hallucinogens, 291

Hamlet, 310
Hammett, Dashiell, 302
Happiness, 327–28
Harvard, 284, 314
Harvey, William, 111
Hates, 238–39
Headhunters, 85
Heart, 111
Heat death (of universe), 336–37
Heavenly bodies, xiv, 180–81. *See also*
　　Stars
Hegel, Georg Wilhelm Friedrich,
　　113, 135, 172n, 177ff., 183, 184,
　　215, 224, 241, 244, 324, 325
　　and Kant's *Critique of Judgment*,
　　341
　　and Napoleon on horseback, 204
Heidegger, Martin, xvi, xvii, xix, xx,
　　37, 43, 57, 68n, 69, 129, 130,
　　134–35ff., 145, 153, 154–55, 179,
　　180, 183ff., 198, 200, 203ff., 211,
　　219, 221, 223, 224–25, 229–51, 282,
　　291, 294, 322, 327
　　-Wittgenstein dialogue, 159ff.,
　　175–76
Hellman, Lillian, 30
Helmholtz, Hermann von, 36
Hilbert (formalist), 90, 91
History, 138, 177, 178, 183ff., 221, 223,
　　310. *See also* Marxism
　　earth's, 336
Hitler, Adolf, 325
Hölderlin, Johann Christian Friedrich
　　von, 170, 240–45
"Hölderlin and the Essence of
　　Poetry," 241
Holland, 31, 129
Homer, 148
Homosexuality, Wittgenstein's, 4, 60
Horror movies, 20
Horror stories. *See* Literature
"How to" manuals, 21–22
Hui-neng, 291, 340
Humanism, 178–79
Human Knowledge, 11
Humboldt, Wilhelm von, 67–68
Hume, David, 6–7, 36–37, 39, 45, 46,
　　126–27, 151

"Hunger Artist, The," 62
Husserl, Edmund, 110, 116–31, 145,
　　153, 190
Huxley, Aldous, 213

Idea(s), 53, 158–59, 184–85ff., 324–25.
　　See also Idealism; specific
　　philosophers
Idealism, 113, 192. *See also*
　　Consciousness
Identity and Difference, 251
Illumination. *See* Light
Immortality, xvii–xviii, 53, 54, 194,
　　247
"Indirect communication," 56
Inertia, 181, 191
Infantile sexuality, 149
Infinite series, infinity, 86, 94
Infinitesimals, 66
Insanity (schizophrenia), 241, 242
Instrument, language as, 166–67, 173
Intentionality, 118–19, 130
*Introduction to Mathematical
　　Philosophy*, 40
Intuitionism, 79–80, 99. *See also*
　　specific philosophers
Inventions, 186
Irish writers, 216
Irrational numbers (quantities),
　　9n–10n, 66, 94, 99
IS, 147
"Is Life Worth Living?," 284–88

James, Henry, 70, 158, 254
James, William, xvi, xvii, xix–xx, 5,
　　10, 14, 31, 60, 61, 66, 135, 144,
　　158–59, 229, 299, 313–14, 329
　　and Chautauqua colony, 307–8
　　and faith to will, 271–94
　　and habit, 301
　　and will to believe, 253–69
Jespersen, Otto, 169
Jesus Christ, 281
Jews and Judaism, 28, 155, 244, 245,
　　281–82, 286
Joyce, James, 168, 250
Judaism. *See* Jews and Judaism
Julien the Hospitaler, St., 216

Kafka, Franz, 4, 62, 63, 122, 149, 280
Kant, Immanuel, xvii–xviii, 7, 19, 34,
    53–54, 77, 86, 99, 124, 163, 164,
    181–82, 193ff., 207, 230, 233, 237,
    246–47, 250, 257, 288, 340–42
Kean (Sartre), 138
Kepler, Johannes, 180–81
Kierkegaard, Søren, 31, 56, 61, 73, 92,
    213, 224, 240, 247, 248, 256, 284
Knife, in Aristotle's metaphysics, 250
Koestler, Arthur, 328

Labor, specialization of, 22–23
Language, 5ff., 18, 96, 142–46, 148,
    150, 153–54, 157–58ff., 240. *See
    also* Logic; specific ideas,
    philosophers, terms
    "games," 65, 67
    and mysticism. *See* Mysticism;
        Wittgenstein, Ludwig
    open, 59–78
    ordinary, 38, 170, 322n. *See also*
        Wittgenstein, Ludwig
Law, 76
    case, 97
Lebenswelt. See "Life world"
Leibniz, Gottfried Wilhelm, Baron
    von, 5, 11, 39, 51, 66, 151, 152
Leisure, 310–11
Lenin, Nikolai, 325
Leningrad, xi
Lessing, and Greeks, 243
Letheia, 148
*Letters from Ludwig Wittgenstein,
    with a Memoir,* 52n
Lewis, Anthony, xi–xii, xvii
Lewis, C. I., 6
"Liar, The" (paradox), 156
Liberalism, religious, 272ff.
Liberty. *See* Freedom
"Life world," 120ff.
Light (illumination), 143, 147ff., 187,
    188
"Limitative theorems," 91, 93
Literature, 21, 70–71, 143, 215–16, 219,
    232, 243, 279, 334. *See also*
    specific authors

Russian, 328, 343. *See also* specific
    authors
    and Walden II, 310
Locke, John, 69
Logic, xviii, 1–50, 64ff., 79ff., 101ff.,
    256. *See also* Mathematics and
    mathematical logic; specific
    philosophers, theories
    and illusion of technique, 1–15
    mystique of, 27–50
    technique, technicians, and
        philosophy, 17–25
"Logical Atomism," 32–50
Logical Positivism. *See* Positivism
"Logical reductionism," 47
Logical Structure of the World, The,
    36
Logos, 37
Logos apophantikos, 37
Loneliness, 213–14, 218
Lonely Crowd, The, 213
Loves, 238–39
Lying, despair, 222n

Mach, Ernst, 36
Machine, the, 20
Madame Bovary, 216
Malcolm, Norman, 61
Man Without Qualities, The, 29
Marcel, Gabriel, 278
Marijuana, 340
Marxism (Marx), xi, 135, 149, 183,
    199, 203, 317–29
Masters and Johnson, 100n
"Material implication," 38
Materialism. *See* Marxism; Science
"Mathematics, Science and
    Language," 79n
Mathematics and mathematical logic,
    xviii, 1–50, 65ff., 79–100, 101ff.,
    112ff., 120, 124, 159, 199–200, 256.
    See also specific philosophers
    arithmetic with frills, 82–89
    conventionalism, 94–100
    mechanization, 89–94
"Mathematics and the Good," 12n
Matter, 9–10. *See also* Two Worlds
Meaning, 68ff., 118, 137, 169. *See also*

Consciousness; specific
philosophers
Meaninglessness. *See* Nihilism
Mechanics, 66, 111, 181
Mechanization, 89–94
Medical technology, 21
Medieval philosophy. *See* Middle
Ages
Meditations on First Philosophy
(Descartes), 115–16
Memory, 173–74
Merleau-Ponty, Sartre and, 335
Metaphors, 88–89, 119, 168, 184. *See
also* specific metaphors;
philosophers
Metaphysics, 46, 116, 191, 203–4, 250,
325. *See also* God (s); specific
ideas, philosophers
Method, 22, 322–23. *See also*
Technology
Metric system, 321
Metropolis (city), 213–14, 218
Micronesians, 179
Middle Ages (medieval philosophy),
114ff., 118, 130, 141, 147, 152, 177,
180, 189, 200, 204, 216, 261. *See
also* specific philosophers
Mill, John Stuart, 3
Mind, 68ff. *See also* Consciousness;
Idea(s); Psychology
Mirror, metaphor of, 34–35, 38, 42–43,
47
Molière, Jean Baptiste Poquelin, 160
Monads, 39
Montaigne, Michel Eyquem, seigneur
de, 279
Moore, G. E., 6, 162–64, 192
"Moral holidays," 293
Morality. *See also* Ethics; Faith;
specific philosophers
moral will, 229–51
Morality plays, 243–44
Morbidity, 60–61
Morrell, Lady Ottoline, 31
Moscow, 326
Moslems, 179
Motivation. *See* Will

Mountain climber, James' example of,
266
Movies, horror, 20
Multiplication, 97
Murdoch, Iris, 70, 71, 72n
Music, 35, 143, 168, 193–94
atonal, 29, 64, 194
and Walden II, 310
Musil, Robert, 29
Mysticism, 3, 51–57, 160, 288–94, 339.
See also specific philosophers
Myths, 20–21

Nabokov, Vladimir, 167, 173
Name, belief in one's own, 277–78
Napoleon, 204
Natural standpoint (natural
consciousness), 117, 131, 190ff.
Nazis(m), 125, 130, 134–35, 155, 192,
231
Neue Sachlichkeit, Die, 217
"Neutral monism," 10
New England, 253–54. *See also* James,
William
New Guinea, 85–86, 179
Newman, John Henry Cardinal, 3, 4
New Math, 80–81, 95
"New Realism, The," 217
New Testament (Gospels), 278
Tolstoi's, 30, 31
Newton, Isaac (Newtonians), xiv, 66,
89, 149, 180
New York
East River, 276
Times Square, 213
New York *Times,* 326
Lewis article in, xi–xii, xvii
Nietzsche, Friedrich, 63, 193ff., 204,
231, 241, 243, 247, 256, 268, 329
Night, 150–54. *See also* Stars
Nihilism, 198, 230, 236–37, 254–55,
268, 285, 286ff. *See also*
Nothingness
faith, freedom, and, 333–45
1984, 306, 329
Nominalism, 173
"No Mind," 340

Nothingness, 12, 242. *See also* Being; Nihilism
Noumena (noumenal realm), 53, 194
Novelists. *See* Literature
Nuclear devices, 336
  bombs (atomic bombs), 185, 198
  thermonuclear war, 223
Numbers and number theory, 82ff. *See also* Mathematics and mathematical language

Occult, the, 291–92
Oedipus, 148–49, 310
Oedipus complex, 148
Open systems. *See* Closed/open systems; Freedom; specific philosophers
"Operant behavior," 73n
Ordinary language, 38, 170, 322n. *See also* Wittgenstein, Ludwig
Orestia, the, 244
Orion, 150, 151
Orwell, George, 213, 306, 329
Our Knowledge of the Eternal World, 9
"Overbeliefs," 277
Overdetermination, 97
Overpopulation, 21
Oxford, 158

Painting, 143, 217–18. *See also* specific painters
Pairing of sets, 85
Pappus, 180
Paradoxes, 87ff., 156
Paris, 214
Parmenides, 185, 186–87, 250
Partisan Review, 317–18
Pascal, Gabriel, 31, 110, 245, 275, 283, 344
  and habit, 301
Passage to India, A, 333–34
Pater, Walter, 218
Pausanias, 148
Pavlov, Ivan, xi, xiii
Pessimism, 221
Pet theories, 237–38
Phainomena, 322

Phenomenalism, 127. *See also* Hume, David
Phenomenology, xvii, 95, 96, 116–20ff., 138, 183. *See also* specific philosophers
Philosophic Investigations, 63–64, 68, 75, 139, 160–61, 164, 176. *See also* Wittgenstein, Ludwig
Phos, 148
Photographs, 341
Physics (physicists), xiv, xvi, 36, 115, 181, 185, 188, 253, 258
Physics (Aristotle), 332
Physis, 188, 189
π, 93–94
Picasso, Pablo, 62, 64
Picture hanging askew, example of, 141, 142, 150, 153
Planets. *See* Heavenly bodies
Planned conditioning. *See* Behavioral scientists, behaviorism
Plato, 86, 99, 135, 231, 319. *See also* Platonism
Platonism, 9, 40, 86, 99, 167, 174, 199. *See also* Russell, Bertrand
Poetry (poets), 173, 214–15, 224–25, 230, 240–45. *See also* specific poets
Poincaré, Jules Henri, 80
Politics, xiii, 223–24, 325. *See also* Marxism
Politics (Aristotle), 320
Positivism and positivists, 6–7, 35–36, 44, 46, 52–53, 56, 72–73, 98, 199–200. *See also* specific philosophers
Possibility, 175
Post, E. L., 91, 93
Power, 197, 199, 204, 205, 222, 225
Pragmatism, xvii, 5–6, 66, 82, 95–96, 144, 158, 240, 255, 272, 286, 294. *See also* James, William
Prayer, 65n, 276, 280–81. *See also* Religion
Principles of Psychology (James), 264, 265
Problems of Philosophy, The, 9
"Programmed society," 324, 327

"Proof of the External World,"
162–64
Propositions, 37. See also Language
Protestantism. See also Christianity;
specific philosophers
Reformation, 177, 178
Proust, Marcel, 70, 138, 216, 279, 305
Psalms of David, 245
Psychic phenomena, 291–92
Psychoanalysis (psychiatrists), 29, 75,
104, 148–49, 232, 238, 261, 267, 343
Psychology, 9, 120ff., 188, 258. See
also Behavioral scientists,
behaviorism; specific
psychologists
Pythagoreans, 66

Rahv, Philip, 317–18
Ramanujan, 82
Rats, 72n–73n
Realism, 39, 42. See also Russell,
Bertrand
Reality vs. appearance. See Two
Worlds
Reductionism, logical, 47
Reference, 118
Reformation, the, 177, 178
Religion, xix, 3, 4, 6off., 75, 139,
152–53, 193ff., 328, 333, 343–45.
See also Bible; Christianity;
Mysticism; specific philosophers,
sects
American businessman and, 204–5
and moral will (see under
Morality)
and morbidity, 60
William James and (see James,
William)
Remembrance of Things Past. See
Proust, Marcel
Renaissance, the, 111, 177, 178–79
Renouvier, Charles Bernard, 264
Res, 249–50
Resistance, 149
Rêve Parisien, 214
Revolution. See Class struggle
Richta, Radovan, 324
Riefenstahl, Leni, 231

Riesman, David, 213
Rilke, Rainer Maria, 205
Rite of Spring, 194
Ritual, 17–18
gesture, 275–76, 279, 282–83, 344,
345
Rocks, 338ff.
Romantic poets, 3, 218. See also
specific poets
Rome, 282
Rosenberg, Harold, 217
Rudimentary language, 168
Rule of types, 12n, 87–88, 100
Runners, 279–80
Russell, Bertrand, 1–15, 25, 27, 29ff.,
38, 40, 42, 57, 61, 64, 78, 79, 82ff.,
100, 105, 144, 149, 162, 167, 188,
192, 255, 256
Russia and Russians (Soviet Union),
xi–xii, 165–66, 246, 297, 298
literature, 215–16, 343. See also
specific writers
shape of future, 317–29
Ryle, Gilbert, 70, 71

Salvation, 117, 139. See also Grace
Santayana, George, 8, 192
Sartre, Jean-Paul, xvii, xx, 76, 93, 118,
138, 165, 261–62, 335
Schelling, Friedrich Wilhelm Joseph
von, 194, 195, 340
Schiller, Johann Cristoph Friedrich
von, 243
Schizophrenia, 241, 242
School, 19. See also New Math
Schopenhauer, Arthur, 194, 195, 197,
243, 285
Schroeder, and calculus of classes, 156
Science, xiiiff., 23, 36–37, 43, 46, 51,
96, 120, 178, 179, 180–82, 199–200,
203–4, 253, 258, 322–23. See also
Technique; Technology; specific
fields, scientists
and "life world," 120–25
and pet theories, 237–38
Science and the Modern World, 180
Science fiction, 20, 213

"Scientific materialism" ("Scientific reductionism"), 47
Selbstbewusst, 195–96
Self. See Alienation
Self-consciousness, 113ff., 178, 195, 217
Self-denial, 304–5
Self-surrender. See Gelassenheit
Semantics, 155–56
Sensation and senses, 10–11, 35, 110, 128
"Sentiment of Rationality, The," 159
Sets, pairing of, 85
Sex, 100n
    infantile sexuality, 149
    manuals, 21–22
Shakespeare, William (Shakespearean tragedy), 196, 241, 343
"Show and tell," 59
Silence, 51, 52, 57
Singer, Isaac Bashevis, 281–82
Sirius, 150
Skinner, B. F., xii, xvii, xviii, 210, 257, 297–300, 301, 304, 306, 311ff.
Skolem (mathematician), 91
Smoking, 74–75
Society for Psychical Research, 291
Socrates, 135, 243
Solzhenitsyn, Alexander, xii–xiii, xvii, xviii, 246, 323
Sophocles, 244, 245
Soul, 71, 72, 189, 328
    "Dasein" and, 234–35
Soviet Union. See Russia and Russians
Sozein ta Phainomena, 181, 322
Space
    concept of, 9
    flight, 134 (see also Astronauts)
Specialization of labor, 22–23
Speech, 344–45. See also Conversation; Language
Spiegel, Der, 135, 244
Stalin, Joseph, 318, 326
Stars, 125, 150–51. See also Heavenly bodies
Stellen, 207
Stoics, 117
Stone Age man, 179

Stranger, The, 236–37
Stravinsky, Igor, 194
"Structure of the Continuum, The," 79n
Subject/object. See Two Worlds
Suebia, 134
Suicide, 264, 285, 292, 345
Suit of clothes, metaphor of, 91–92
Sullivan, Harry Stack, 345
Summae (Thomas Aquinas), 99
Sun, 336, 337
Superman, Nietzsche's, 204
Suspension, 117. See also Bracketing
Suzuki, D. T., 340
Swedenborg, Emanuel, xv
Système du Monde, Le, 322
Systematic doubt, 112. See also Descartes, René, and Cartesian philosophy

Tables
    Eddington's, 109
    and existence, 127–28
Tao and Taoism, 291, 340, 343
Tarnev, 30
Tarski, Alfred, 91, 156
"Technik, Technologie," 18
Technique, xiii, xv, xviii–xix, xxi–106, 221. See also specific writers
    illusion of, 1–15
    mathematics and mechanism, 79–100
    and mysticism, 51–57
    and mystique of logic, 27–50
    and open language, 59–78
    technicians, philosophy, and, 17–25
"Technique, technologie," 18
Technology, xix, 18ff., 101ff., 134, 211, 221ff. See also Behavioral scientists, behaviorism; Technique
    as human destiny, 177–201
Telephone Company, 102–3
Television, 222
Themis, 196
Themistocles, 148
Theology. See Religion

Thermodynamics, law of, 336
Thermonuclear war, 223
Third World, 326
Thomas Aquinas, St., 99, 130
Thucydides I, 322n
Time, 9, 146, 175. *See also* Day
Times Square, 213
Tolstoi, Count Leo, 30, 31, 209,
    235–36, 287
Tool, language as, 166–67, 173
Torquemada, Tomás de, 328
Totalitarianism, 105, 149–50, 298–99,
    315. *See also* Communists and
    Communism
Tractatus Logico-Philosophicus,
    30–50, 51–57, 63, 64, 66, 75, 98,
    160
Tradition of the New, 217
"Transcendental subjectivity." *See*
    Bracketing
Trees, 338ff.
Trilling, Lionel, 232
Trinity, the, 274
Triumph of the Will, The, 231
Truth, 113, 140–56, 160, 169, 180, 197,
    236, 237, 243. *See also* Tao and
    Taoism; Two Worlds; specific
    philosophers
    -tables, 40
Turing (logician), 91
Two Worlds, 9, 46–47, 67, 109–31,
    162. *See also* Descartes, René, and
    Cartesian philosophy

Unconscious, the, 232
Undecidability, 91, 102–3
United States and Americans, 5, 6,
    118, 165–66, 192, 325–26. *See also*
    specific persons
    businessman, 204–5
    shape of future, 297–315
Universe. *See also* Heavenly bodies
    death of, 336–37
Untruth. *See* Truth
Ur-Sein, 195
Utopia, 203–19
    Marxism and, 327
    Walden II, 297ff., 306–15

Utopia or Oblivion, 209

Valéry, Paul, 303
Varieties of Religious Experience, 31,
    262–63, 271ff., 282, 283. *See also*
    James, Williams
Venn diagrams, 38n, 40–42
Victorianism, 232
Vienna, 4, 27–29, 79
Visions, 290–91
Voltaire, François Marie Arouet de,
    23
Voluntas, 231
Von Wright, G. H., 60, 61

Walden II, 297ff., 306–15
War, 223, 323. *See also* specific wars
Waste Land, The, 214–15
Weierstrass, Karl Theodor, 66
Weltgeist, 204
Whistling, 69
Whitehead, Alfred, 1–15, 25, 34, 35,
    38, 47, 105, 149, 180, 182, 186, 255,
    269, 335–36, 337
Whitman, Walt, 293
Wiener, Norbert, 210
Will, 73ff., 115, 204ff., 222, 229–94,
    340. *See also* Freedom; specific
    philosophers
    to believe, 253–69
    faith to, 271–94
    moral, 229–51
    philosophy of the, 192–98
    to power. *See* Power
Will to Believe, The, 265–66
Winckelmann, Johann Joachim, 243
Wirklichkeit, 249
Wisdom, John, 61
Wittgenstein, Ludwig, xvi, xviii, xix,
    1–15, 25, 27–100, 105, 119, 136,
    151–52, 159ff., 239, 255–56, 277,
    284, 288
    and mathematics and mechanism,
    79–100
    and mysticism, 51–57
    and mystique of logic, 27–50
    and open language, 59–78
    sister Hermine, 27, 29, 59, 60

Wordsworth, William, 3, 342
World War I, 30
World War II (Second World
    War), 85, 169–70
Writers. See Literature; Poetry

Young Men's Christian Association,
    284–85
Yurok Indians, 17–18

Zen Buddhism, 291, 340, 343
Zoology, 40, 42

69692